RADIANT

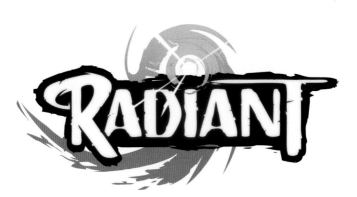

TONY VALENTE

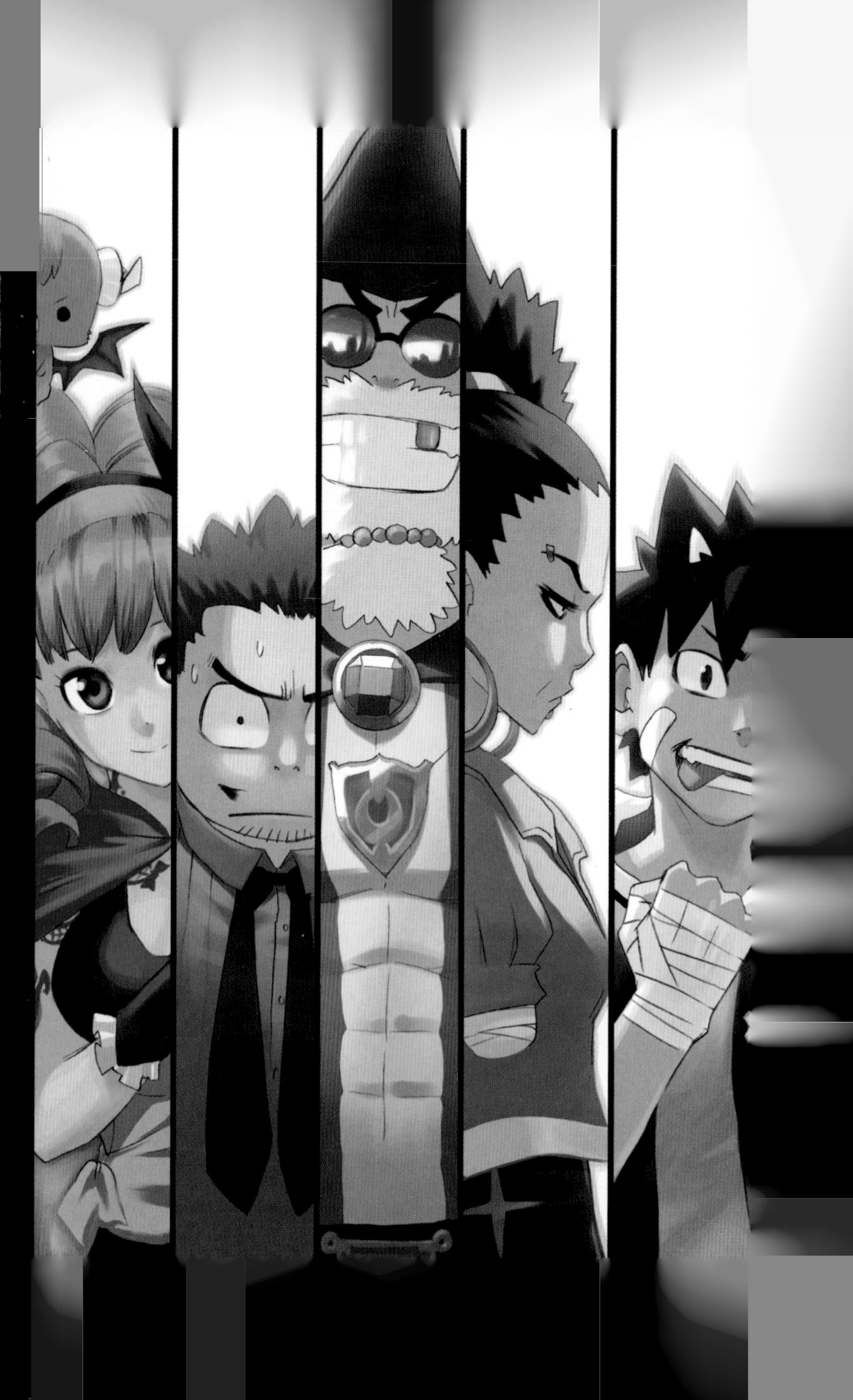

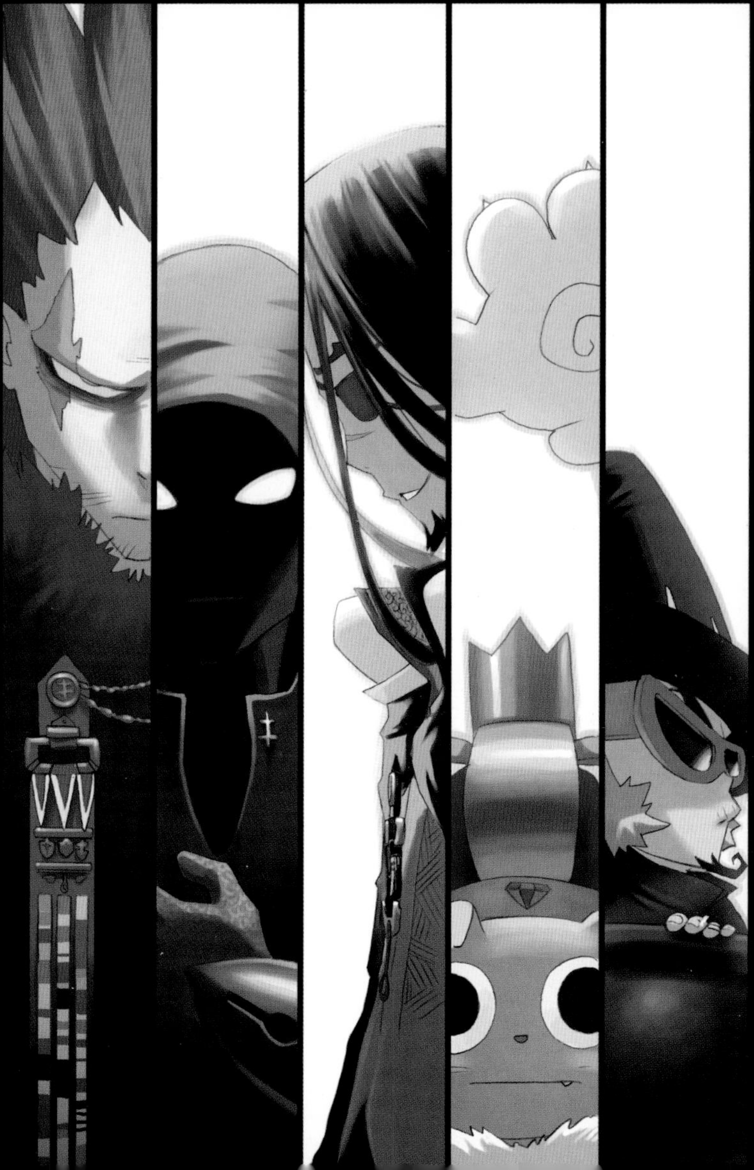

CONTENTS

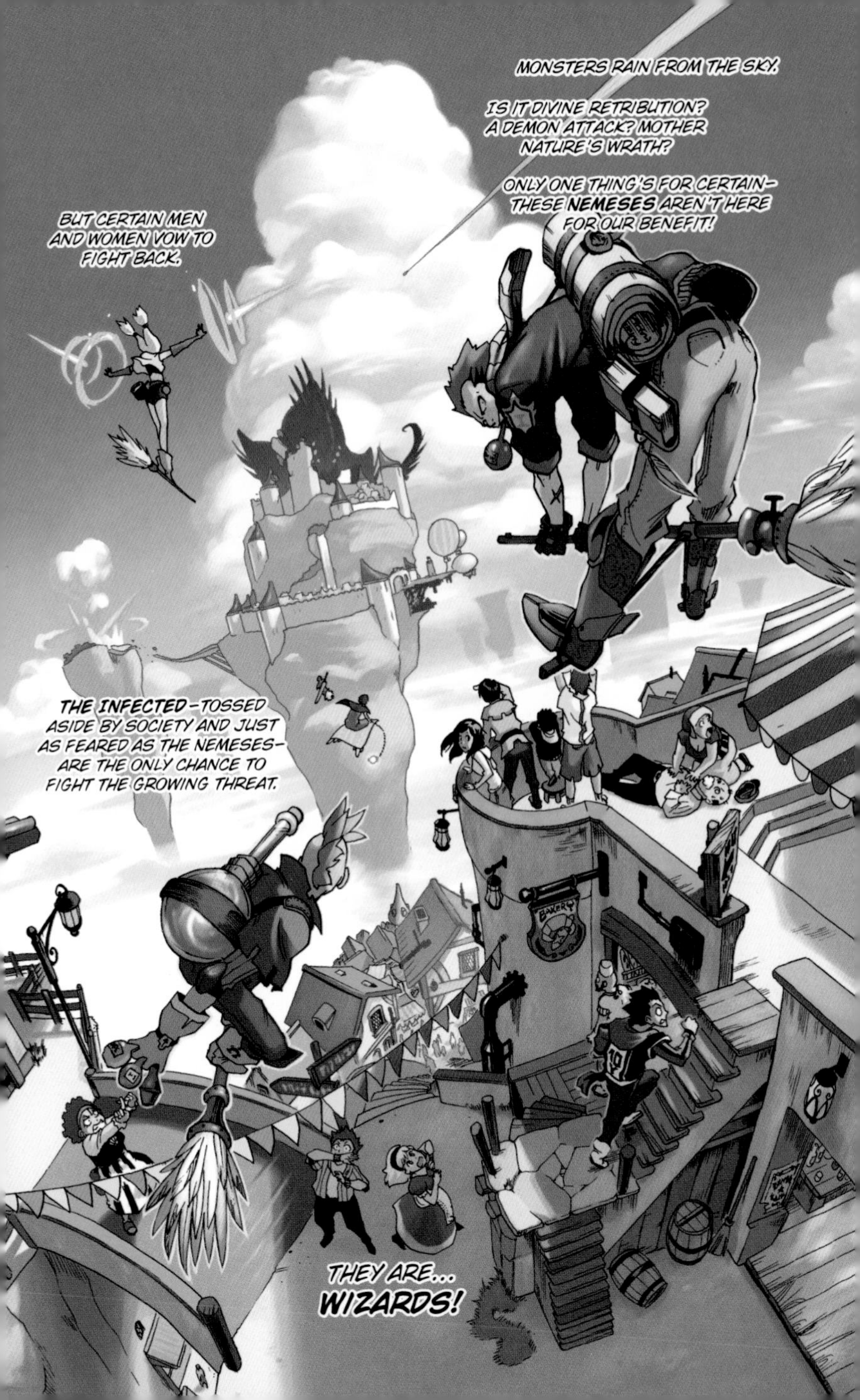
MONSTERS RAIN FROM THE SKY.
IS IT DIVINE RETRIBUTION? A DEMON ATTACK? MOTHER NATURE'S WRATH?
ONLY ONE THING'S FOR CERTAIN–THESE NEMESES AREN'T HERE FOR OUR BENEFIT!
BUT CERTAIN MEN AND WOMEN VOW TO FIGHT BACK.
THE INFECTED–TOSSED ASIDE BY SOCIETY AND JUST AS FEARED AS THE NEMESES–ARE THE ONLY CHANCE TO FIGHT THE GROWING THREAT.
THEY ARE... WIZARDS!

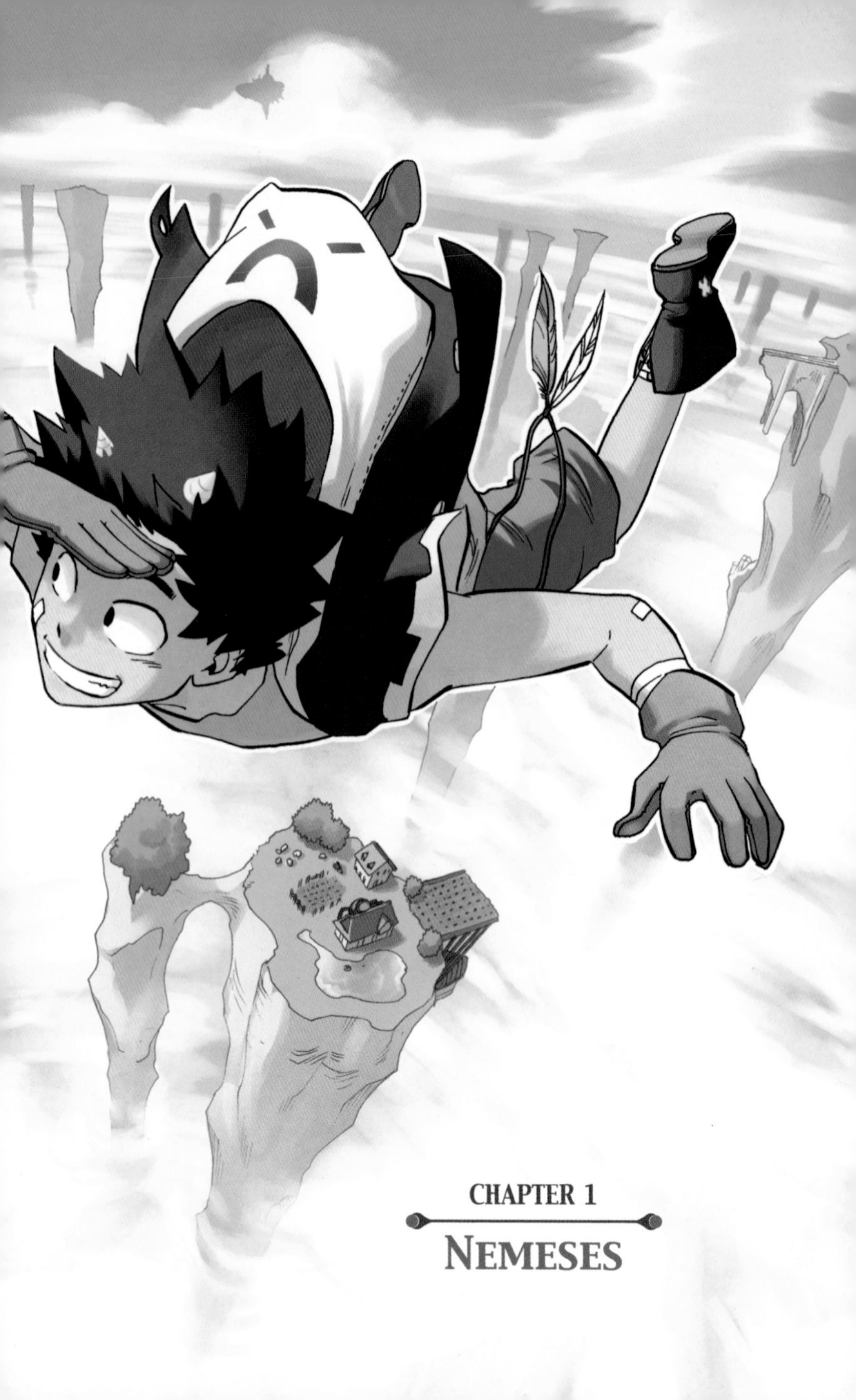

CHAPTER 1

NEMESES

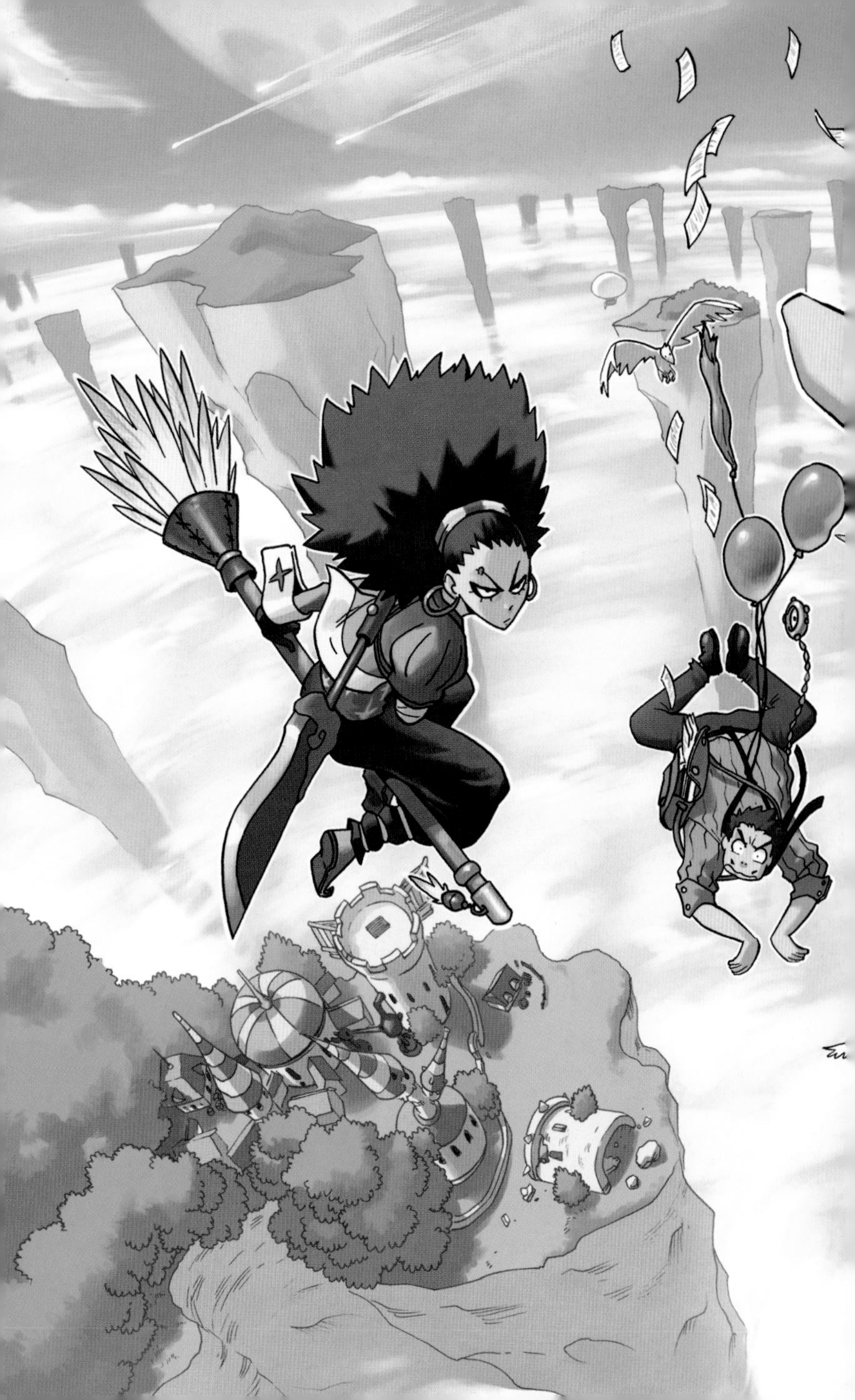

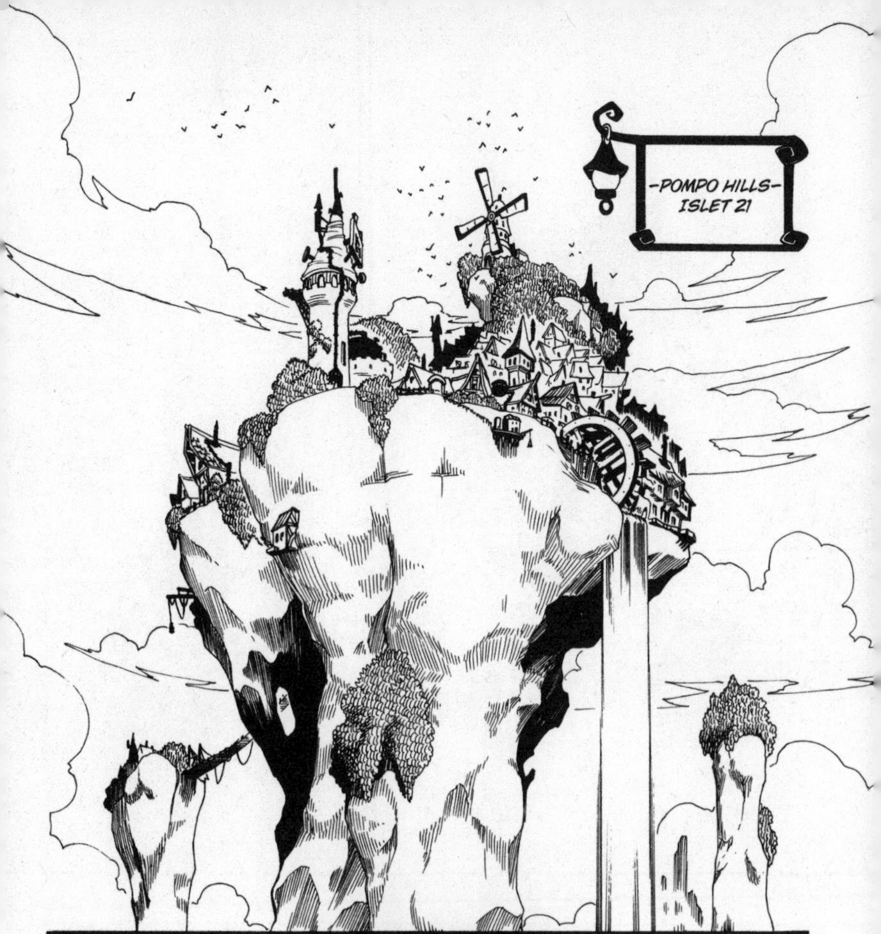
-POMPO HILLS-
ISLET 21

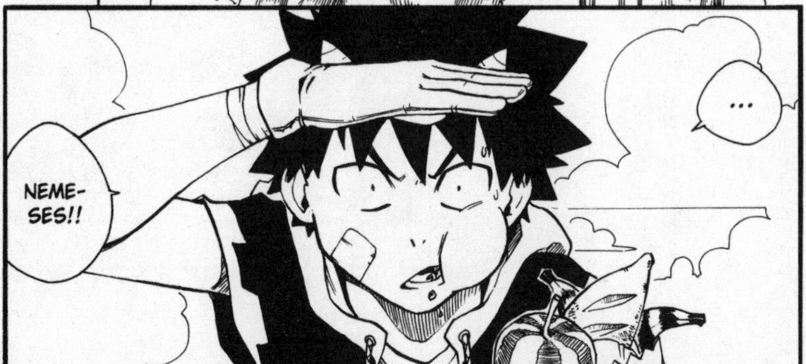
...
NEME-
SES!!

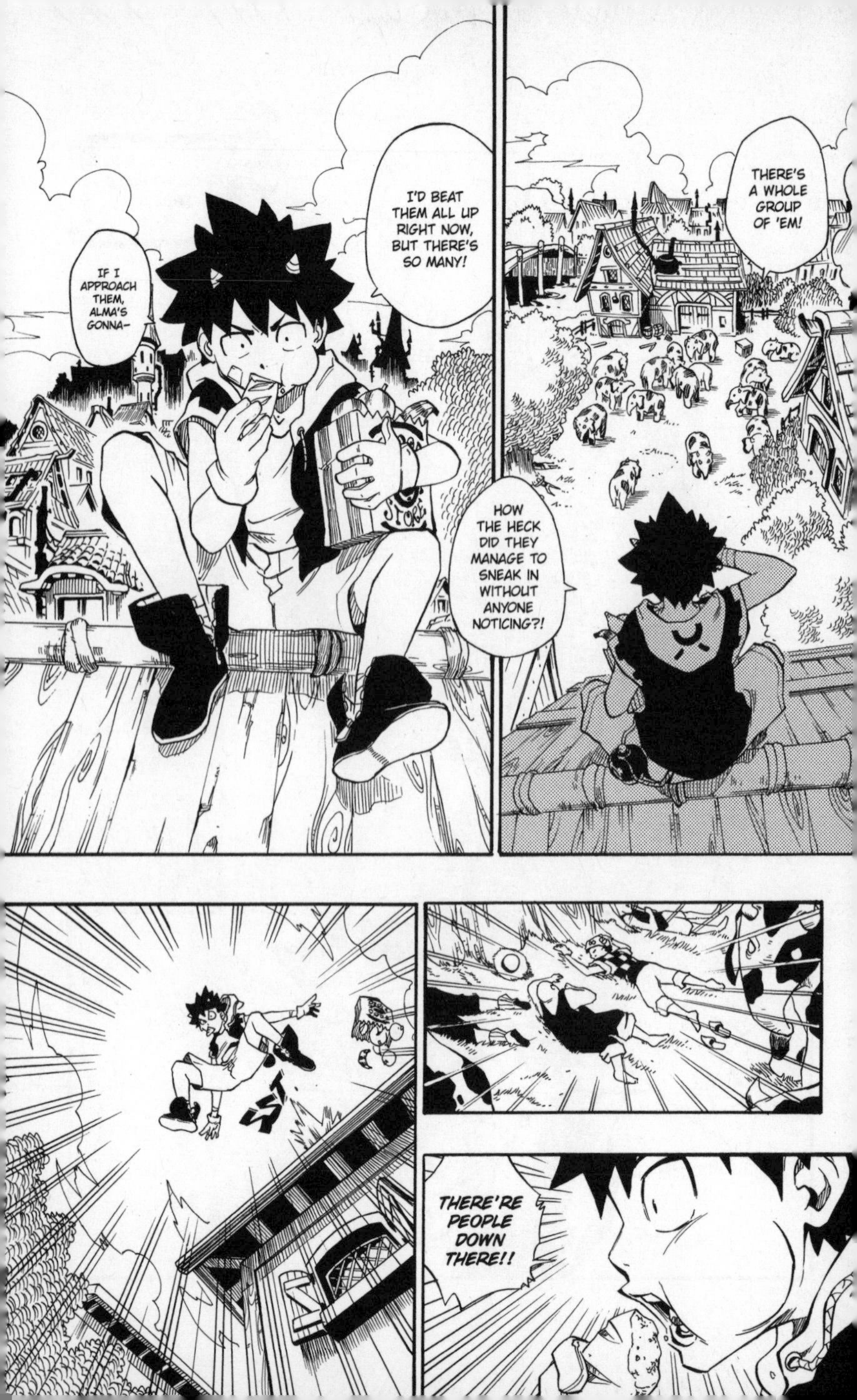
THERE'S A WHOLE GROUP OF 'EM!
HOW THE HECK DID THEY MANAGE TO SNEAK IN WITHOUT ANYONE NOTICING?!
I'D BEAT THEM ALL UP RIGHT NOW, BUT THERE'S SO MANY!
IF I APPROACH THEM, ALMA'S GONNA-
THERE'RE PEOPLE DOWN THERE!!

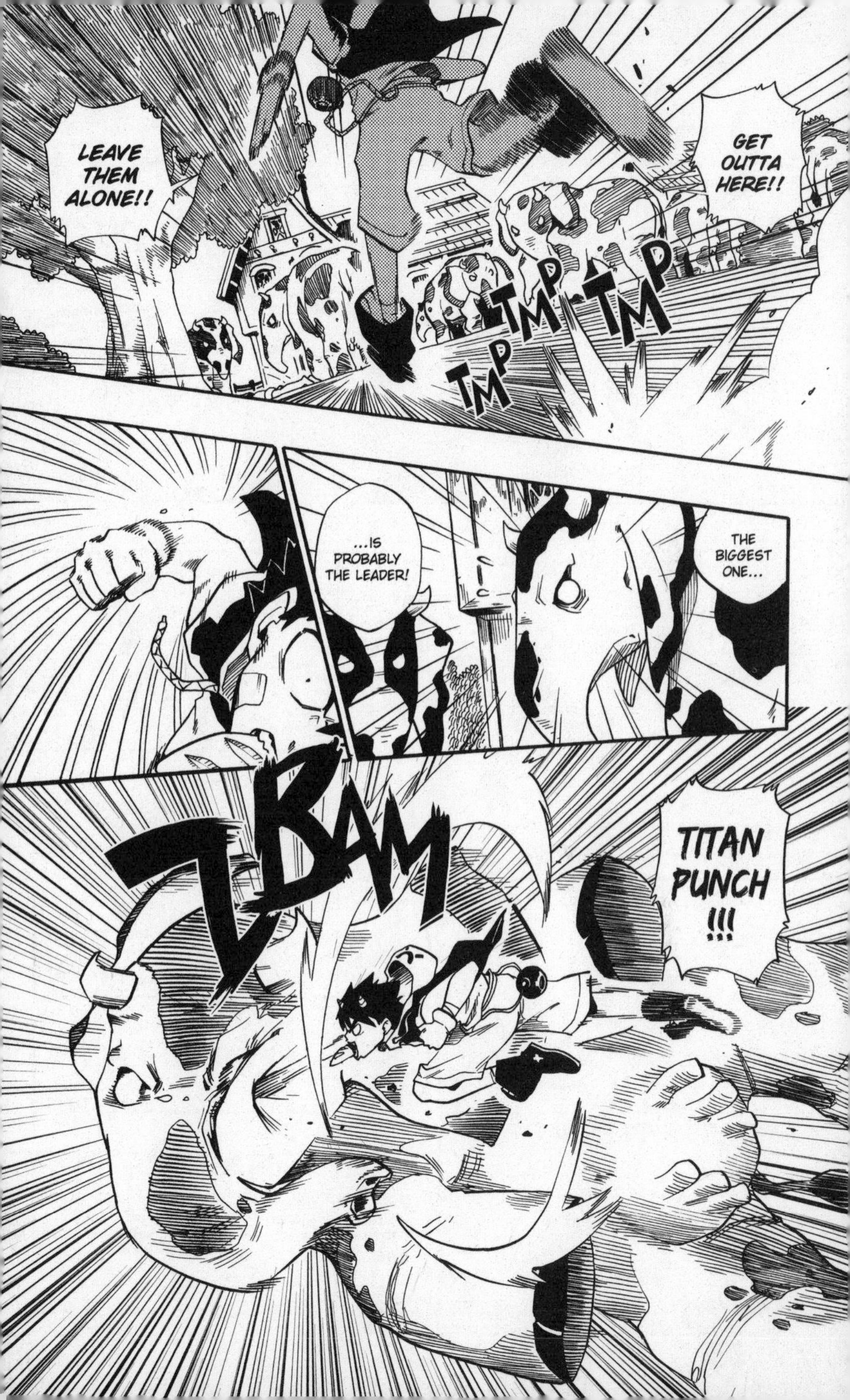
GET OUTTA HERE!!
LEAVE THEM ALONE!!
TMP TMP TMP TMP
THE BIGGEST ONE...
...IS PROBABLY THE LEADER!
TITAN PUNCH!!!
ZBAM

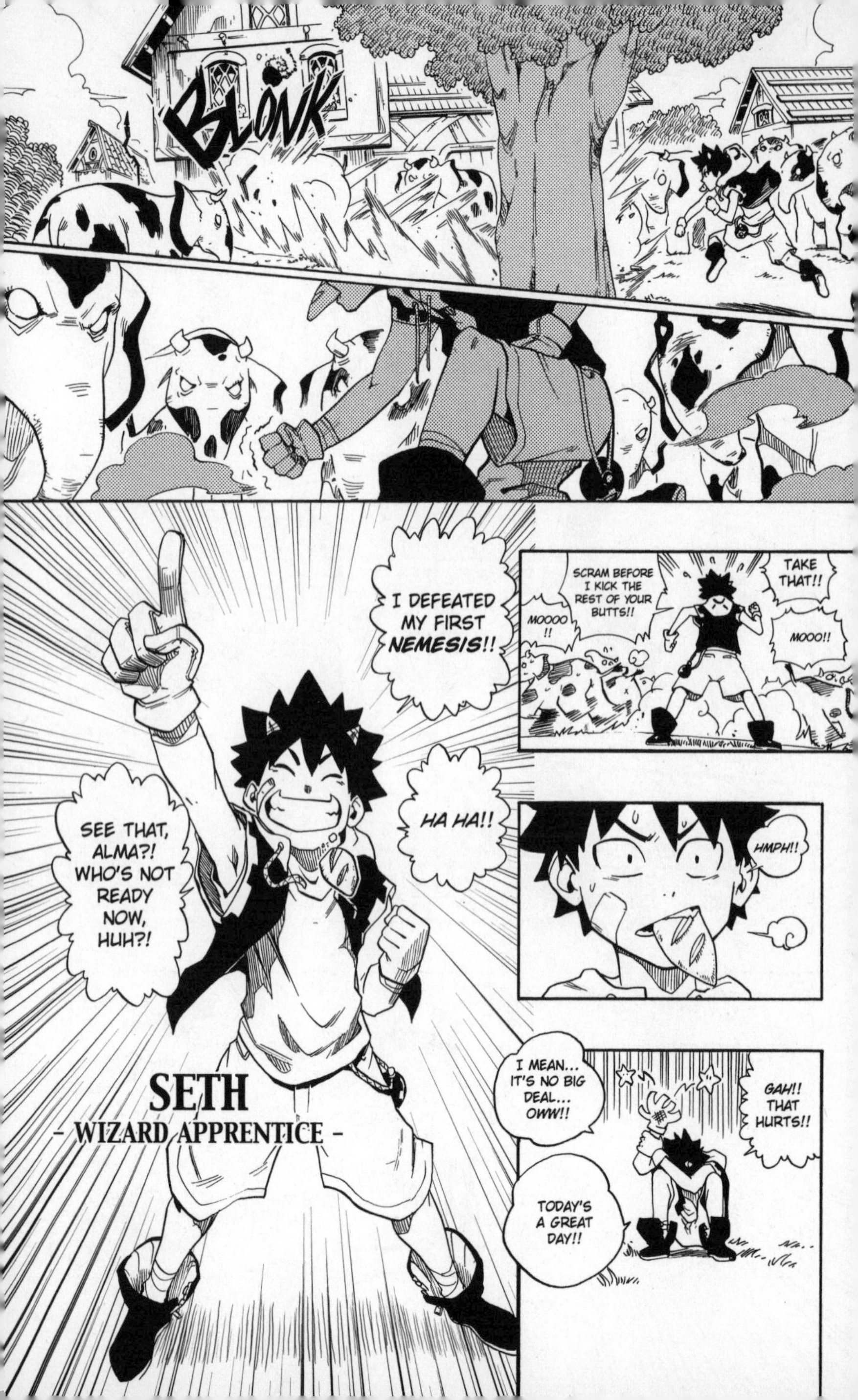
BLONK
TAKE THAT!!
SCRAM BEFORE I KICK THE REST OF YOUR BUTTS!!
MOOO!!
MOOOO!!
HMPH!!
GAH!! THAT HURTS!!
I MEAN... IT'S NO BIG DEAL... OWW!!
TODAY'S A GREAT DAY!!
I DEFEATED MY FIRST NEMESIS!!
HA HA!!
SEE THAT, ALMA?! WHO'S NOT READY NOW, HUH?!
SETH
- WIZARD APPRENTICE -

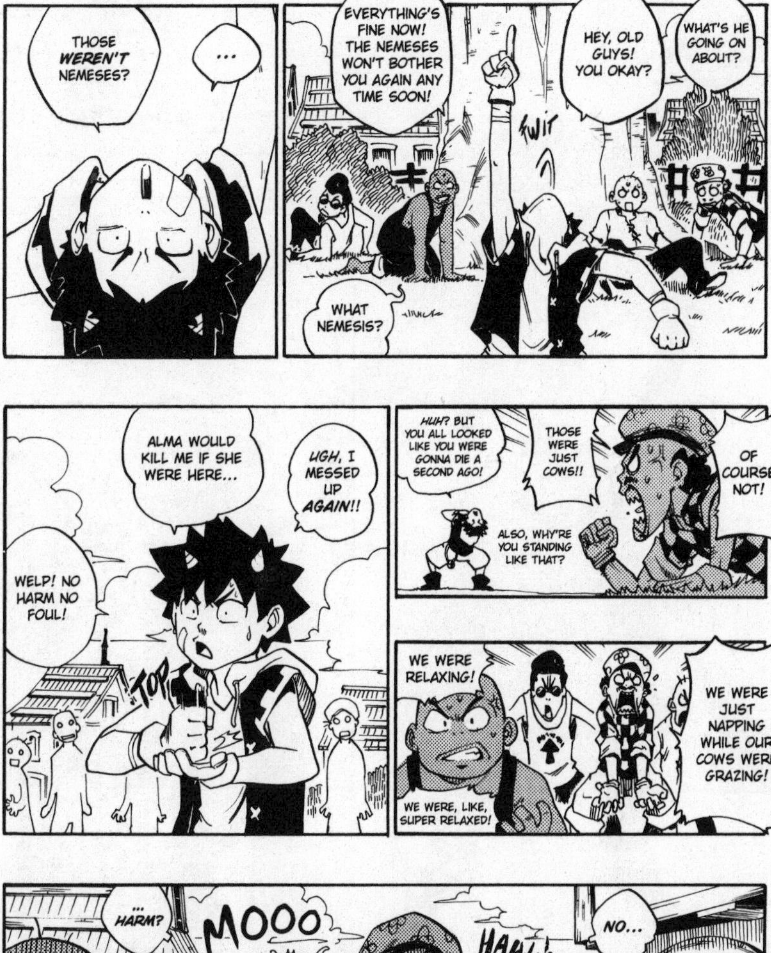

WHAT'S HE GOING ON ABOUT?
HEY, OLD GUYS! YOU OKAY?
EVERYTHING'S FINE NOW! THE NEMESES WON'T BOTHER YOU AGAIN ANY TIME SOON!
FWIT
WHAT NEMESIS?
...
THOSE *WEREN'T* NEMESES?
OF COURSE NOT!
THOSE WERE JUST COWS!!
HUH? BUT YOU ALL LOOKED LIKE YOU WERE GONNA DIE A SECOND AGO!
ALSO, WHY'RE YOU STANDING LIKE THAT?
WE WERE JUST NAPPING WHILE OUR COWS WERE GRAZING!
WE WERE RELAXING!
WE WERE, LIKE, SUPER RELAXED!
UGH, I MESSED UP *AGAIN*!!
ALMA WOULD KILL ME IF SHE WERE HERE...
WELP! NO HARM NO FOUL!
TOP
NO...
MOOOO
MOOO
... *HARM*?

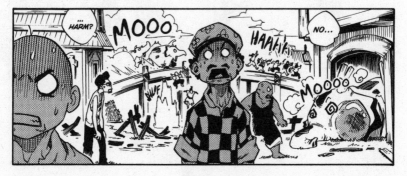

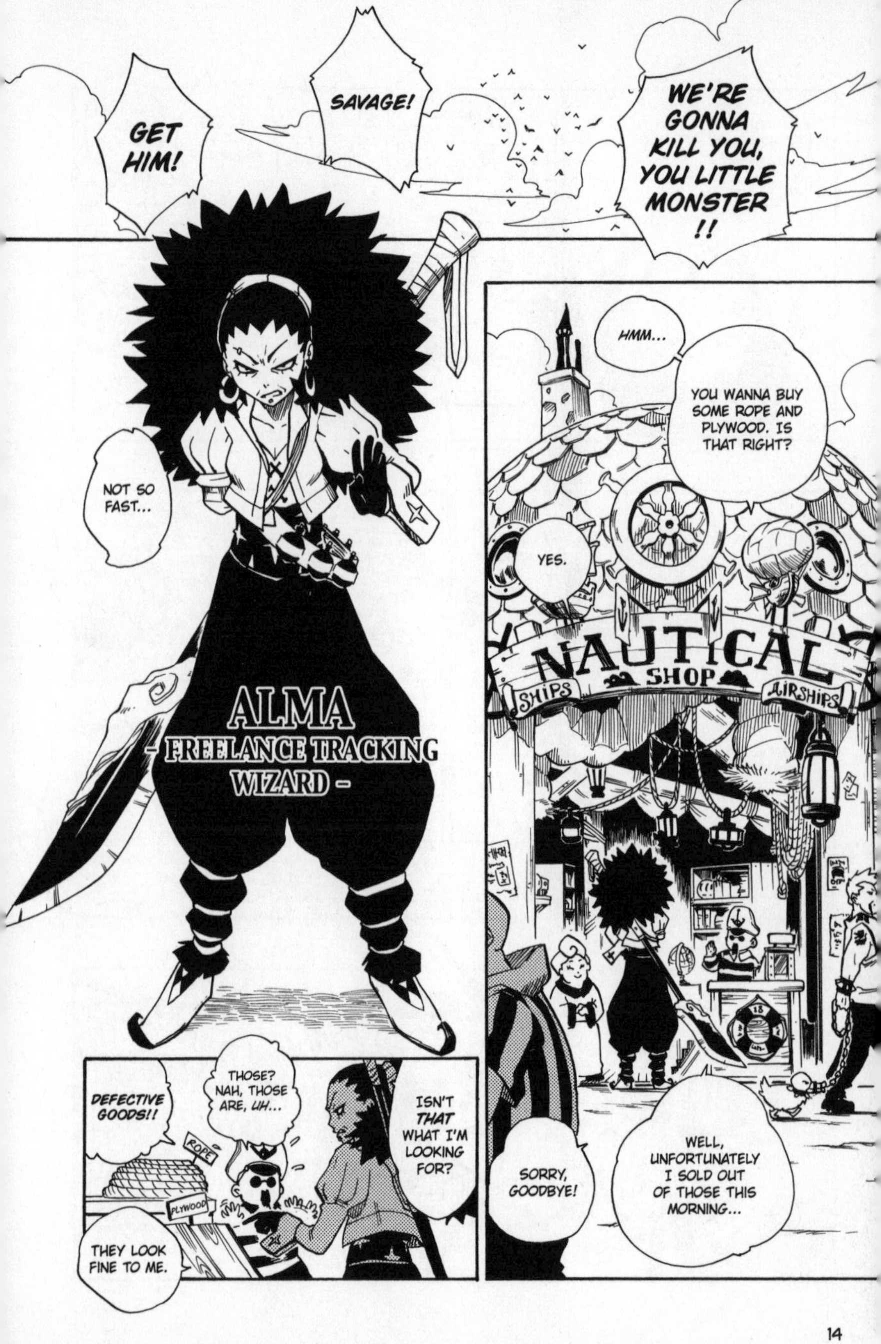
WE'RE GONNA KILL YOU, YOU LITTLE MONSTER!!
SAVAGE!
GET HIM!
HMM...
YOU WANNA BUY SOME ROPE AND PLYWOOD. IS THAT RIGHT?
YES.
NAUTICAL SHOP
SHIPS
AIRSHIPS
WELL, UNFORTUNATELY I SOLD OUT OF THOSE THIS MORNING...
SORRY, GOODBYE!
NOT SO FAST...
ALMA
- FREELANCE TRACKING WIZARD -
ISN'T THAT WHAT I'M LOOKING FOR?
THOSE? NAH, THOSE ARE, UH...
DEFECTIVE GOODS!!
ROPE
PLYWOOD
THEY LOOK FINE TO ME.

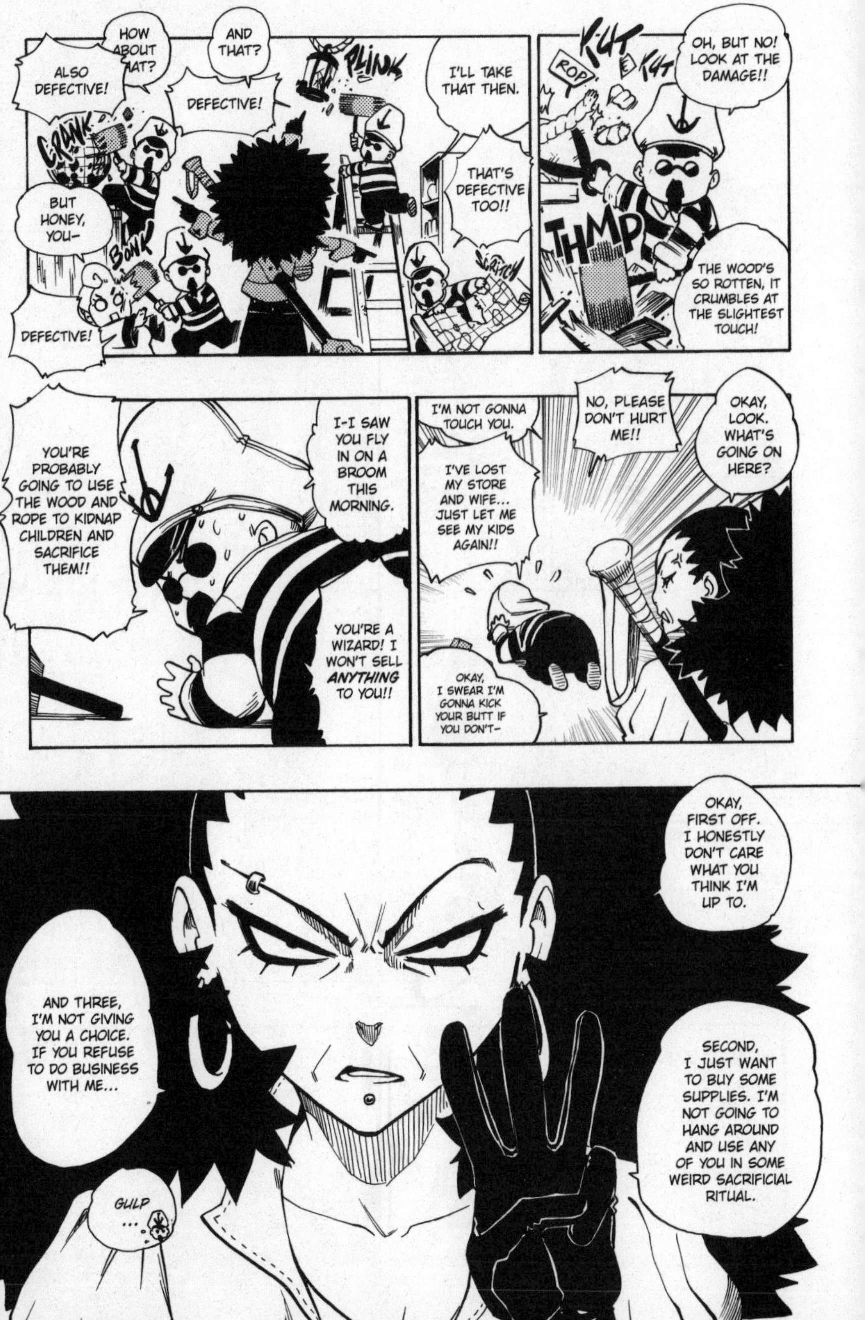
OH, BUT NO! LOOK AT THE DAMAGE!!
K-LUT
ROP
K-LUT
THMP
THE WOOD'S SO ROTTEN, IT CRUMBLES AT THE SLIGHTEST TOUCH!
I'LL TAKE THAT THEN.
THAT'S DEFECTIVE TOO!!
PLINK
AND THAT?
DEFECTIVE!
HOW ABOUT THAT?
ALSO DEFECTIVE!
CRANK
BUT HONEY, YOU-
BONK
SCRITCH
DEFECTIVE!
OKAY, LOOK. WHAT'S GOING ON HERE?
NO, PLEASE DON'T HURT ME!!
I'M NOT GONNA TOUCH YOU.
I'VE LOST MY STORE AND WIFE... JUST LET ME SEE MY KIDS AGAIN!!
OKAY, I SWEAR I'M GONNA KICK YOUR BUTT IF YOU DON'T-
I-I SAW YOU FLY IN ON A BROOM THIS MORNING.
YOU'RE PROBABLY GOING TO USE THE WOOD AND ROPE TO KIDNAP CHILDREN AND SACRIFICE THEM!!
YOU'RE A WIZARD! I WON'T SELL *ANYTHING* TO YOU!!
OKAY, FIRST OFF. I HONESTLY DON'T CARE WHAT YOU THINK I'M UP TO.
SECOND, I JUST WANT TO BUY SOME SUPPLIES. I'M NOT GOING TO HANG AROUND AND USE ANY OF YOU IN SOME WEIRD SACRIFICIAL RITUAL.
AND THREE, I'M NOT GIVING YOU A CHOICE. IF YOU REFUSE TO DO BUSINESS WITH ME...
GULP...

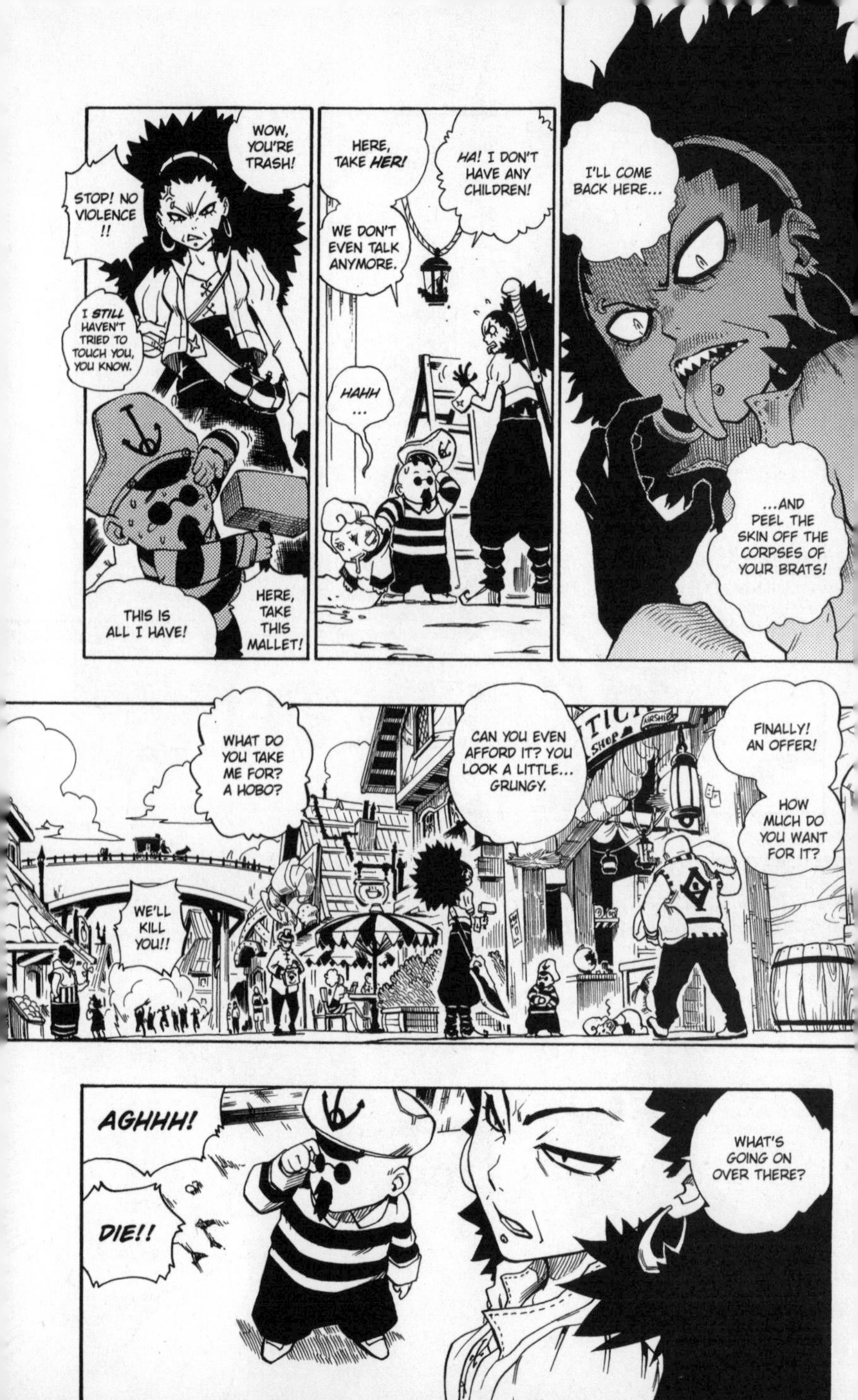

I'LL COME BACK HERE...
...AND PEEL THE SKIN OFF THE CORPSES OF YOUR BRATS!
HA! I DON'T HAVE ANY CHILDREN!
HERE, TAKE HER!
WE DON'T EVEN TALK ANYMORE.
HAHH...
WOW, YOU'RE TRASH!
STOP! NO VIOLENCE!!
I STILL HAVEN'T TRIED TO TOUCH YOU, YOU KNOW.
HERE, TAKE THIS MALLET!
THIS IS ALL I HAVE!
FINALLY! AN OFFER!
HOW MUCH DO YOU WANT FOR IT?
CAN YOU EVEN AFFORD IT? YOU LOOK A LITTLE... GRUNGY.
WHAT DO YOU TAKE ME FOR? A HOBO?
WE'LL KILL YOU!!
WHAT'S GOING ON OVER THERE?
AGHHH!
DIE!!

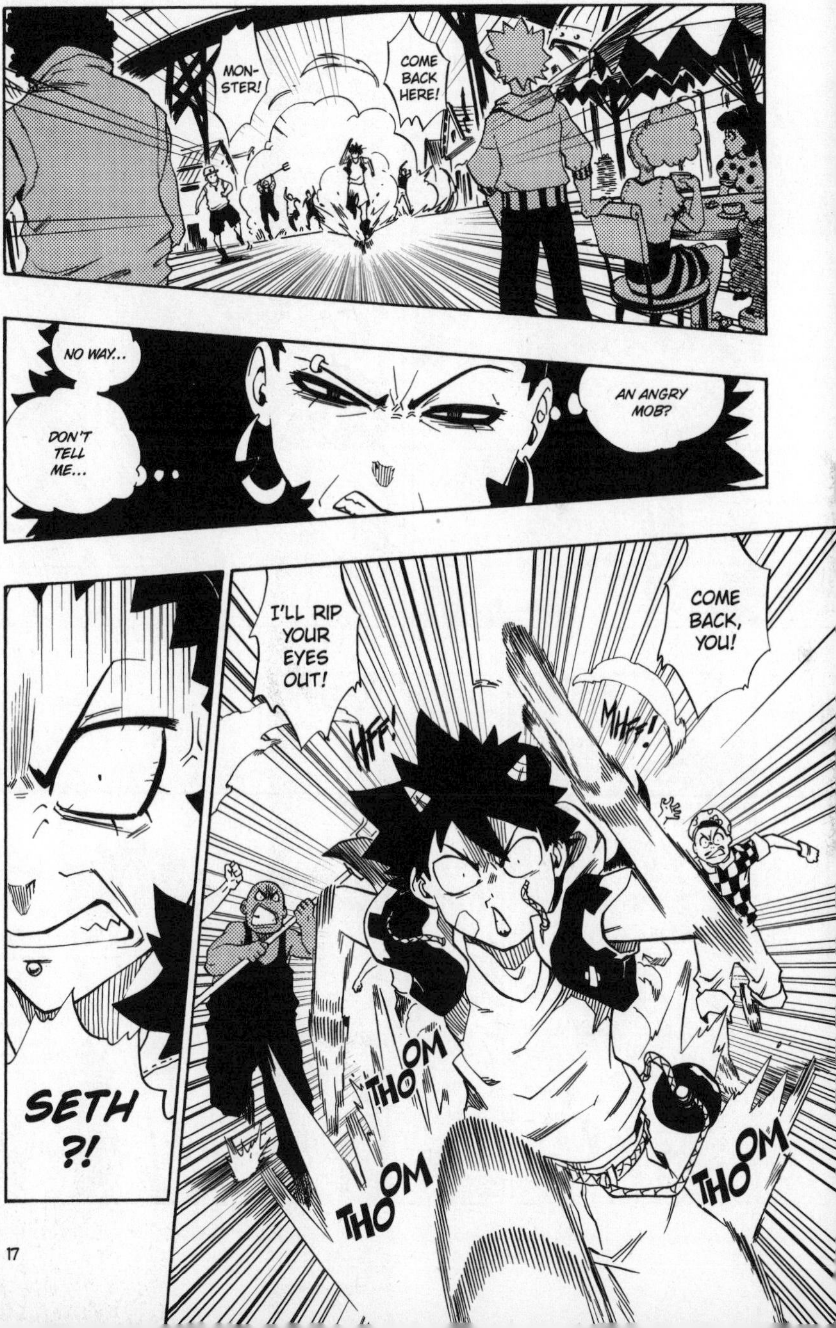

COME BACK HERE!
MON-STER!
NO WAY...
DON'T TELL ME...
AN ANGRY MOB?
COME BACK, YOU!
I'LL RIP YOUR EYES OUT!
MHFF!
HFF!
THOOM
THOOM
THOOM
SETH ?!

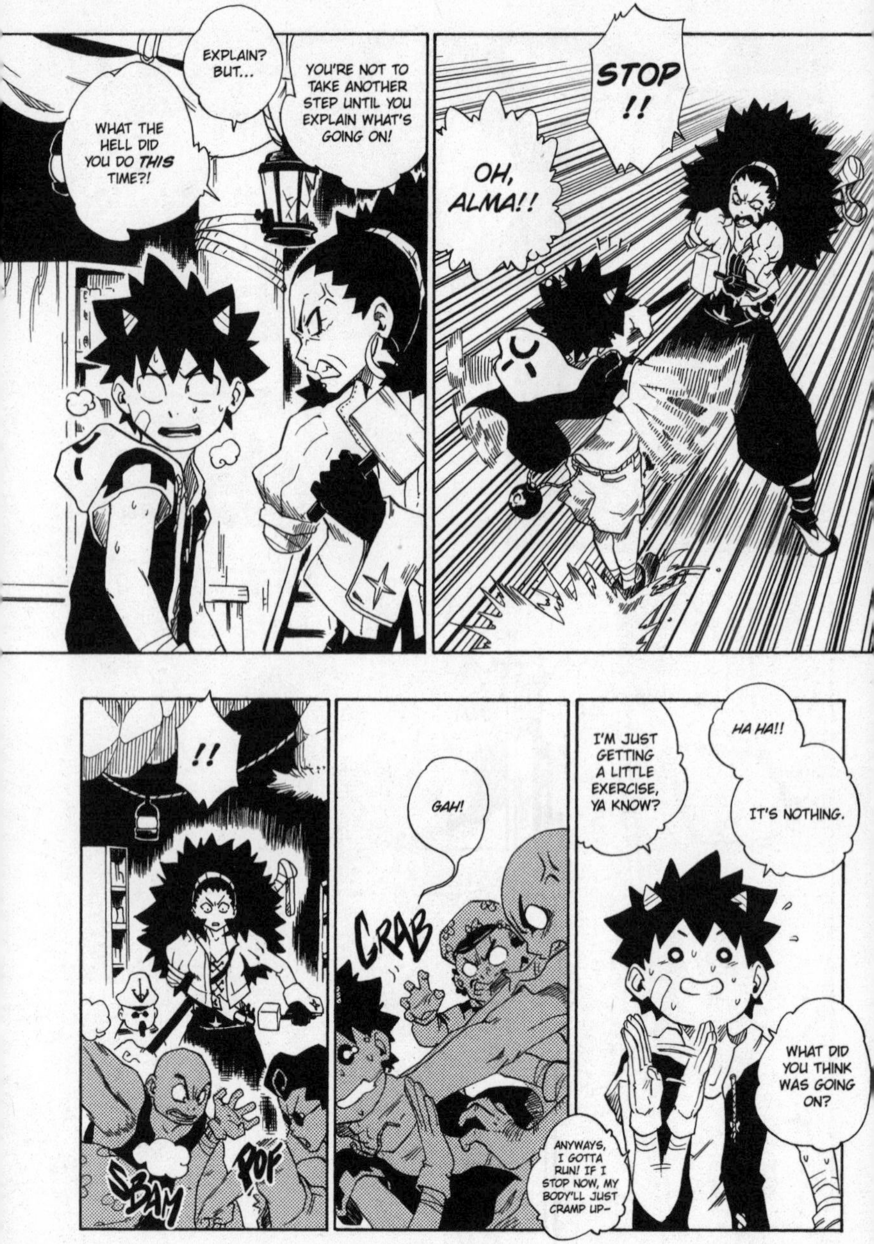
STOP!!
OH, ALMA!!
YOU'RE NOT TO TAKE ANOTHER STEP UNTIL YOU EXPLAIN WHAT'S GOING ON!
EXPLAIN? BUT...
WHAT THE HELL DID YOU DO *THIS* TIME?!
HA HA!!
IT'S NOTHING.
I'M JUST GETTING A LITTLE EXERCISE, YA KNOW?
WHAT DID YOU THINK WAS GOING ON?
ANYWAYS, I GOTTA RUN! IF I STOP NOW, MY BODY'LL JUST CRAMP UP–
GAH!
GRAB
!!
POF
SBAM

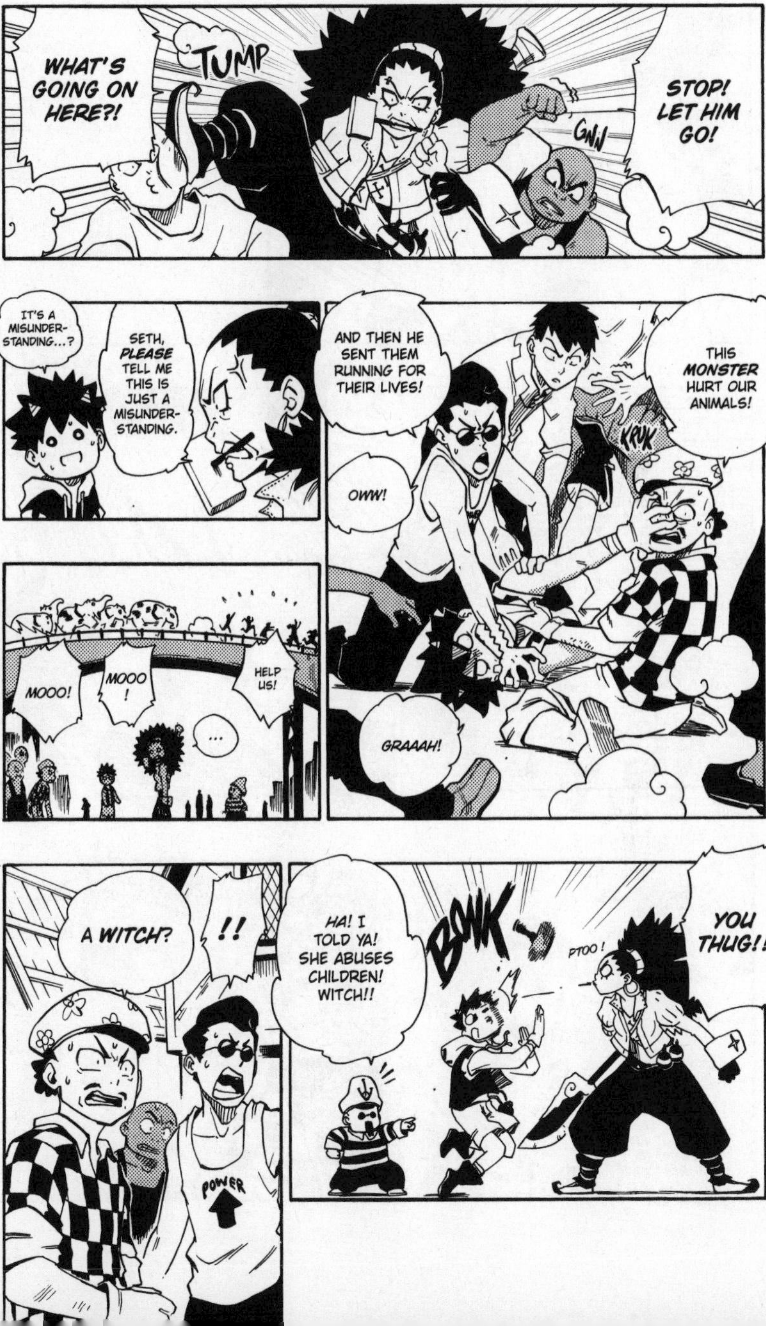
STOP! LET HIM GO!
TUMP
GNN
WHAT'S GOING ON HERE?!
THIS MONSTER HURT OUR ANIMALS!
AND THEN HE SENT THEM RUNNING FOR THEIR LIVES!
KRUK
OWW!
GRAAAH!
SETH, PLEASE TELL ME THIS IS JUST A MISUNDER-STANDING.
IT'S A MISUNDER-STANDING...?
HELP US!
MOOO!
MOOO!
MOOO!
...
YOU THUG!!
PTOO!
BONK
HA! I TOLD YA! SHE ABUSES CHILDREN! WITCH!!
!!
A WITCH?
POWER

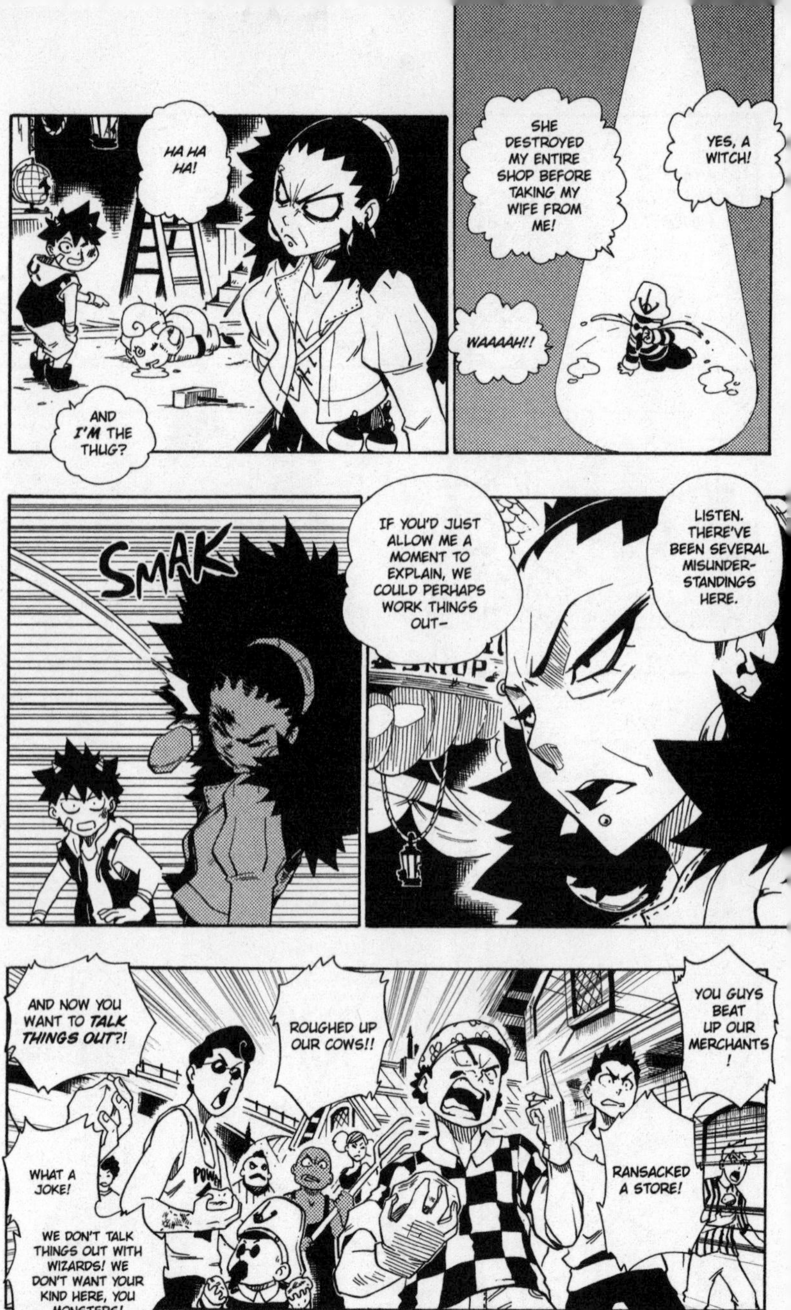
YES, A WITCH!
SHE DESTROYED MY ENTIRE SHOP BEFORE TAKING MY WIFE FROM ME!
WAAAAH!!
HA HA HA!
AND I'M THE THUG?
LISTEN. THERE'VE BEEN SEVERAL MISUNDER-STANDINGS HERE.
IF YOU'D JUST ALLOW ME A MOMENT TO EXPLAIN, WE COULD PERHAPS WORK THINGS OUT-
SMAK
YOU GUYS BEAT UP OUR MERCHANTS!
ROUGHED UP OUR COWS!!
AND NOW YOU WANT TO TALK THINGS OUT?!
RANSACKED A STORE!
WHAT A JOKE!
WE DON'T TALK THINGS OUT WITH WIZARDS! WE DON'T WANT YOUR KIND HERE, YOU MONSTERS!

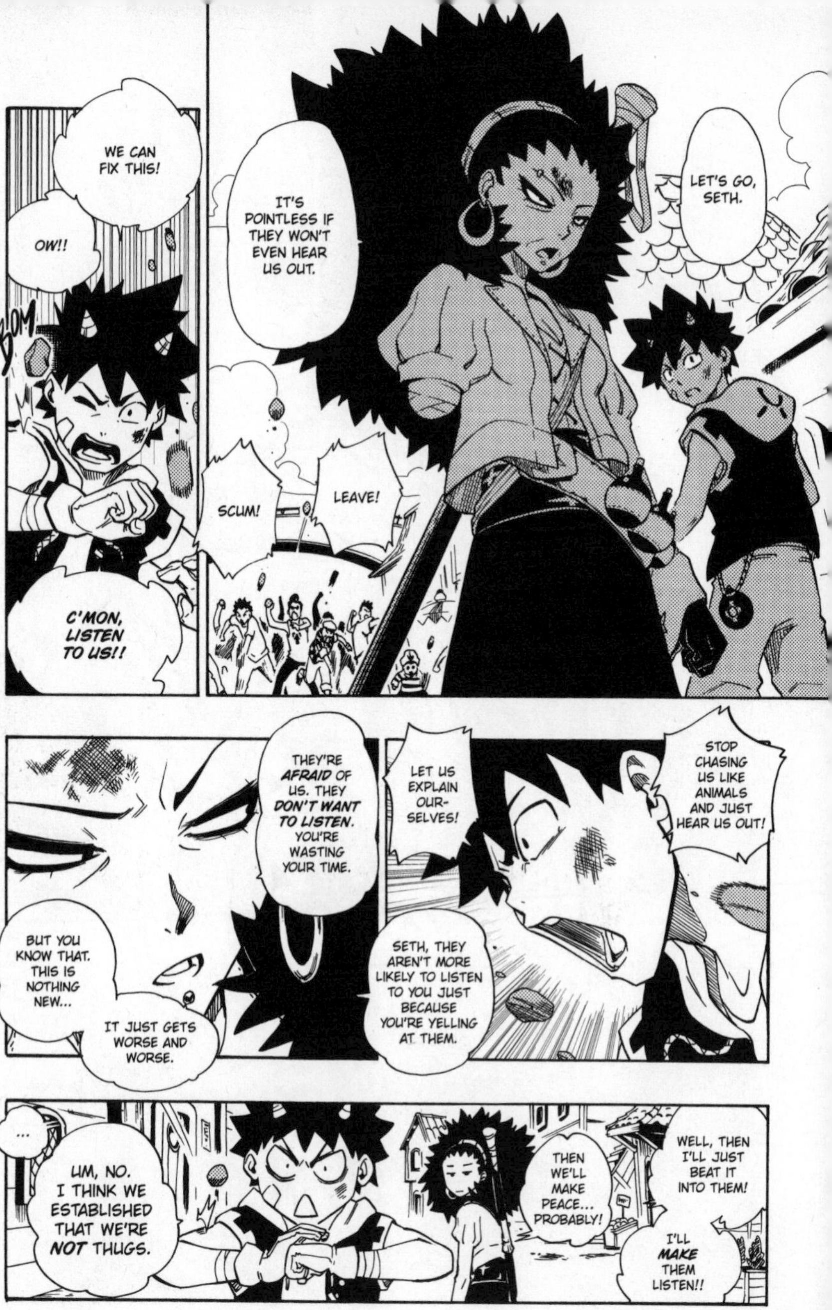
LET'S GO, SETH.
IT'S POINTLESS IF THEY WON'T EVEN HEAR US OUT.
LEAVE!
SCUM!
WE CAN FIX THIS!
OW!!
BOM
C'MON, LISTEN TO US!!
STOP CHASING US LIKE ANIMALS AND JUST HEAR US OUT!
LET US EXPLAIN OUR-SELVES!
SETH, THEY AREN'T MORE LIKELY TO LISTEN TO YOU JUST BECAUSE YOU'RE YELLING AT THEM.
THEY'RE AFRAID OF US. THEY DON'T WANT TO LISTEN. YOU'RE WASTING YOUR TIME.
BUT YOU KNOW THAT. THIS IS NOTHING NEW...
IT JUST GETS WORSE AND WORSE.
WELL, THEN I'LL JUST BEAT IT INTO THEM!
I'LL MAKE THEM LISTEN!!
THEN WE'LL MAKE PEACE... PROBABLY!
...
UM, NO. I THINK WE ESTABLISHED THAT WE'RE NOT THUGS.

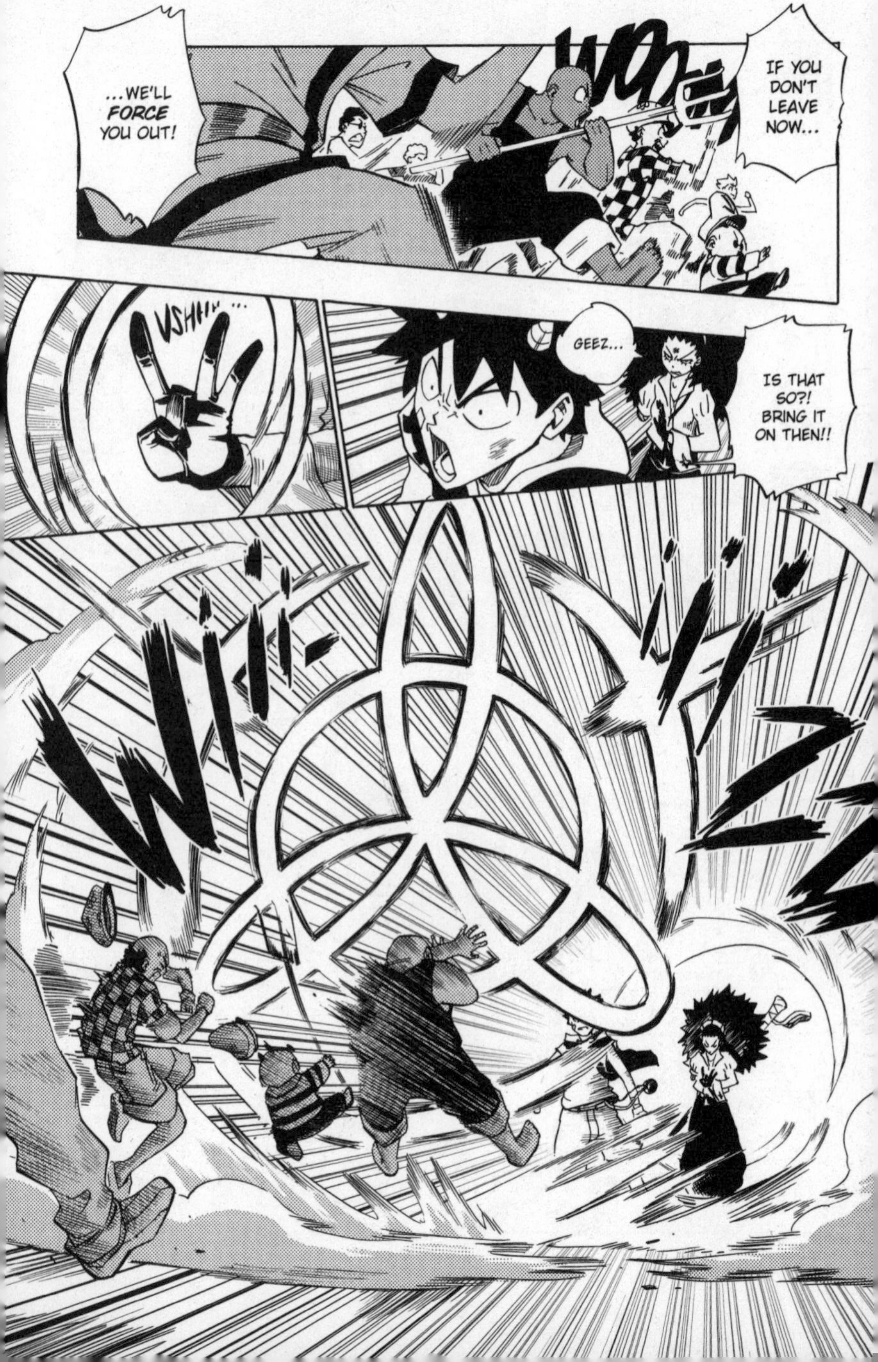
IF YOU DON'T LEAVE NOW...
...WE'LL FORCE YOU OUT!
IS THAT SO?! BRING IT ON THEN!!
GEEZ...

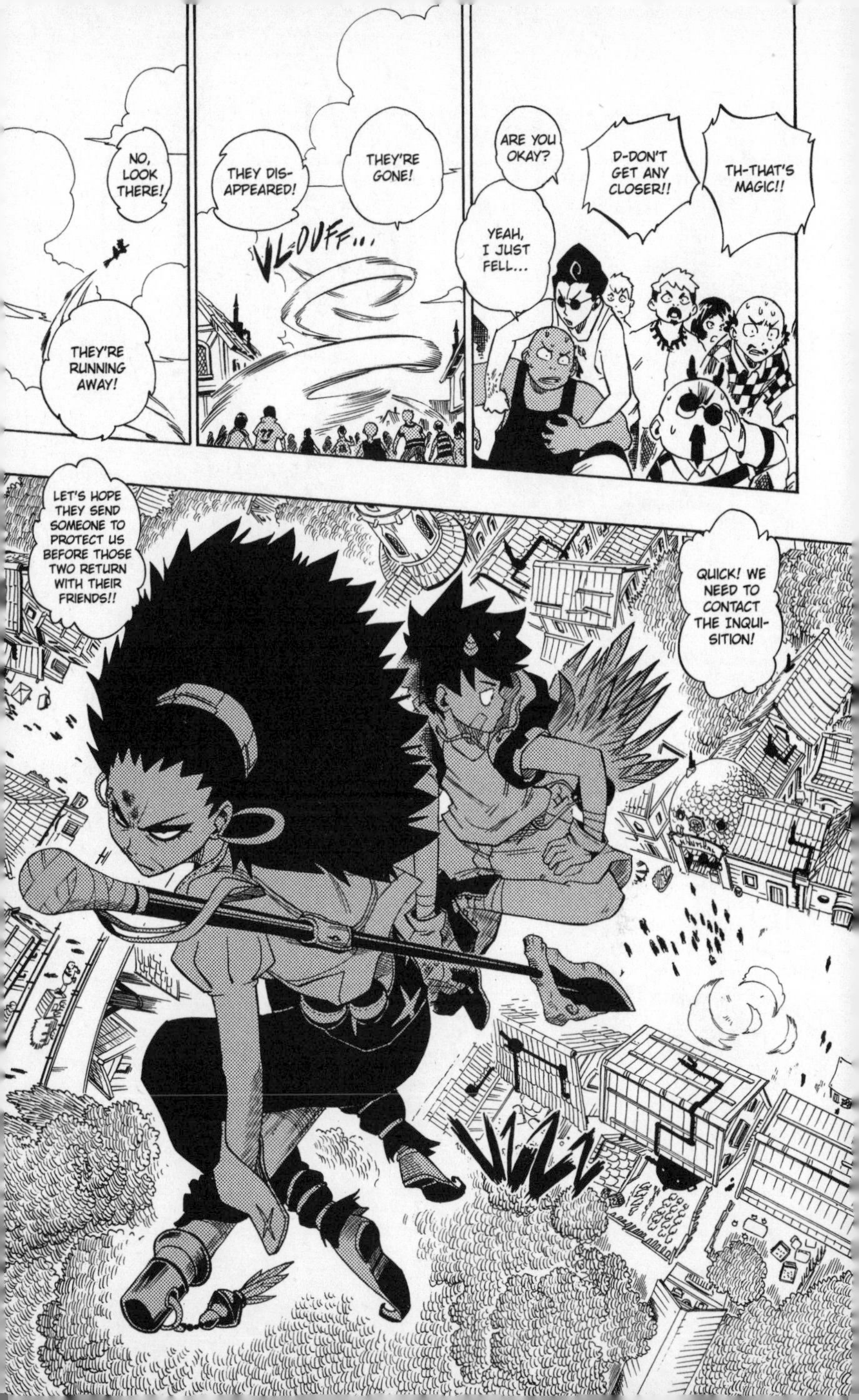
TH-THAT'S MAGIC!!
D-DON'T GET ANY CLOSER!!
ARE YOU OKAY?
YEAH, I JUST FELL...
THEY'RE GONE!
THEY DIS-APPEARED!
VLOUFF...
NO, LOOK THERE!
THEY'RE RUNNING AWAY!
QUICK! WE NEED TO CONTACT THE INQUISITION!
LET'S HOPE THEY SEND SOMEONE TO PROTECT US BEFORE THOSE TWO RETURN WITH THEIR FRIENDS!!

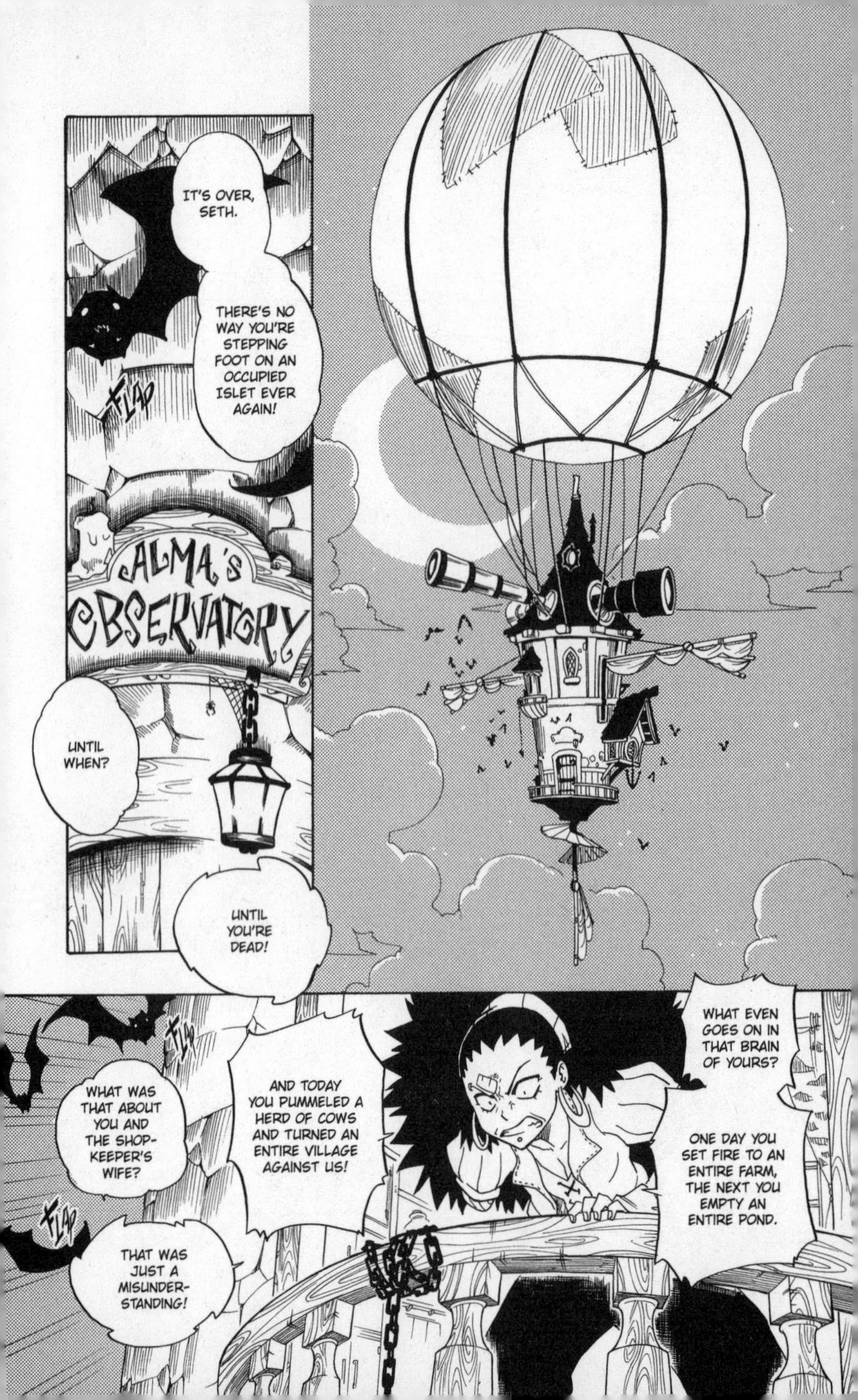
IT'S OVER, SETH.
THERE'S NO WAY YOU'RE STEPPING FOOT ON AN OCCUPIED ISLET EVER AGAIN!
FLAP
ALMA'S OBSERVATORY
UNTIL WHEN?
UNTIL YOU'RE DEAD!
WHAT EVEN GOES ON IN THAT BRAIN OF YOURS?
ONE DAY YOU SET FIRE TO AN ENTIRE FARM, THE NEXT YOU EMPTY AN ENTIRE POND.
AND TODAY YOU PUMMELED A HERD OF COWS AND TURNED AN ENTIRE VILLAGE AGAINST US!
FLAP
WHAT WAS THAT ABOUT YOU AND THE SHOP-KEEPER'S WIFE?
FLAP
THAT WAS JUST A MISUNDER-STANDING!

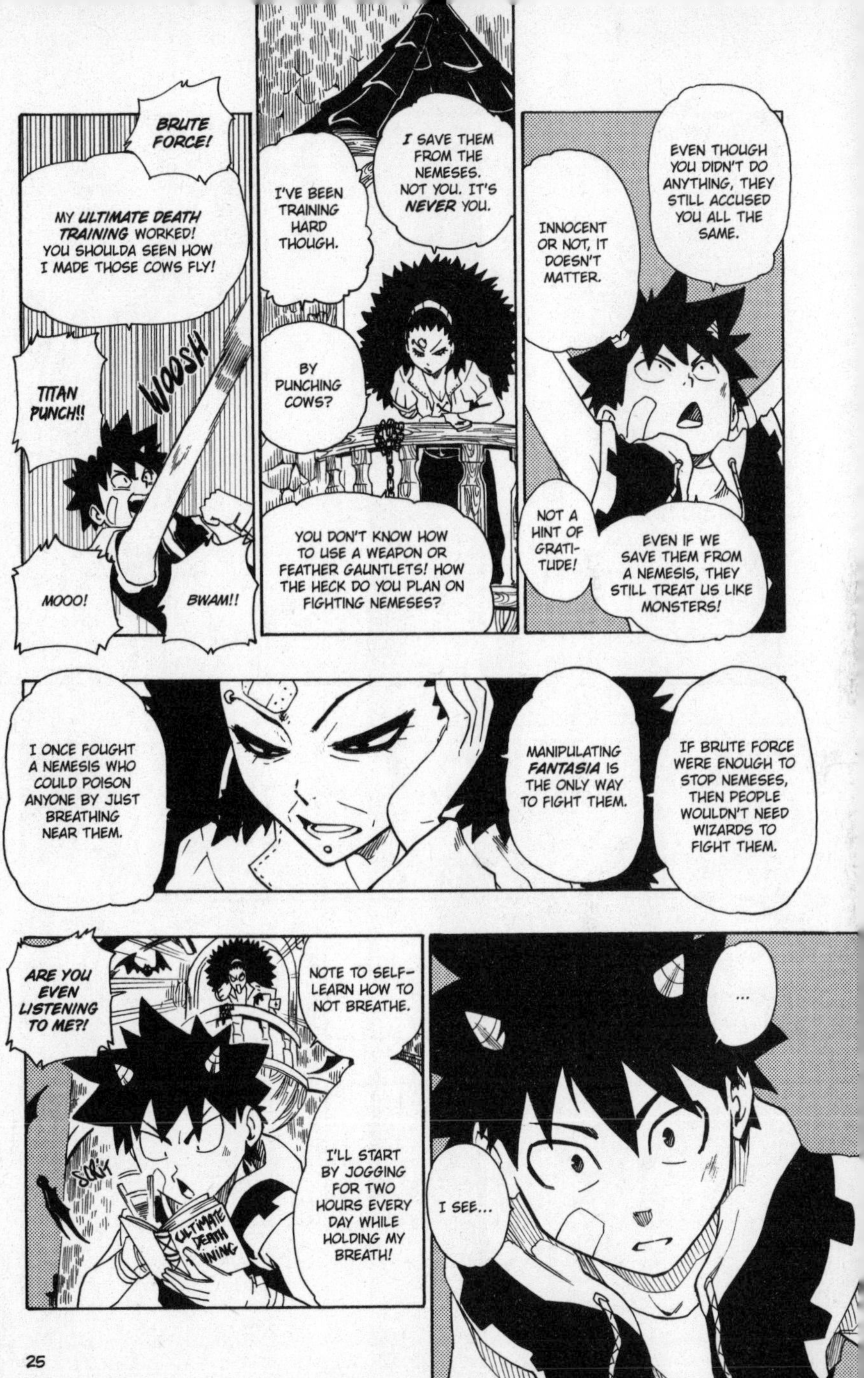

EVEN THOUGH YOU DIDN'T DO ANYTHING, THEY STILL ACCUSED YOU ALL THE SAME.
INNOCENT OR NOT, IT DOESN'T MATTER.
EVEN IF WE SAVE THEM FROM A NEMESIS, THEY STILL TREAT US LIKE MONSTERS!
NOT A HINT OF GRATI-TUDE!
I SAVE THEM FROM THE NEMESES. NOT YOU. IT'S ***NEVER*** YOU.
I'VE BEEN TRAINING HARD THOUGH.
BY PUNCHING COWS?
YOU DON'T KNOW HOW TO USE A WEAPON OR FEATHER GAUNTLETS! HOW THE HECK DO YOU PLAN ON FIGHTING NEMESES?
BRUTE FORCE!
MY ***ULTIMATE DEATH TRAINING*** WORKED! YOU SHOULDA SEEN HOW I MADE THOSE COWS FLY!
WOOSH
TITAN PUNCH!!
BWAM!!
MOOO!
IF BRUTE FORCE WERE ENOUGH TO STOP NEMESES, THEN PEOPLE WOULDN'T NEED WIZARDS TO FIGHT THEM.
MANIPULATING ***FANTASIA*** IS THE ONLY WAY TO FIGHT THEM.
I ONCE FOUGHT A NEMESIS WHO COULD POISON ANYONE BY JUST BREATHING NEAR THEM.
...
I SEE...
NOTE TO SELF-LEARN HOW TO NOT BREATHE.
ARE YOU EVEN LISTENING TO ME?!
I'LL START BY JOGGING FOR TWO HOURS EVERY DAY WHILE HOLDING MY BREATH!

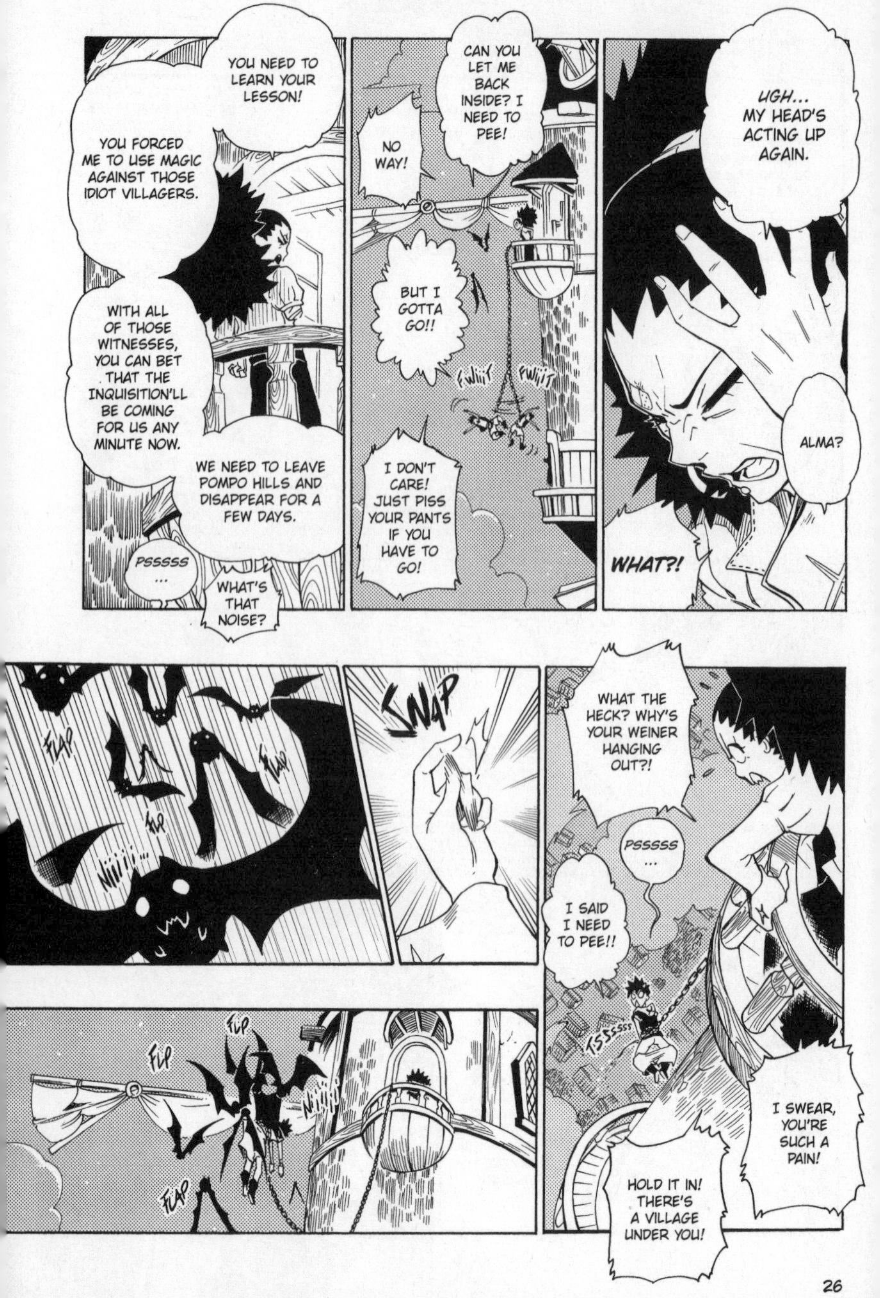
UGH... MY HEAD'S ACTING UP AGAIN.
ALMA?
WHAT?!
CAN YOU LET ME BACK INSIDE? I NEED TO PEE!
NO WAY!
BUT I GOTTA GO!!
FWIIT FWIIT
I DON'T CARE! JUST PISS YOUR PANTS IF YOU HAVE TO GO!
YOU NEED TO LEARN YOUR LESSON!
YOU FORCED ME TO USE MAGIC AGAINST THOSE IDIOT VILLAGERS.
WITH ALL OF THOSE WITNESSES, YOU CAN BET THAT THE INQUISITION'LL BE COMING FOR US ANY MINUTE NOW.
WE NEED TO LEAVE POMPO HILLS AND DISAPPEAR FOR A FEW DAYS.
PSSSSS ...
WHAT'S THAT NOISE?
WHAT THE HECK? WHY'S YOUR WEINER HANGING OUT?!
PSSSSS ...
I SAID I NEED TO PEE!!
TSSSSS
I SWEAR, YOU'RE SUCH A PAIN!
HOLD IT IN! THERE'S A VILLAGE UNDER YOU!
SNAP
FLAP
FLAP
NIIII...
FLIP
FLIP
NIIII
FLAP

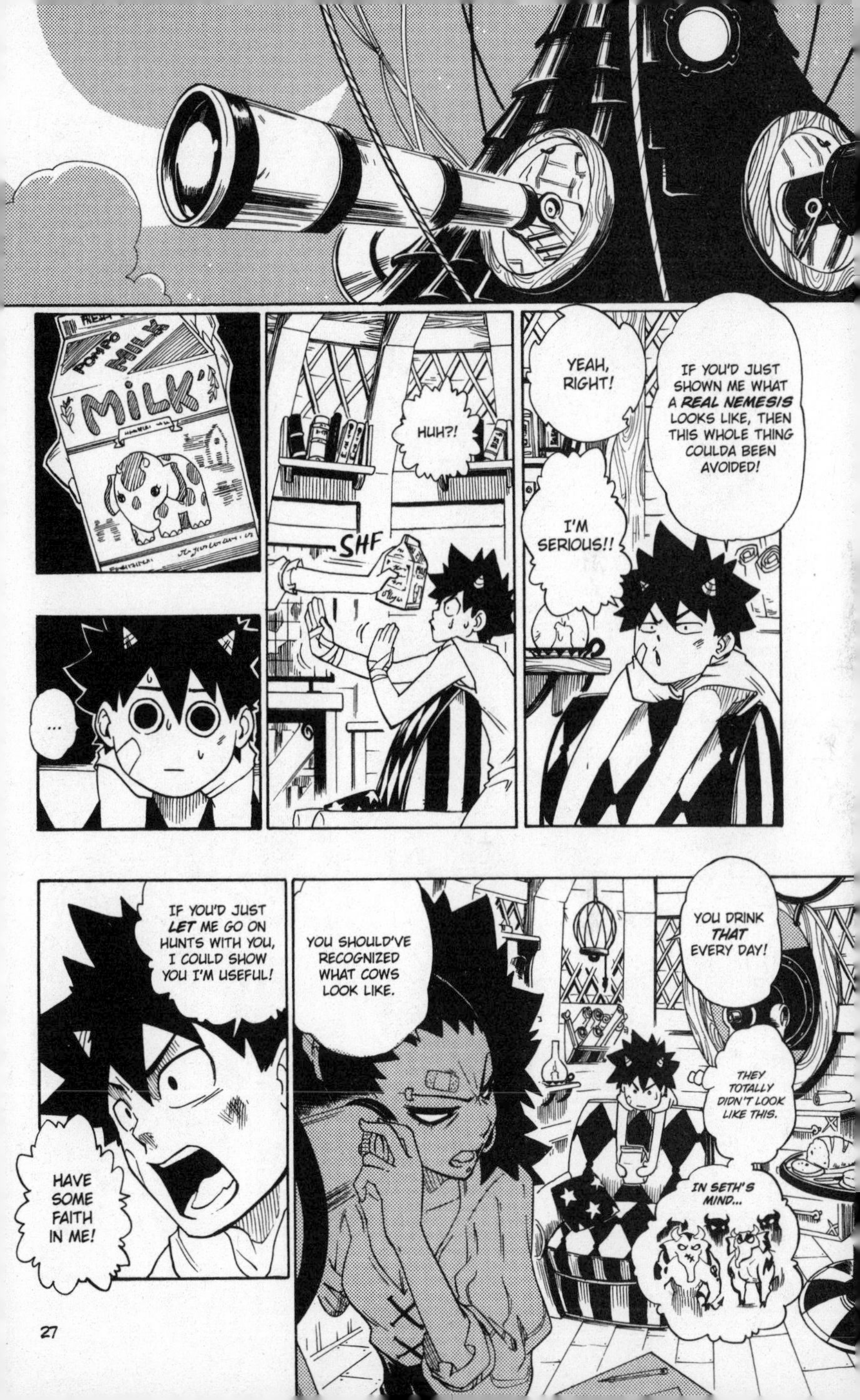
IF YOU'D JUST SHOWN ME WHAT A REAL NEMESIS LOOKS LIKE, THEN THIS WHOLE THING COULDA BEEN AVOIDED!
YEAH, RIGHT!
I'M SERIOUS!!
HUH?!
SHF
POMPO MILK
MiLK
...
YOU DRINK THAT EVERY DAY!
THEY TOTALLY DIDN'T LOOK LIKE THIS.
IN SETH'S MIND...
YOU SHOULD'VE RECOGNIZED WHAT COWS LOOK LIKE.
IF YOU'D JUST LET ME GO ON HUNTS WITH YOU, I COULD SHOW YOU I'M USEFUL!
HAVE SOME FAITH IN ME!

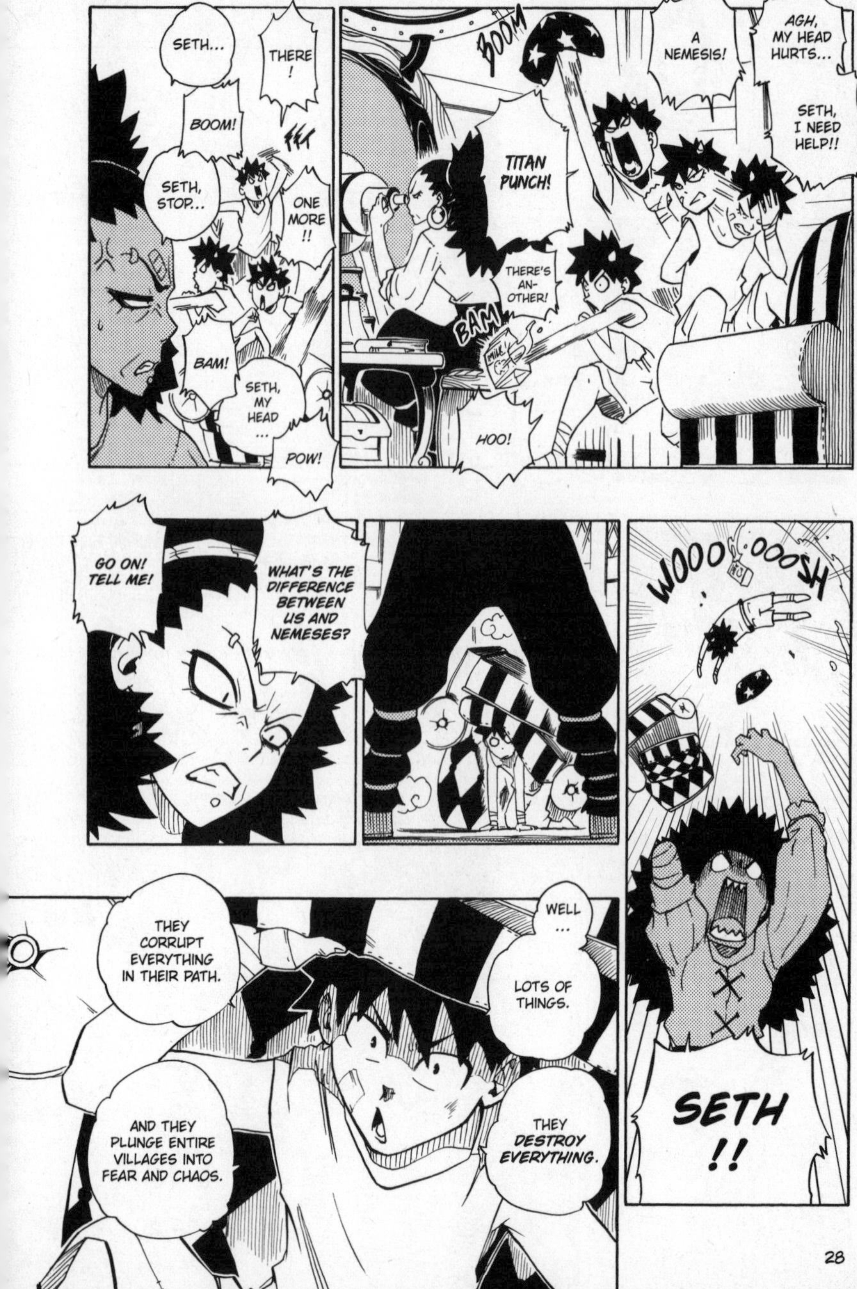
AGH, MY HEAD HURTS...
SETH, I NEED HELP!!
A NEMESIS!
BOOM
TITAN PUNCH!
THERE'S AN-OTHER!
BAM
HOO!
THERE !
SETH...
BOOM!
ONE MORE !!
SETH, STOP...
BAM!
SETH, MY HEAD ...
POW!
WOOOOOOSH
SETH !!
WHAT'S THE DIFFERENCE BETWEEN US AND NEMESES?
GO ON! TELL ME!
WELL ...
LOTS OF THINGS.
THEY CORRUPT EVERYTHING IN THEIR PATH.
THEY DESTROY EVERYTHING.
AND THEY PLUNGE ENTIRE VILLAGES INTO FEAR AND CHAOS.

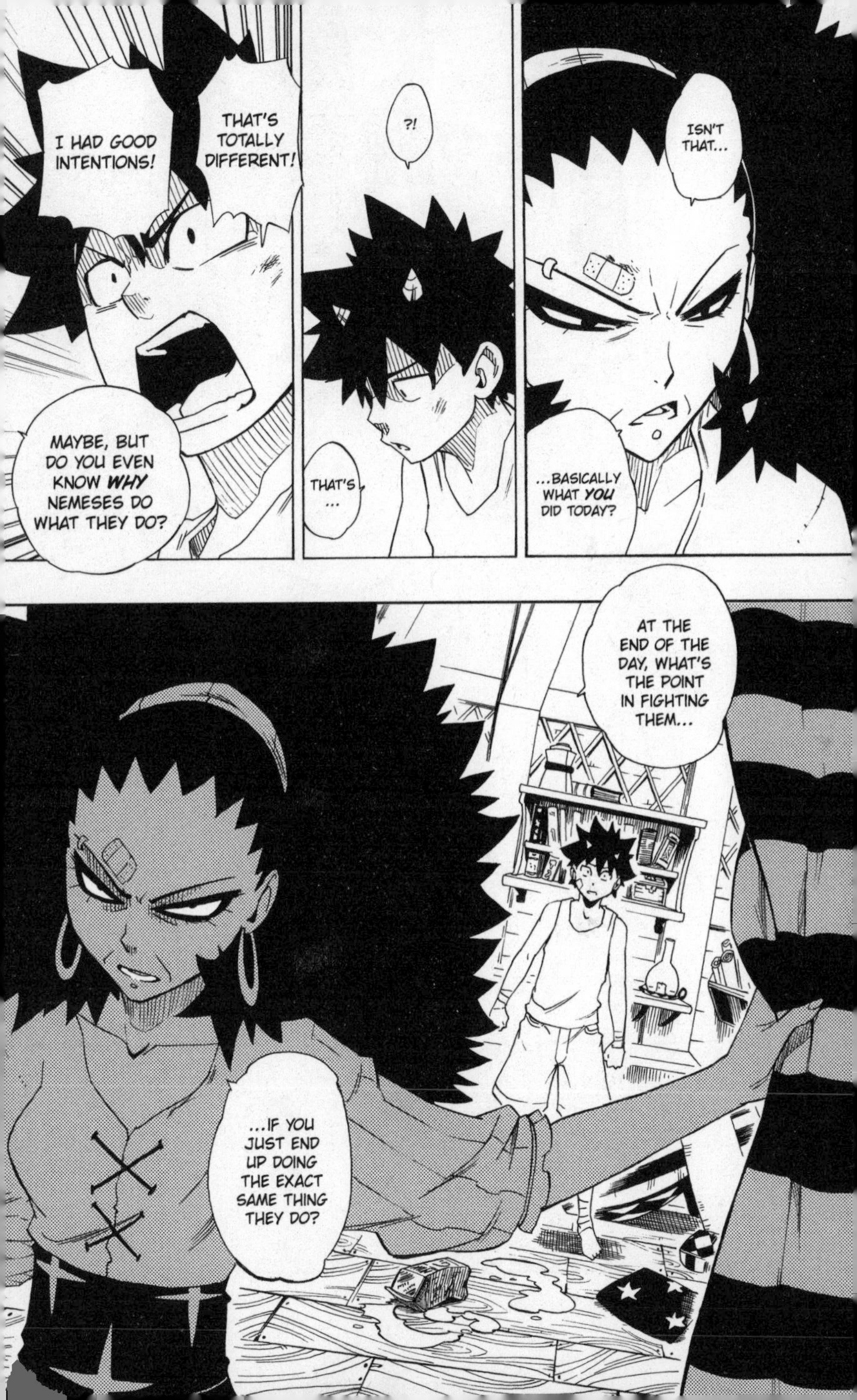
ISN'T THAT...
...BASICALLY WHAT YOU DID TODAY?
?!
THAT'S ...
THAT'S TOTALLY DIFFERENT!
I HAD GOOD INTENTIONS!
MAYBE, BUT DO YOU EVEN KNOW WHY NEMESES DO WHAT THEY DO?
AT THE END OF THE DAY, WHAT'S THE POINT IN FIGHTING THEM...
...IF YOU JUST END UP DOING THE EXACT SAME THING THEY DO?

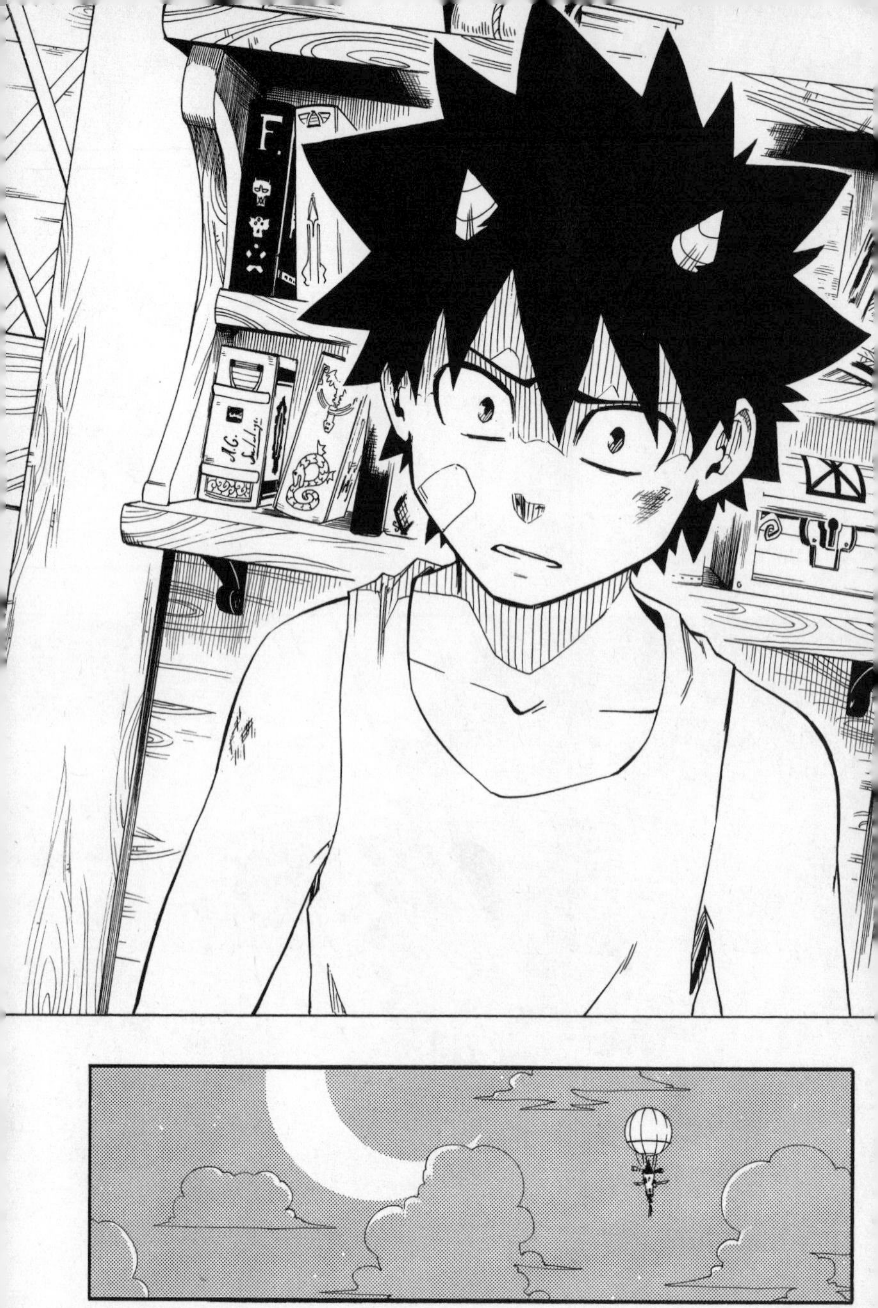
F.

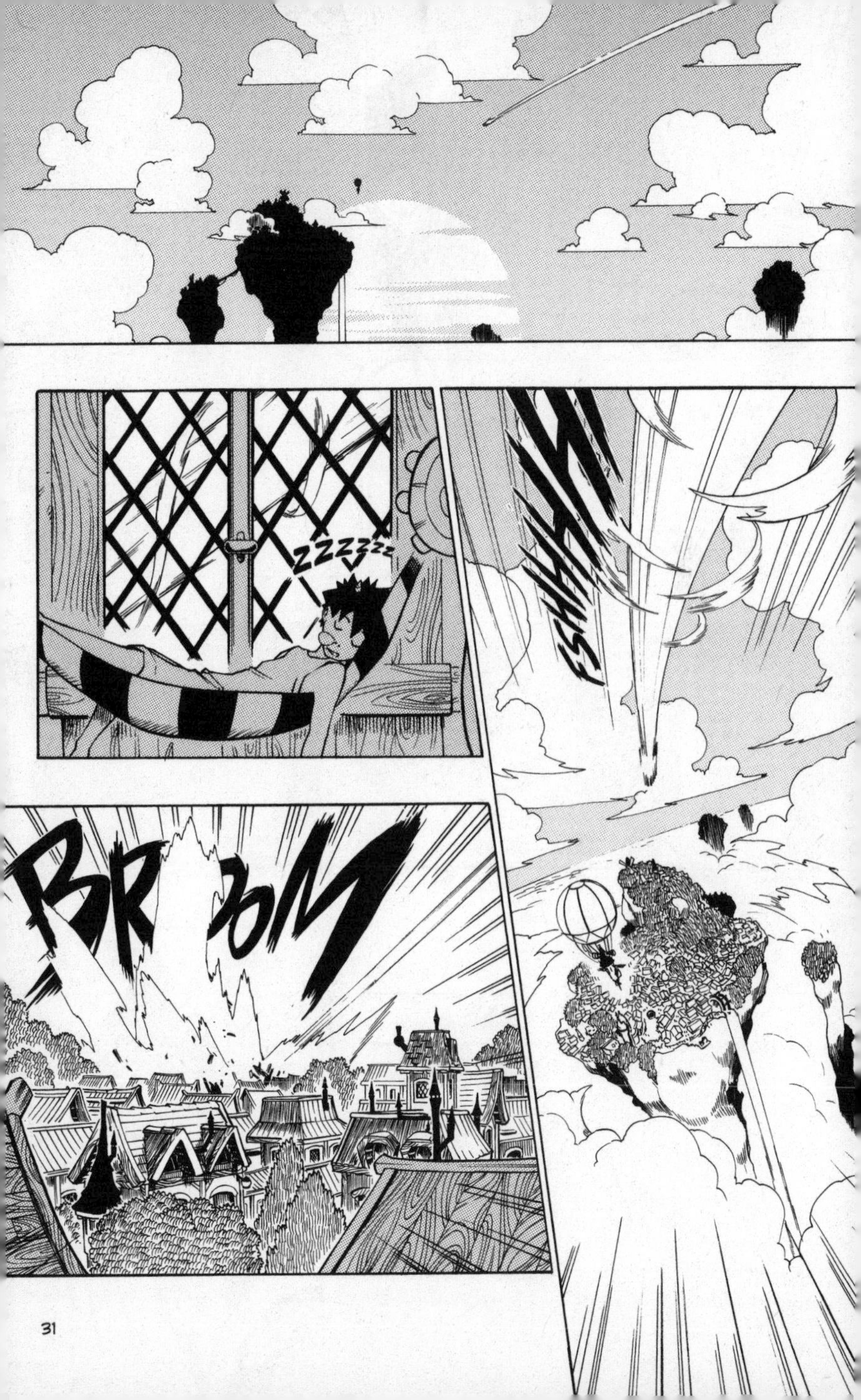
FSHWHH
ZZZZZZ
BROOM

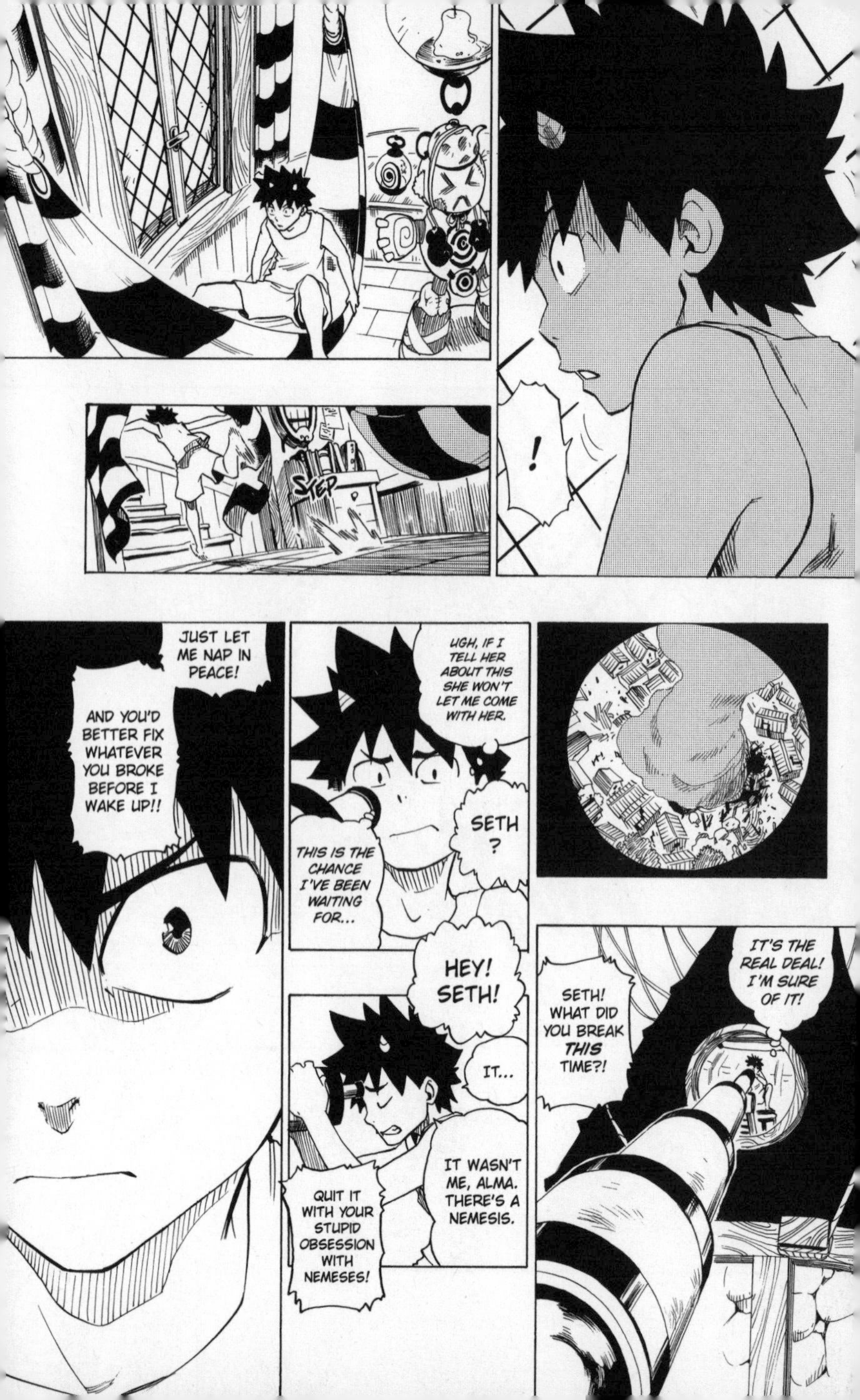
!
STEP
IT'S THE REAL DEAL! I'M SURE OF IT!
SETH! WHAT DID YOU BREAK THIS TIME?!
UGH, IF I TELL HER ABOUT THIS SHE WON'T LET ME COME WITH HER.
SETH?
THIS IS THE CHANCE I'VE BEEN WAITING FOR...
HEY! SETH!
IT...
IT WASN'T ME, ALMA. THERE'S A NEMESIS.
QUIT IT WITH YOUR STUPID OBSESSION WITH NEMESES!
JUST LET ME NAP IN PEACE!
AND YOU'D BETTER FIX WHATEVER YOU BROKE BEFORE I WAKE UP!!

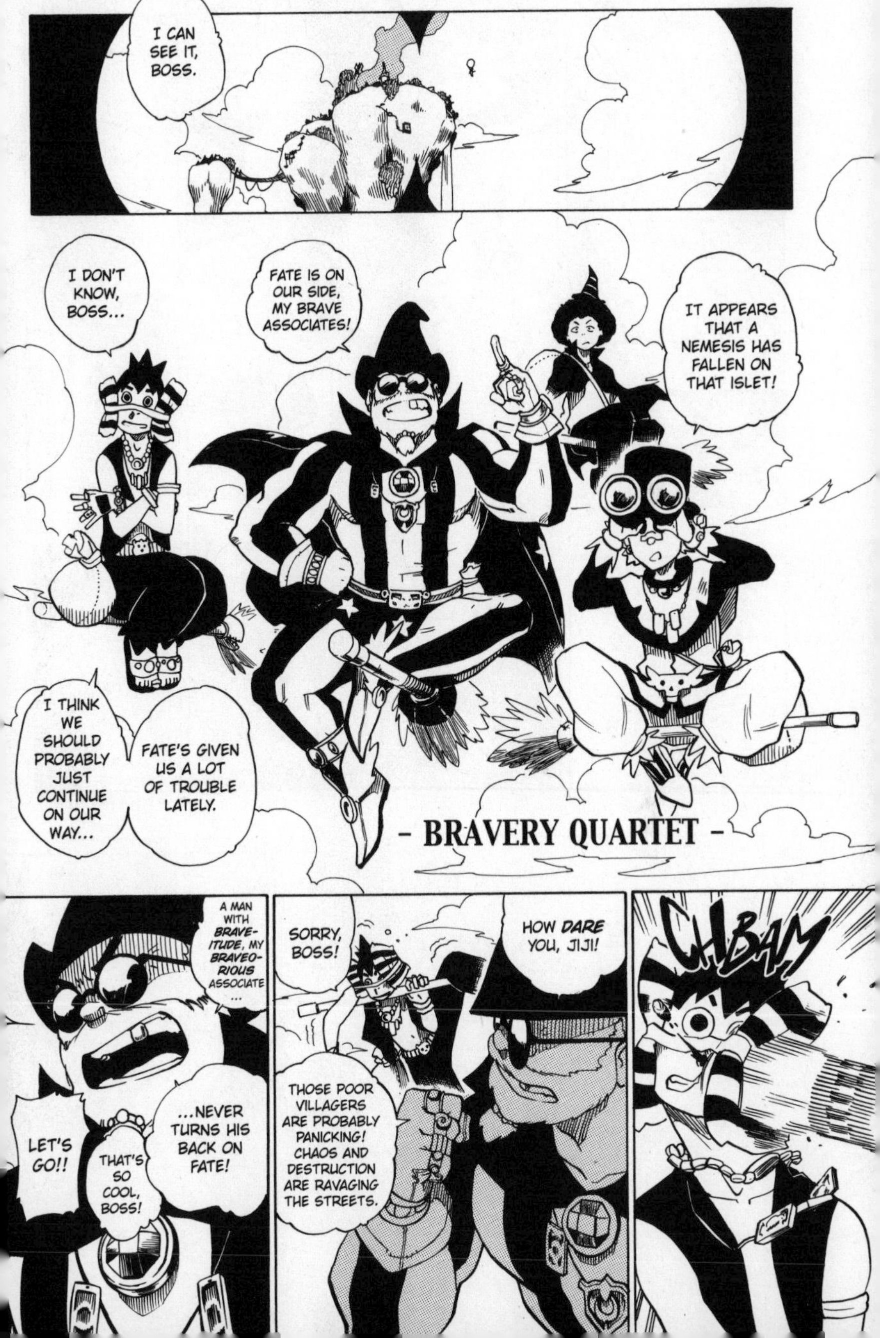
I CAN SEE IT, BOSS.
IT APPEARS THAT A NEMESIS HAS FALLEN ON THAT ISLET!
FATE IS ON OUR SIDE, MY BRAVE ASSOCIATES!
I DON'T KNOW, BOSS...
FATE'S GIVEN US A LOT OF TROUBLE LATELY.
I THINK WE SHOULD PROBABLY JUST CONTINUE ON OUR WAY...
- BRAVERY QUARTET -
CHBAM
HOW DARE YOU, JIJI!
SORRY, BOSS!
THOSE POOR VILLAGERS ARE PROBABLY PANICKING! CHAOS AND DESTRUCTION ARE RAVAGING THE STREETS.
A MAN WITH BRAVE-ITUDE, MY BRAVEO-RIOUS ASSOCIATE ...
...NEVER TURNS HIS BACK ON FATE!
THAT'S SO COOL, BOSS!
LET'S GO!!

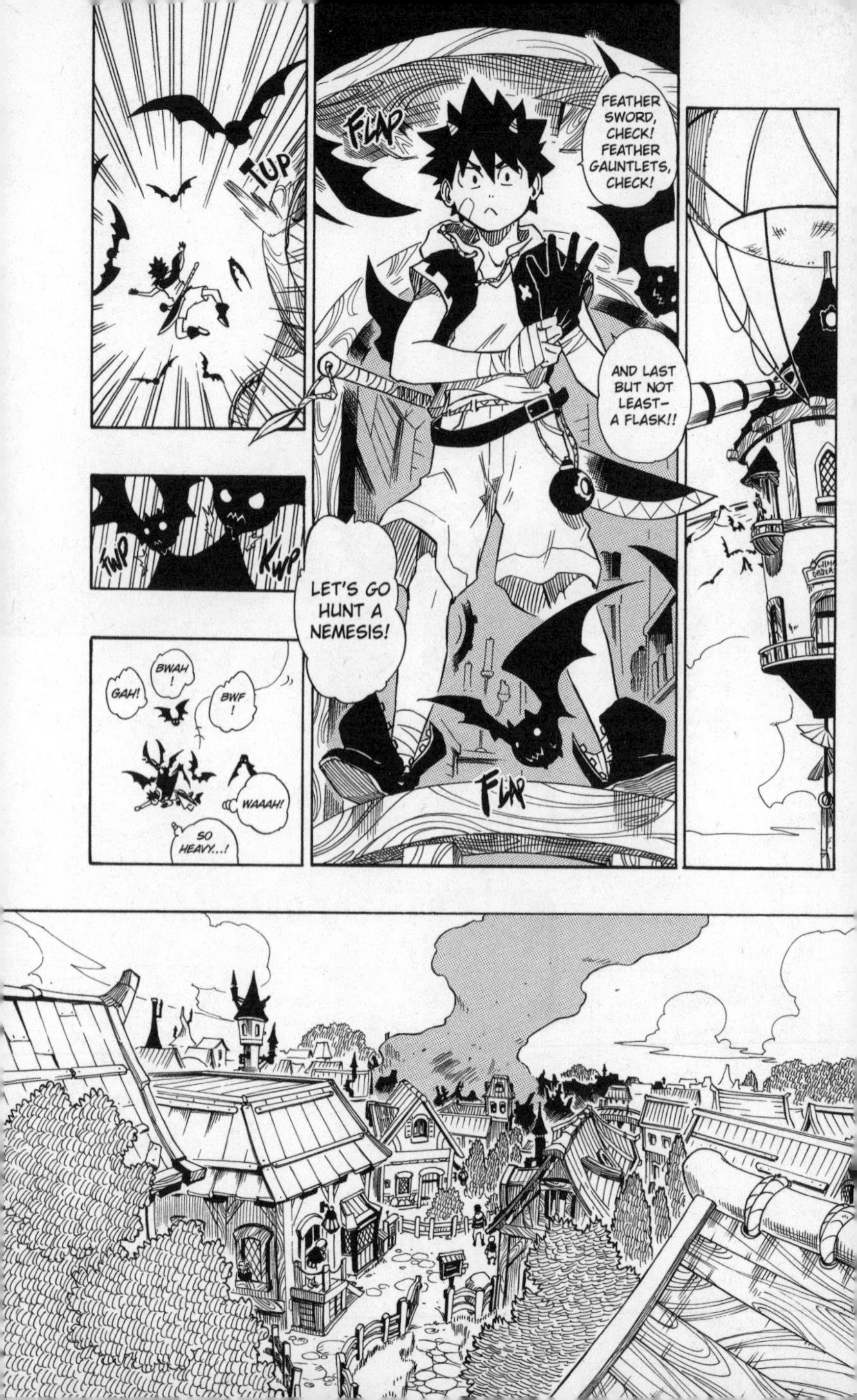
FLAP
FEATHER SWORD, CHECK! FEATHER GAUNTLETS, CHECK!
AND LAST BUT NOT LEAST— A FLASK!!
LET'S GO HUNT A NEMESIS!
FLAP
TUP
FWP
KWP
BWAH!
GAH!
BWF!
WAAAH!
SO HEAVY...!

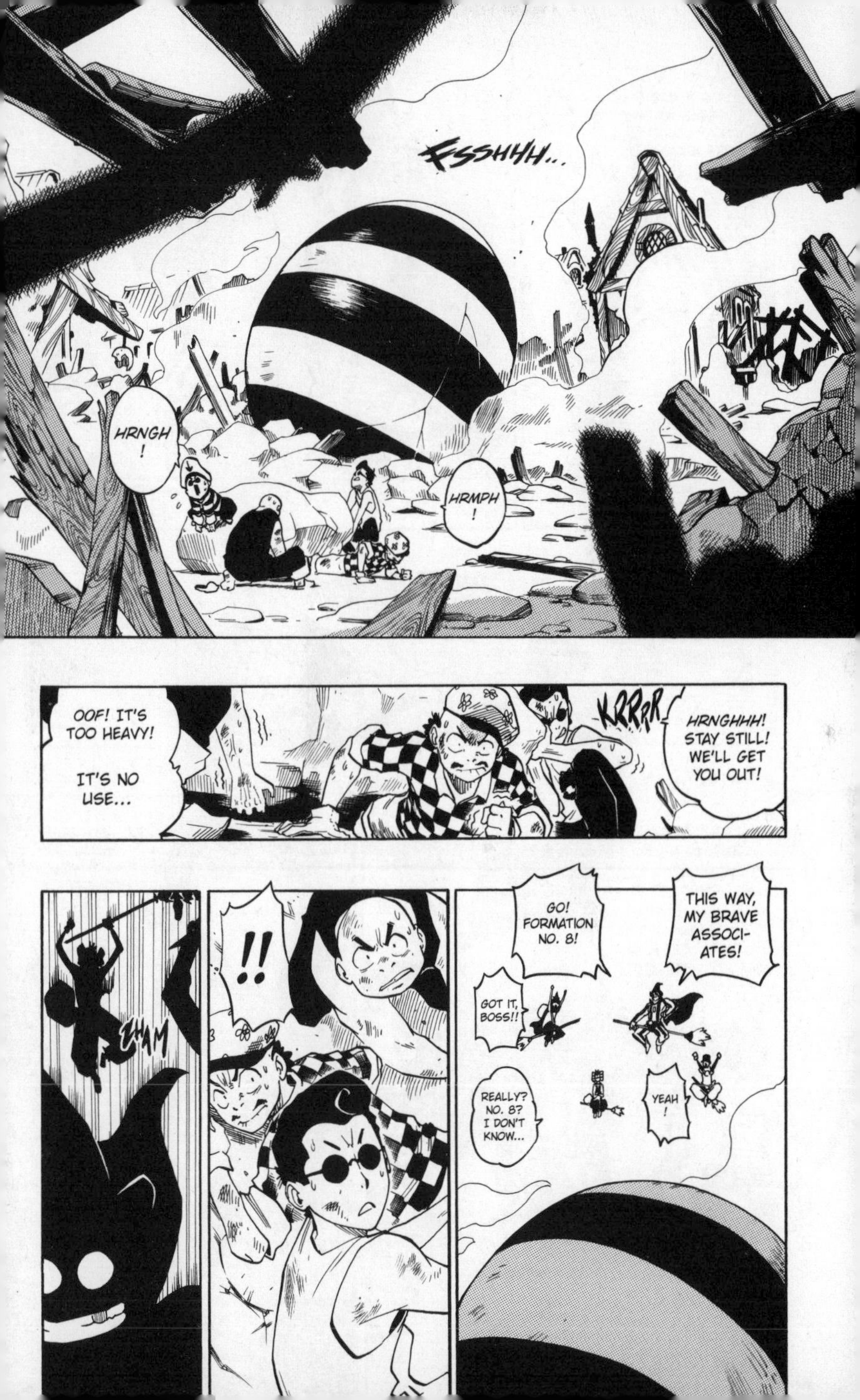
FSSHHH...
HRMPH!
HRNGH!
KRRRR
HRNGHHH! STAY STILL! WE'LL GET YOU OUT!
OOF! IT'S TOO HEAVY!
IT'S NO USE...
THIS WAY, MY BRAVE ASSOCI-ATES!
GO! FORMATION NO. 8!
YEAH!
GOT IT, BOSS!!
REALLY? NO. 8? I DON'T KNOW...
!!
ZHAM

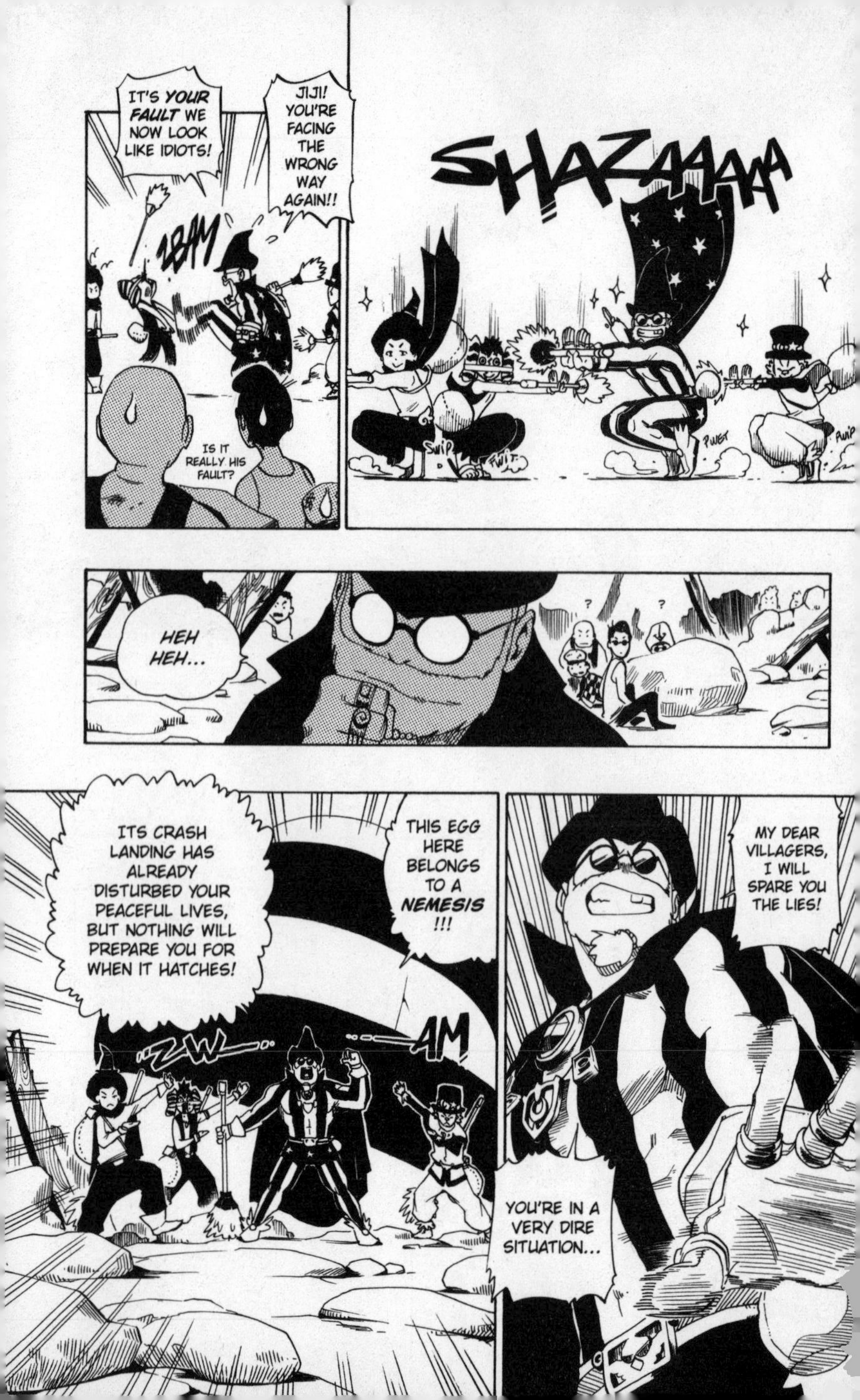
SHAZAAAAA
JIJI! YOU'RE FACING THE WRONG WAY AGAIN!!
IT'S YOUR FAULT WE NOW LOOK LIKE IDIOTS!
IS IT REALLY HIS FAULT?
HEH HEH...
MY DEAR VILLAGERS, I WILL SPARE YOU THE LIES!
YOU'RE IN A VERY DIRE SITUATION...
THIS EGG HERE BELONGS TO A NEMESIS!!!
ITS CRASH LANDING HAS ALREADY DISTURBED YOUR PEACEFUL LIVES, BUT NOTHING WILL PREPARE YOU FOR WHEN IT HATCHES!

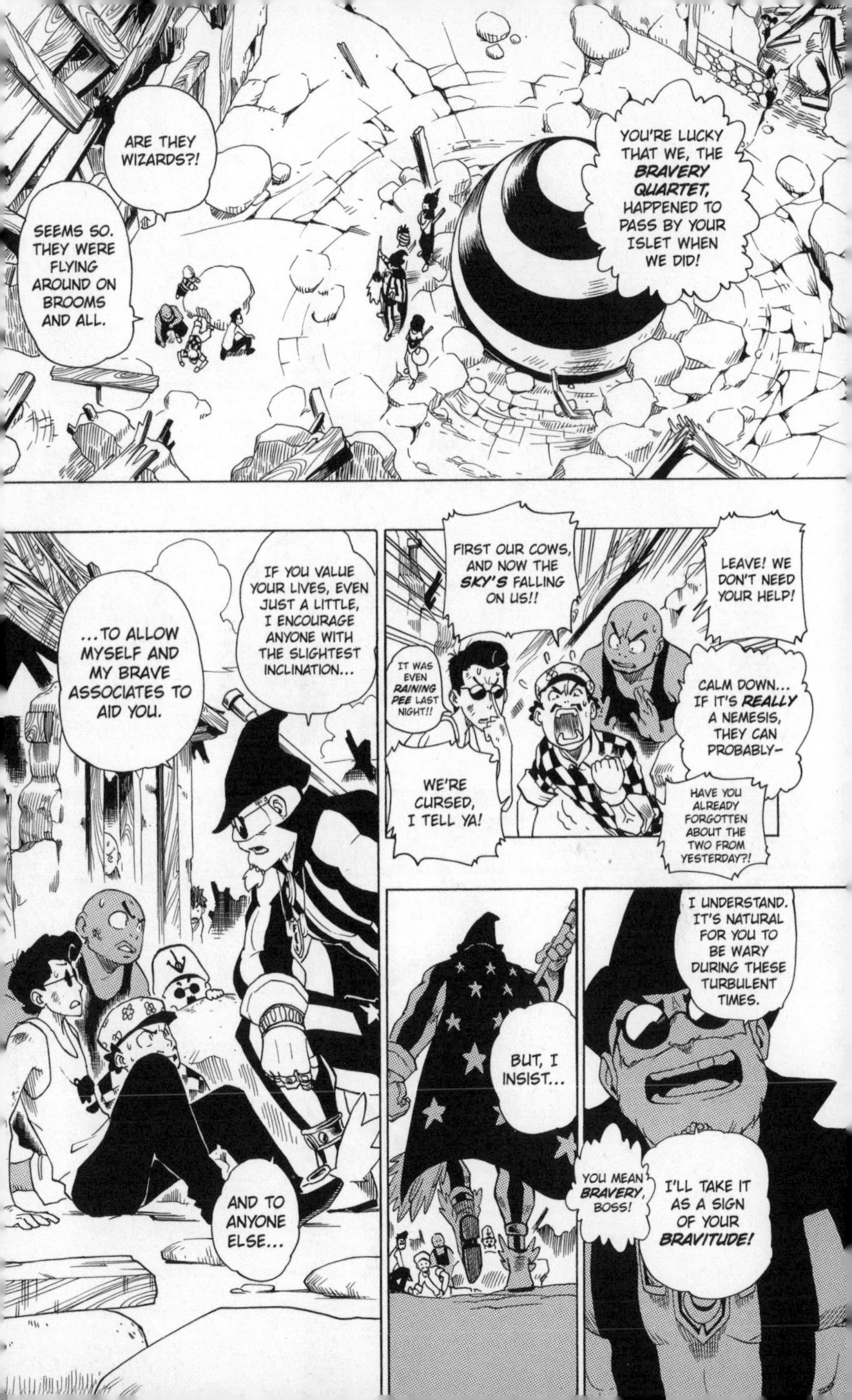

YOU'RE LUCKY THAT WE, THE ***BRAVERY QUARTET,*** HAPPENED TO PASS BY YOUR ISLET WHEN WE DID!
ARE THEY WIZARDS?!
SEEMS SO. THEY WERE FLYING AROUND ON BROOMS AND ALL.
LEAVE! WE DON'T NEED YOUR HELP!
FIRST OUR COWS, AND NOW THE ***SKY'S*** FALLING ON US!!
IT WAS EVEN ***RAINING PEE*** LAST NIGHT!!
CALM DOWN... IF IT'S ***REALLY*** A NEMESIS, THEY CAN PROBABLY-
HAVE YOU ALREADY FORGOTTEN ABOUT THE TWO FROM YESTERDAY?!
WE'RE CURSED, I TELL YA!
I UNDERSTAND. IT'S NATURAL FOR YOU TO BE WARY DURING THESE TURBULENT TIMES.
I'LL TAKE IT AS A SIGN OF YOUR ***BRAVITUDE!***
YOU MEAN ***BRAVERY,*** BOSS!
BUT, I INSIST...
IF YOU VALUE YOUR LIVES, EVEN JUST A LITTLE, I ENCOURAGE ANYONE WITH THE SLIGHTEST INCLINATION...
...TO ALLOW MYSELF AND MY BRAVE ASSOCIATES TO AID YOU.
AND TO ANYONE ELSE...

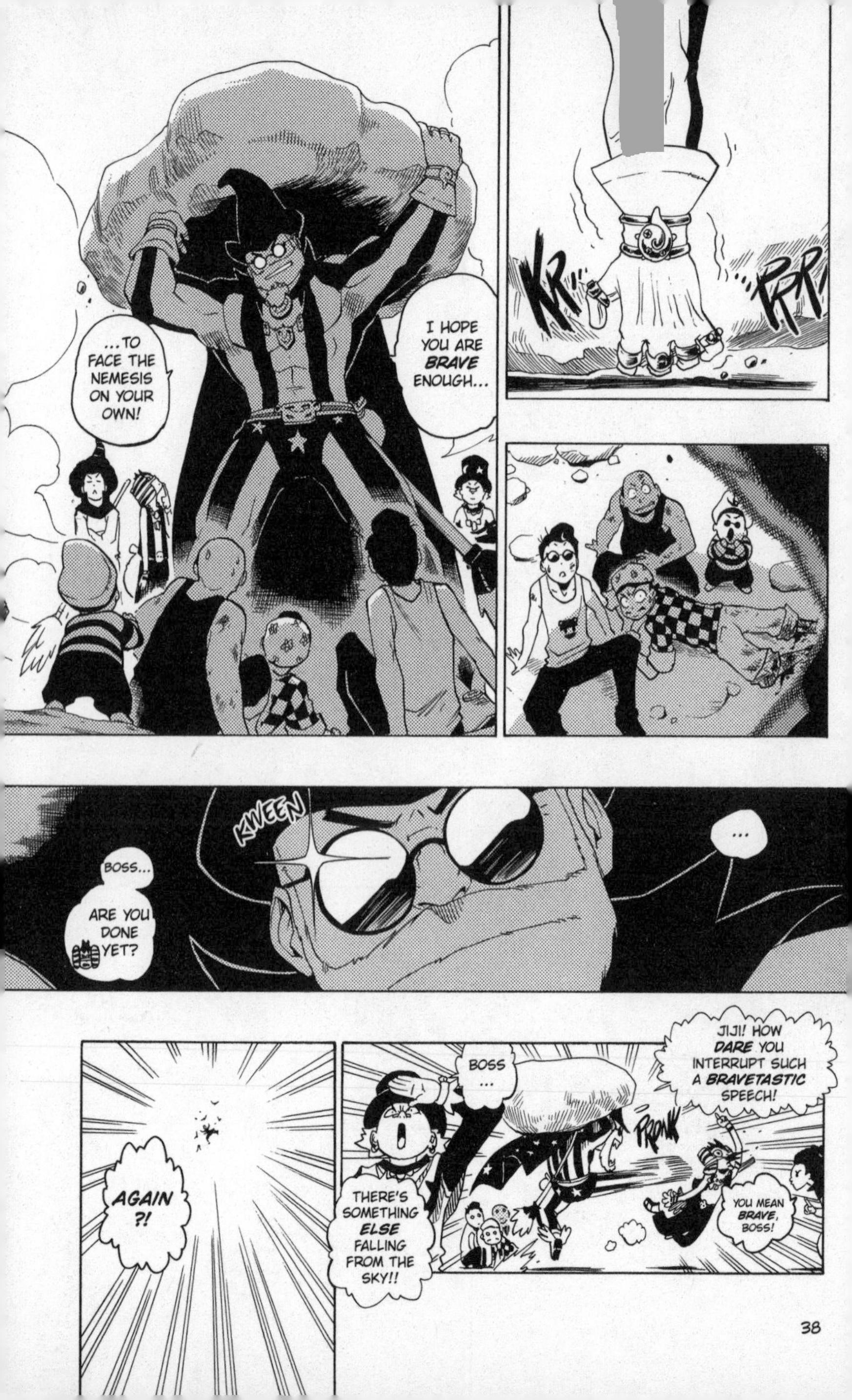
KR... PPP
I HOPE YOU ARE *BRAVE* ENOUGH...
...TO FACE THE NEMESIS ON YOUR OWN!
...
KWEEN
BOSS...
ARE YOU DONE YET?
JIJI! HOW *DARE* YOU INTERRUPT SUCH A *BRAVETASTIC* SPEECH!
BOSS ...
PRONK
YOU MEAN *BRAVE*, BOSS!
THERE'S SOMETHING *ELSE* FALLING FROM THE SKY!!
AGAIN ?!

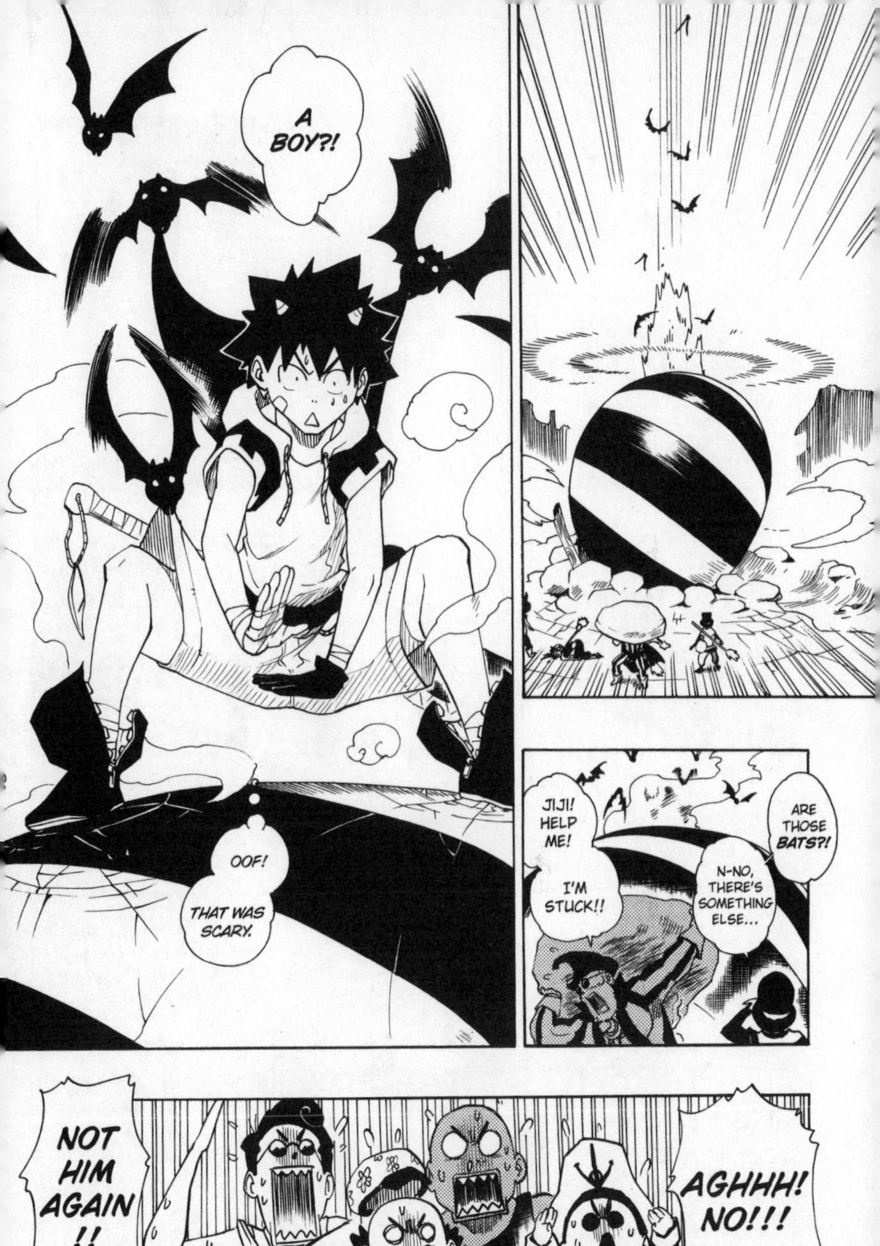
ARE THOSE BATS?!
N-NO, THERE'S SOMETHING ELSE...
JIJI! HELP ME!
I'M STUCK!!
A BOY?!
OOF!
THAT WAS SCARY.
AGHHH! NO!!!
NOT HIM AGAIN!!

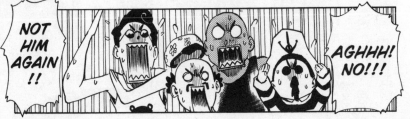

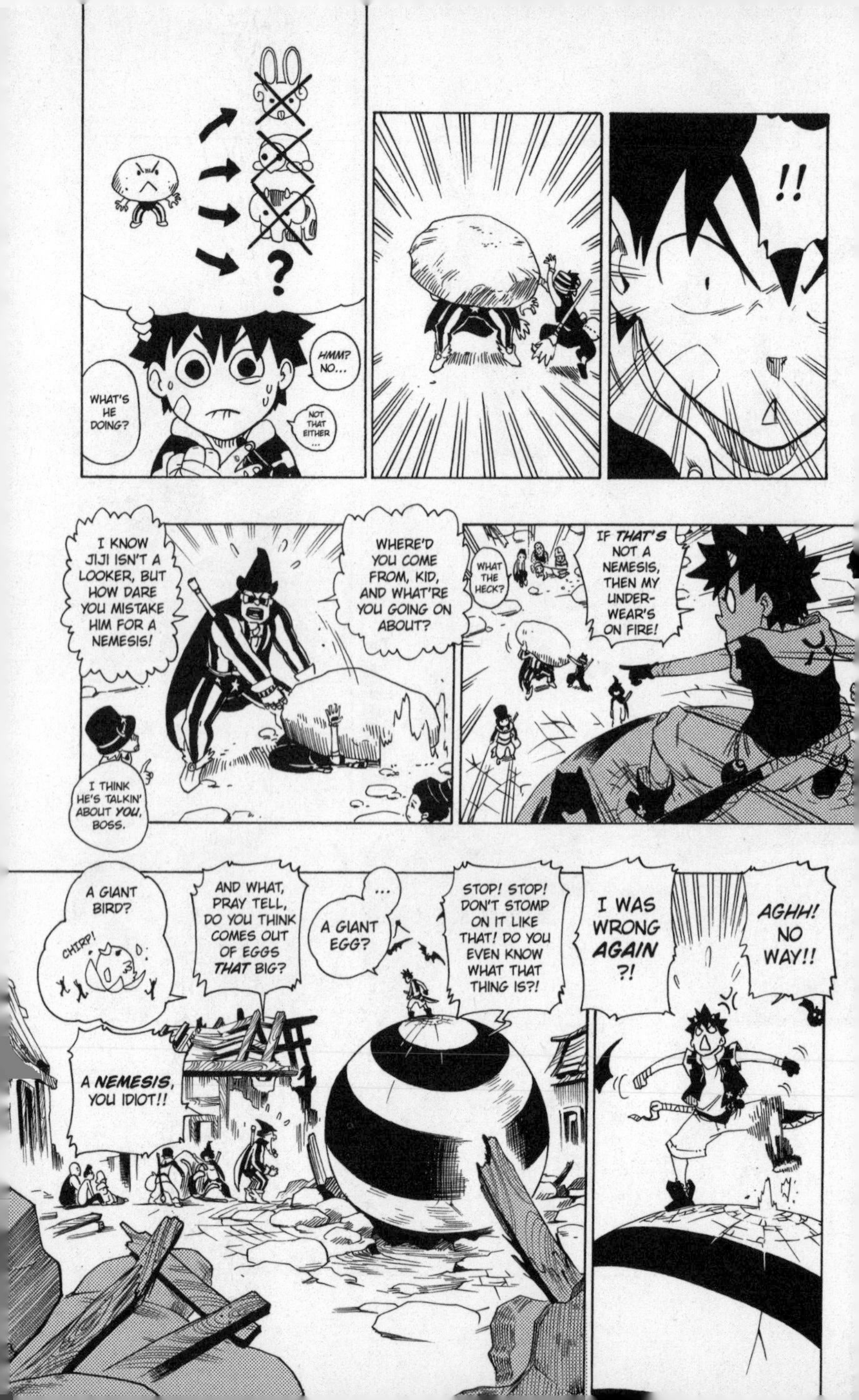
!!
HMM? NO...
WHAT'S HE DOING?
NOT THAT EITHER...
IF THAT'S NOT A NEMESIS, THEN MY UNDER-WEAR'S ON FIRE!
WHAT THE HECK?
WHERE'D YOU COME FROM, KID, AND WHAT'RE YOU GOING ON ABOUT?
I KNOW JIJI ISN'T A LOOKER, BUT HOW DARE YOU MISTAKE HIM FOR A NEMESIS!
I THINK HE'S TALKIN' ABOUT YOU, BOSS.
AGHH! NO WAY!!
I WAS WRONG AGAIN?!
STOP! STOP! DON'T STOMP ON IT LIKE THAT! DO YOU EVEN KNOW WHAT THAT THING IS?!
...
A GIANT EGG?
AND WHAT, PRAY TELL, DO YOU THINK COMES OUT OF EGGS THAT BIG?
A GIANT BIRD?
CHIRP!
A NEMESIS, YOU IDIOT!!

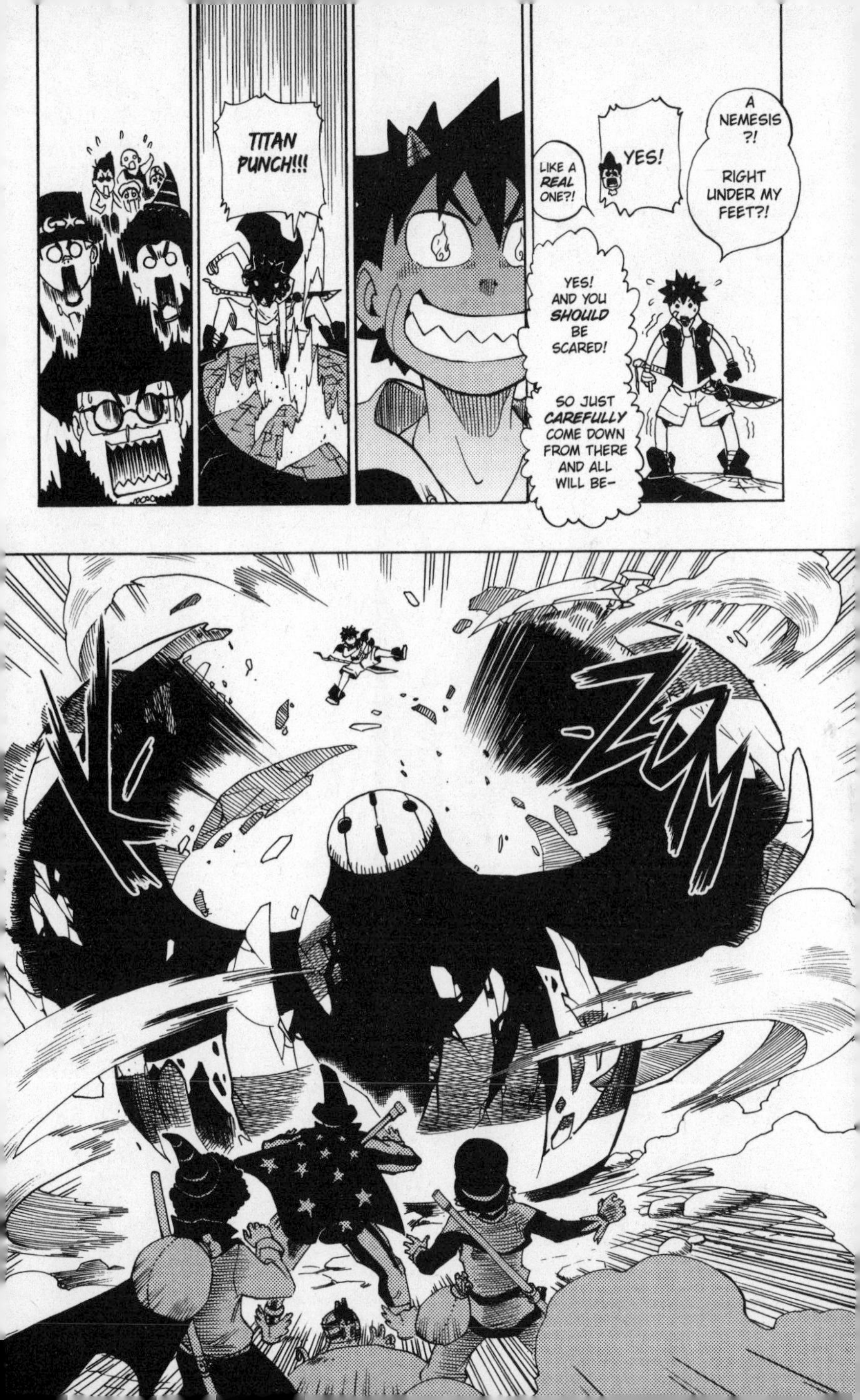
A NEMESIS ?!
RIGHT UNDER MY FEET?!
YES!
LIKE A REAL ONE?!
YES! AND YOU SHOULD BE SCARED!
SO JUST CAREFULLY COME DOWN FROM THERE AND ALL WILL BE-
TITAN PUNCH!!!
-ZOM

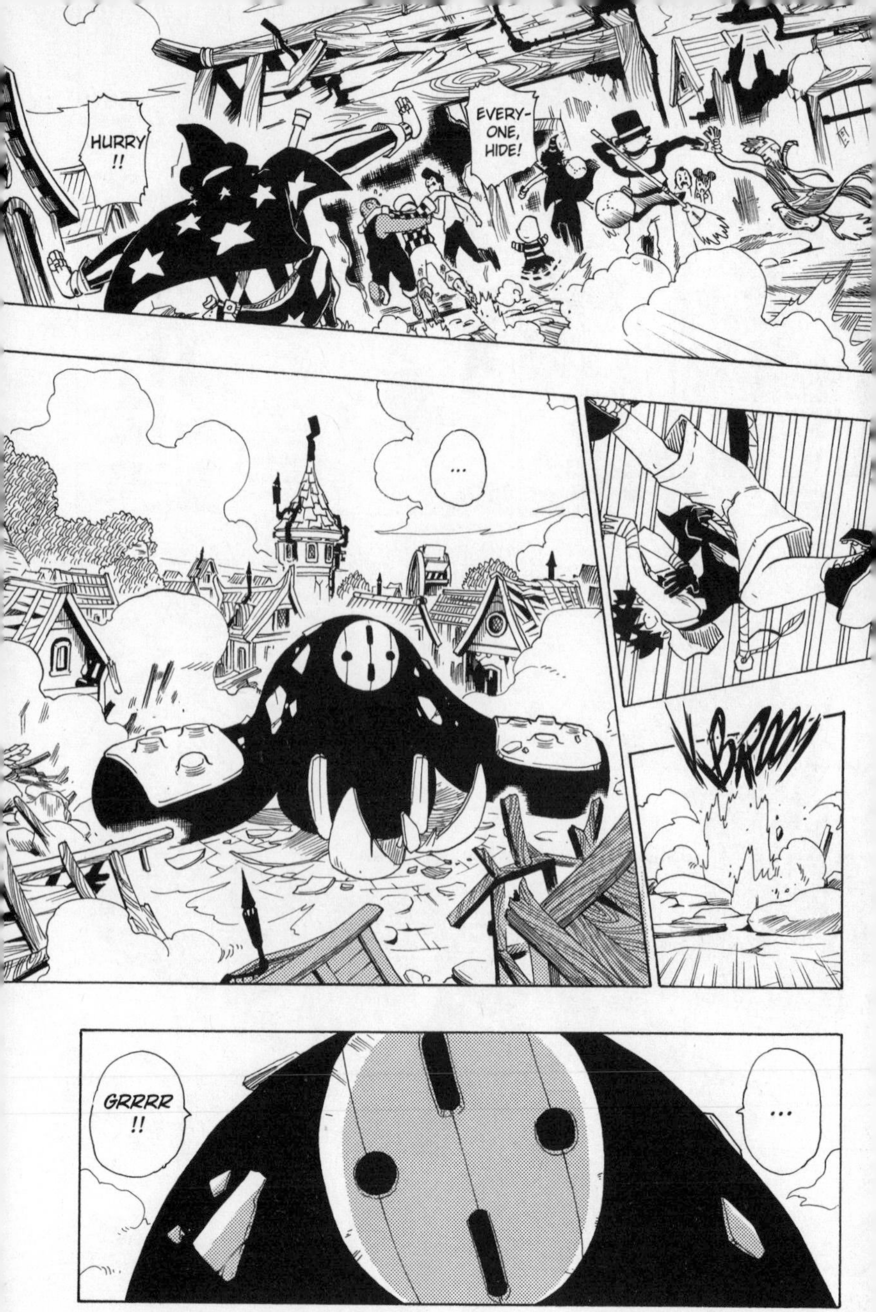
EVERY-ONE, HIDE!
HURRY!!
VBROOM
...
...
GRRRR!!

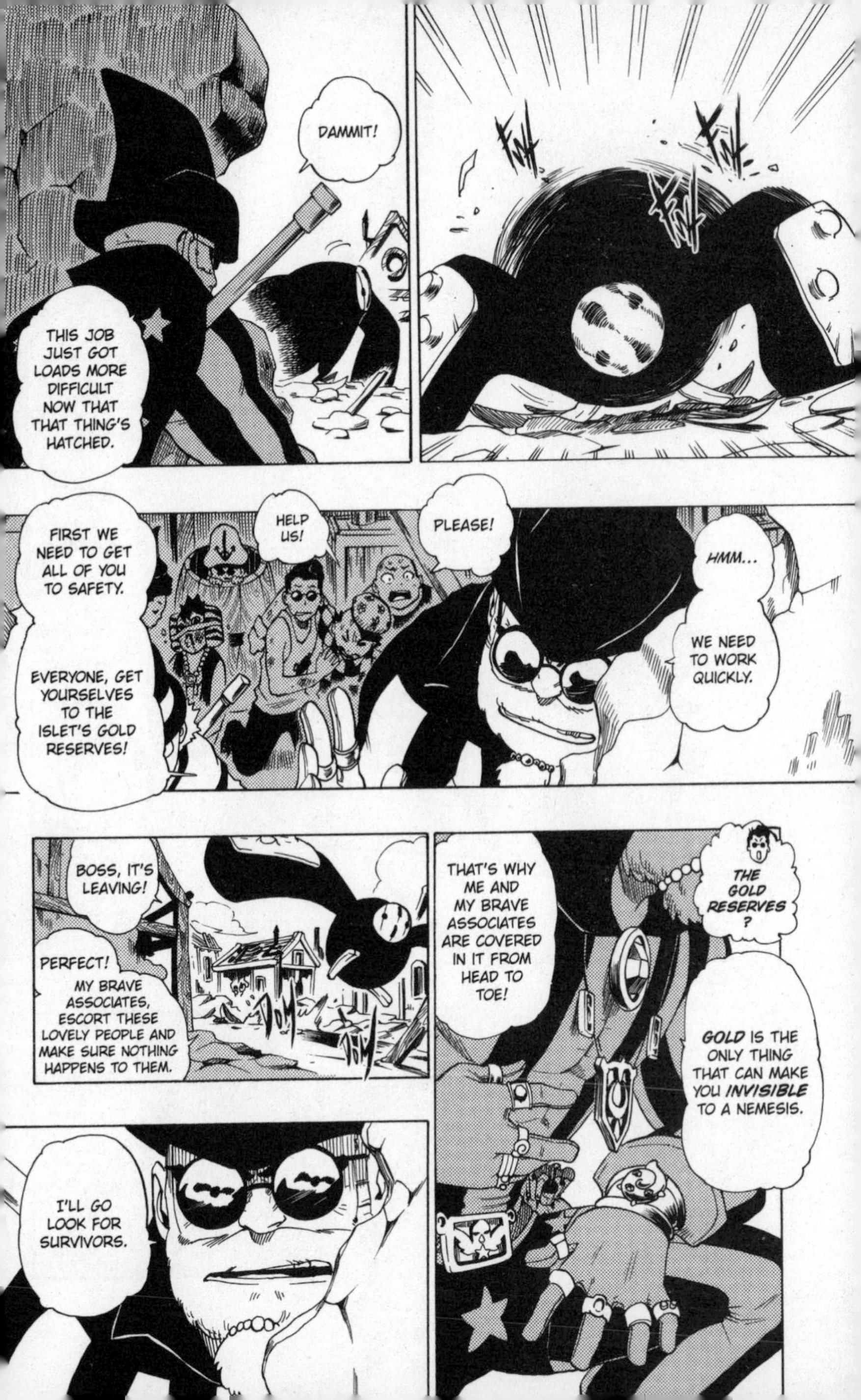
DAMMIT!
THIS JOB JUST GOT LOADS MORE DIFFICULT NOW THAT THAT THING'S HATCHED.
HMM...
WE NEED TO WORK QUICKLY.
PLEASE!
HELP US!
FIRST WE NEED TO GET ALL OF YOU TO SAFETY.
EVERYONE, GET YOURSELVES TO THE ISLET'S GOLD RESERVES!
THE GOLD RESERVES?
GOLD IS THE ONLY THING THAT CAN MAKE YOU INVISIBLE TO A NEMESIS.
THAT'S WHY ME AND MY BRAVE ASSOCIATES ARE COVERED IN IT FROM HEAD TO TOE!
BOSS, IT'S LEAVING!
PERFECT!
MY BRAVE ASSOCIATES, ESCORT THESE LOVELY PEOPLE AND MAKE SURE NOTHING HAPPENS TO THEM.
I'LL GO LOOK FOR SURVIVORS.

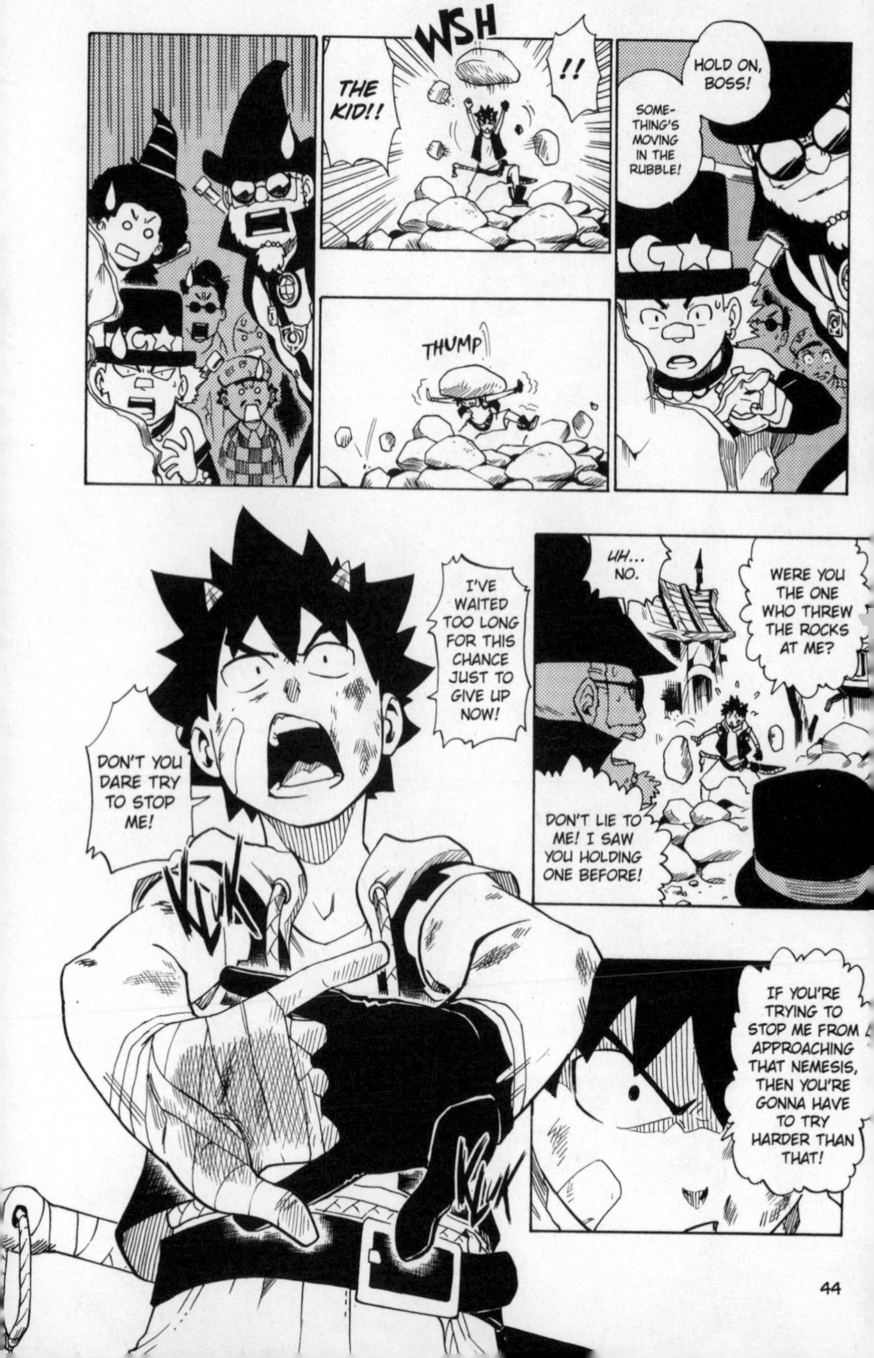
HOLD ON, BOSS!
SOME-THING'S MOVING IN THE RUBBLE!
!!
WSH
THE KID!!
THUMP
WERE YOU THE ONE WHO THREW THE ROCKS AT ME?
UH... NO.
DON'T LIE TO ME! I SAW YOU HOLDING ONE BEFORE!
IF YOU'RE TRYING TO STOP ME FROM APPROACHING THAT NEMESIS, THEN YOU'RE GONNA HAVE TO TRY HARDER THAN THAT!
I'VE WAITED TOO LONG FOR THIS CHANCE JUST TO GIVE UP NOW!
DON'T YOU DARE TRY TO STOP ME!

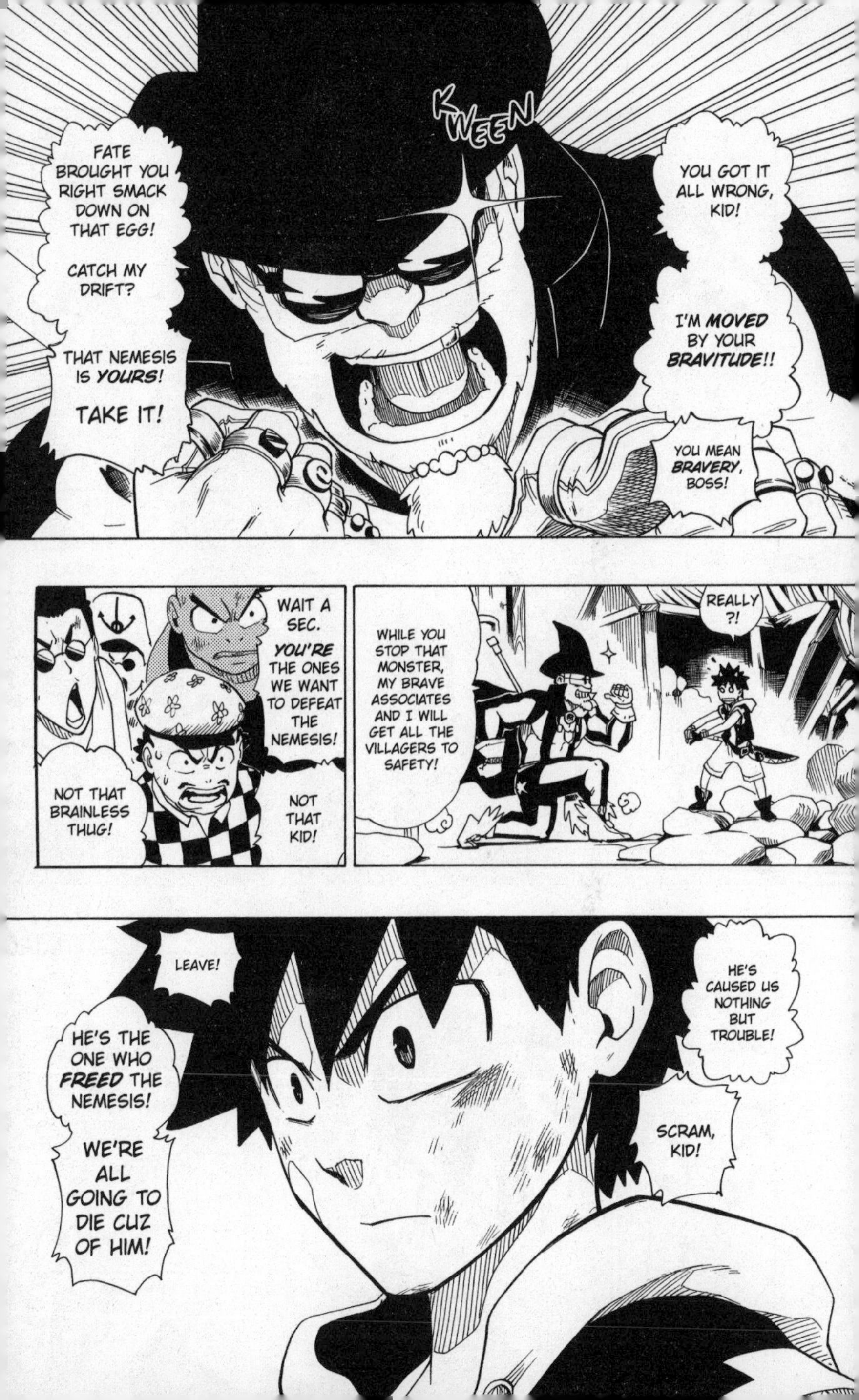
KWEEN
YOU GOT IT ALL WRONG, KID!
FATE BROUGHT YOU RIGHT SMACK DOWN ON THAT EGG!
CATCH MY DRIFT?
THAT NEMESIS IS YOURS!
TAKE IT!
I'M MOVED BY YOUR BRAVITUDE!!
YOU MEAN BRAVERY, BOSS!
REALLY?!
WHILE YOU STOP THAT MONSTER, MY BRAVE ASSOCIATES AND I WILL GET ALL THE VILLAGERS TO SAFETY!
WAIT A SEC. YOU'RE THE ONES WE WANT TO DEFEAT THE NEMESIS!
NOT THAT KID!
NOT THAT BRAINLESS THUG!
HE'S CAUSED US NOTHING BUT TROUBLE!
LEAVE!
HE'S THE ONE WHO FREED THE NEMESIS!
SCRAM, KID!
WE'RE ALL GOING TO DIE CUZ OF HIM!

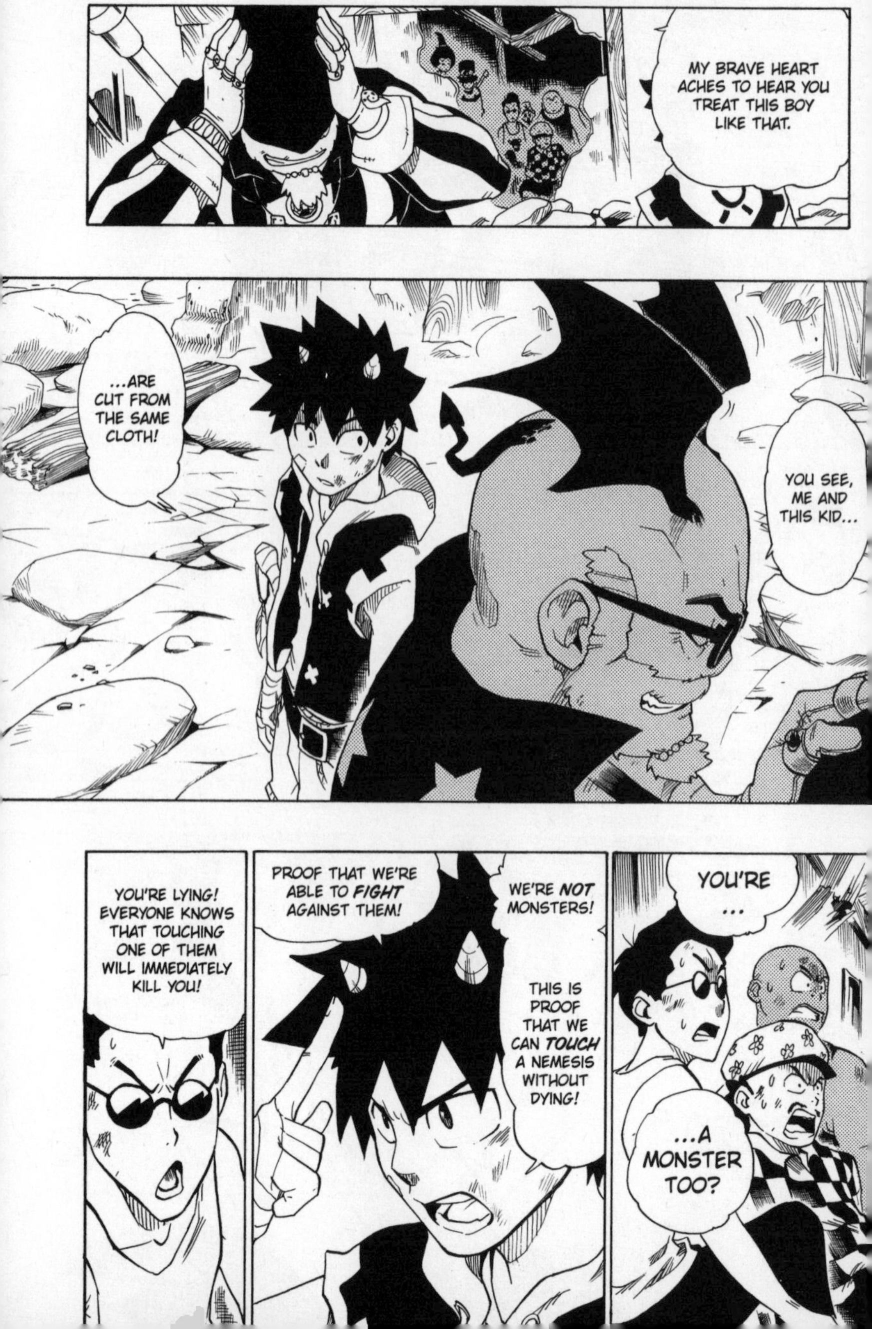
MY BRAVE HEART ACHES TO HEAR YOU TREAT THIS BOY LIKE THAT.
YOU SEE, ME AND THIS KID...
...ARE CUT FROM THE SAME CLOTH!
YOU'RE ...
...A MONSTER TOO?
WE'RE *NOT* MONSTERS!
THIS IS PROOF THAT WE CAN *TOUCH* A NEMESIS WITHOUT DYING!
PROOF THAT WE'RE ABLE TO *FIGHT* AGAINST THEM!
YOU'RE LYING! EVERYONE KNOWS THAT TOUCHING ONE OF THEM WILL IMMEDIATELY KILL YOU!

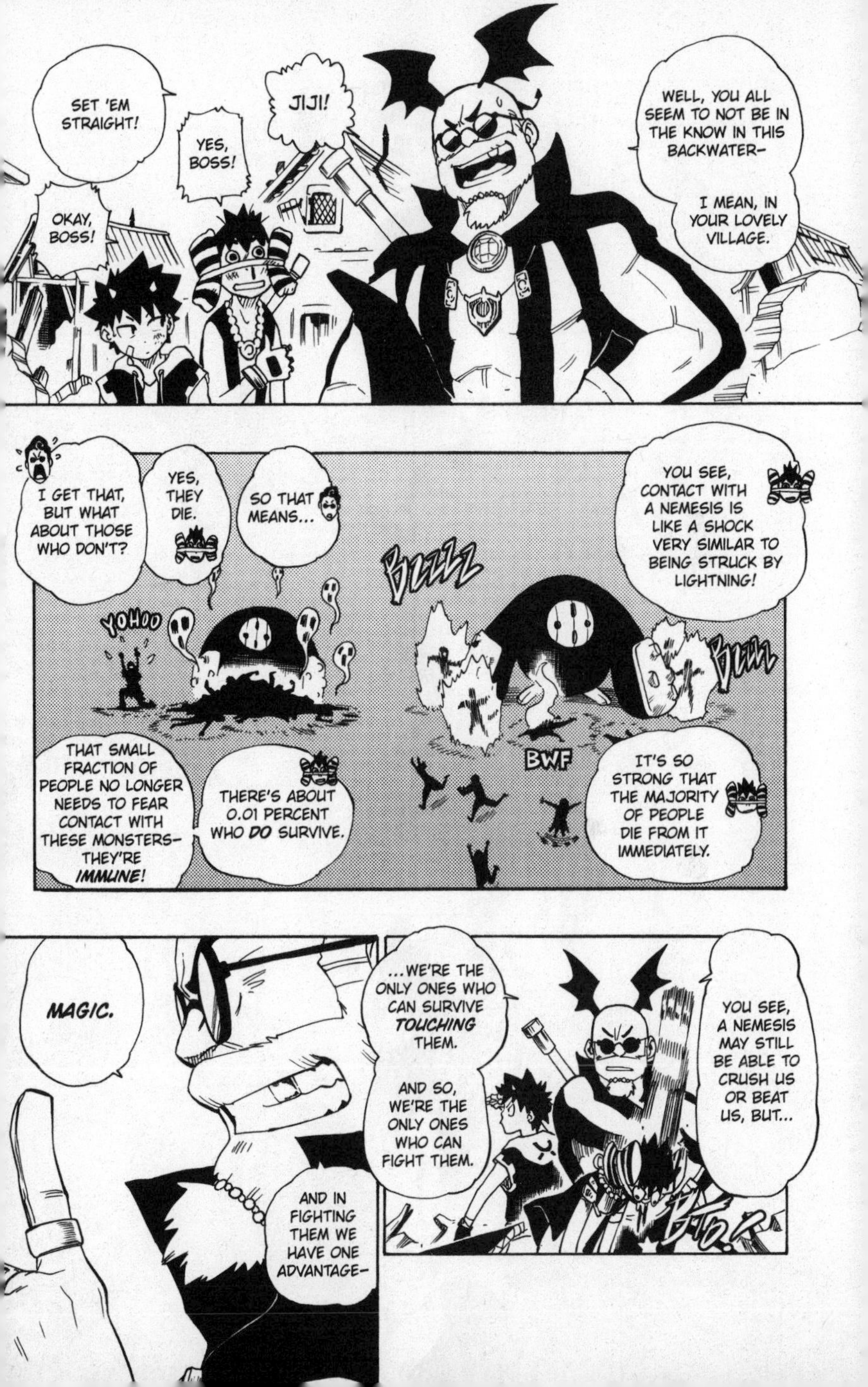

WELL, YOU ALL SEEM TO NOT BE IN THE KNOW IN THIS BACKWATER—
I MEAN, IN YOUR LOVELY VILLAGE.
JIJI!
YES, BOSS!
SET 'EM STRAIGHT!
OKAY, BOSS!
YOU SEE, CONTACT WITH A NEMESIS IS LIKE A SHOCK VERY SIMILAR TO BEING STRUCK BY LIGHTNING!
IT'S SO STRONG THAT THE MAJORITY OF PEOPLE DIE FROM IT IMMEDIATELY.
BWF
SO THAT MEANS...
YES, THEY DIE.
I GET THAT, BUT WHAT ABOUT THOSE WHO DON'T?
YOHOO
THERE'S ABOUT 0.01 PERCENT WHO *DO* SURVIVE.
THAT SMALL FRACTION OF PEOPLE NO LONGER NEEDS TO FEAR CONTACT WITH THESE MONSTERS— THEY'RE *IMMUNE*!
YOU SEE, A NEMESIS MAY STILL BE ABLE TO CRUSH US OR BEAT US, BUT...
...WE'RE THE ONLY ONES WHO CAN SURVIVE *TOUCHING* THEM.
AND SO, WE'RE THE ONLY ONES WHO CAN FIGHT THEM.
AND IN FIGHTING THEM WE HAVE ONE ADVANTAGE—
MAGIC.

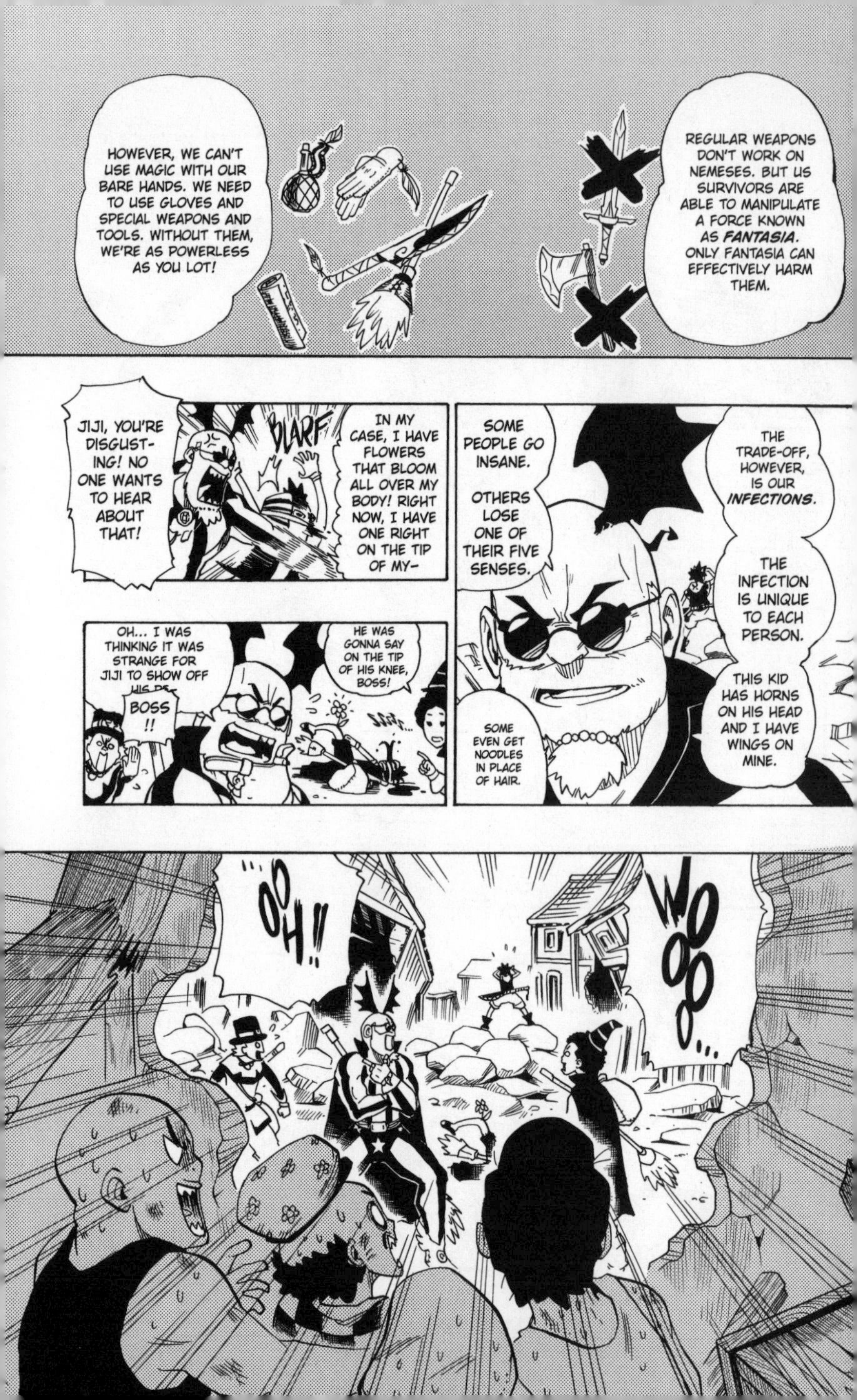
REGULAR WEAPONS DON'T WORK ON NEMESES. BUT US SURVIVORS ARE ABLE TO MANIPULATE A FORCE KNOWN AS *FANTASIA*. ONLY FANTASIA CAN EFFECTIVELY HARM THEM.
HOWEVER, WE CAN'T USE MAGIC WITH OUR BARE HANDS. WE NEED TO USE GLOVES AND SPECIAL WEAPONS AND TOOLS. WITHOUT THEM, WE'RE AS POWERLESS AS YOU LOT!
THE TRADE-OFF, HOWEVER, IS OUR *INFECTIONS*.
THE INFECTION IS UNIQUE TO EACH PERSON.
THIS KID HAS HORNS ON HIS HEAD AND I HAVE WINGS ON MINE.
SOME PEOPLE GO INSANE.
OTHERS LOSE ONE OF THEIR FIVE SENSES.
SOME EVEN GET NOODLES IN PLACE OF HAIR.
IN MY CASE, I HAVE FLOWERS THAT BLOOM ALL OVER MY BODY! RIGHT NOW, I HAVE ONE RIGHT ON THE TIP OF MY–
BLARF
JIJI, YOU'RE DISGUSTING! NO ONE WANTS TO HEAR ABOUT THAT!
HE WAS GONNA SAY ON THE TIP OF HIS KNEE, BOSS!
OH... I WAS THINKING IT WAS STRANGE FOR JIJI TO SHOW OFF
BOSS!!
WOOOO...
OOH!!

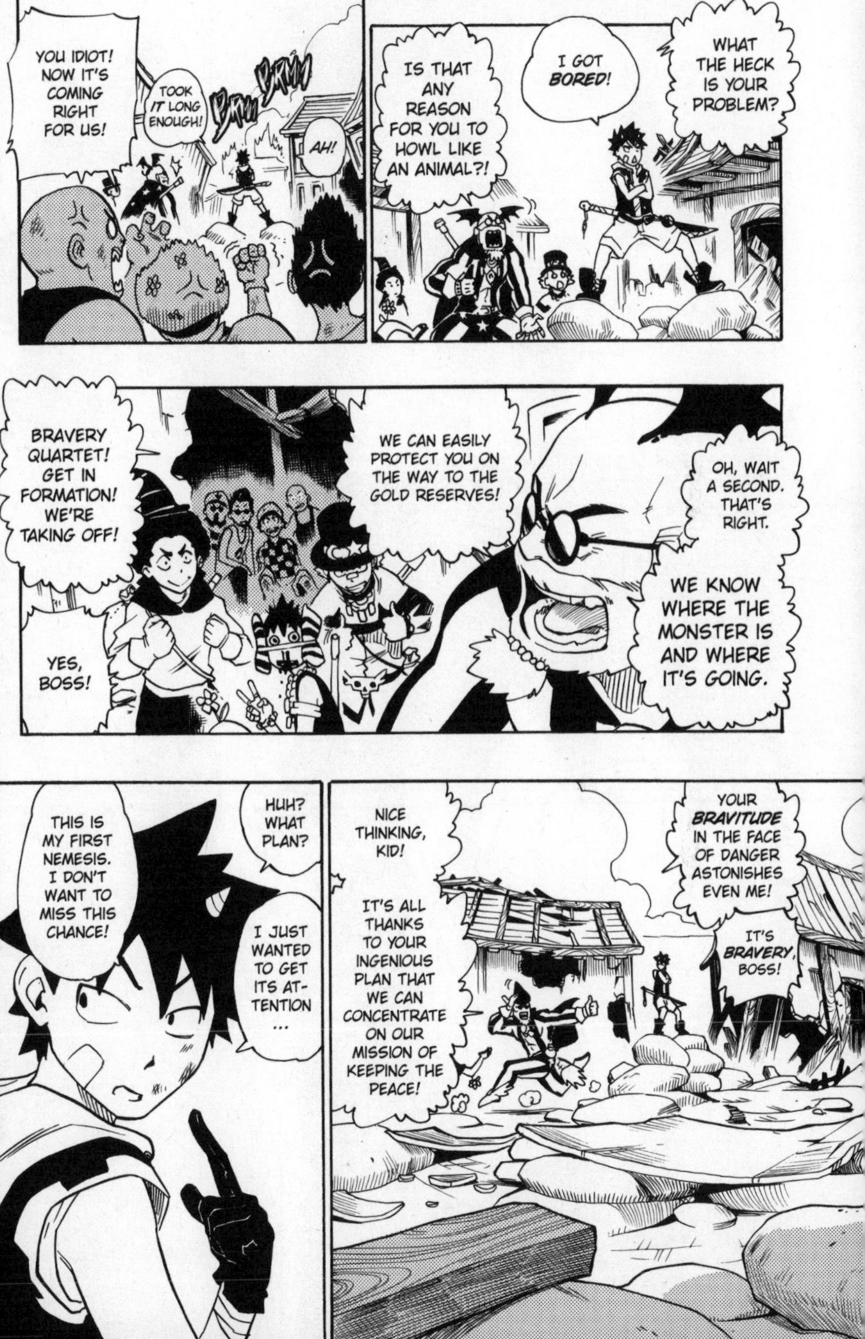
WHAT THE HECK IS YOUR PROBLEM?
I GOT BORED!
IS THAT ANY REASON FOR YOU TO HOWL LIKE AN ANIMAL?!
AH!
TOOK IT LONG ENOUGH!
YOU IDIOT! NOW IT'S COMING RIGHT FOR US!
OH, WAIT A SECOND. THAT'S RIGHT.
WE KNOW WHERE THE MONSTER IS AND WHERE IT'S GOING.
WE CAN EASILY PROTECT YOU ON THE WAY TO THE GOLD RESERVES!
BRAVERY QUARTET! GET IN FORMATION! WE'RE TAKING OFF!
YES, BOSS!
YOUR BRAVITUDE IN THE FACE OF DANGER ASTONISHES EVEN ME!
IT'S BRAVERY, BOSS!
NICE THINKING, KID!
IT'S ALL THANKS TO YOUR INGENIOUS PLAN THAT WE CAN CONCENTRATE ON OUR MISSION OF KEEPING THE PEACE!
HUH? WHAT PLAN?
I JUST WANTED TO GET ITS ATTENTION...
THIS IS MY FIRST NEMESIS. I DON'T WANT TO MISS THIS CHANCE!

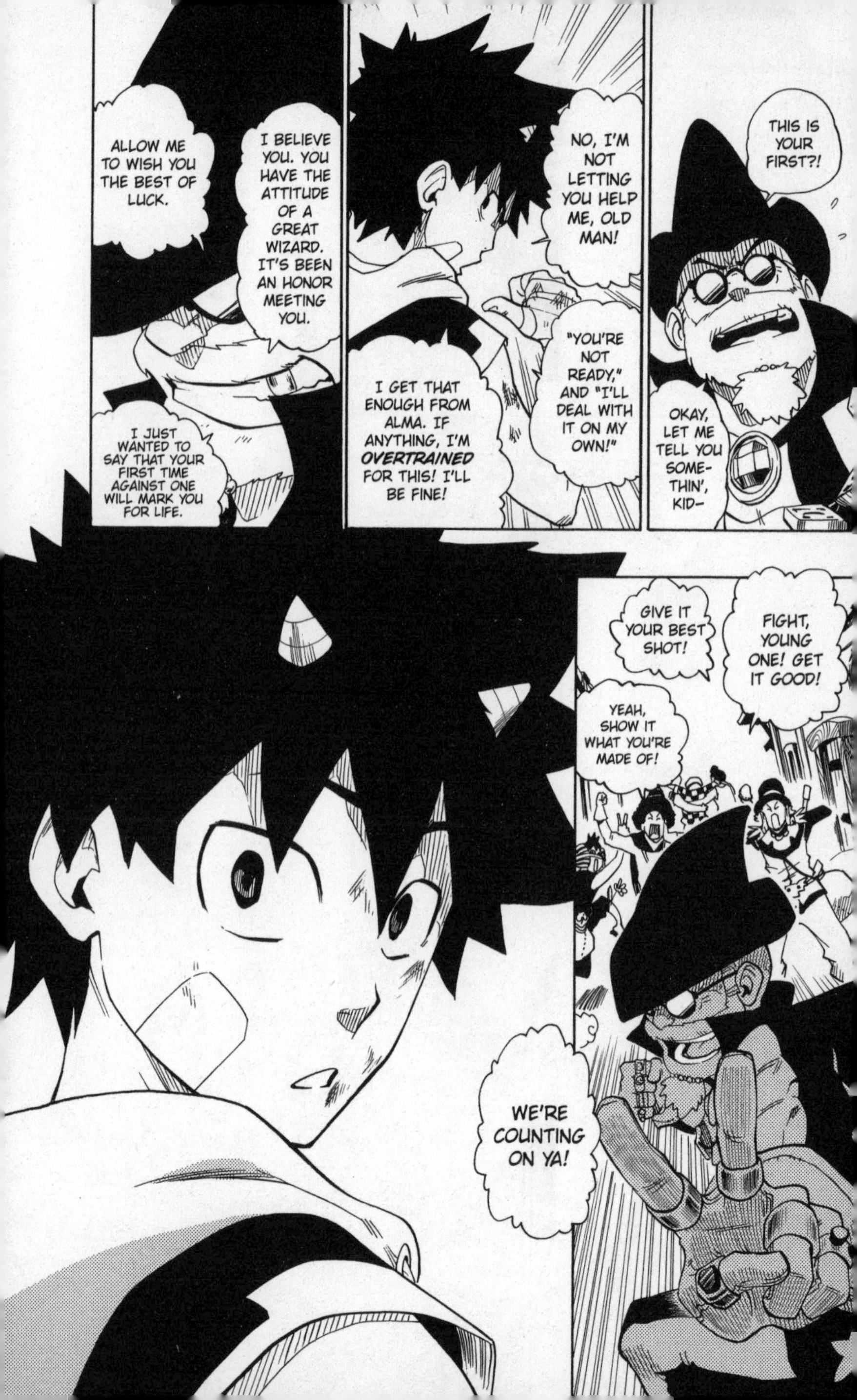
THIS IS YOUR FIRST?!
OKAY, LET ME TELL YOU SOME-THIN', KID-
NO, I'M NOT LETTING YOU HELP ME, OLD MAN!
"YOU'RE NOT READY," AND "I'LL DEAL WITH IT ON MY OWN!"
I GET THAT ENOUGH FROM ALMA. IF ANYTHING, I'M **OVERTRAINED** FOR THIS! I'LL BE FINE!
I BELIEVE YOU. YOU HAVE THE ATTITUDE OF A GREAT WIZARD. IT'S BEEN AN HONOR MEETING YOU.
ALLOW ME TO WISH YOU THE BEST OF LUCK.
I JUST WANTED TO SAY THAT YOUR FIRST TIME AGAINST ONE WILL MARK YOU FOR LIFE.
FIGHT, YOUNG ONE! GET IT GOOD!
GIVE IT YOUR BEST SHOT!
YEAH, SHOW IT WHAT YOU'RE MADE OF!
WE'RE COUNTING ON YA!

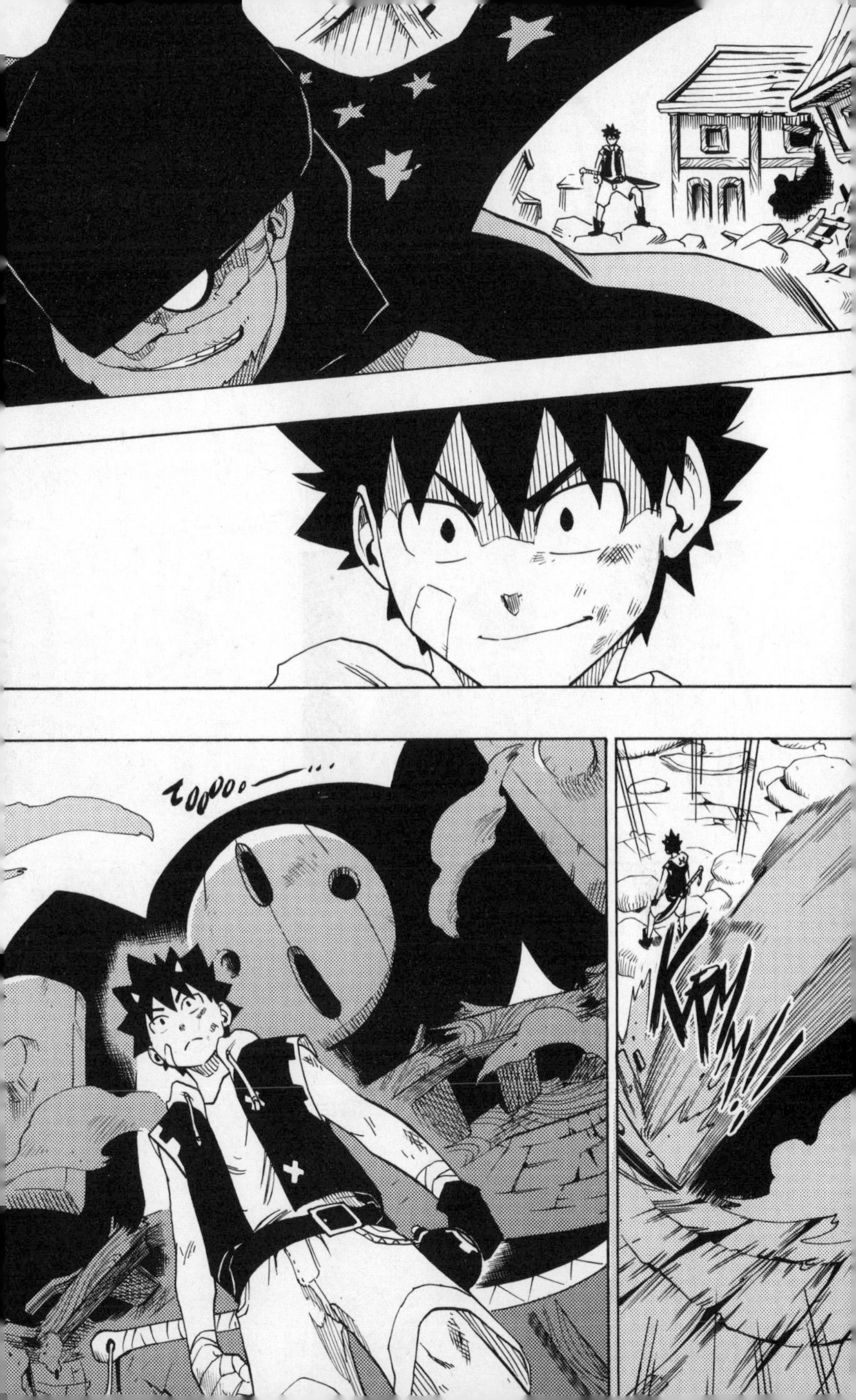
ZOOOOO—...

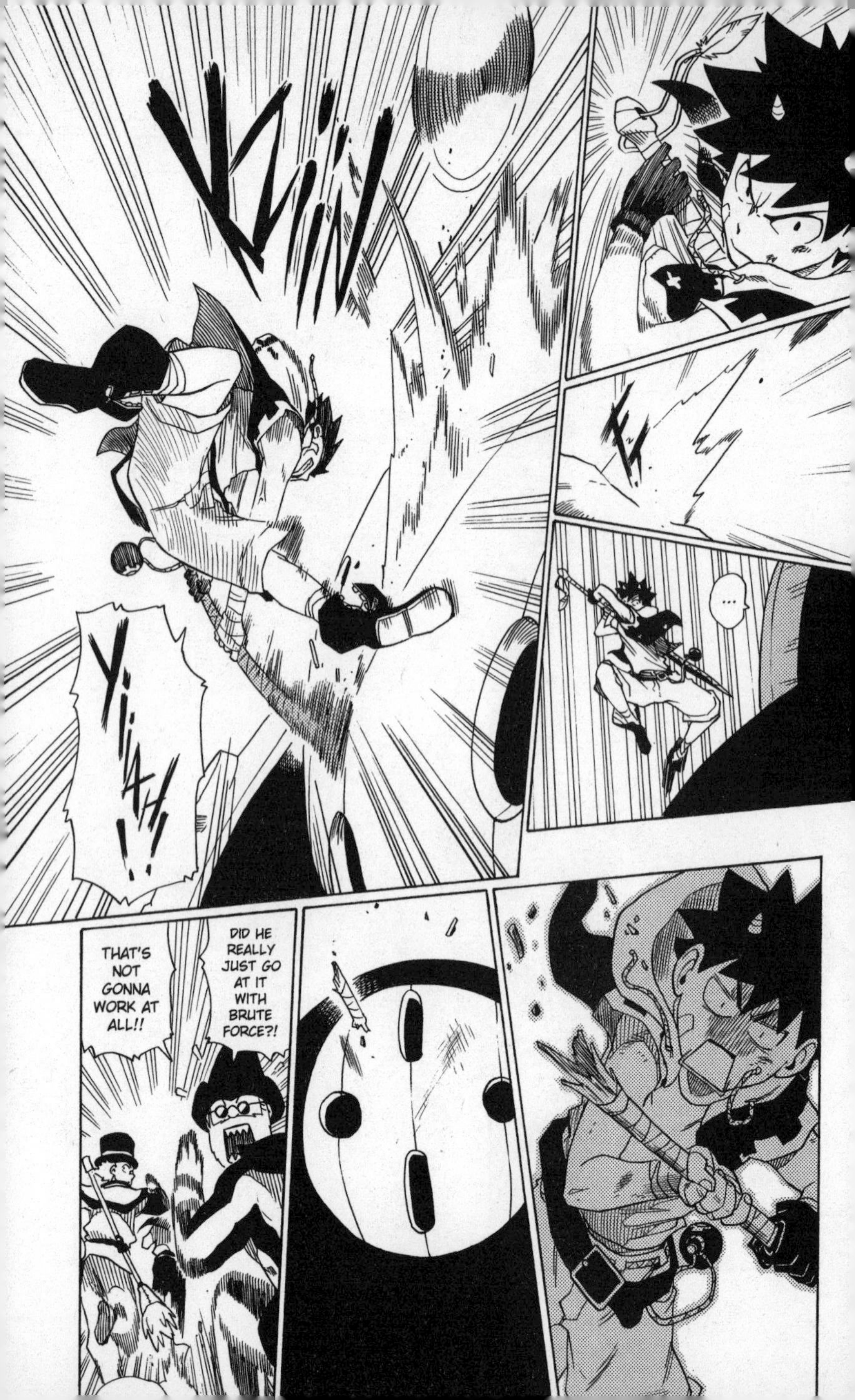
...
YiiiAH!!
DID HE REALLY JUST GO AT IT WITH BRUTE FORCE?!
THAT'S NOT GONNA WORK AT ALL!!

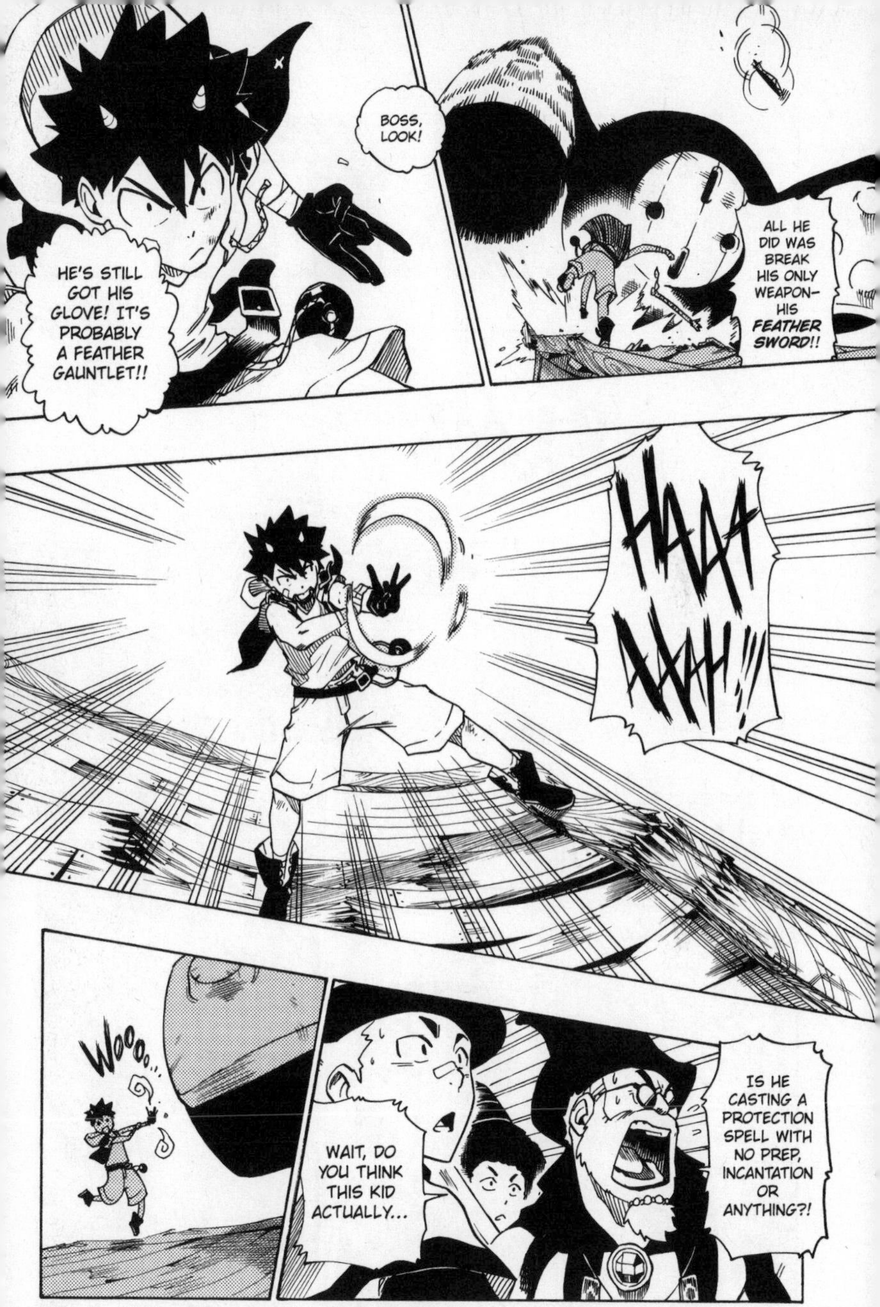
BOSS, LOOK!
ALL HE DID WAS BREAK HIS ONLY WEAPON—HIS FEATHER SWORD!!
HE'S STILL GOT HIS GLOVE! IT'S PROBABLY A FEATHER GAUNTLET!!
HAAAAAAH!!
IS HE CASTING A PROTECTION SPELL WITH NO PREP, INCANTATION OR ANYTHING?!
WAIT, DO YOU THINK THIS KID ACTUALLY...
WOOOO...

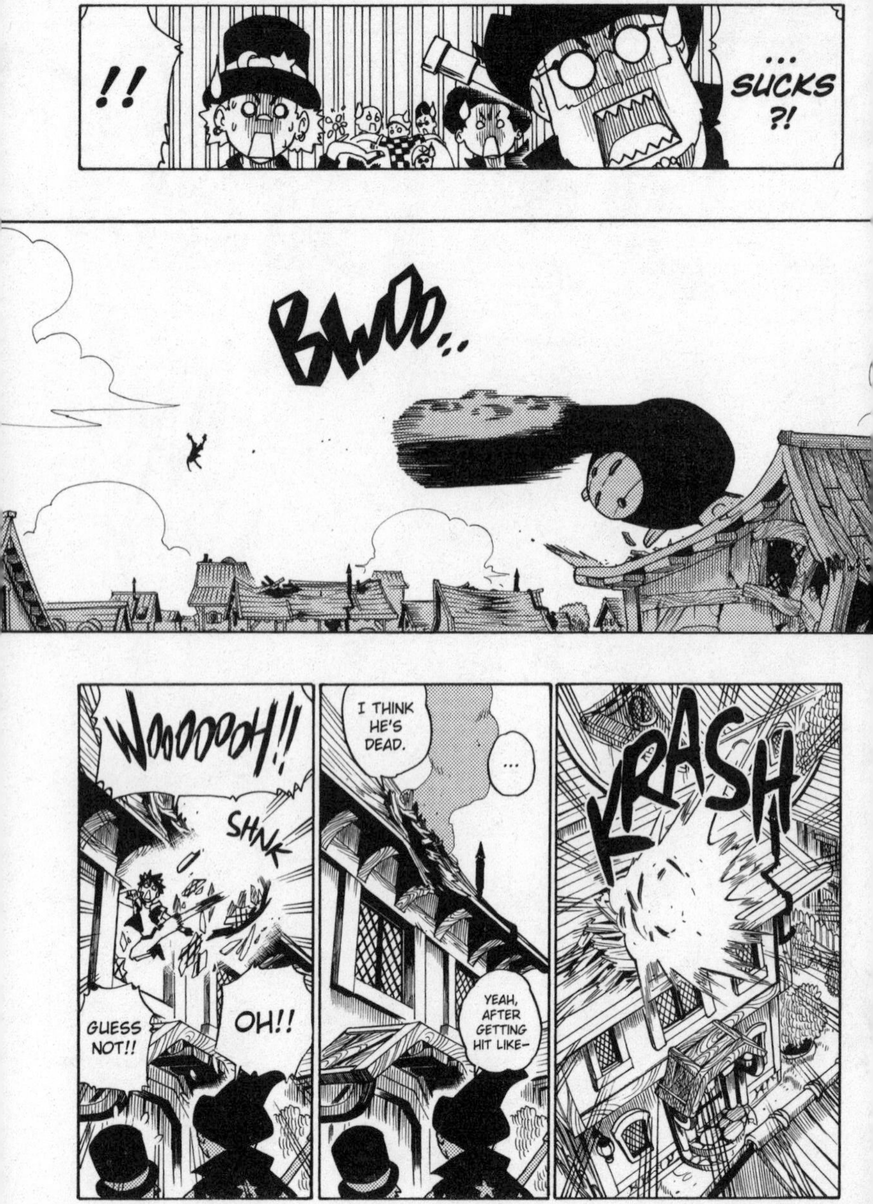

... SUCKS ?!
!!
BWOO...
KRASH
I THINK HE'S DEAD.
...
YEAH, AFTER GETTING HIT LIKE-
WOOOOOOH!!
SHNK
OH!!
GUESS NOT!!

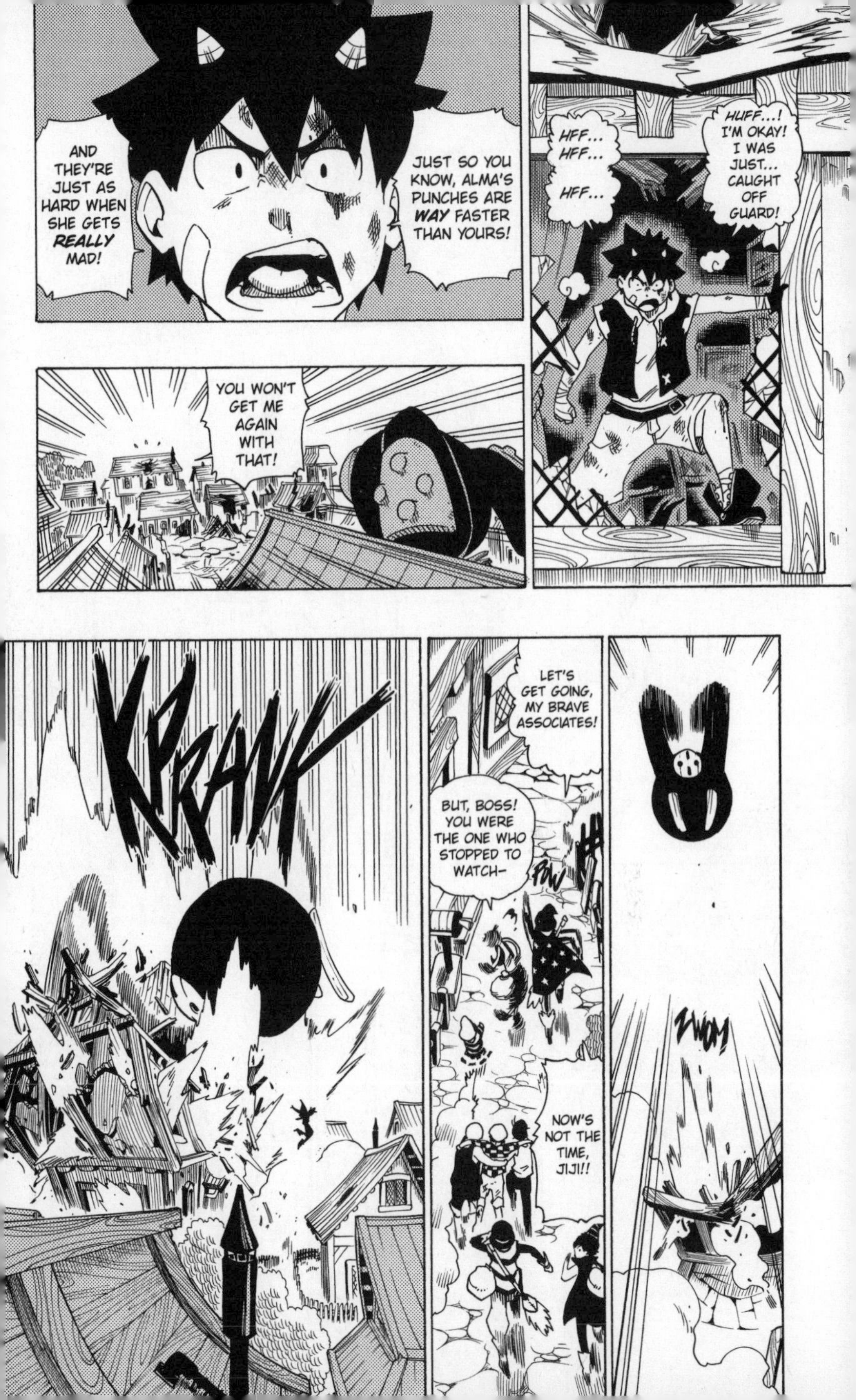
HUFF...! I'M OKAY! I WAS JUST... CAUGHT OFF GUARD!
HFF... HFF... HFF...
JUST SO YOU KNOW, ALMA'S PUNCHES ARE WAY FASTER THAN YOURS!
AND THEY'RE JUST AS HARD WHEN SHE GETS REALLY MAD!
YOU WON'T GET ME AGAIN WITH THAT!
ZWOM
LET'S GET GOING, MY BRAVE ASSOCIATES!
BUT, BOSS! YOU WERE THE ONE WHO STOPPED TO WATCH-
POW
NOW'S NOT THE TIME, JIJI!!
KRANK

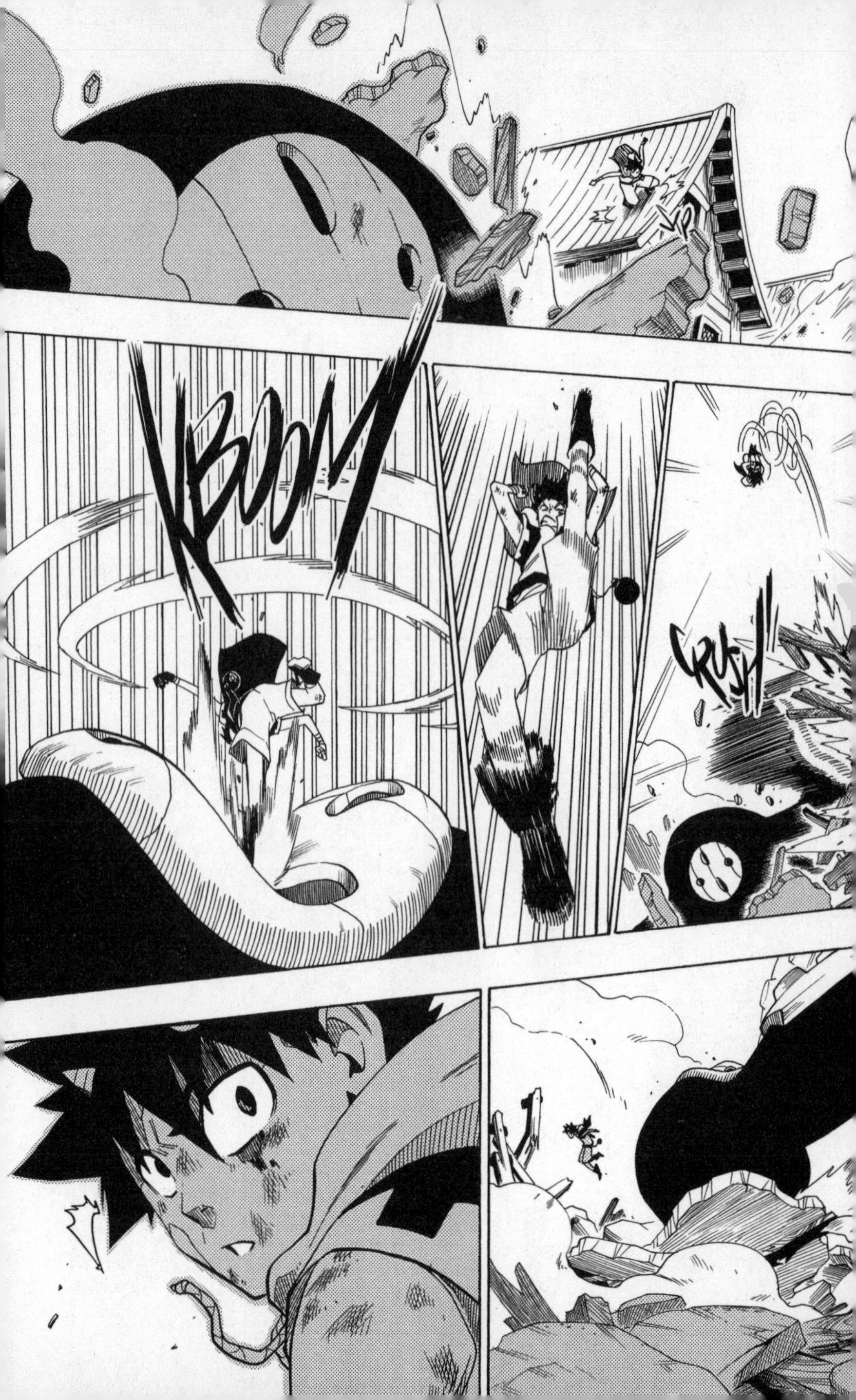
VIP
CRUSH!!
KBOOM

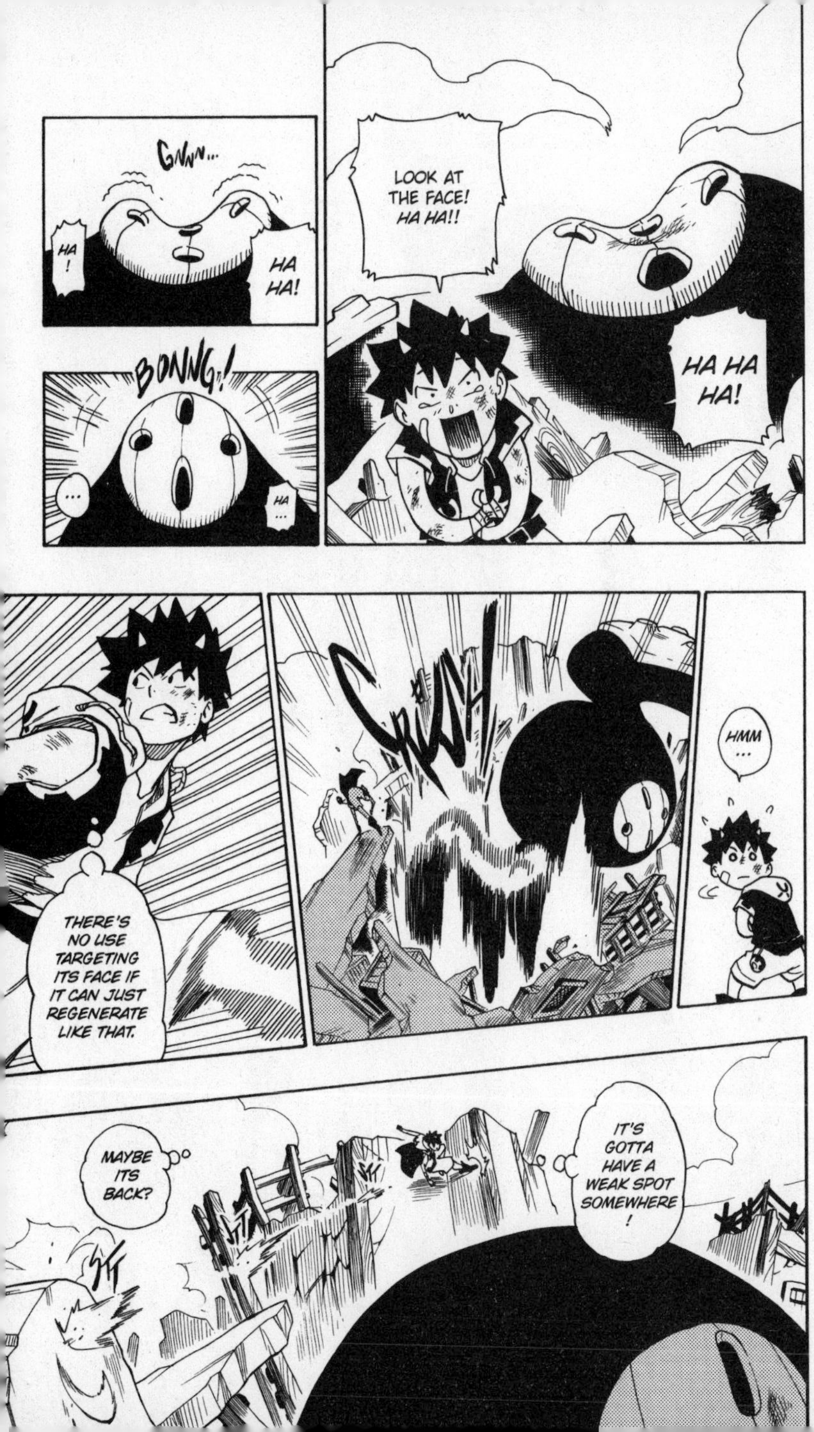
LOOK AT THE FACE! HA HA!!
HA HA HA!
GNNN...
HA HA!
HA!
BONNG!!
HA...
...
HMM...
CRUSH
THERE'S NO USE TARGETING ITS FACE IF IT CAN JUST REGENERATE LIKE THAT.
IT'S GOTTA HAVE A WEAK SPOT SOMEWHERE!
MAYBE ITS BACK?

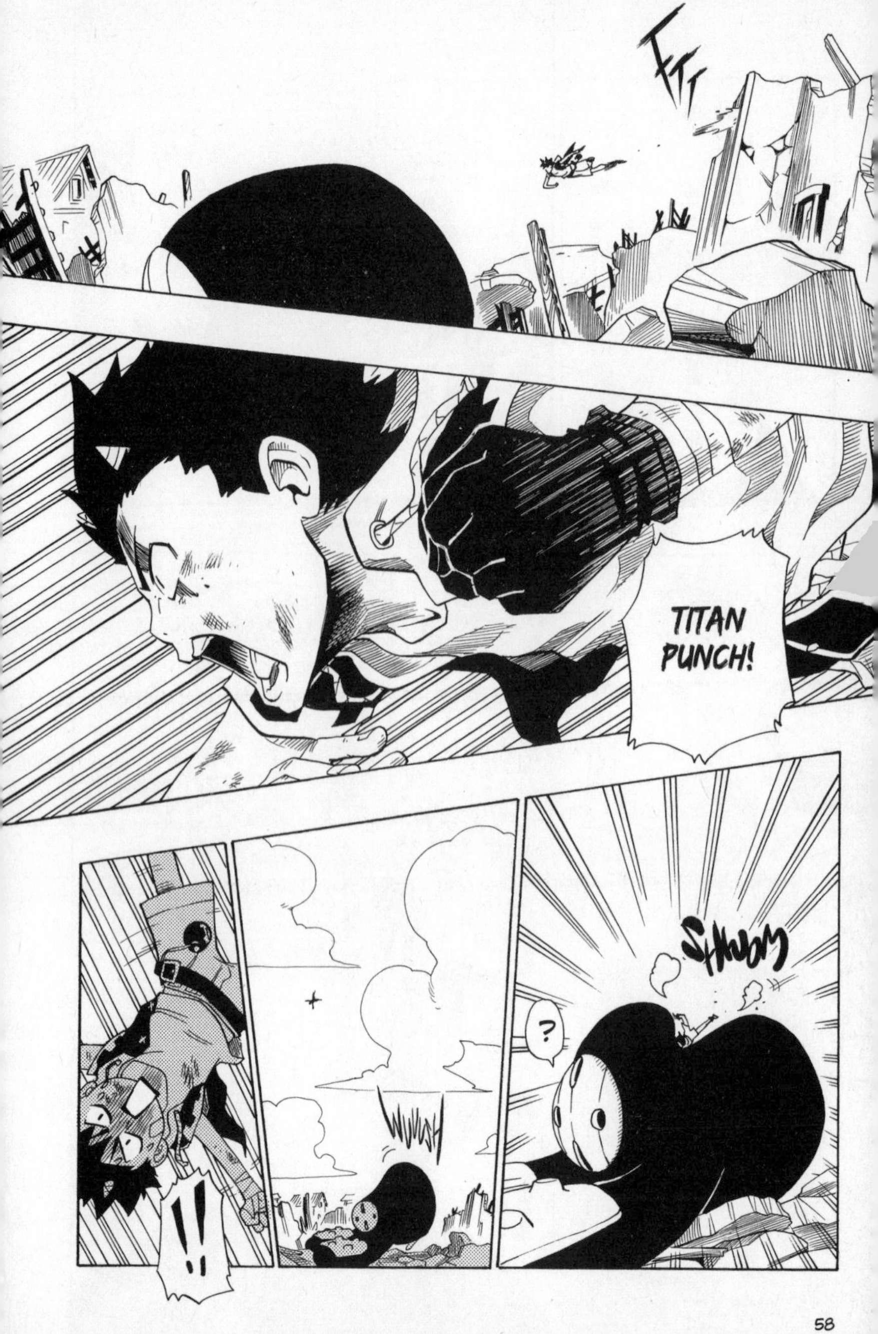
TITAN PUNCH!
SHWOOM
?
WHUUSH
!!

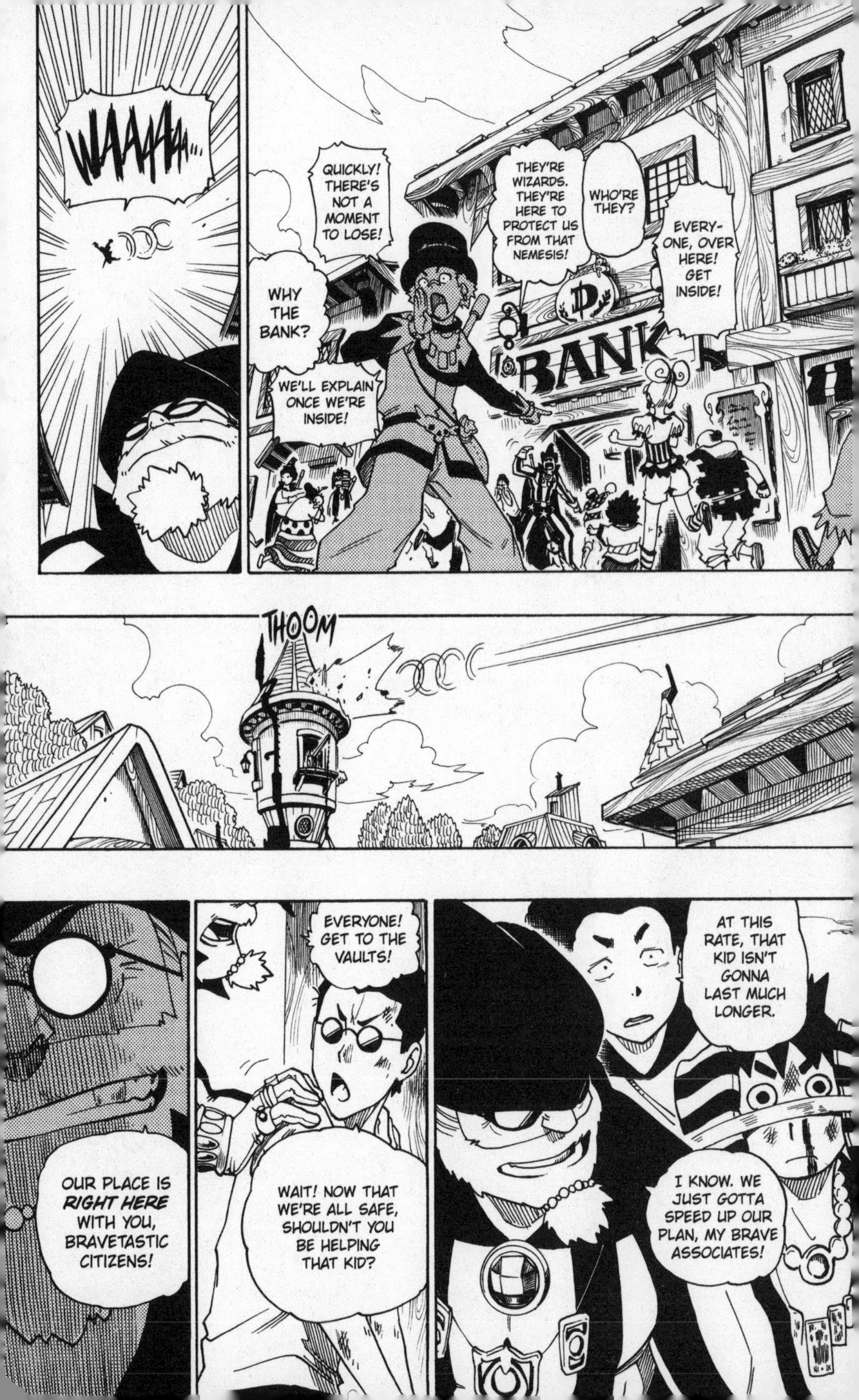
EVERY-ONE, OVER HERE! GET INSIDE!
WHO'RE THEY?
THEY'RE WIZARDS. THEY'RE HERE TO PROTECT US FROM THAT NEMESIS!
QUICKLY! THERE'S NOT A MOMENT TO LOSE!
BANK
WHY THE BANK?
WE'LL EXPLAIN ONCE WE'RE INSIDE!
WAAAAA...
THOOM
AT THIS RATE, THAT KID ISN'T GONNA LAST MUCH LONGER.
I KNOW. WE JUST GOTTA SPEED UP OUR PLAN, MY BRAVE ASSOCIATES!
EVERYONE! GET TO THE VAULTS!
WAIT! NOW THAT WE'RE ALL SAFE, SHOULDN'T YOU BE HELPING THAT KID?
OUR PLACE IS *RIGHT HERE* WITH YOU, BRAVETASTIC CITIZENS!

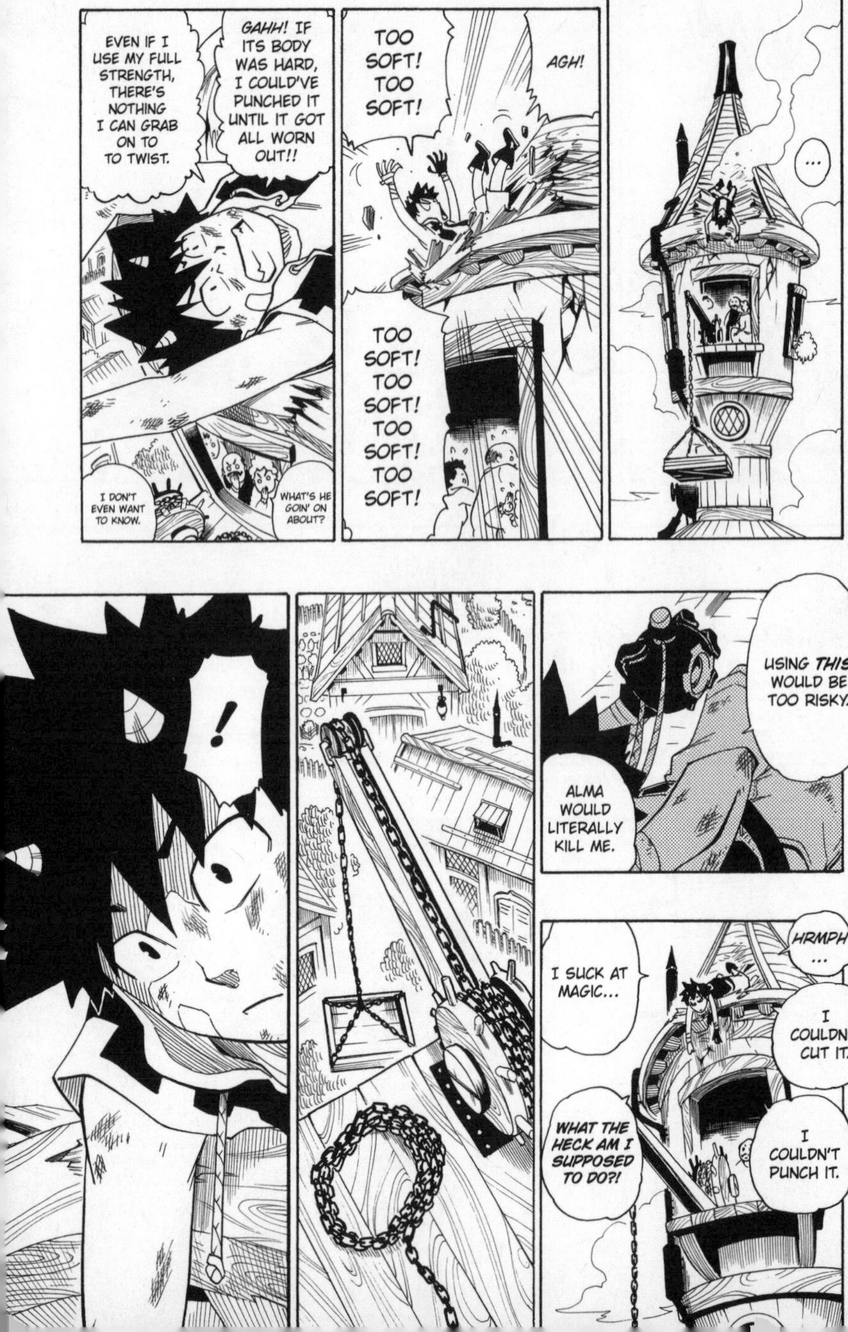
...
AGH!
TOO SOFT! TOO SOFT!
TOO SOFT! TOO SOFT! TOO SOFT! TOO SOFT!
GAHH! IF ITS BODY WAS HARD, I COULD'VE PUNCHED IT UNTIL IT GOT ALL WORN OUT!!
EVEN IF I USE MY FULL STRENGTH, THERE'S NOTHING I CAN GRAB ON TO TO TWIST.
WHAT'S HE GOIN' ON ABOUT?
I DON'T EVEN WANT TO KNOW.
USING *THIS* WOULD BE TOO RISKY.
ALMA WOULD LITERALLY KILL ME.
HRMPH...
I COULDN'T CUT IT.
I COULDN'T PUNCH IT.
I SUCK AT MAGIC...
WHAT THE HECK AM I SUPPOSED TO DO?!
!

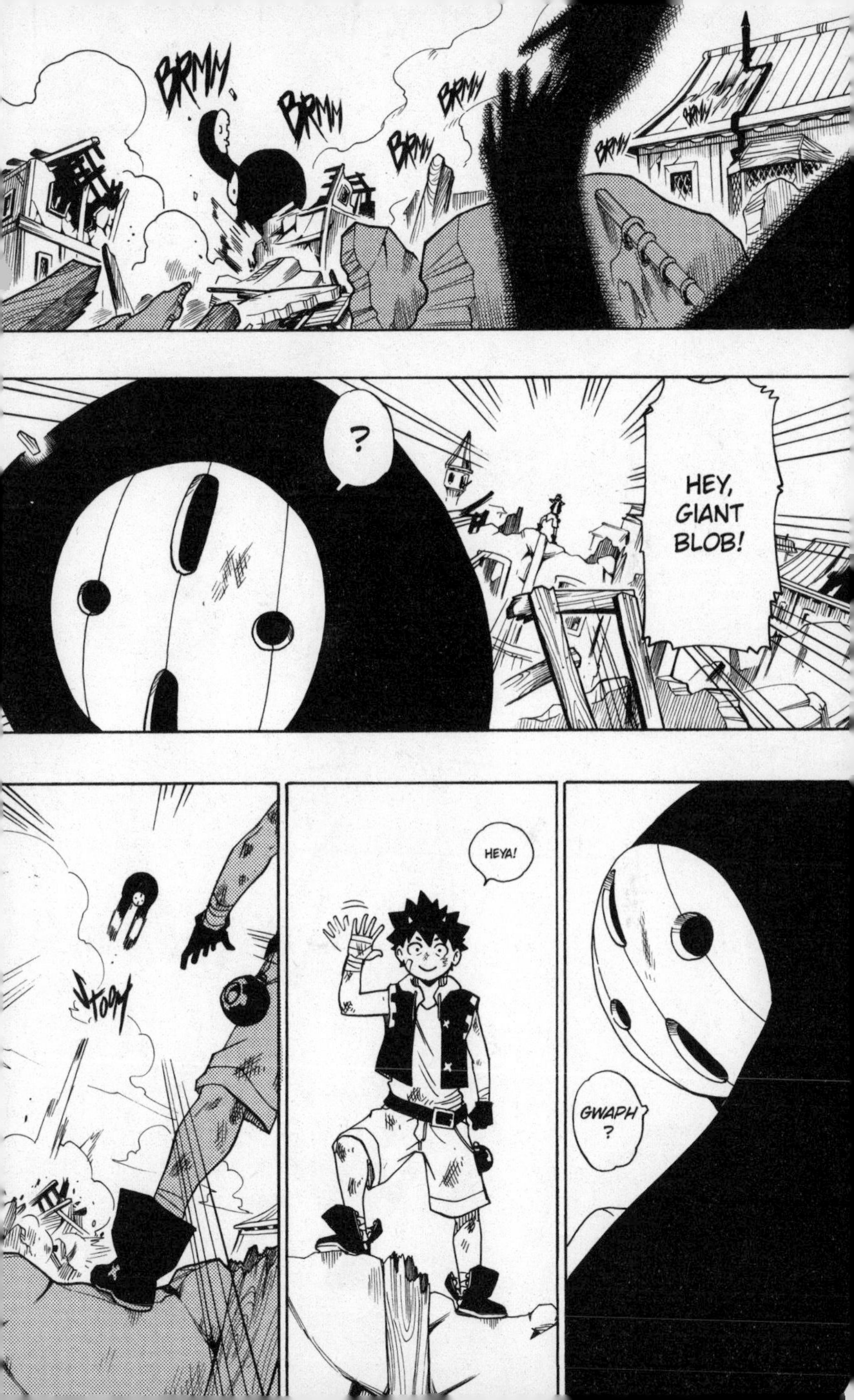
BRMM
BRMM
BRMM
BRMM
BRMM
BRMM
HEY, GIANT BLOB!
?
GWAPH ?
HEYA!
STOMP

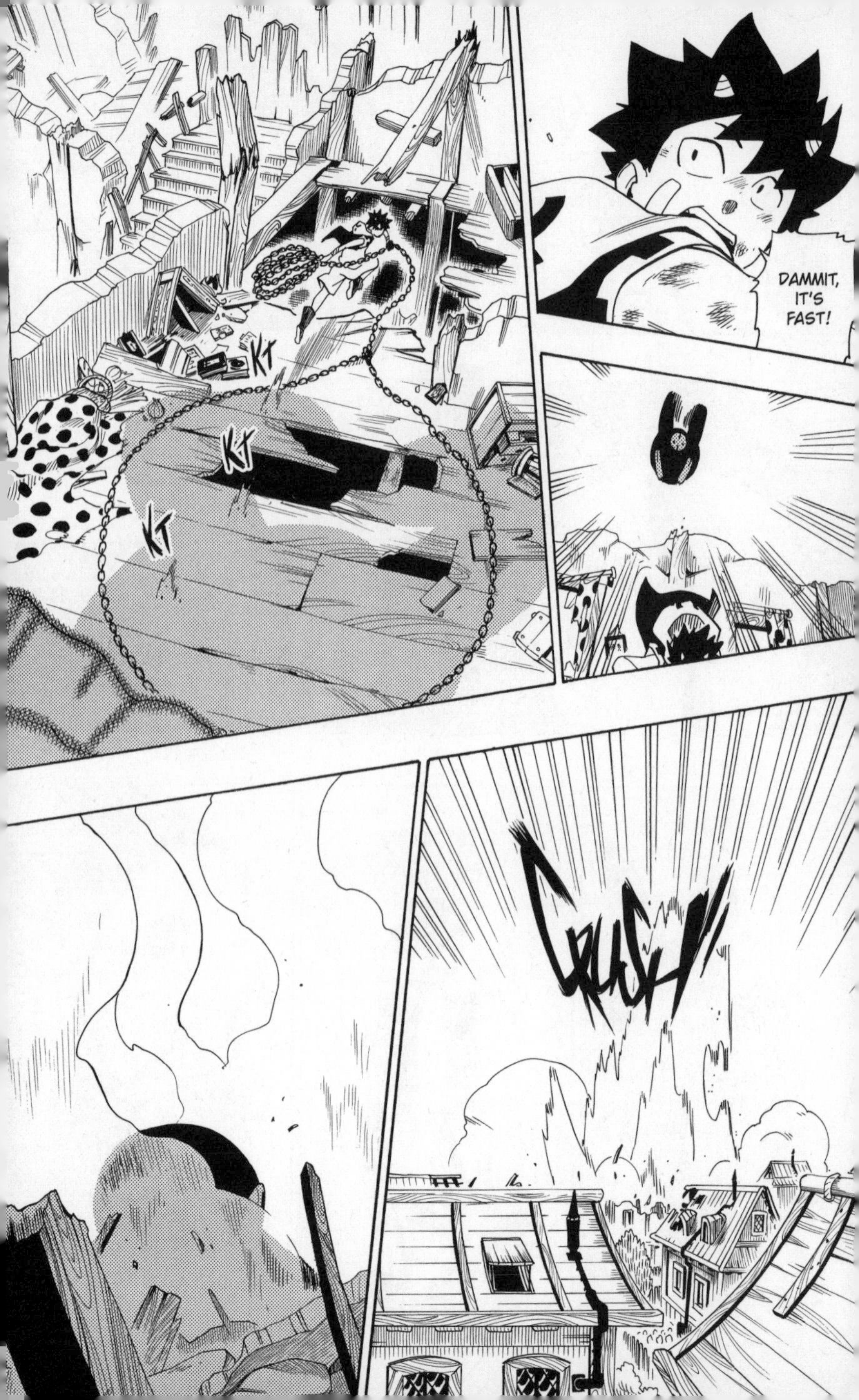
DAMMIT, IT'S FAST!
KT
KT
KT
CRUSH

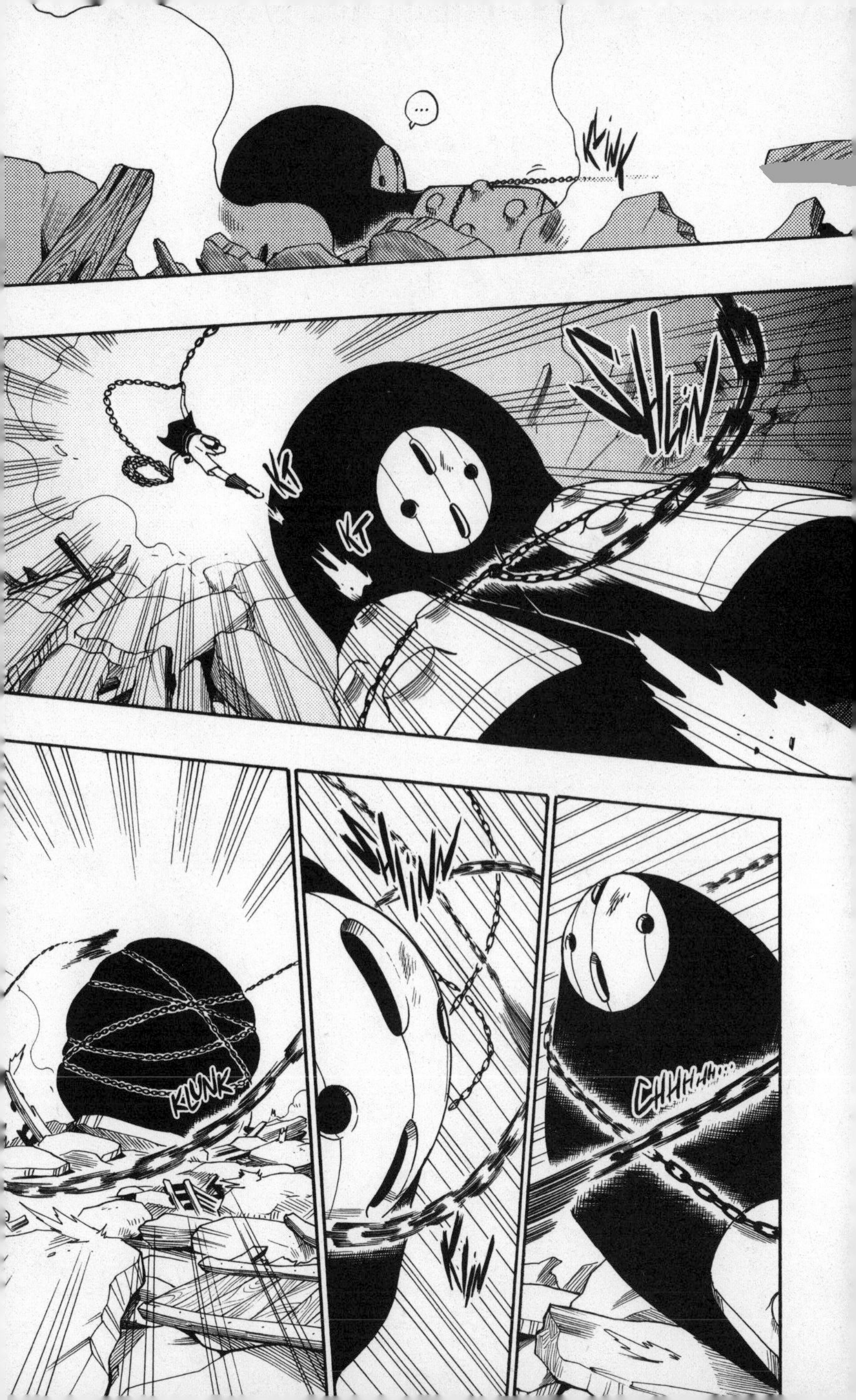
...
KLINK
SHLINN
KT
KT
CHHH...
SHLINN
KLIN
KLUNK

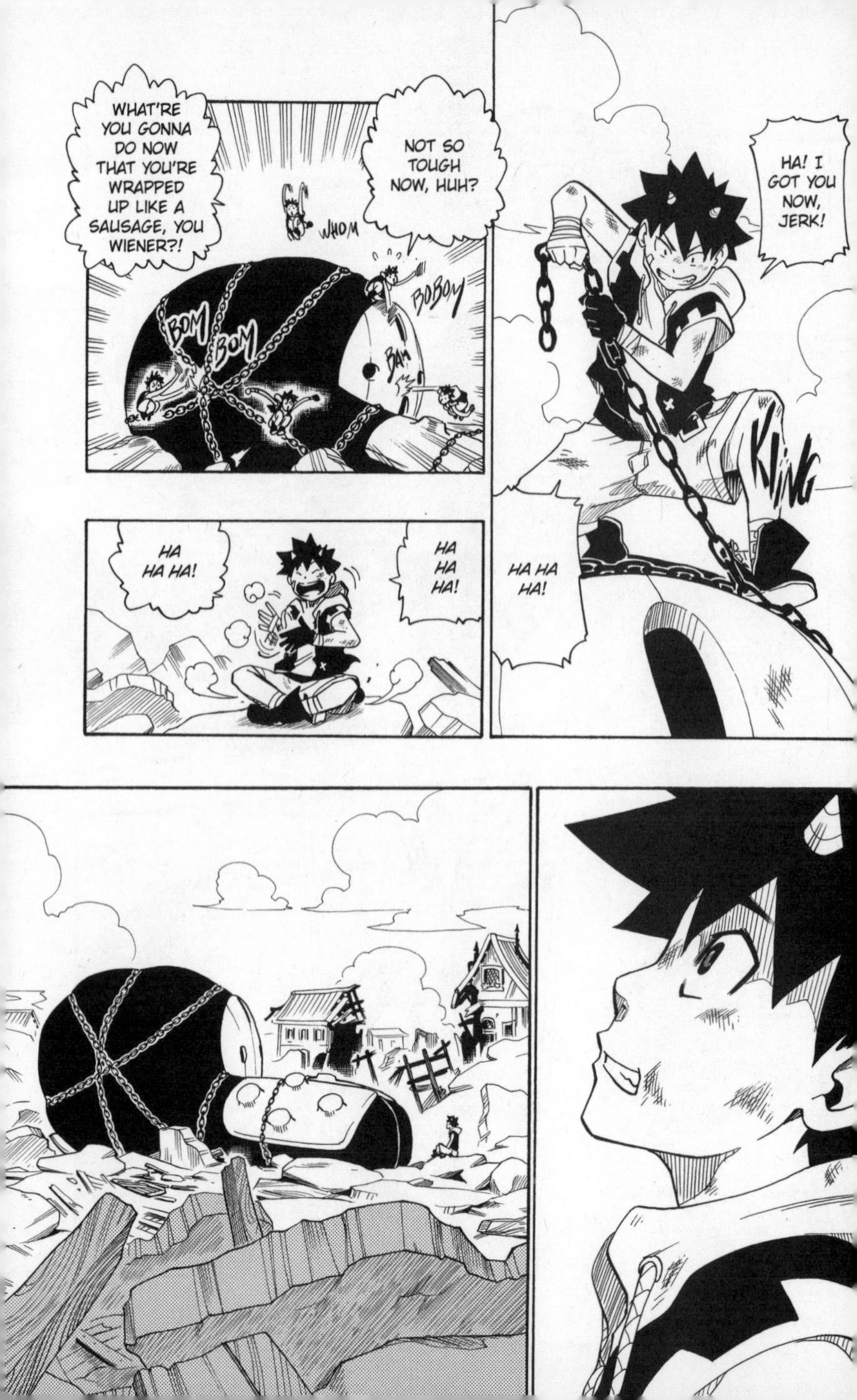
HA! I GOT YOU NOW, JERK!
KING
HA HA HA!
NOT SO TOUGH NOW, HUH?
WHAT'RE YOU GONNA DO NOW THAT YOU'RE WRAPPED UP LIKE A SAUSAGE, YOU WIENER?!
WHOM
BOBOM
BOM
BOM
BAM
HA HA HA!
HA HA HA!

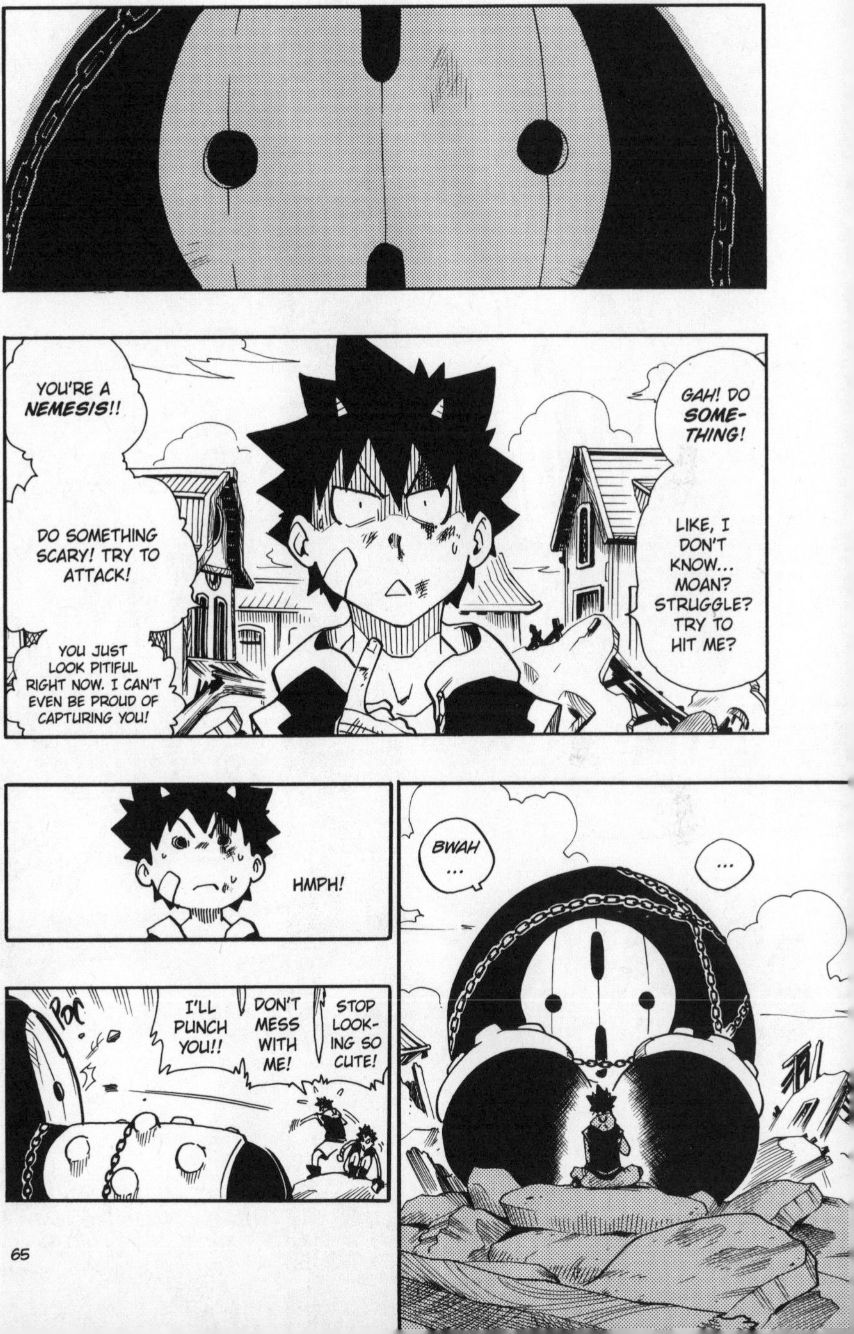
GAH! DO SOMETHING!
LIKE, I DON'T KNOW... MOAN? STRUGGLE? TRY TO HIT ME?
YOU'RE A NEMESIS!!
DO SOMETHING SCARY! TRY TO ATTACK!
YOU JUST LOOK PITIFUL RIGHT NOW. I CAN'T EVEN BE PROUD OF CAPTURING YOU!
...
BWAH ...
HMPH!
STOP LOOKING SO CUTE!
DON'T MESS WITH ME!
I'LL PUNCH YOU!!
POC

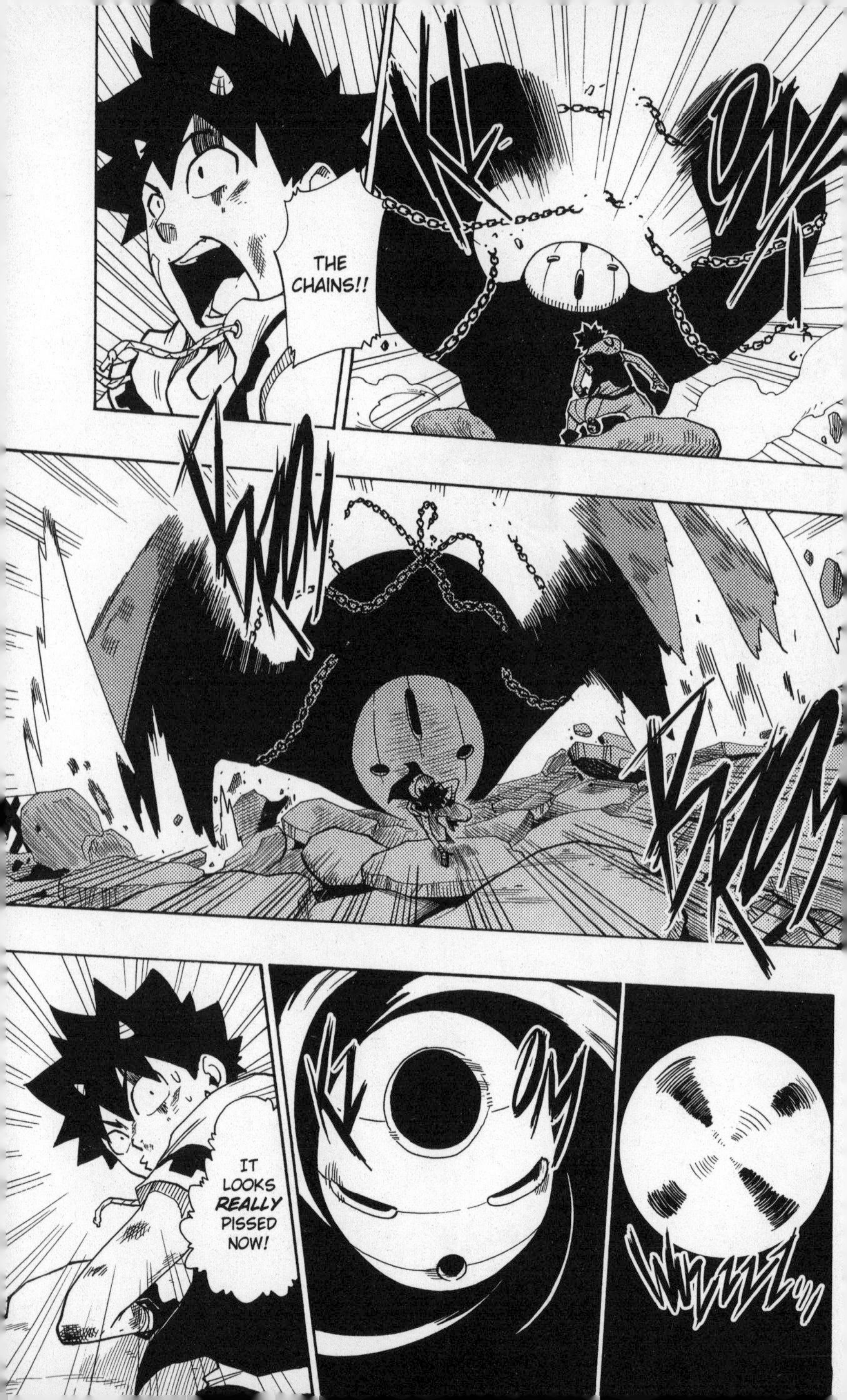
THE CHAINS!!
IT LOOKS **REALLY** PISSED NOW!

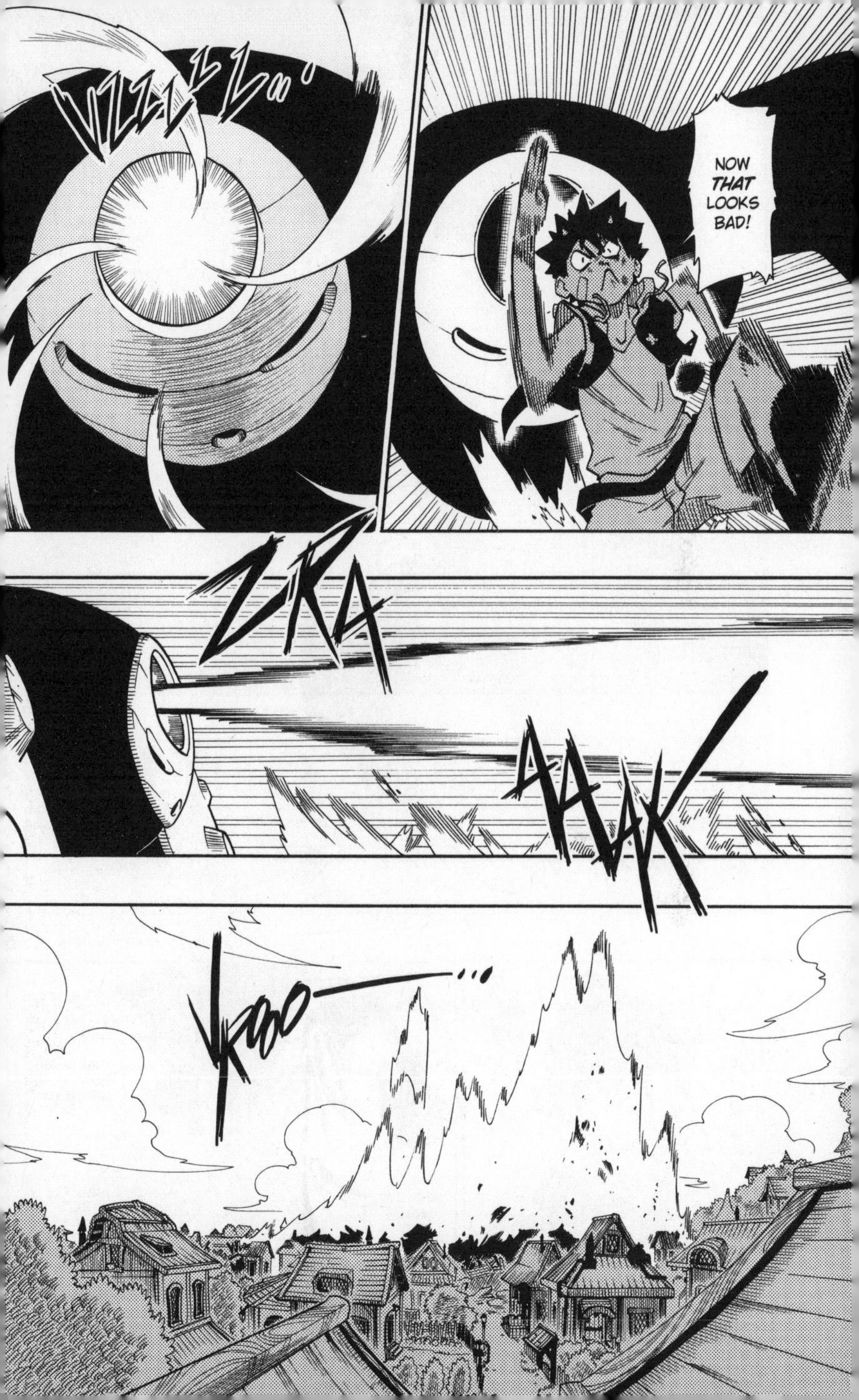
NOW THAT LOOKS BAD!
VZZZZZZM..
ZRAAAAK
VKROO—..

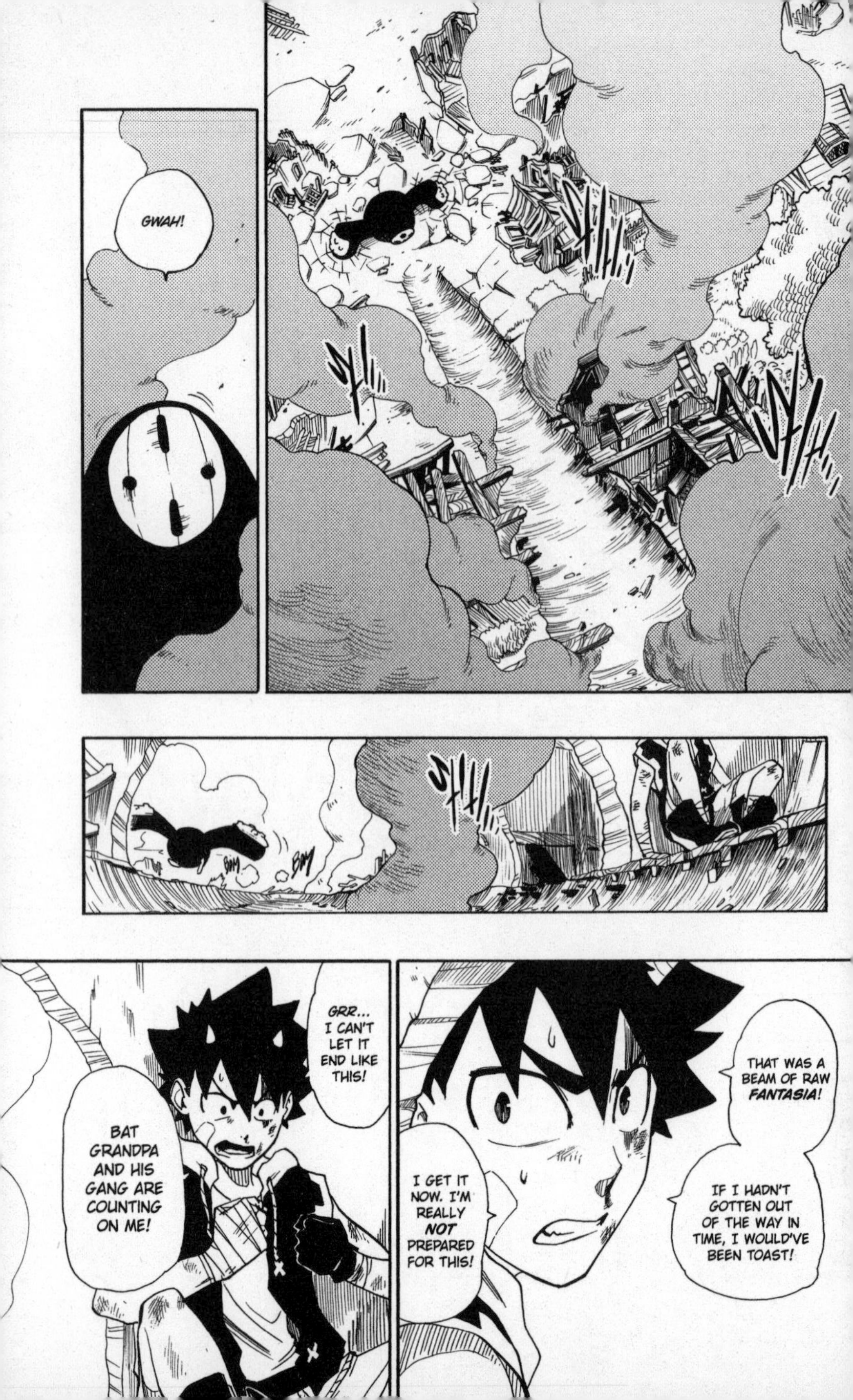
GWAH!
BAM
BAM
THAT WAS A BEAM OF RAW *FANTASIA*!
IF I HADN'T GOTTEN OUT OF THE WAY IN TIME, I WOULD'VE BEEN TOAST!
I GET IT NOW. I'M REALLY ***NOT*** PREPARED FOR THIS!
GRR... I CAN'T LET IT END LIKE THIS!
BAT GRANDPA AND HIS GANG ARE COUNTING ON ME!

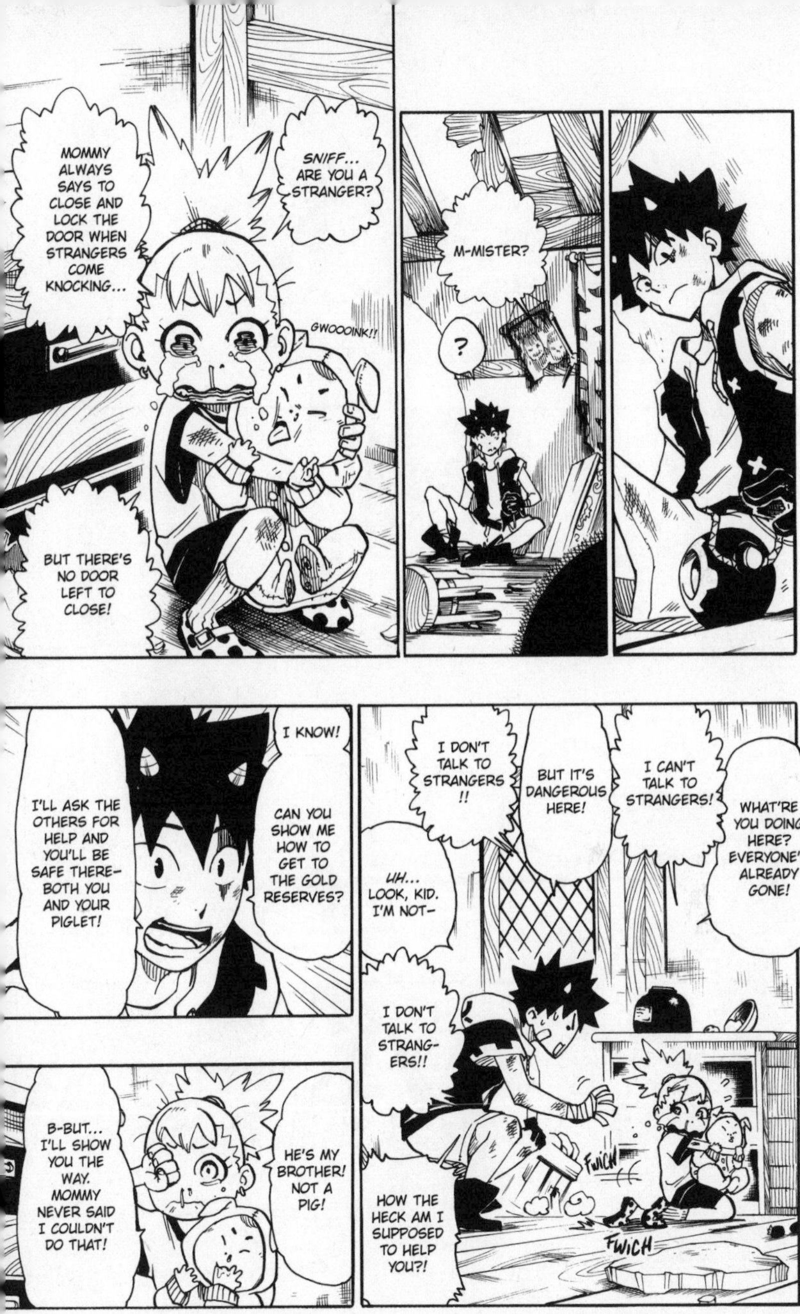
M-MISTER?
?
SNIFF... ARE YOU A STRANGER?
MOMMY ALWAYS SAYS TO CLOSE AND LOCK THE DOOR WHEN STRANGERS COME KNOCKING...
GWOOOINK!!
BUT THERE'S NO DOOR LEFT TO CLOSE!
WHAT'RE YOU DOING HERE? EVERYONE'S ALREADY GONE!
I CAN'T TALK TO STRANGERS!
BUT IT'S DANGEROUS HERE!
I DON'T TALK TO STRANGERS!!
UH... LOOK, KID. I'M NOT-
I DON'T TALK TO STRANG-ERS!!
FWICH
FWICH
HOW THE HECK AM I SUPPOSED TO HELP YOU?!
I KNOW!
CAN YOU SHOW ME HOW TO GET TO THE GOLD RESERVES?
I'LL ASK THE OTHERS FOR HELP AND YOU'LL BE SAFE THERE-BOTH YOU AND YOUR PIGLET!
HE'S MY BROTHER! NOT A PIG!
B-BUT... I'LL SHOW YOU THE WAY. MOMMY NEVER SAID I COULDN'T DO THAT!

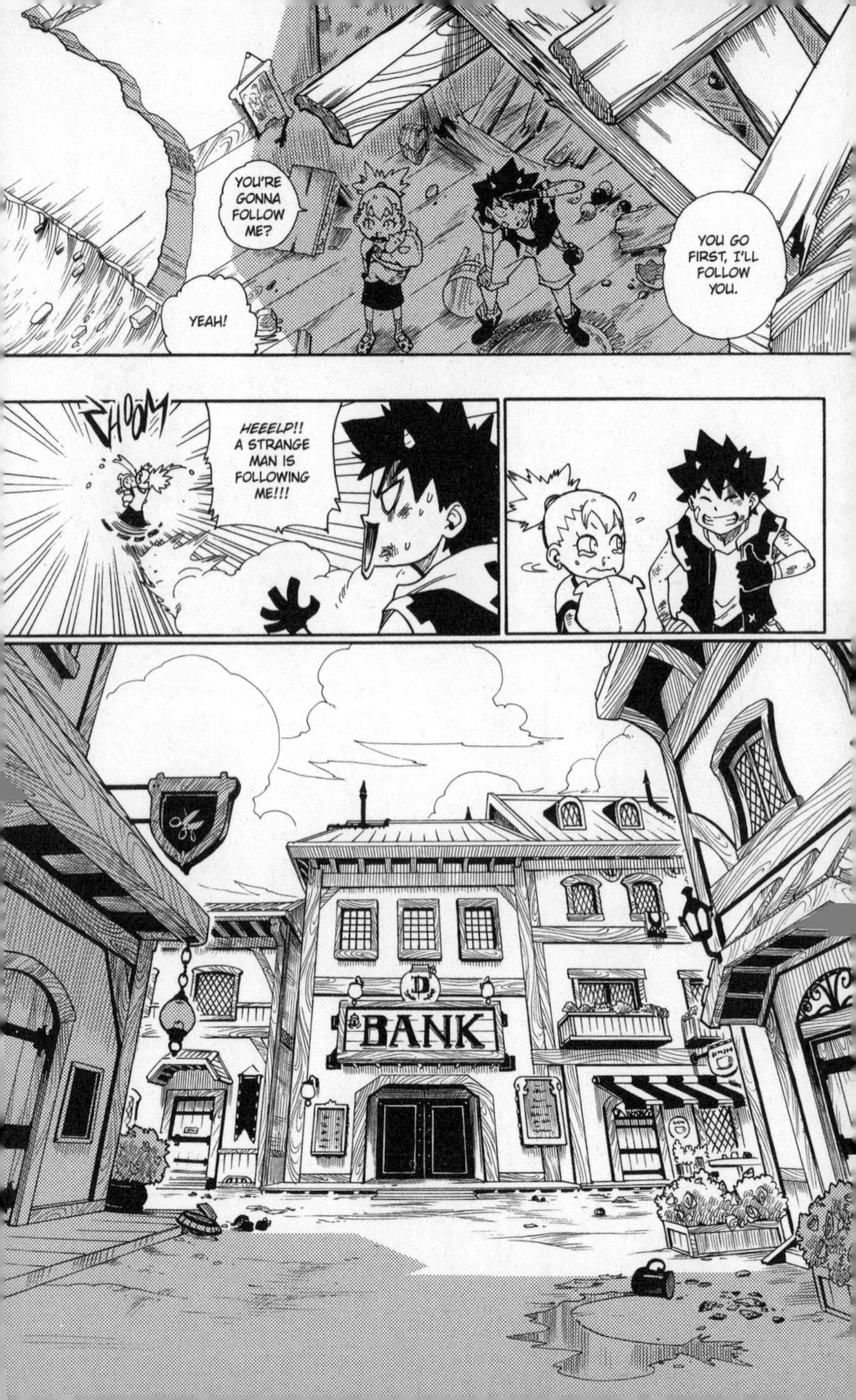
YOU GO FIRST, I'LL FOLLOW YOU.
YOU'RE GONNA FOLLOW ME?
YEAH!
ZHOOM
HEEELP!! A STRANGE MAN IS FOLLOWING ME!!!
BANK

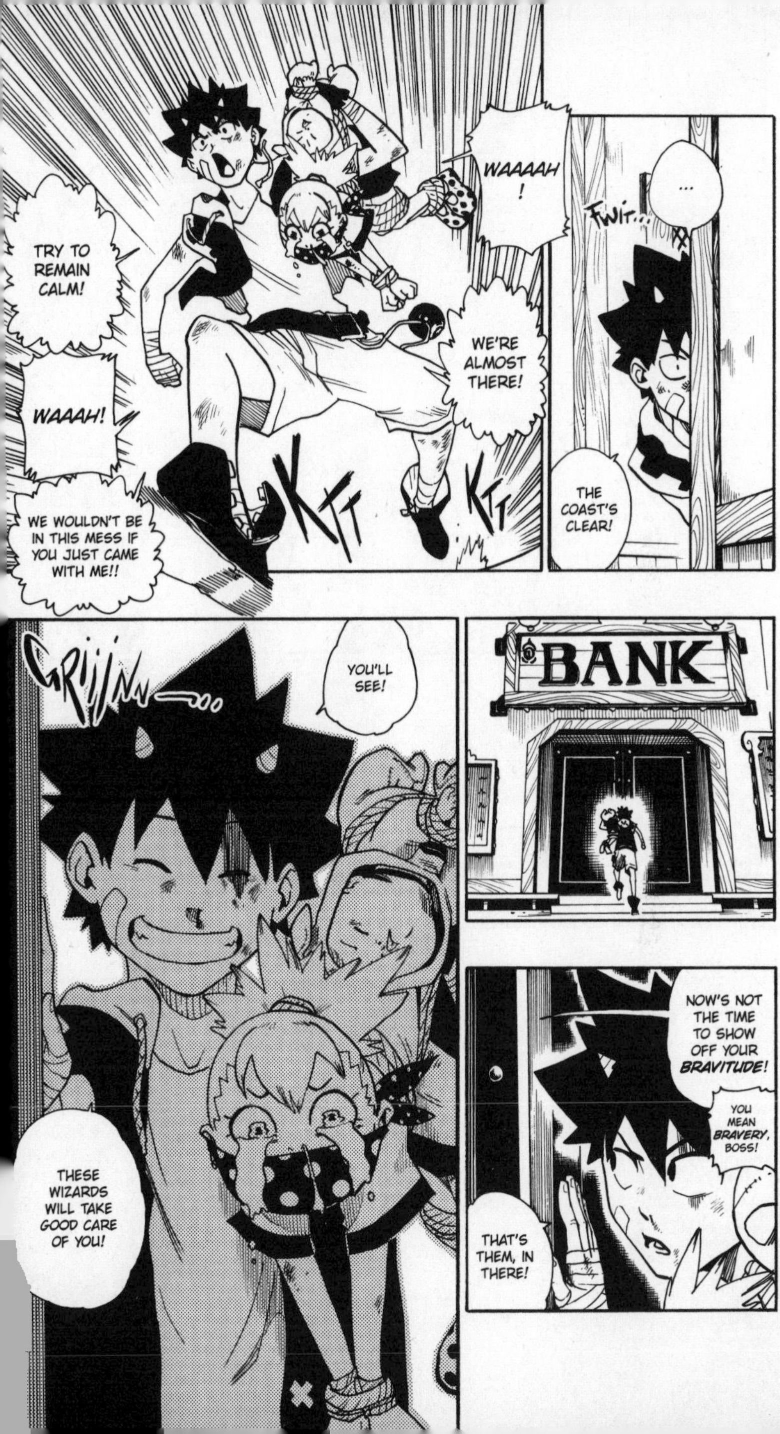
...
FWIT...
THE COAST'S CLEAR!
WAAAAH!
TRY TO REMAIN CALM!
WE'RE ALMOST THERE!
WAAAH!
KTT
KTT
WE WOULDN'T BE IN THIS MESS IF YOU JUST CAME WITH ME!!
BANK
NOW'S NOT THE TIME TO SHOW OFF YOUR BRAVITUDE!
YOU MEAN BRAVERY, BOSS!
THAT'S THEM, IN THERE!
YOU'LL SEE!
GRIIINN
THESE WIZARDS WILL TAKE GOOD CARE OF YOU!

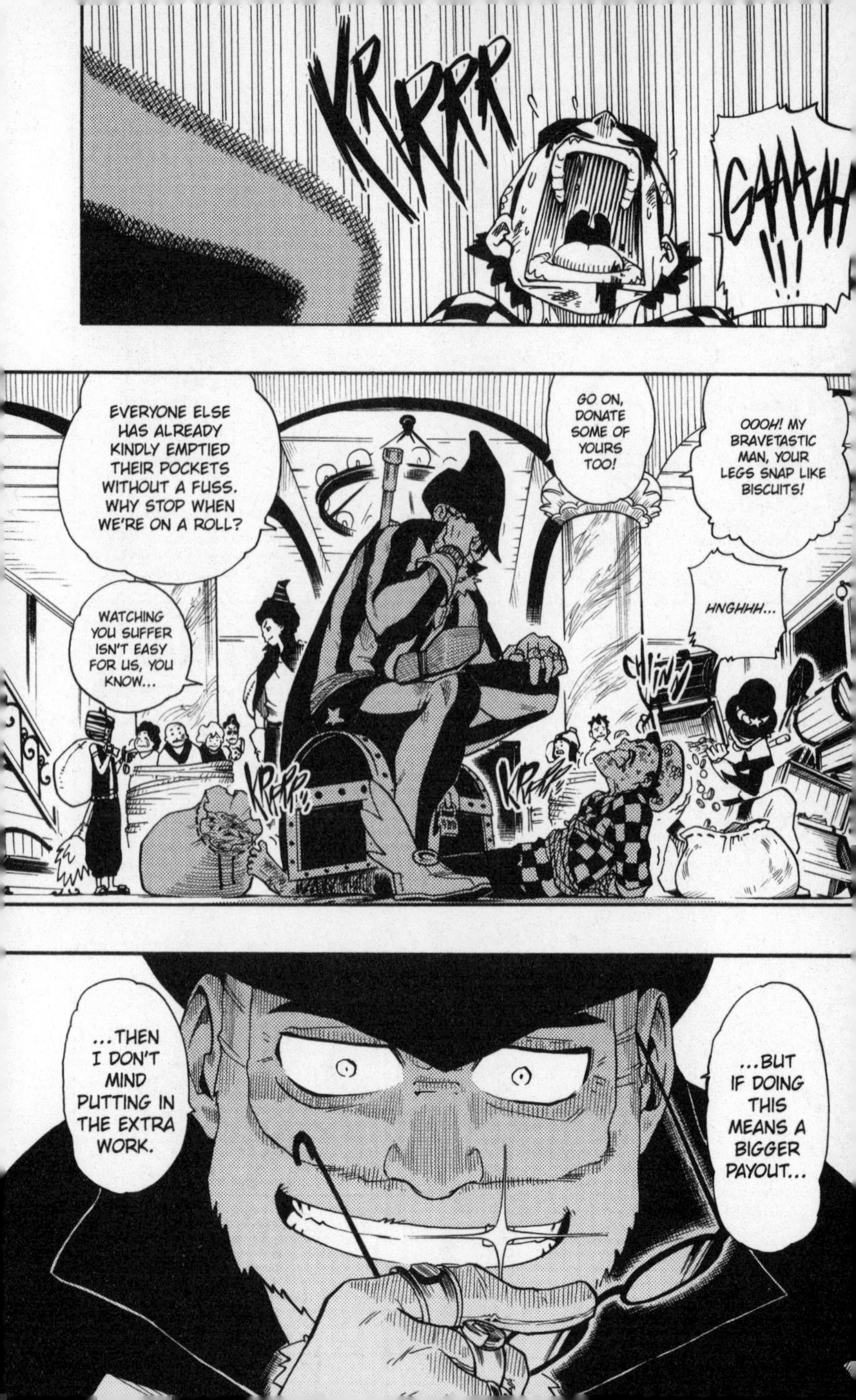
GAAAAH!!!
KRRRR
OOOH! MY BRAVETASTIC MAN, YOUR LEGS SNAP LIKE BISCUITS!
GO ON, DONATE SOME OF YOURS TOO!
EVERYONE ELSE HAS ALREADY KINDLY EMPTIED THEIR POCKETS WITHOUT A FUSS. WHY STOP WHEN WE'RE ON A ROLL?
HNGHHH...
WATCHING YOU SUFFER ISN'T EASY FOR US, YOU KNOW...
...BUT IF DOING THIS MEANS A BIGGER PAYOUT...
...THEN I DON'T MIND PUTTING IN THE EXTRA WORK.

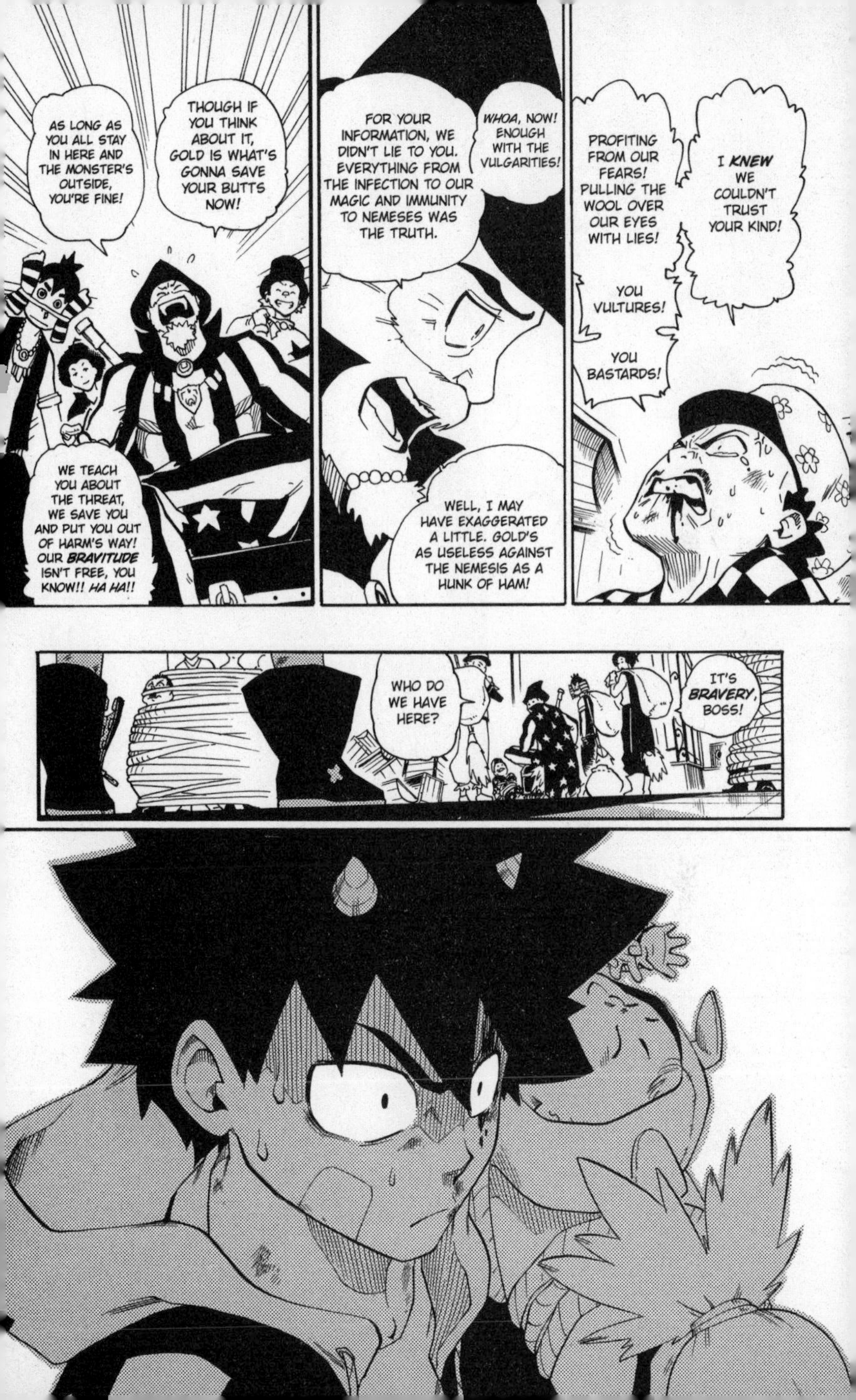
I *KNEW* WE COULDN'T TRUST YOUR KIND!
PROFITING FROM OUR FEARS! PULLING THE WOOL OVER OUR EYES WITH LIES!
YOU VULTURES!
YOU BASTARDS!
WHOA, NOW! ENOUGH WITH THE VULGARITIES!
FOR YOUR INFORMATION, WE DIDN'T LIE TO YOU. EVERYTHING FROM THE INFECTION TO OUR MAGIC AND IMMUNITY TO NEMESES WAS THE TRUTH.
WELL, I MAY HAVE EXAGGERATED A LITTLE. GOLD'S AS USELESS AGAINST THE NEMESIS AS A HUNK OF HAM!
THOUGH IF YOU THINK ABOUT IT, GOLD IS WHAT'S GONNA SAVE YOUR BUTTS NOW!
AS LONG AS YOU ALL STAY IN HERE AND THE MONSTER'S OUTSIDE, YOU'RE FINE!
WE TEACH YOU ABOUT THE THREAT, WE SAVE YOU AND PUT YOU OUT OF HARM'S WAY! OUR *BRAVITUDE* ISN'T FREE, YOU KNOW!! *HA HA*!!
IT'S *BRAVERY*, BOSS!
WHO DO WE HAVE HERE?

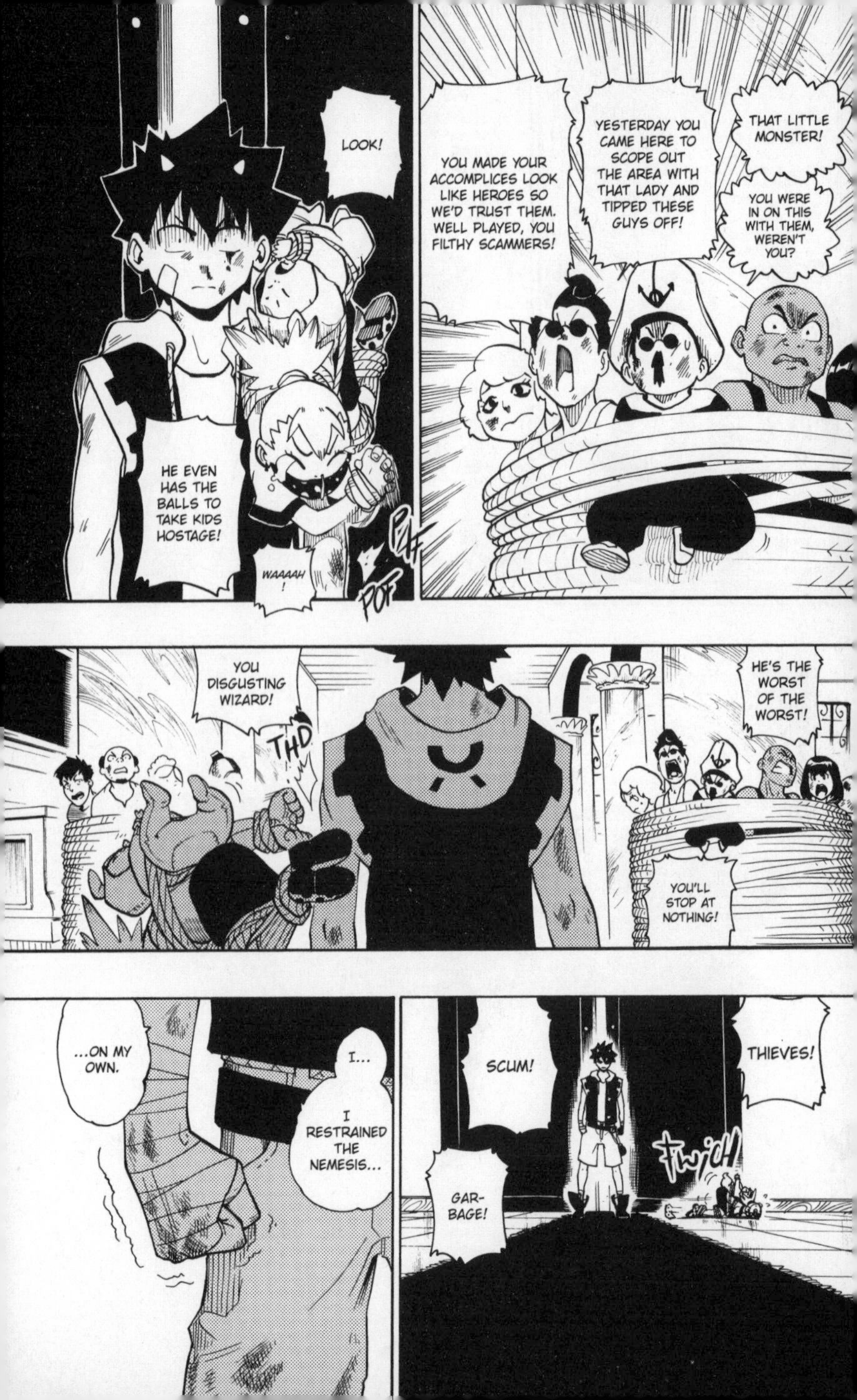
THAT LITTLE MONSTER!
YOU WERE IN ON THIS WITH THEM, WEREN'T YOU?
YESTERDAY YOU CAME HERE TO SCOPE OUT THE AREA WITH THAT LADY AND TIPPED THESE GUYS OFF!
YOU MADE YOUR ACCOMPLICES LOOK LIKE HEROES SO WE'D TRUST THEM. WELL PLAYED, YOU FILTHY SCAMMERS!
LOOK!
HE EVEN HAS THE BALLS TO TAKE KIDS HOSTAGE!
WAAAAH!
PFF
POF
HE'S THE WORST OF THE WORST!
YOU'LL STOP AT NOTHING!
YOU DISGUSTING WIZARD!
THD
THIEVES!
SCUM!
TWITCH
GAR-BAGE!
I...
I RESTRAINED THE NEMESIS...
...ON MY OWN.

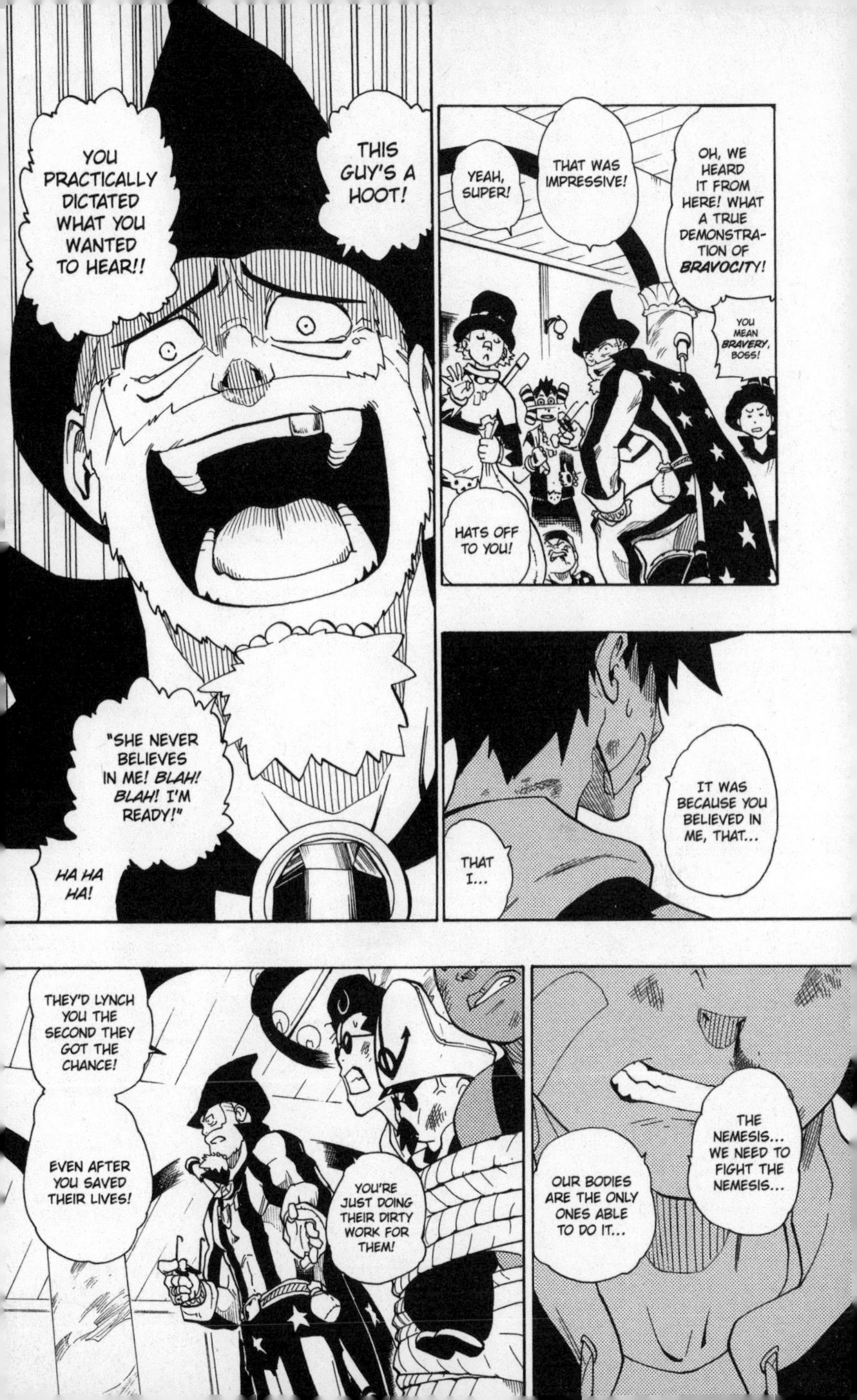
OH, WE HEARD IT FROM HERE! WHAT A TRUE DEMONSTRATION OF *BRAVOCITY*!
THAT WAS IMPRESSIVE!
YEAH, SUPER!
YOU MEAN *BRAVERY*, BOSS!
HATS OFF TO YOU!
IT WAS BECAUSE YOU BELIEVED IN ME, THAT...
THAT I...
THIS GUY'S A HOOT!
YOU PRACTICALLY DICTATED WHAT YOU WANTED TO HEAR!!
"SHE NEVER BELIEVES IN ME! *BLAH! BLAH!* I'M READY!"
HA HA HA!
THE NEMESIS... WE NEED TO FIGHT THE NEMESIS...
OUR BODIES ARE THE ONLY ONES ABLE TO DO IT...
THEY'D LYNCH YOU THE SECOND THEY GOT THE CHANCE!
EVEN AFTER YOU SAVED THEIR LIVES!
YOU'RE JUST DOING THEIR DIRTY WORK FOR THEM!

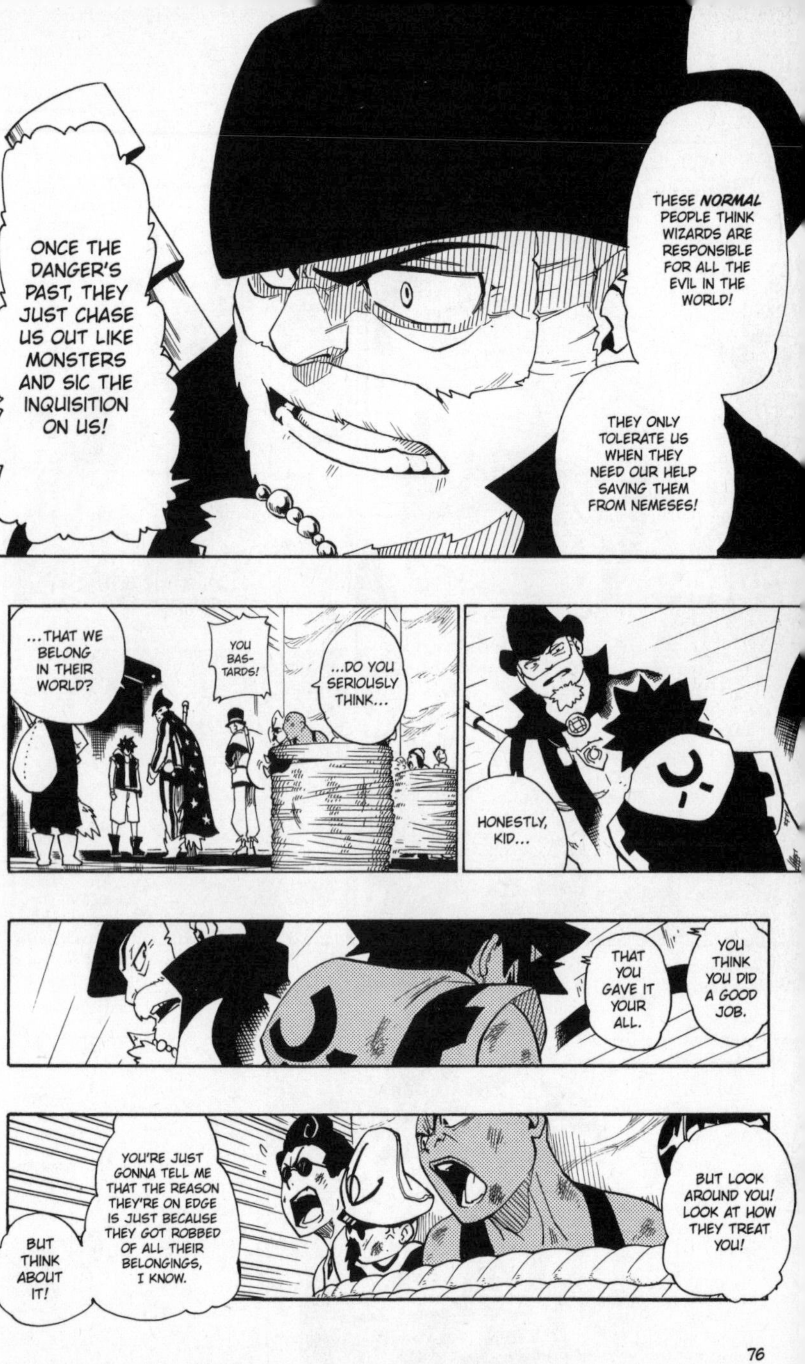
THESE ***NORMAL*** PEOPLE THINK WIZARDS ARE RESPONSIBLE FOR ALL THE EVIL IN THE WORLD!
THEY ONLY TOLERATE US WHEN THEY NEED OUR HELP SAVING THEM FROM NEMESES!
ONCE THE DANGER'S PAST, THEY JUST CHASE US OUT LIKE MONSTERS AND SIC THE INQUISITION ON US!
HONESTLY, KID...
...DO YOU SERIOUSLY THINK...
YOU BAS-TARDS!
...THAT WE BELONG IN THEIR WORLD?
YOU THINK YOU DID A GOOD JOB.
THAT YOU GAVE IT YOUR ALL.
BUT LOOK AROUND YOU! LOOK AT HOW THEY TREAT YOU!
YOU'RE JUST GONNA TELL ME THAT THE REASON THEY'RE ON EDGE IS JUST BECAUSE THEY GOT ROBBED OF ALL THEIR BELONGINGS, I KNOW.
BUT THINK ABOUT IT!

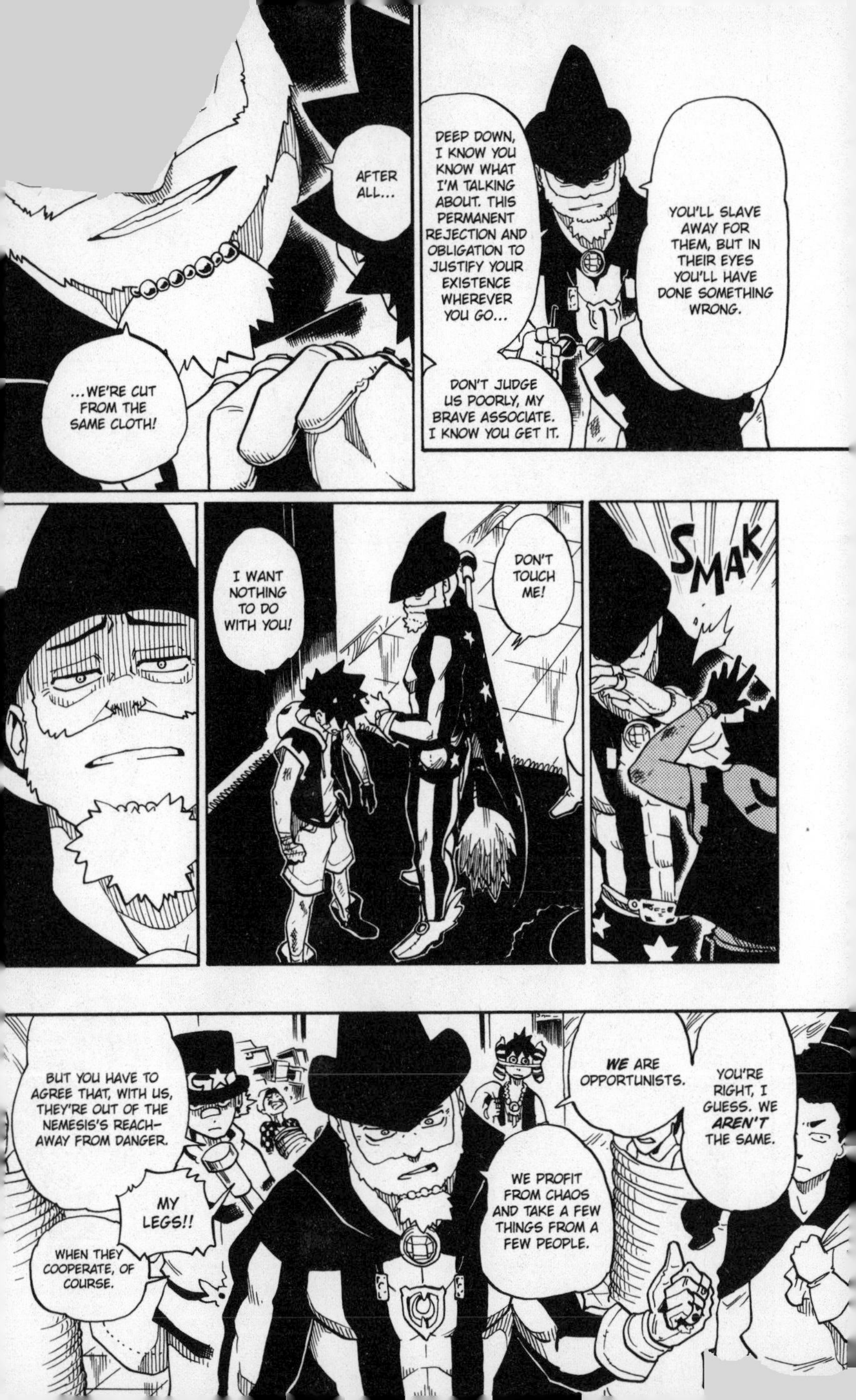
YOU'LL SLAVE AWAY FOR THEM, BUT IN THEIR EYES YOU'LL HAVE DONE SOMETHING WRONG.
DEEP DOWN, I KNOW YOU KNOW WHAT I'M TALKING ABOUT. THIS PERMANENT REJECTION AND OBLIGATION TO JUSTIFY YOUR EXISTENCE WHEREVER YOU GO...
DON'T JUDGE US POORLY, MY BRAVE ASSOCIATE. I KNOW YOU GET IT.
AFTER ALL...
...WE'RE CUT FROM THE SAME CLOTH!
SMAK
DON'T TOUCH ME!
I WANT NOTHING TO DO WITH YOU!
YOU'RE RIGHT, I GUESS. WE AREN'T THE SAME.
WE ARE OPPORTUNISTS.
WE PROFIT FROM CHAOS AND TAKE A FEW THINGS FROM A FEW PEOPLE.
BUT YOU HAVE TO AGREE THAT, WITH US, THEY'RE OUT OF THE NEMESIS'S REACH—AWAY FROM DANGER.
MY LEGS!!
WHEN THEY COOPERATE, OF COURSE.

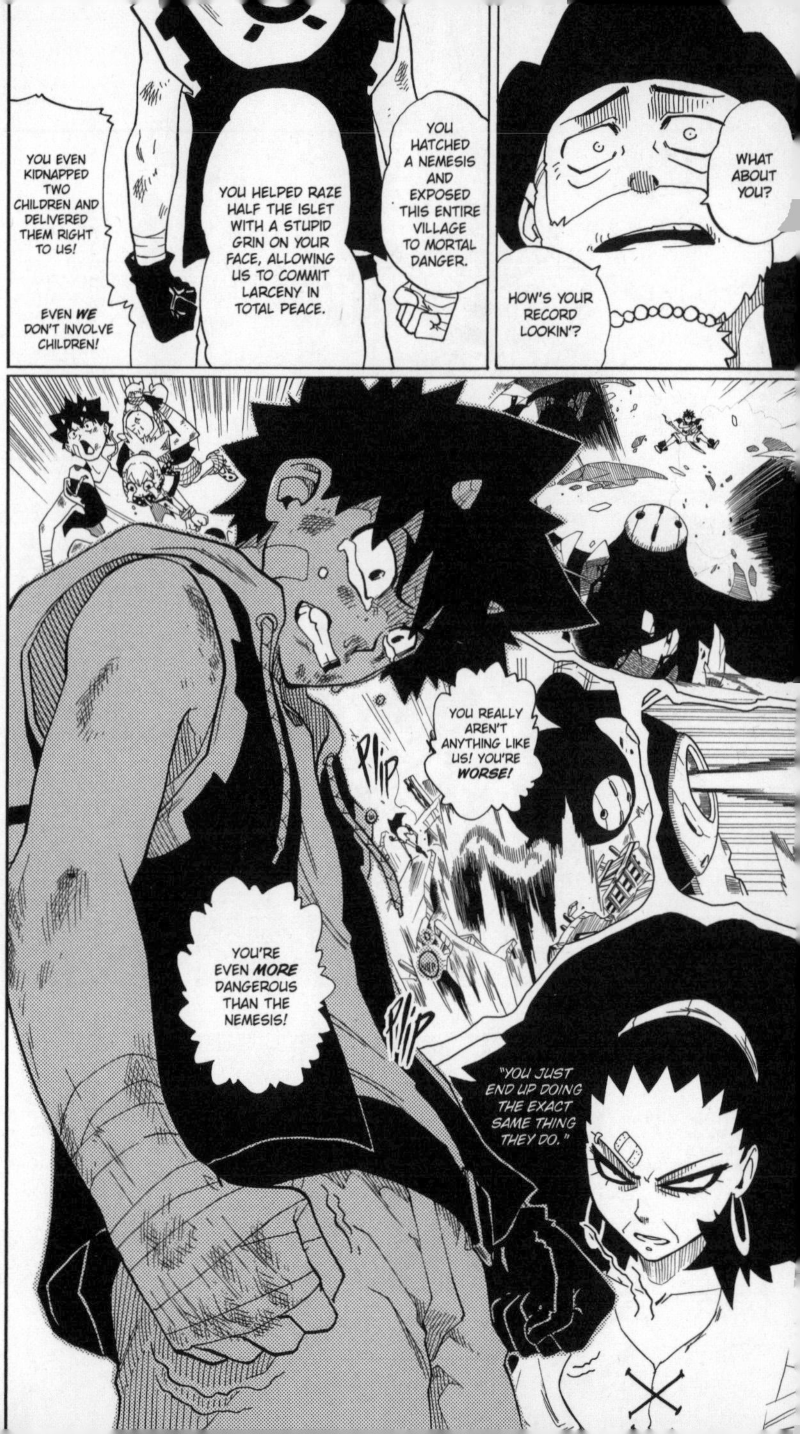
WHAT ABOUT YOU?
HOW'S YOUR RECORD LOOKIN'?
YOU HATCHED A NEMESIS AND EXPOSED THIS ENTIRE VILLAGE TO MORTAL DANGER.
YOU HELPED RAZE HALF THE ISLET WITH A STUPID GRIN ON YOUR FACE, ALLOWING US TO COMMIT LARCENY IN TOTAL PEACE.
YOU EVEN KIDNAPPED TWO CHILDREN AND DELIVERED THEM RIGHT TO US!
EVEN WE DON'T INVOLVE CHILDREN!
YOU REALLY AREN'T ANYTHING LIKE US! YOU'RE WORSE!
PLIP
YOU'RE EVEN MORE DANGEROUS THAN THE NEMESIS!
PLIP
"YOU JUST END UP DOING THE EXACT SAME THING THEY DO."

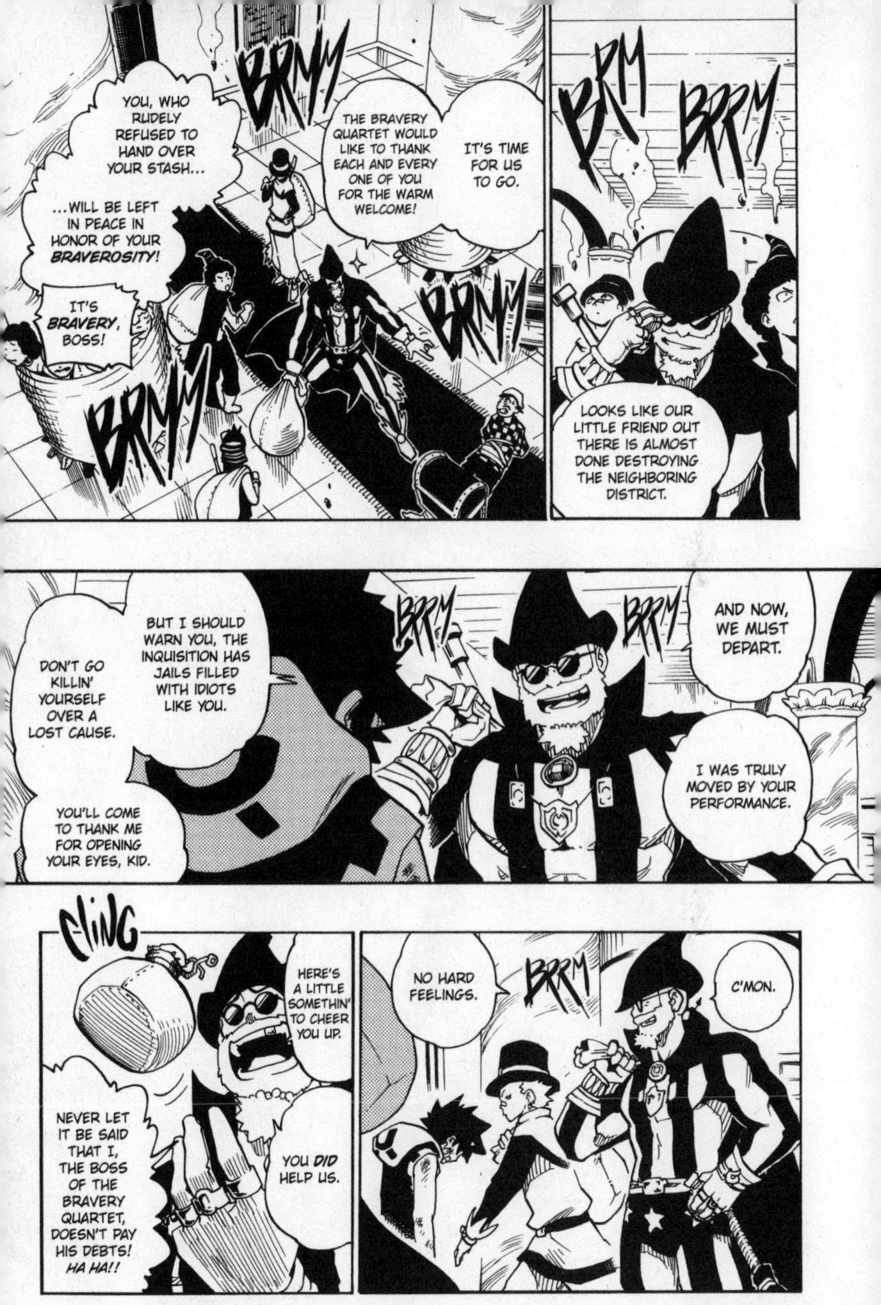
BRM
BRRM
LOOKS LIKE OUR LITTLE FRIEND OUT THERE IS ALMOST DONE DESTROYING THE NEIGHBORING DISTRICT.
IT'S TIME FOR US TO GO.
THE BRAVERY QUARTET WOULD LIKE TO THANK EACH AND EVERY ONE OF YOU FOR THE WARM WELCOME!
BRMM
YOU, WHO RUDELY REFUSED TO HAND OVER YOUR STASH...
...WILL BE LEFT IN PEACE IN HONOR OF YOUR *BRAVEROSITY*!
BRMM
IT'S *BRAVERY*, BOSS!
BRMM
AND NOW, WE MUST DEPART.
BRRM
BRRM
I WAS TRULY MOVED BY YOUR PERFORMANCE.
BUT I SHOULD WARN YOU, THE INQUISITION HAS JAILS FILLED WITH IDIOTS LIKE YOU.
DON'T GO KILLIN' YOURSELF OVER A LOST CAUSE.
YOU'LL COME TO THANK ME FOR OPENING YOUR EYES, KID.
C'MON.
BRRM
NO HARD FEELINGS.
HERE'S A LITTLE SOMETHIN' TO CHEER YOU UP.
CLING
YOU *DID* HELP US.
NEVER LET IT BE SAID THAT I, THE BOSS OF THE BRAVERY QUARTET, DOESN'T PAY HIS DEBTS! *HA HA!!*

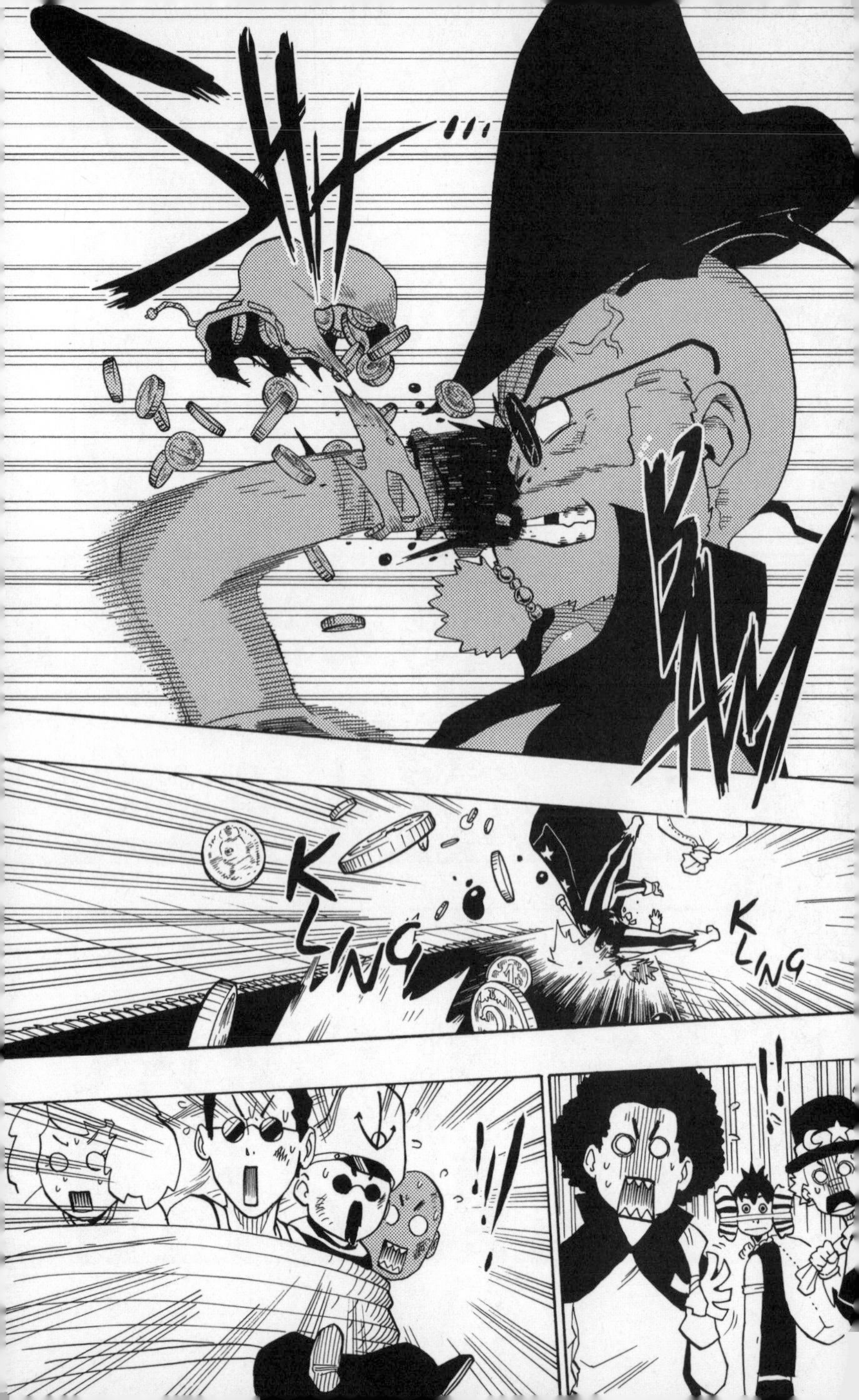
BAM
SHH...
KLING
KLING
!!
!!

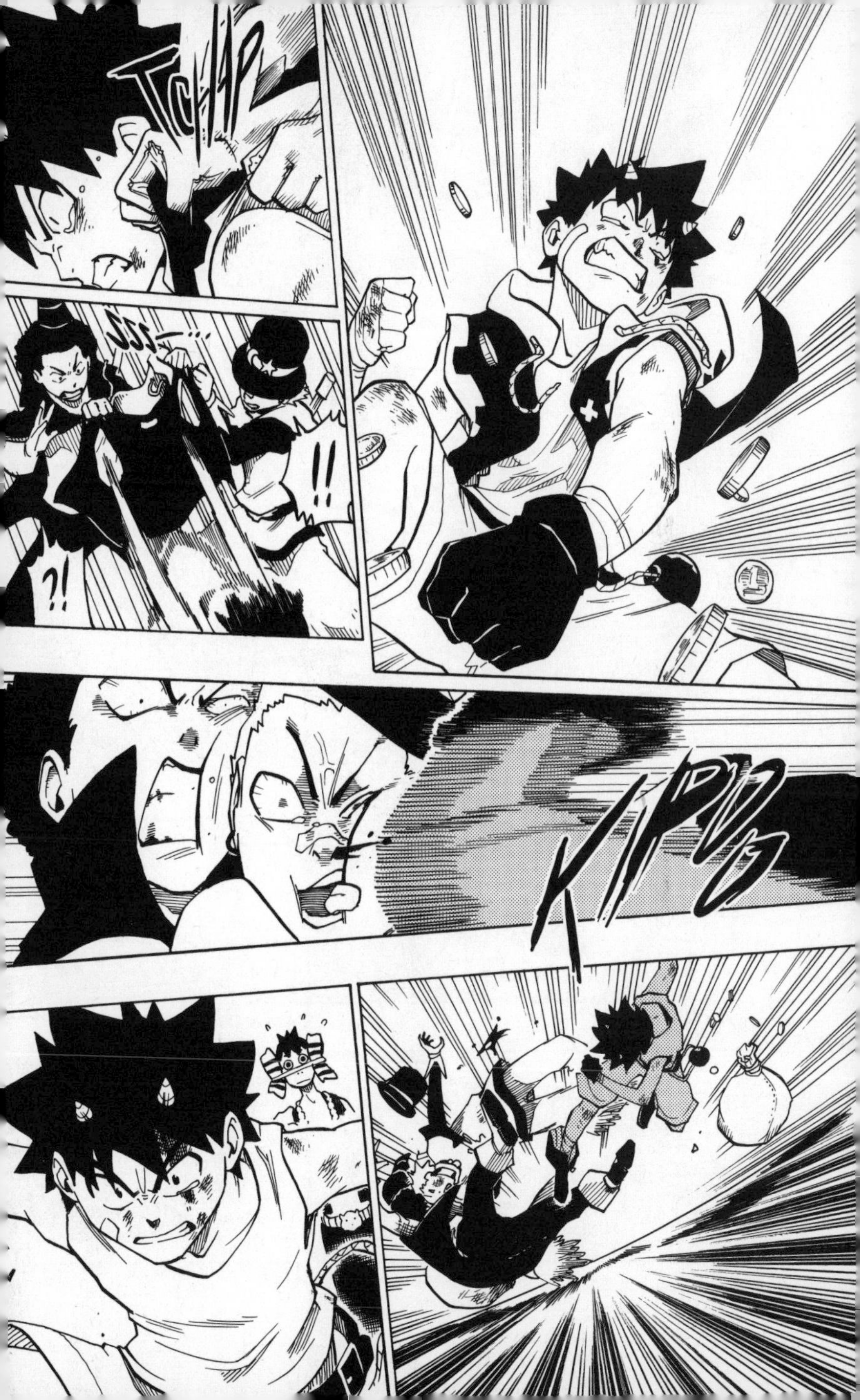
TCHAP
SSS—...
!!
?!

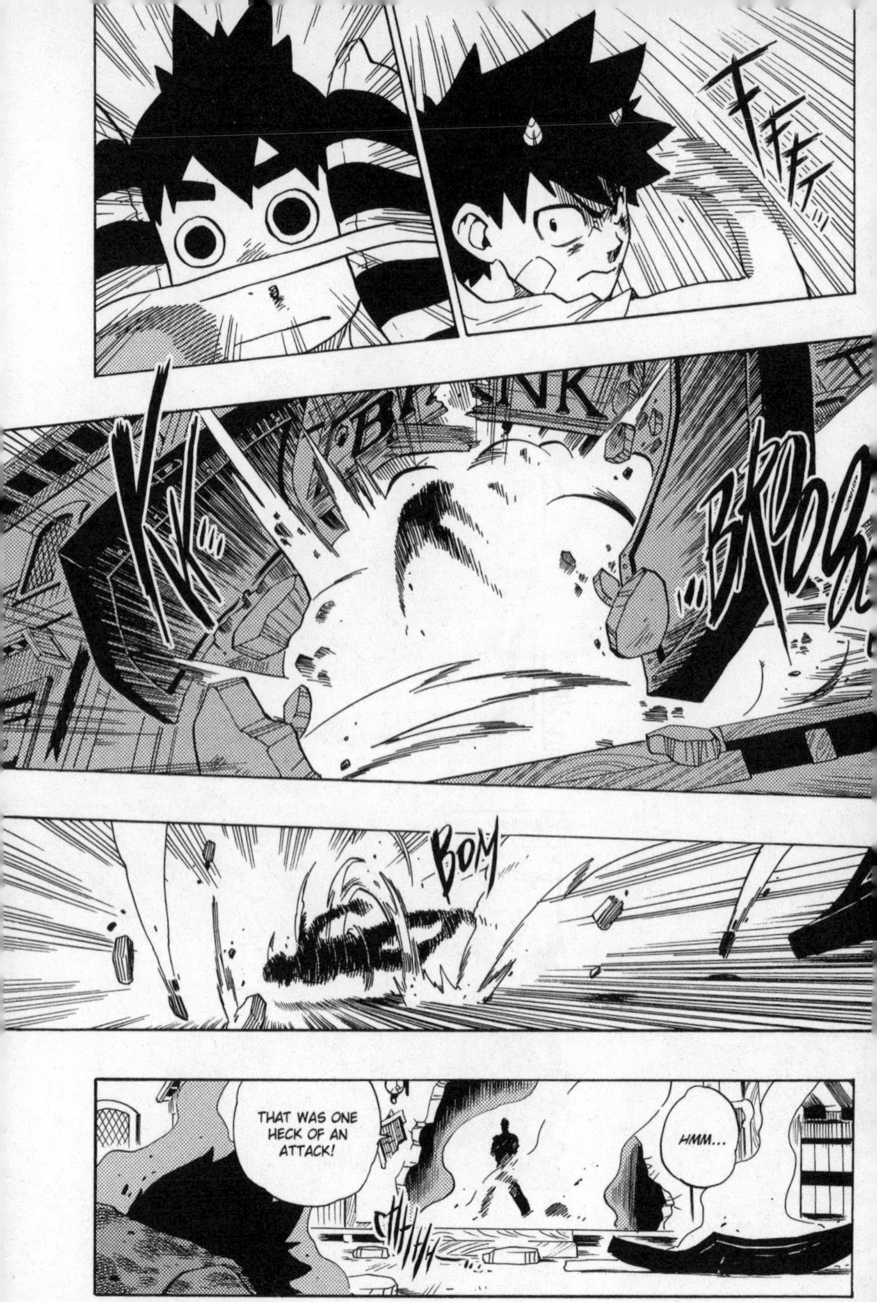
BOM
HMM...
THAT WAS ONE HECK OF AN ATTACK!

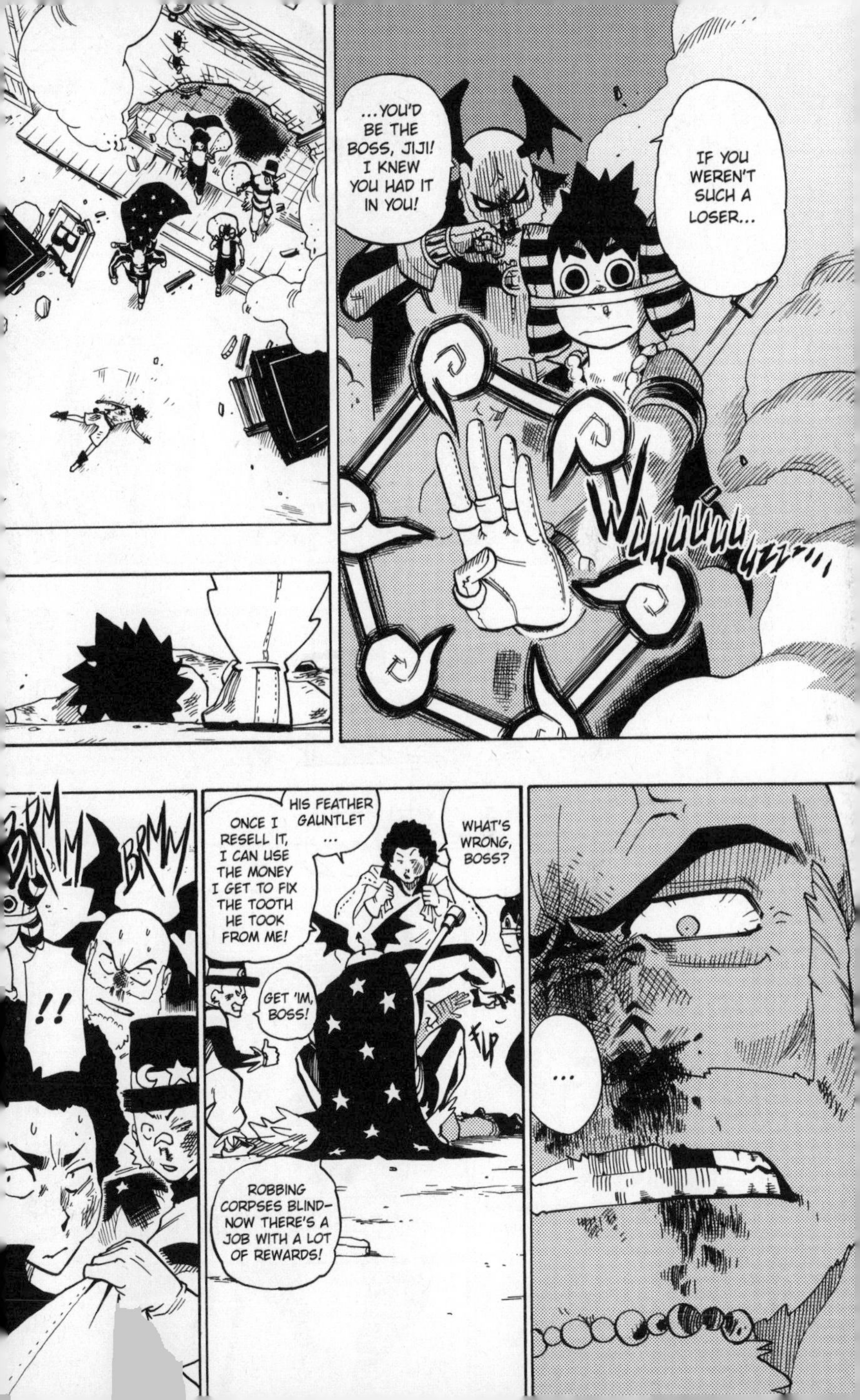
IF YOU WEREN'T SUCH A LOSER...
...YOU'D BE THE BOSS, JIJI! I KNEW YOU HAD IT IN YOU!
...
WHAT'S WRONG, BOSS?
HIS FEATHER GAUNTLET ...
ONCE I RESELL IT, I CAN USE THE MONEY I GET TO FIX THE TOOTH HE TOOK FROM ME!
GET 'IM, BOSS!
FLIP
ROBBING CORPSES BLIND— NOW THERE'S A JOB WITH A LOT OF REWARDS!
BRMM
BRMM
!!

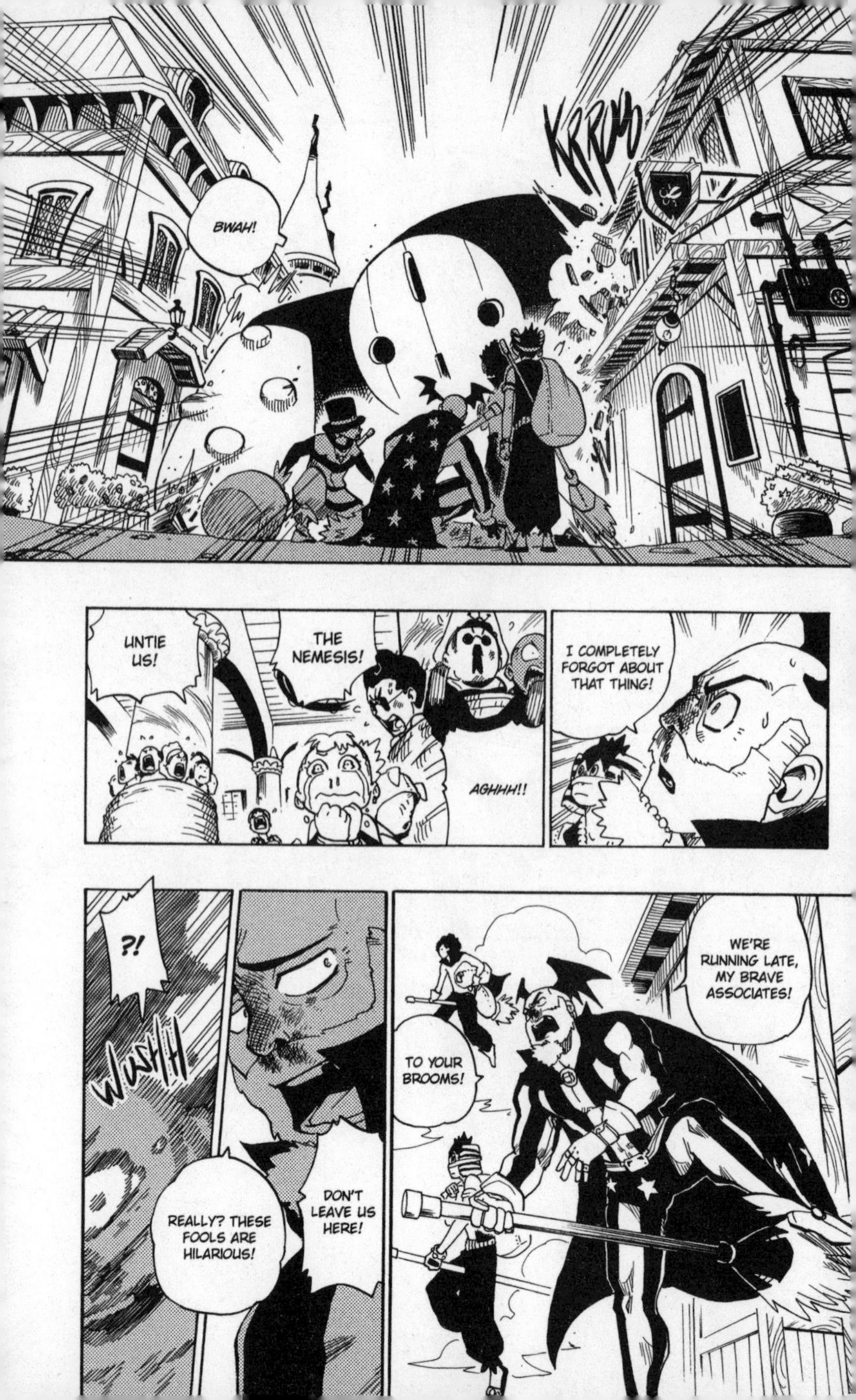
KRRUSH
BWAH!
I COMPLETELY FORGOT ABOUT THAT THING!
THE NEMESIS!
UNTIE US!
AGHHH!!
WE'RE RUNNING LATE, MY BRAVE ASSOCIATES!
TO YOUR BROOMS!
?!
DON'T LEAVE US HERE!
REALLY? THESE FOOLS ARE HILARIOUS!

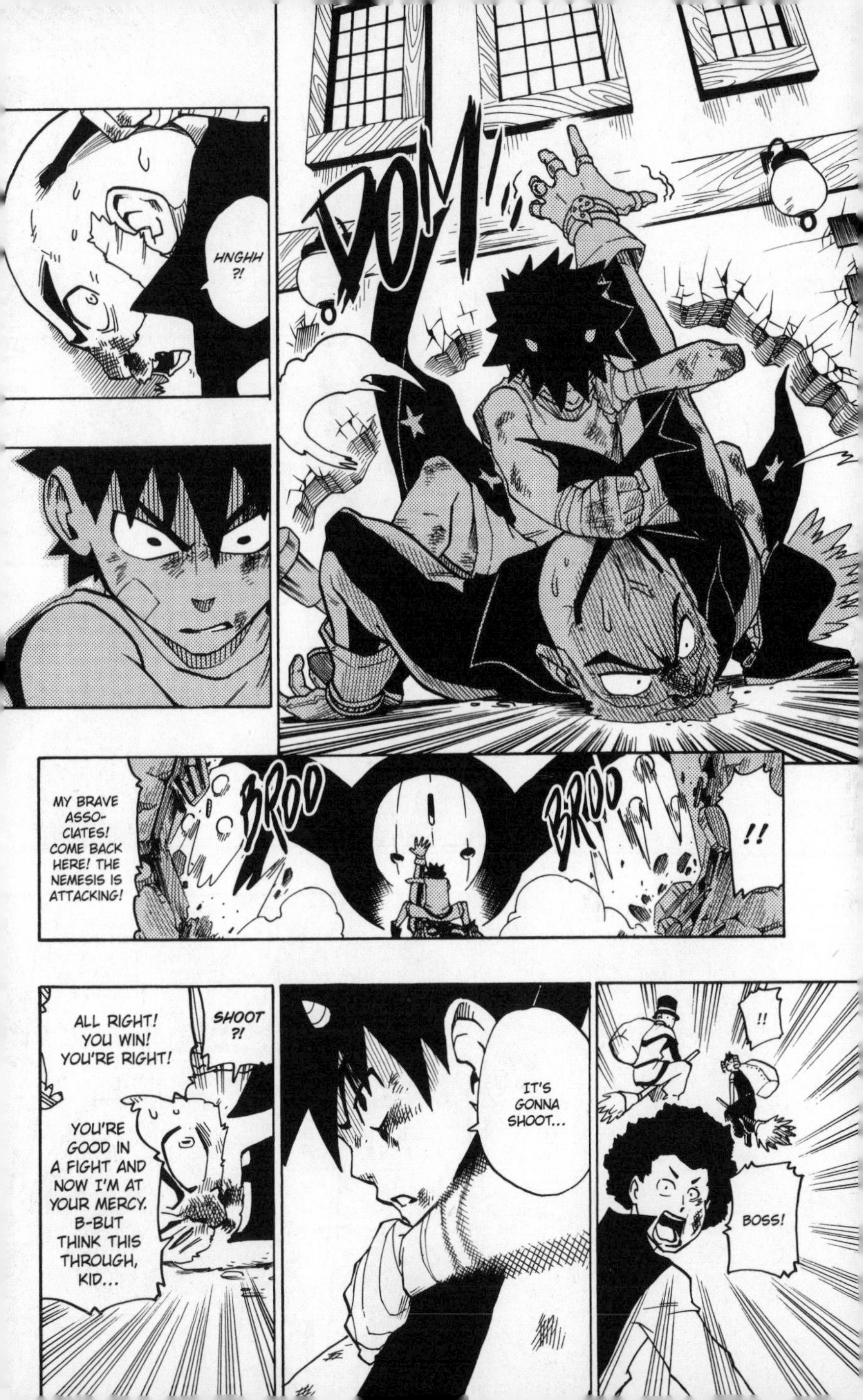
DOM
HNGHH ?!
!!
BROO
BROO
MY BRAVE ASSO-CIATES! COME BACK HERE! THE NEMESIS IS ATTACKING!
!!
BOSS!
IT'S GONNA SHOOT...
SHOOT ?!
ALL RIGHT! YOU WIN! YOU'RE RIGHT!
YOU'RE GOOD IN A FIGHT AND NOW I'M AT YOUR MERCY. B-BUT THINK THIS THROUGH, KID...

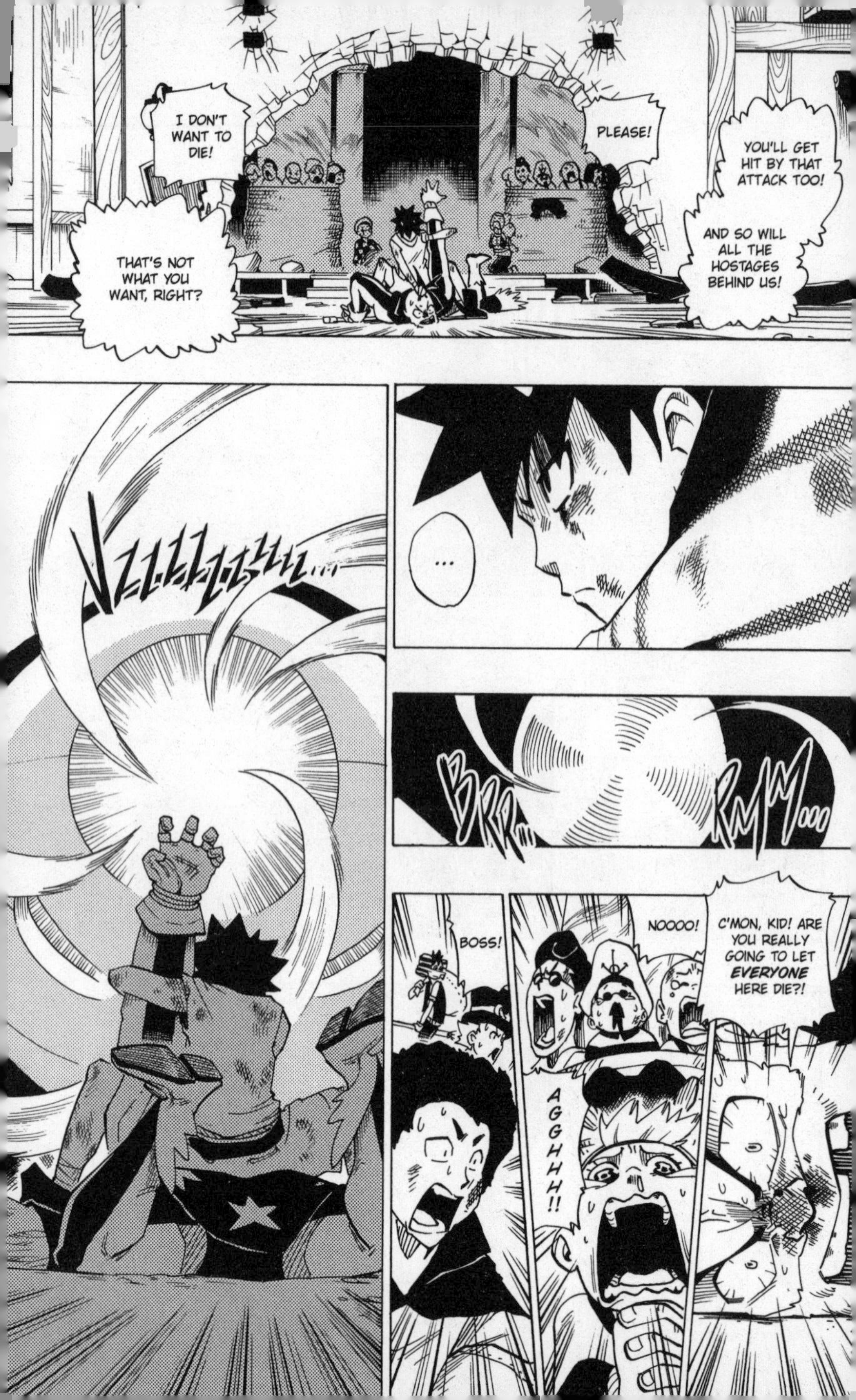
YOU'LL GET HIT BY THAT ATTACK TOO!
AND SO WILL ALL THE HOSTAGES BEHIND US!
PLEASE!
I DON'T WANT TO DIE!
THAT'S NOT WHAT YOU WANT, RIGHT?
...
BRR...
RMM...
C'MON, KID! ARE YOU REALLY GOING TO LET **EVERYONE** HERE DIE?!
NOOOO!
BOSS!
AGGHHHH!!
VZZZZZZZZZZZ...

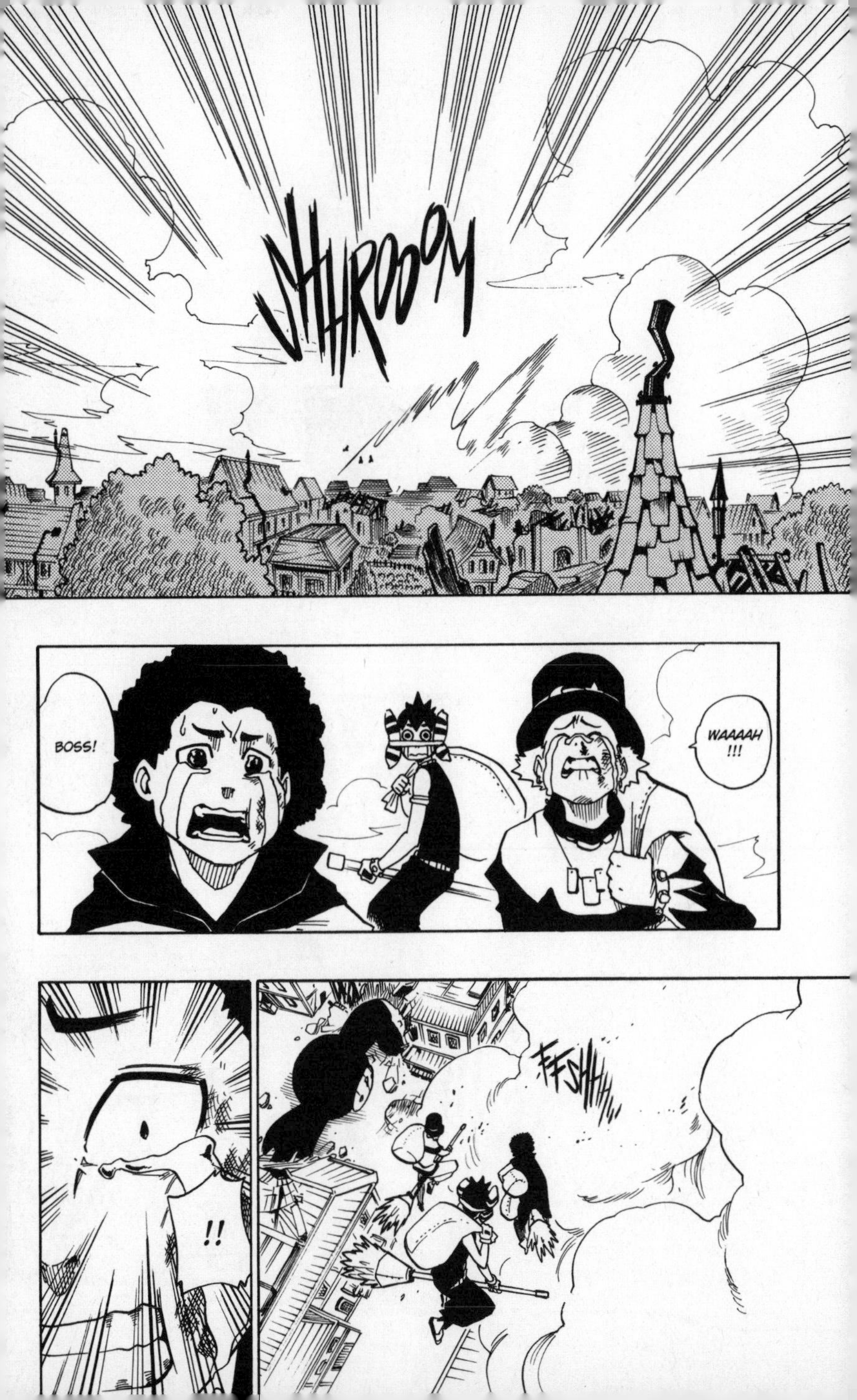
SHHROOOM
WAAAAH !!!
BOSS!
FFSHH
!!

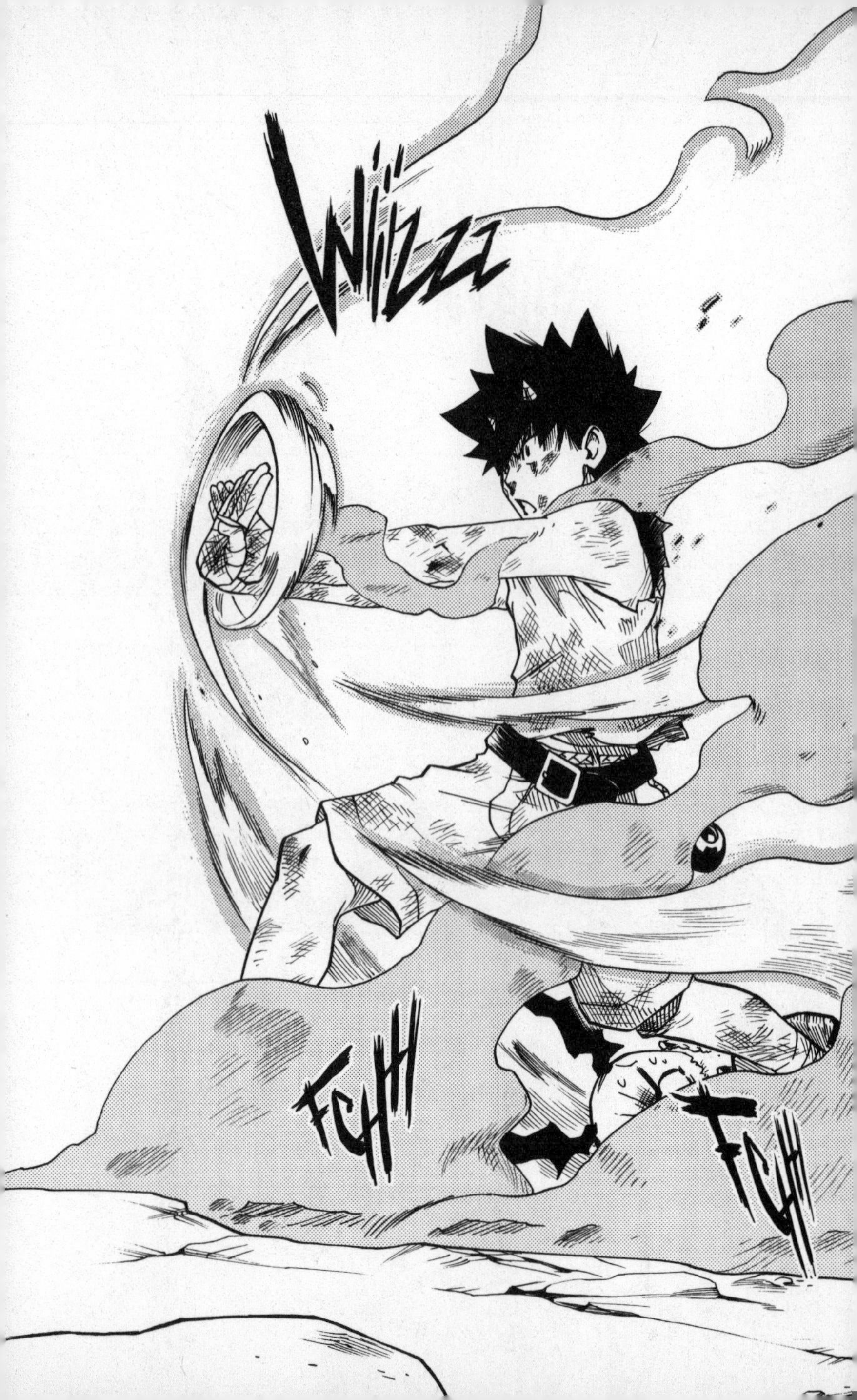
WHIZZZ
FCHH
FCHH

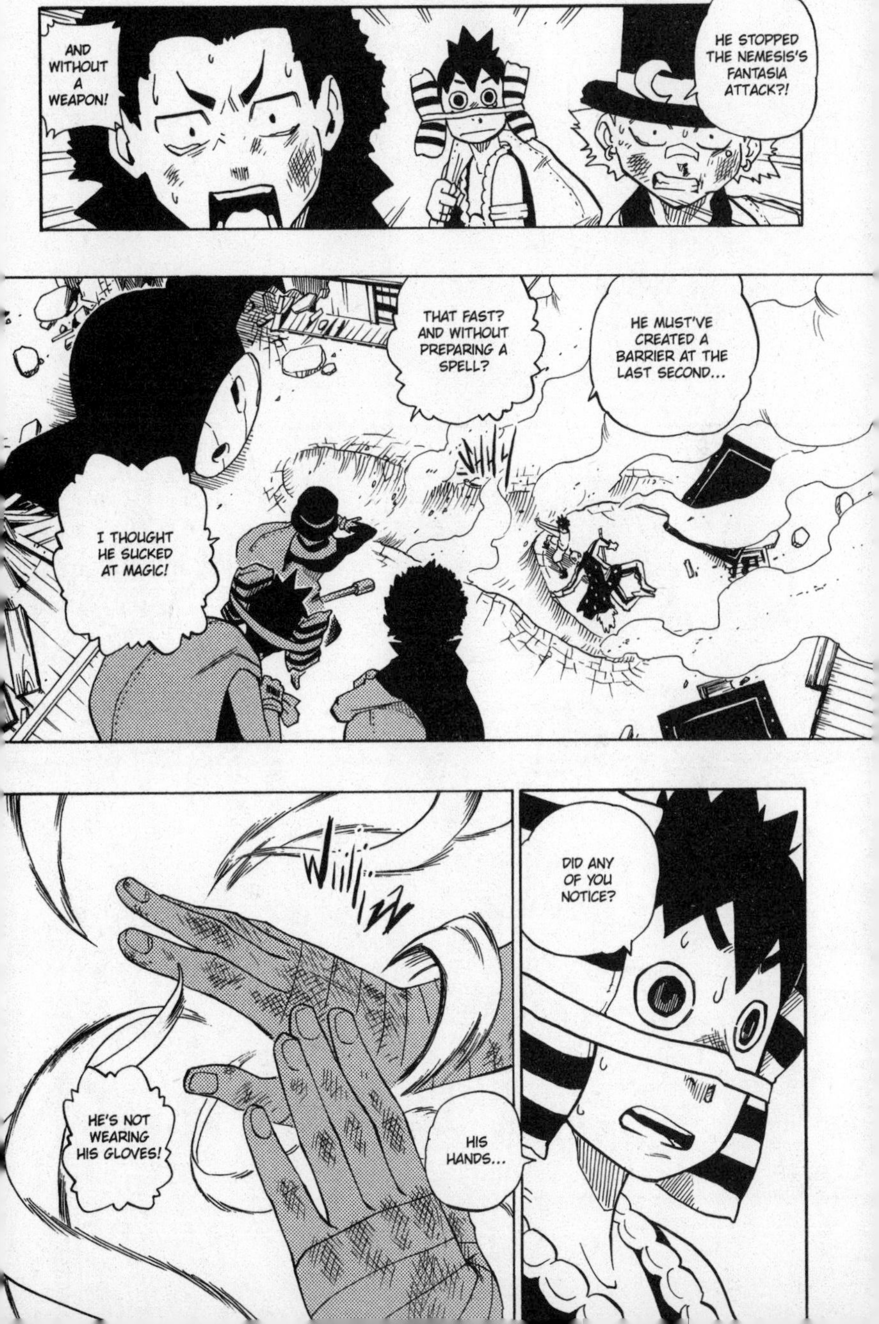
HE STOPPED THE NEMESIS'S FANTASIA ATTACK?!
AND WITHOUT A WEAPON!
HE MUST'VE CREATED A BARRIER AT THE LAST SECOND...
THAT FAST? AND WITHOUT PREPARING A SPELL?
I THOUGHT HE SUCKED AT MAGIC!
DID ANY OF YOU NOTICE?
HIS HANDS...
HE'S NOT WEARING HIS GLOVES!

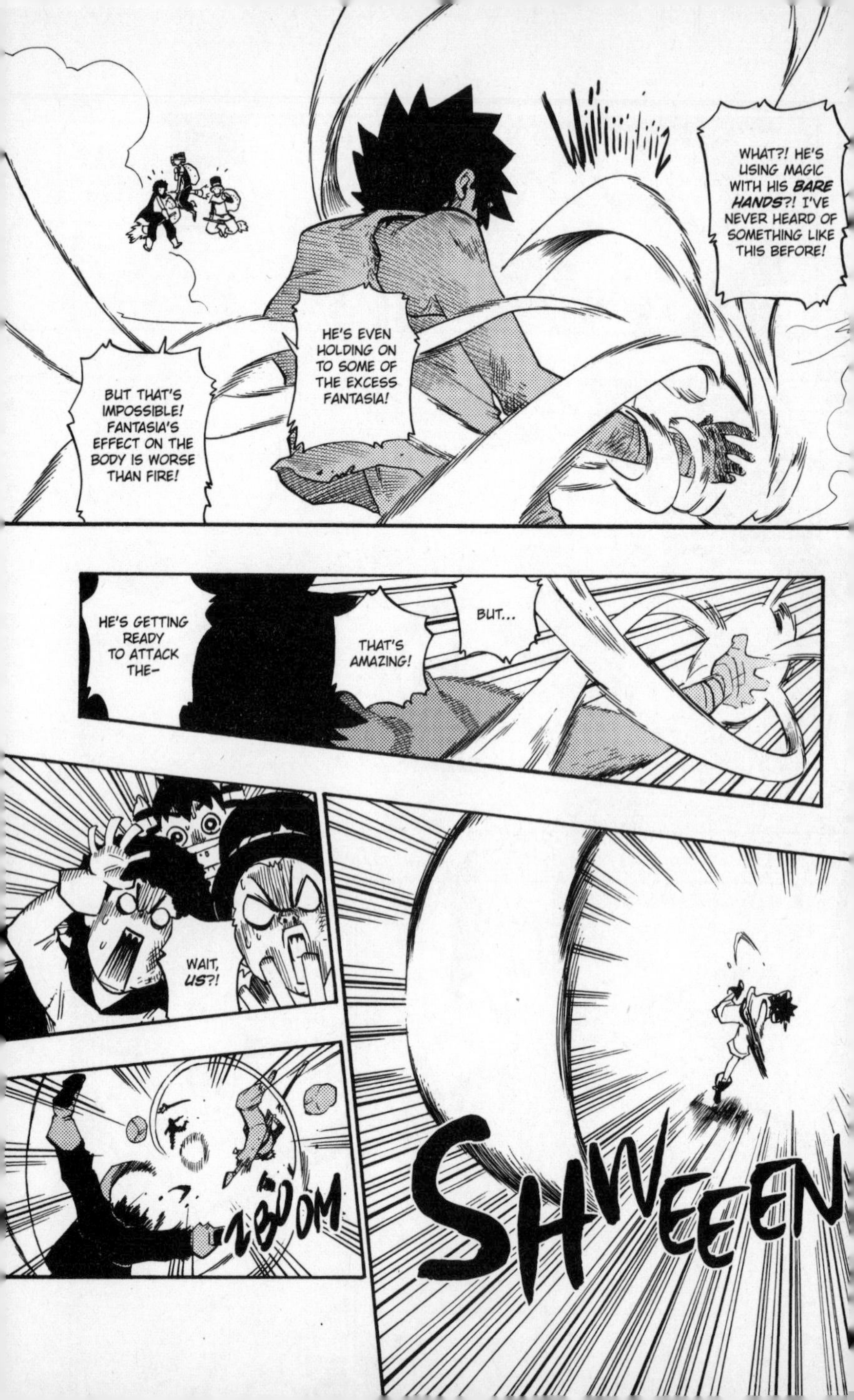
WHAT?! HE'S USING MAGIC WITH HIS **BARE HANDS**?! I'VE NEVER HEARD OF SOMETHING LIKE THIS BEFORE!
HE'S EVEN HOLDING ON TO SOME OF THE EXCESS FANTASIA!
BUT THAT'S IMPOSSIBLE! FANTASIA'S EFFECT ON THE BODY IS WORSE THAN FIRE!
BUT...
THAT'S AMAZING!
HE'S GETTING READY TO ATTACK THE-
SHWEEEN
WAIT, **US**?!
ZBOOM

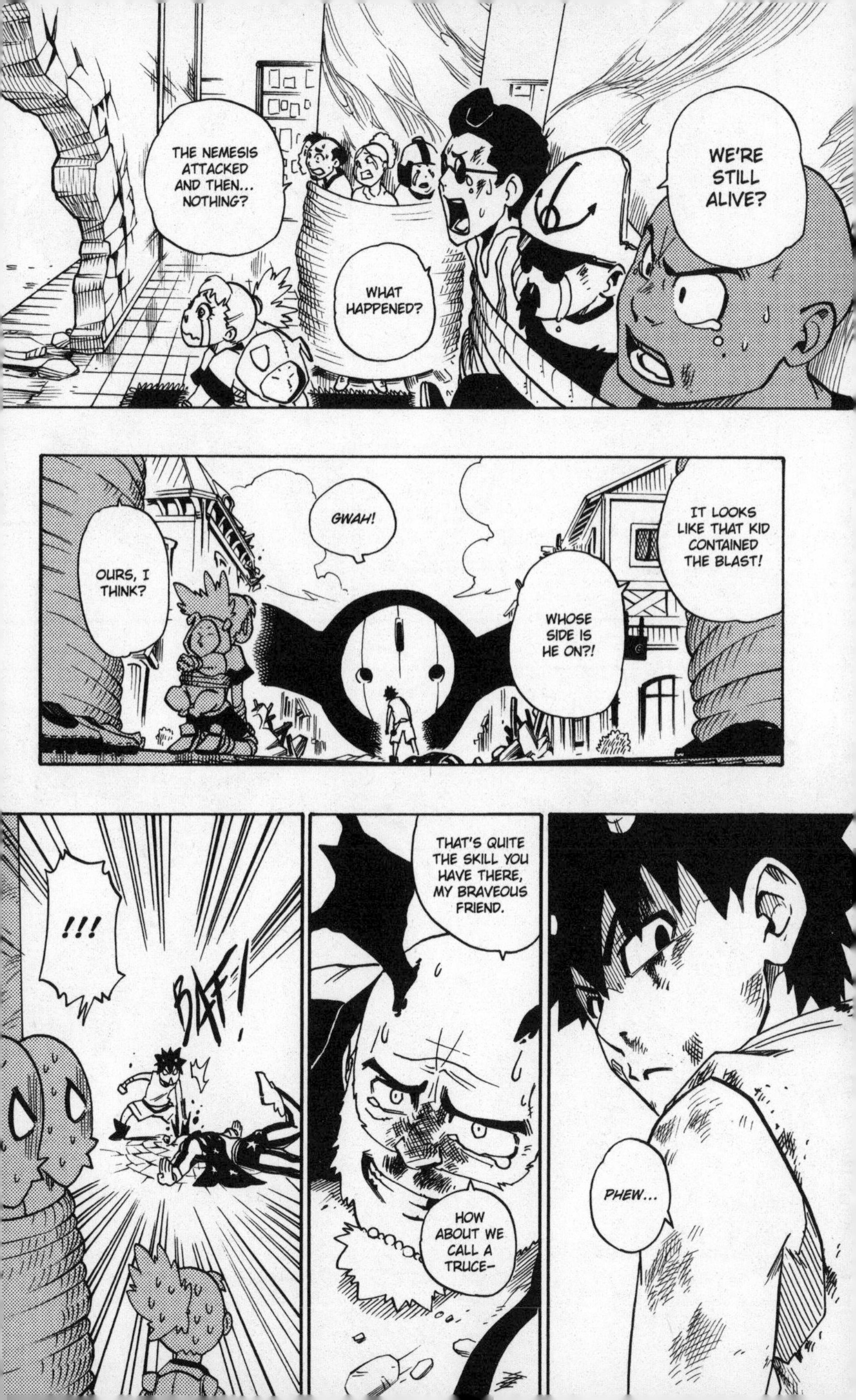
WE'RE STILL ALIVE?
WHAT HAPPENED?
THE NEMESIS ATTACKED AND THEN... NOTHING?
IT LOOKS LIKE THAT KID CONTAINED THE BLAST!
WHOSE SIDE IS HE ON?!
GWAH!
OURS, I THINK?
PHEW...
THAT'S QUITE THE SKILL YOU HAVE THERE, MY BRAVEOUS FRIEND.
HOW ABOUT WE CALL A TRUCE-
!!!
BAF!

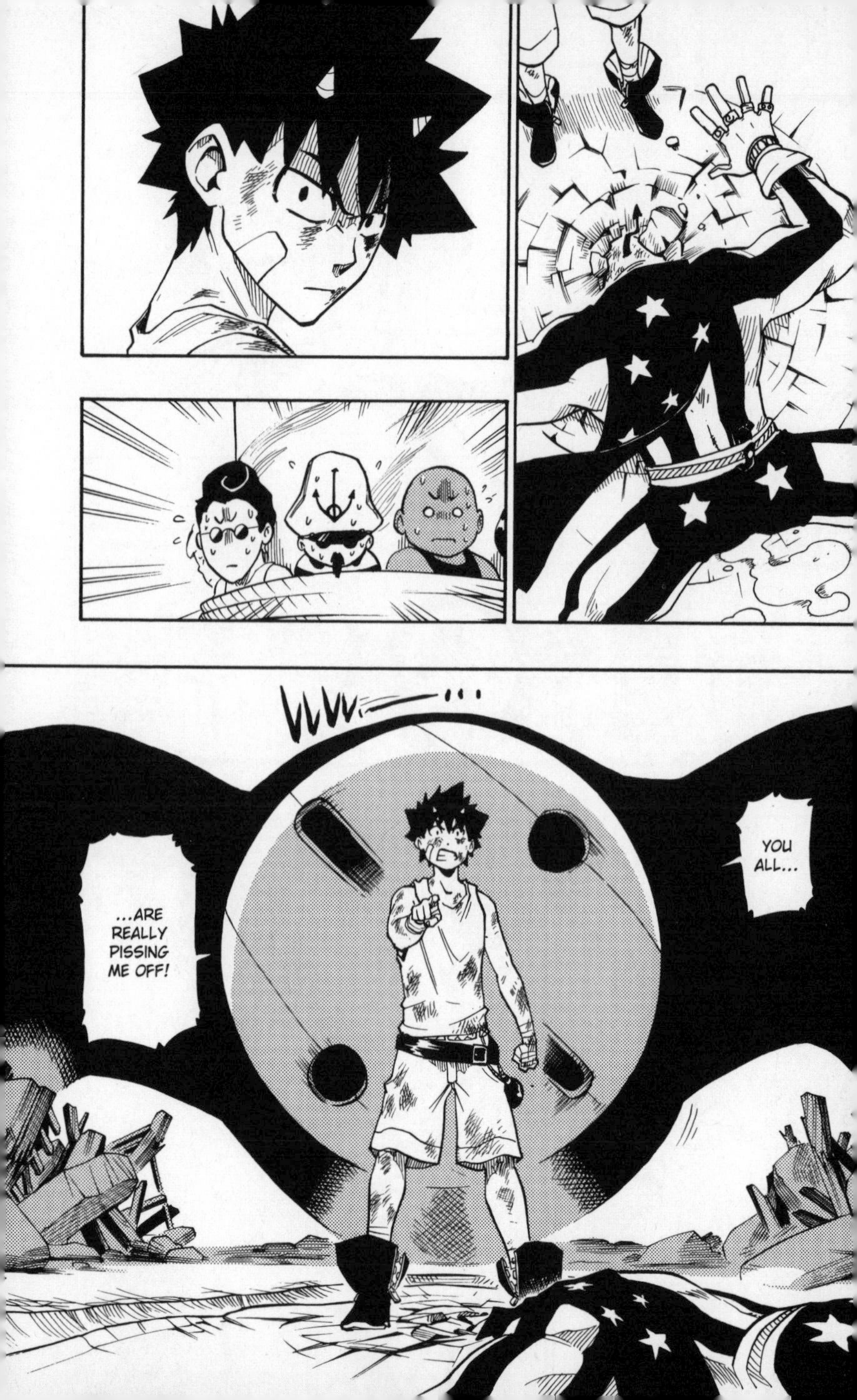
YOU ALL...
...ARE REALLY PISSING ME OFF!

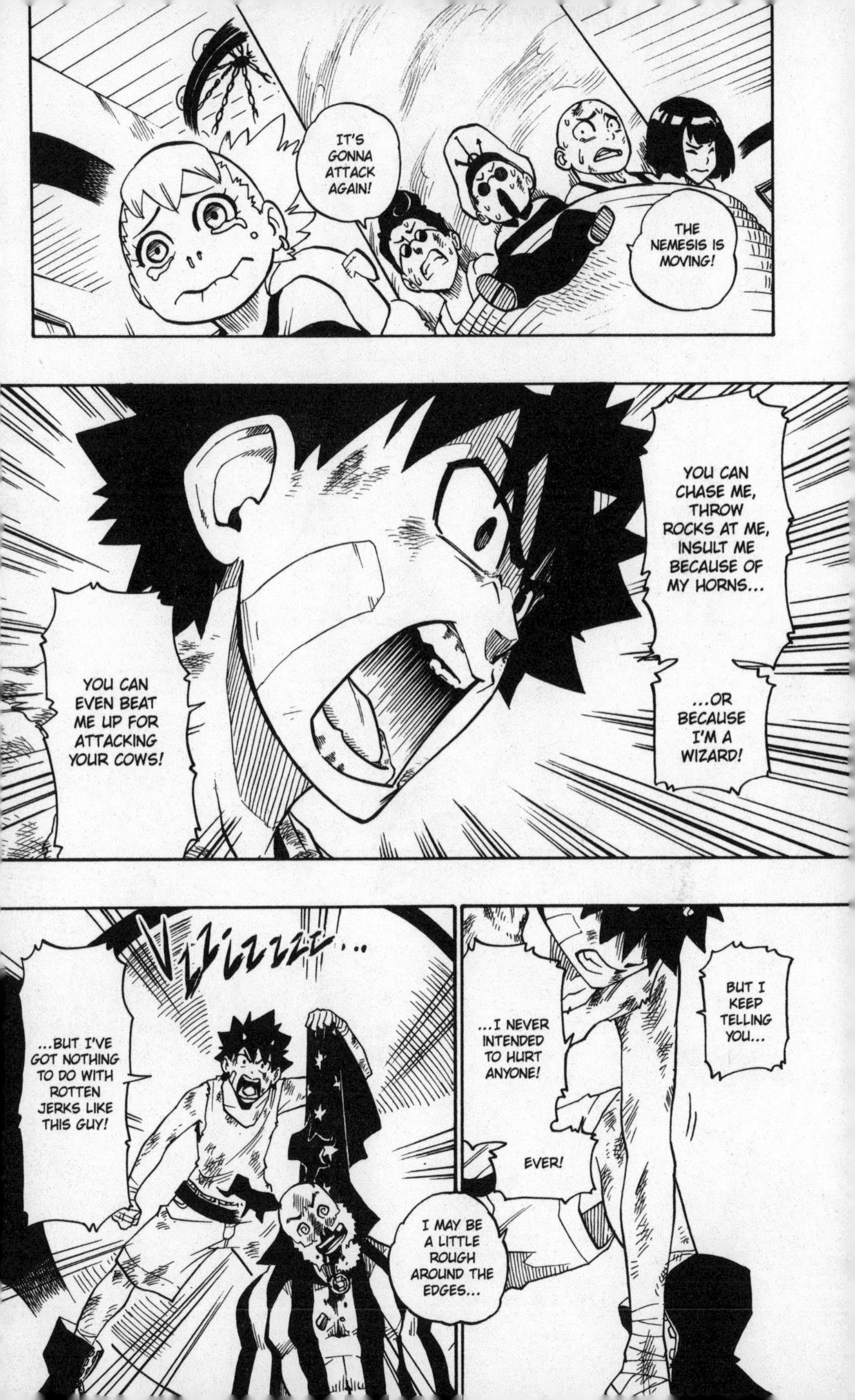
THE NEMESIS IS MOVING!
IT'S GONNA ATTACK AGAIN!
YOU CAN CHASE ME, THROW ROCKS AT ME, INSULT ME BECAUSE OF MY HORNS...
...OR BECAUSE I'M A WIZARD!
YOU CAN EVEN BEAT ME UP FOR ATTACKING YOUR COWS!
BUT I KEEP TELLING YOU...
...I NEVER INTENDED TO HURT ANYONE!
EVER!
Vzzzzzzz...
I MAY BE A LITTLE ROUGH AROUND THE EDGES...
...BUT I'VE GOT NOTHING TO DO WITH ROTTEN JERKS LIKE THIS GUY!

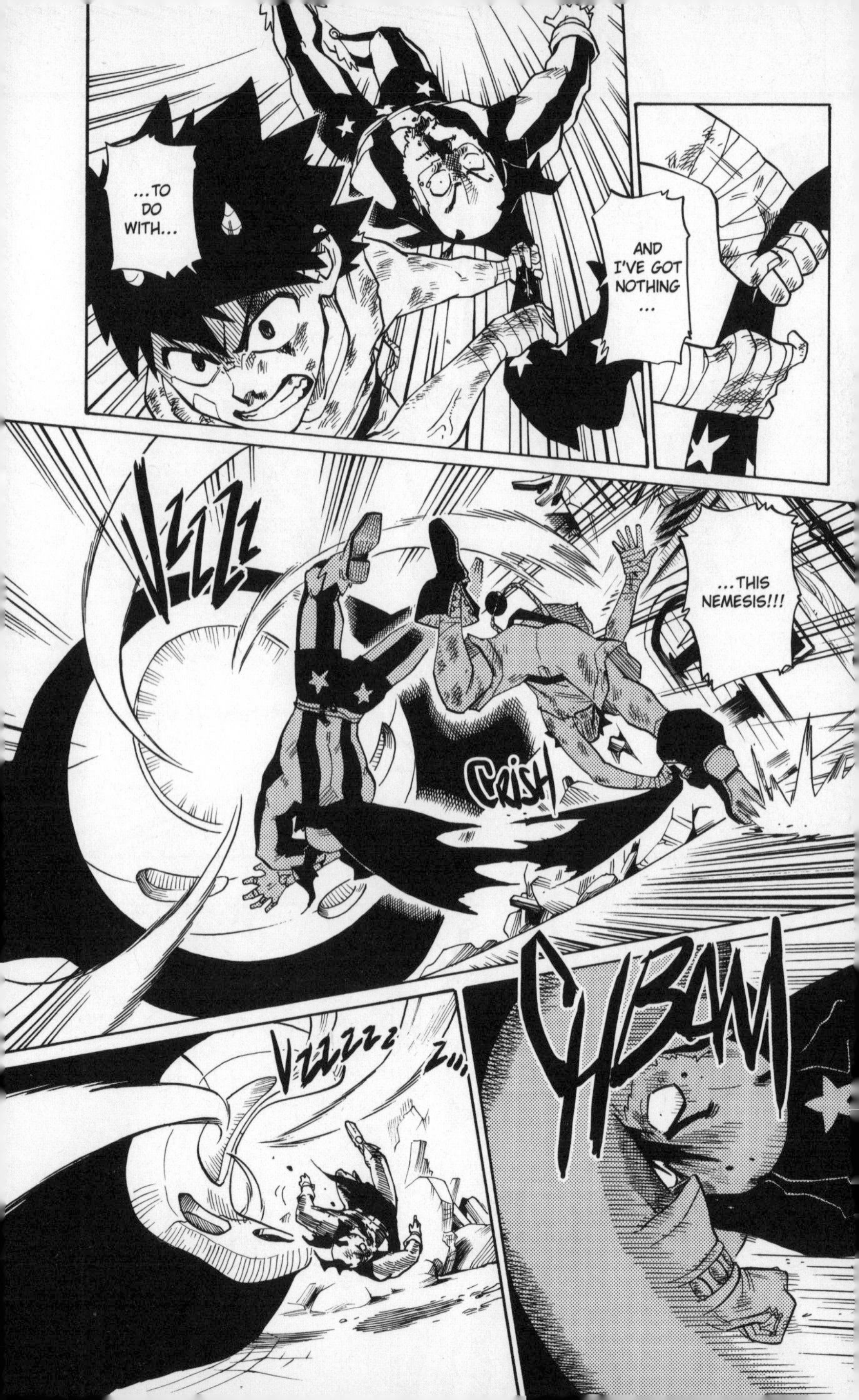
AND I'VE GOT NOTHING ...
...TO DO WITH...
...THIS NEMESIS!!!
VZZZZ
CRISH
BAM
VZZZZZZ ZZ...

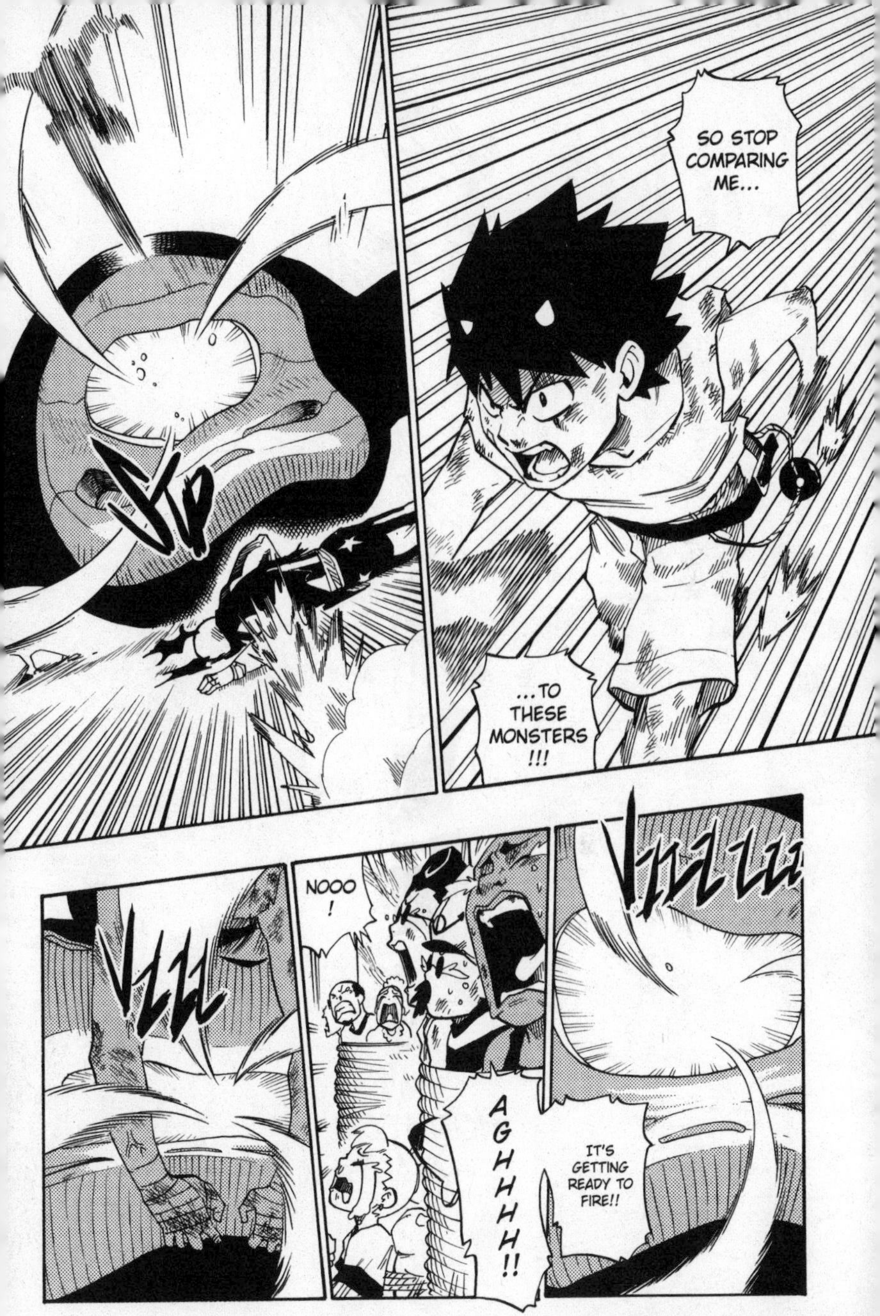
SO STOP COMPARING ME...
...TO THESE MONSTERS!!!
IT'S GETTING READY TO FIRE!!
NOOO!
AGHHHH!!

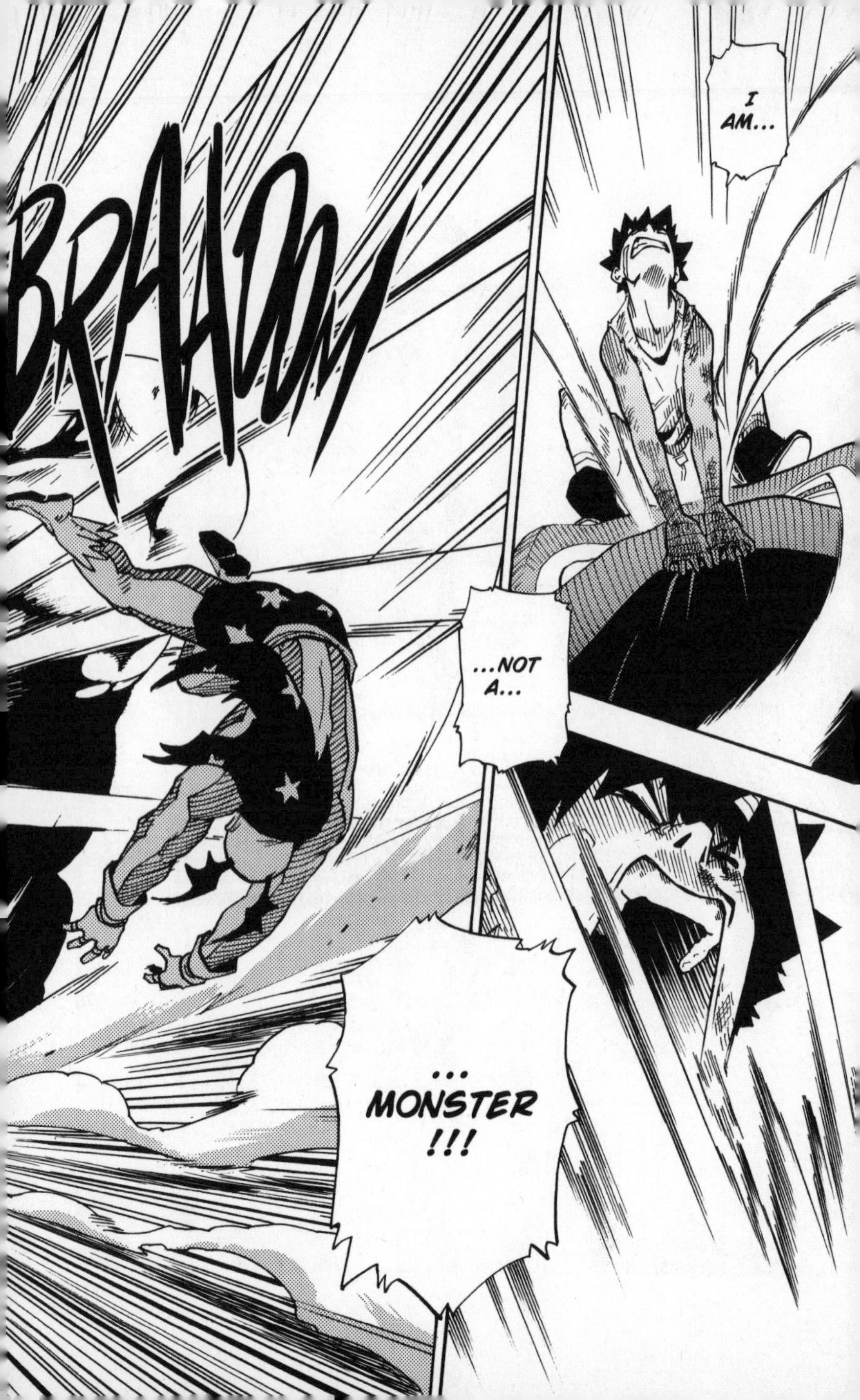
I AM...
...NOT A...
... MONSTER !!!

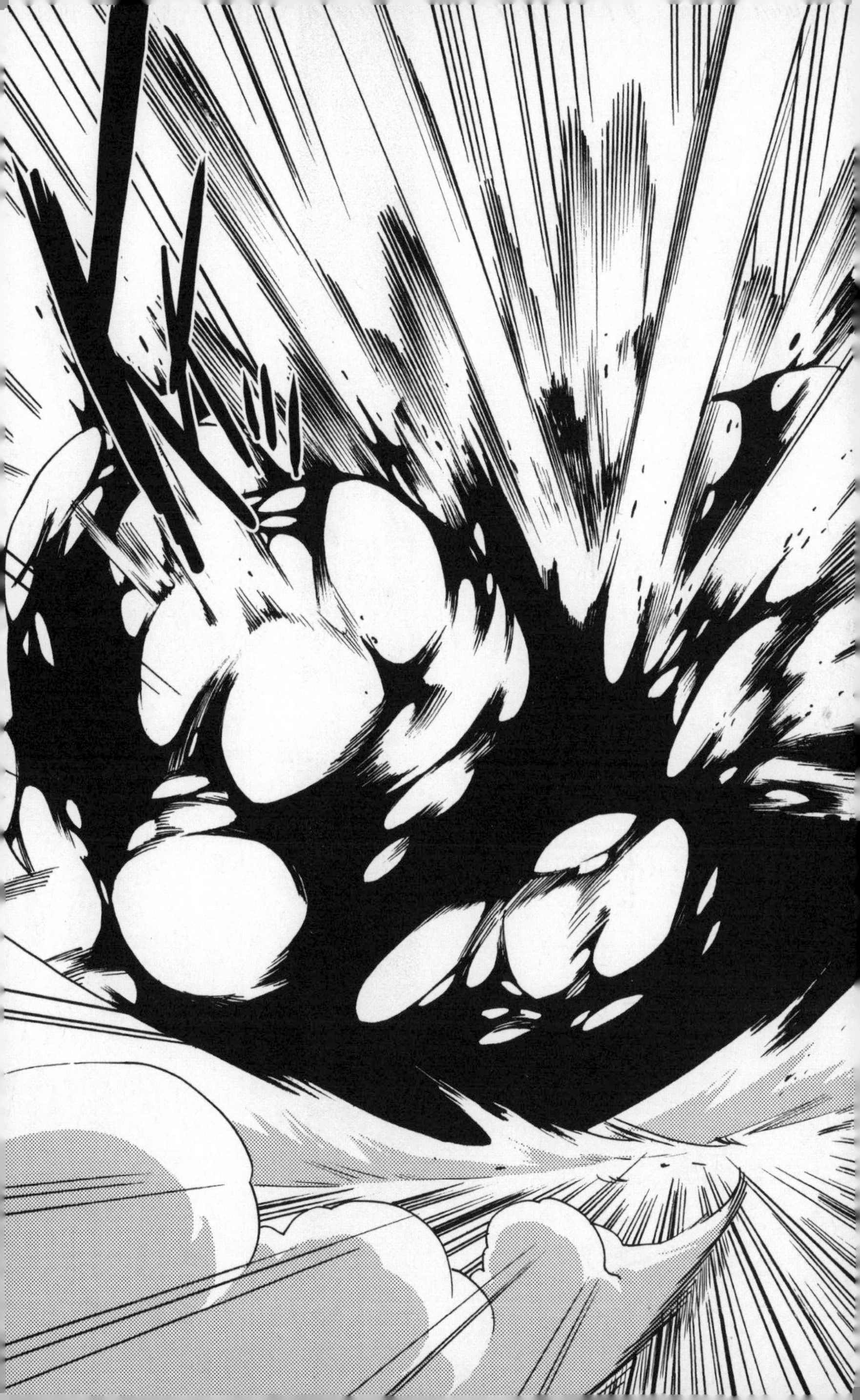

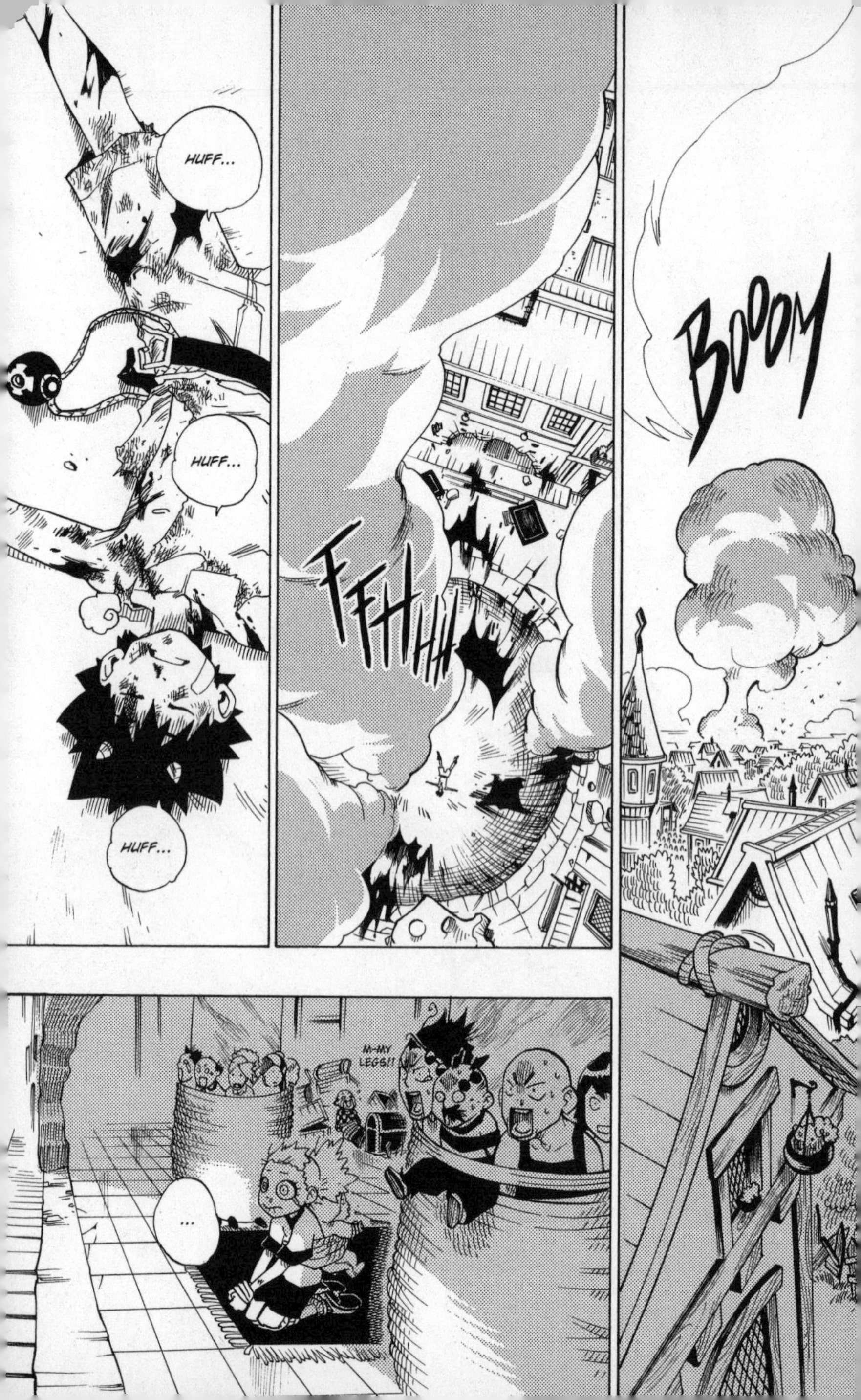
BOOOM
FFHHH
HUFF...
HUFF...
HUFF...
M-MY LEGS!!
...

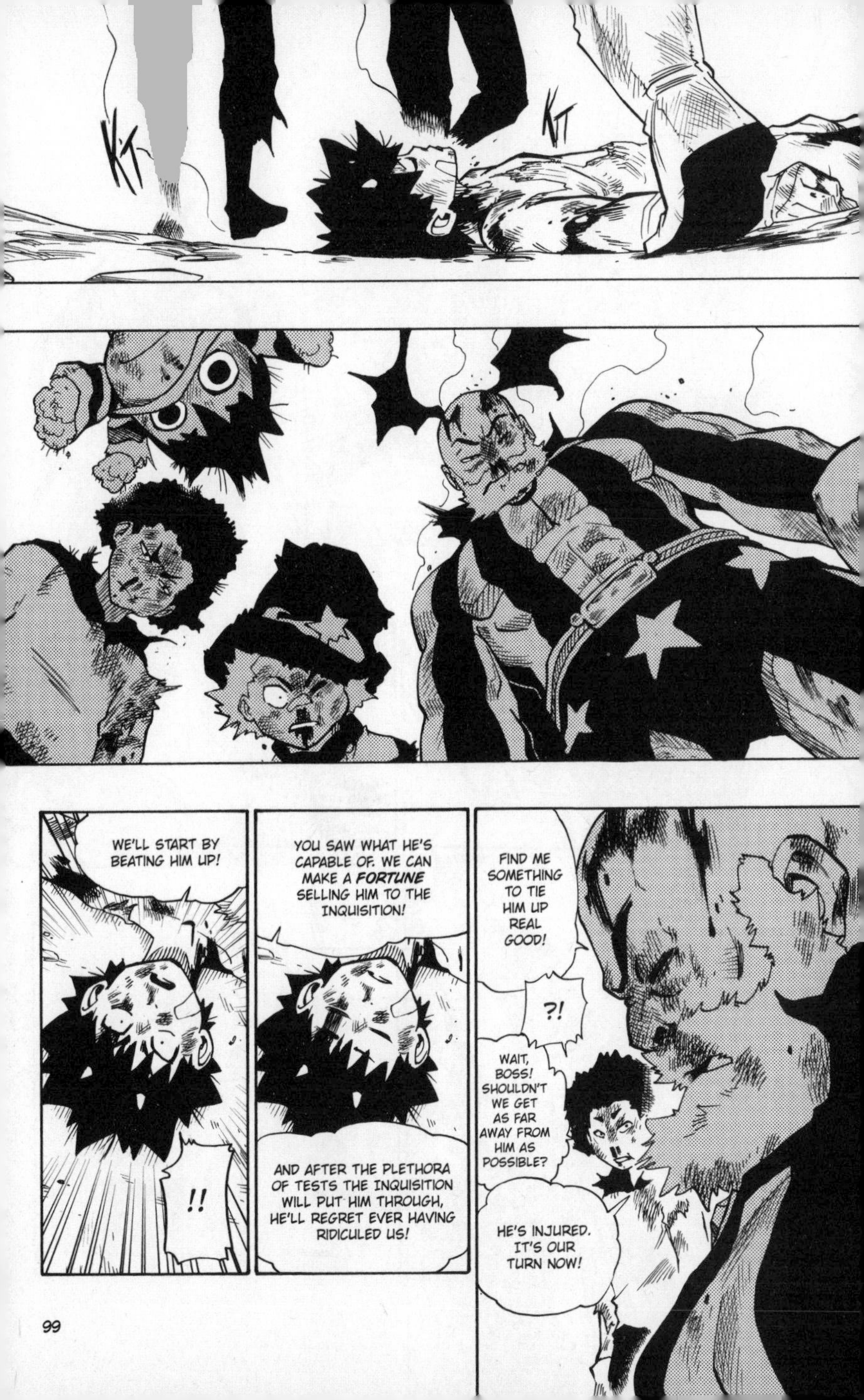
FIND ME SOMETHING TO TIE HIM UP REAL GOOD!
?!
WAIT, BOSS! SHOULDN'T WE GET AS FAR AWAY FROM HIM AS POSSIBLE?
HE'S INJURED. IT'S OUR TURN NOW!
YOU SAW WHAT HE'S CAPABLE OF. WE CAN MAKE A ***FORTUNE*** SELLING HIM TO THE INQUISITION!
AND AFTER THE PLETHORA OF TESTS THE INQUISITION WILL PUT HIM THROUGH, HE'LL REGRET EVER HAVING RIDICULED US!
WE'LL START BY BEATING HIM UP!
!!

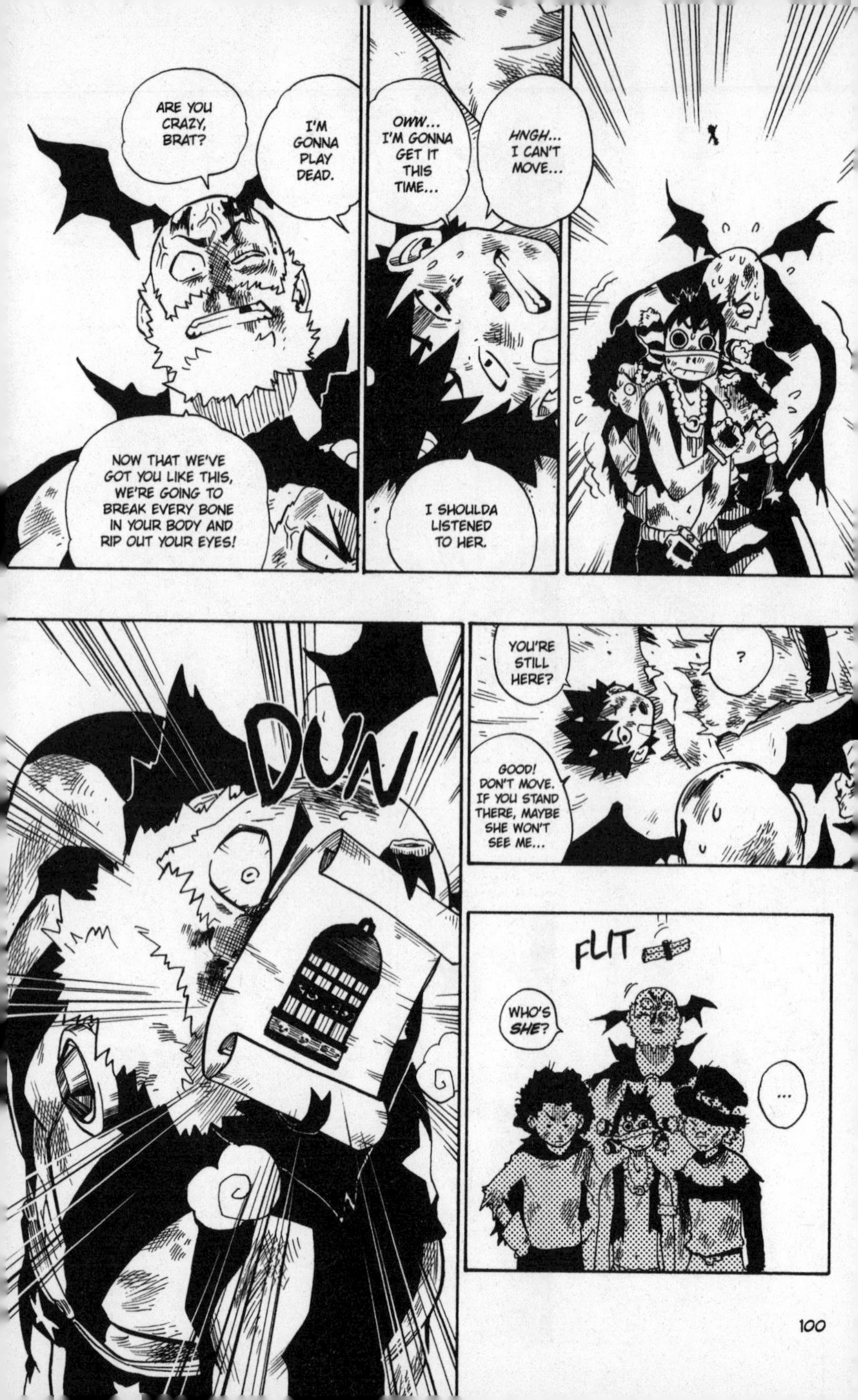
HNGH... I CAN'T MOVE...
OWW... I'M GONNA GET IT THIS TIME...
I SHOULDA LISTENED TO HER.
I'M GONNA PLAY DEAD.
ARE YOU CRAZY, BRAT?
NOW THAT WE'VE GOT YOU LIKE THIS, WE'RE GOING TO BREAK EVERY BONE IN YOUR BODY AND RIP OUT YOUR EYES!
?
YOU'RE STILL HERE?
GOOD! DON'T MOVE. IF YOU STAND THERE, MAYBE SHE WON'T SEE ME...
FLIT
WHO'S SHE?
...
DUN

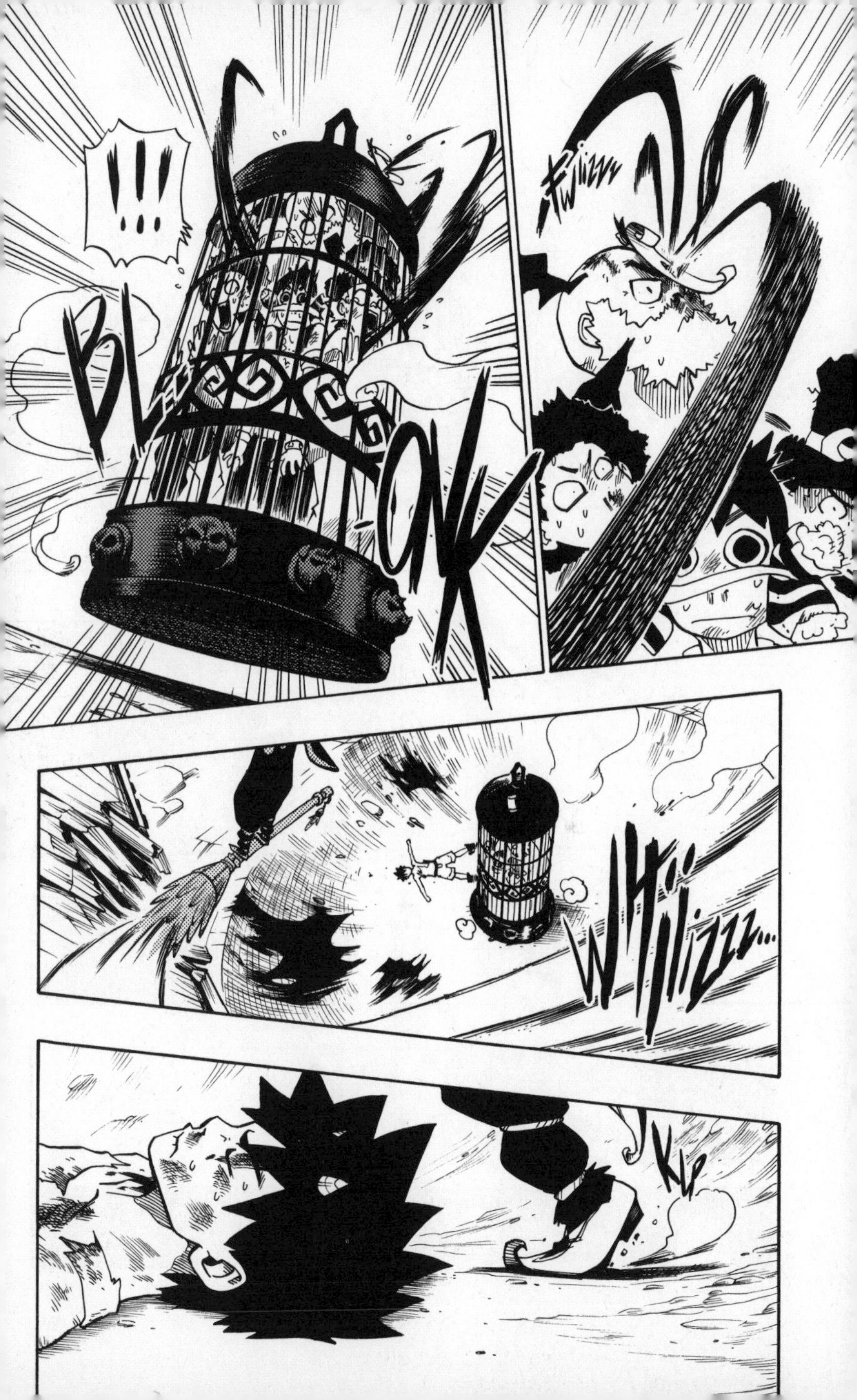
FWIIZZZ
!!!
BLONK
WHIIIZZZ...
KLP

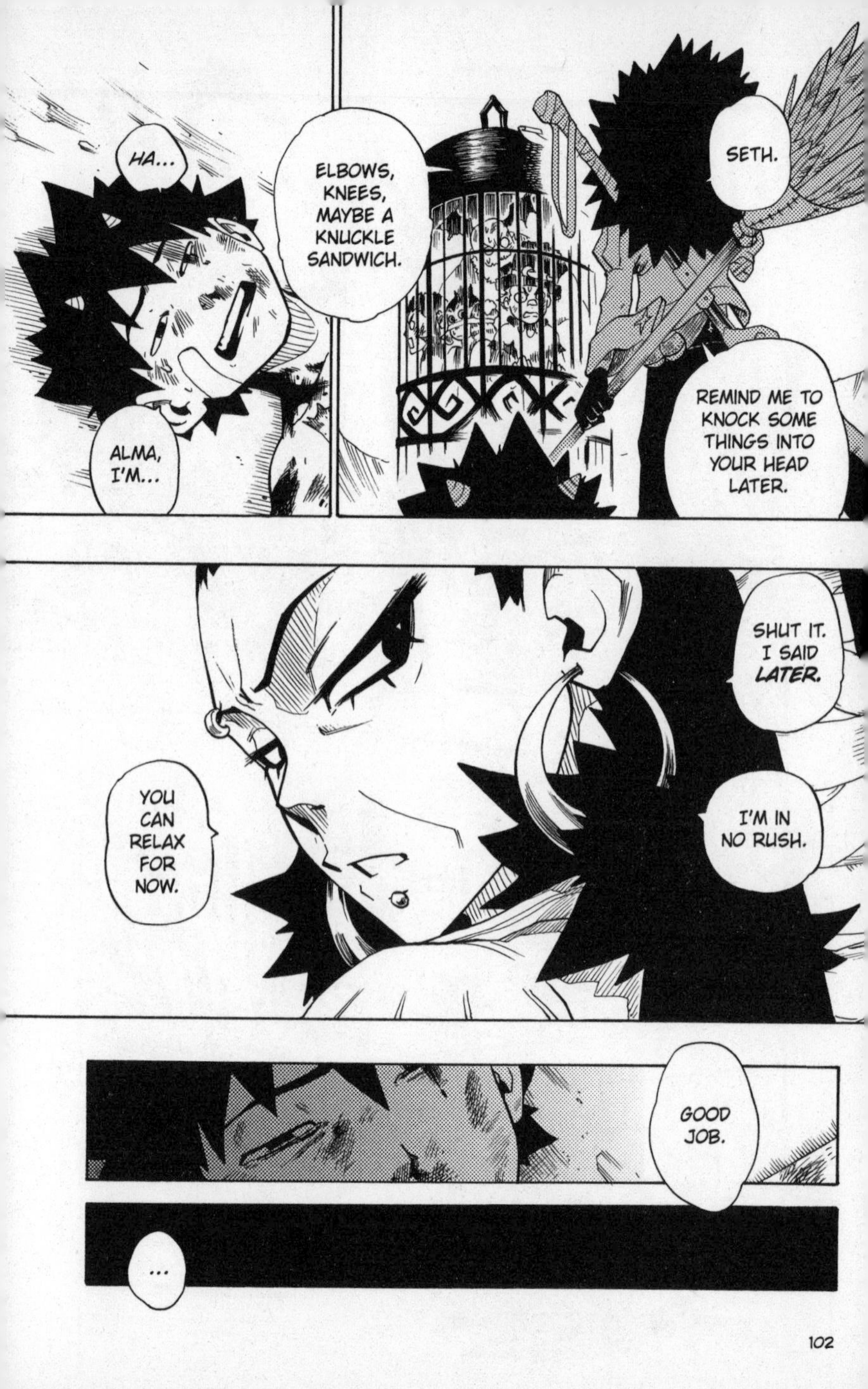
SETH.
ELBOWS, KNEES, MAYBE A KNUCKLE SANDWICH.
REMIND ME TO KNOCK SOME THINGS INTO YOUR HEAD LATER.
HA...
ALMA, I'M...
SHUT IT. I SAID *LATER.*
I'M IN NO RUSH.
YOU CAN RELAX FOR NOW.
GOOD JOB.
...

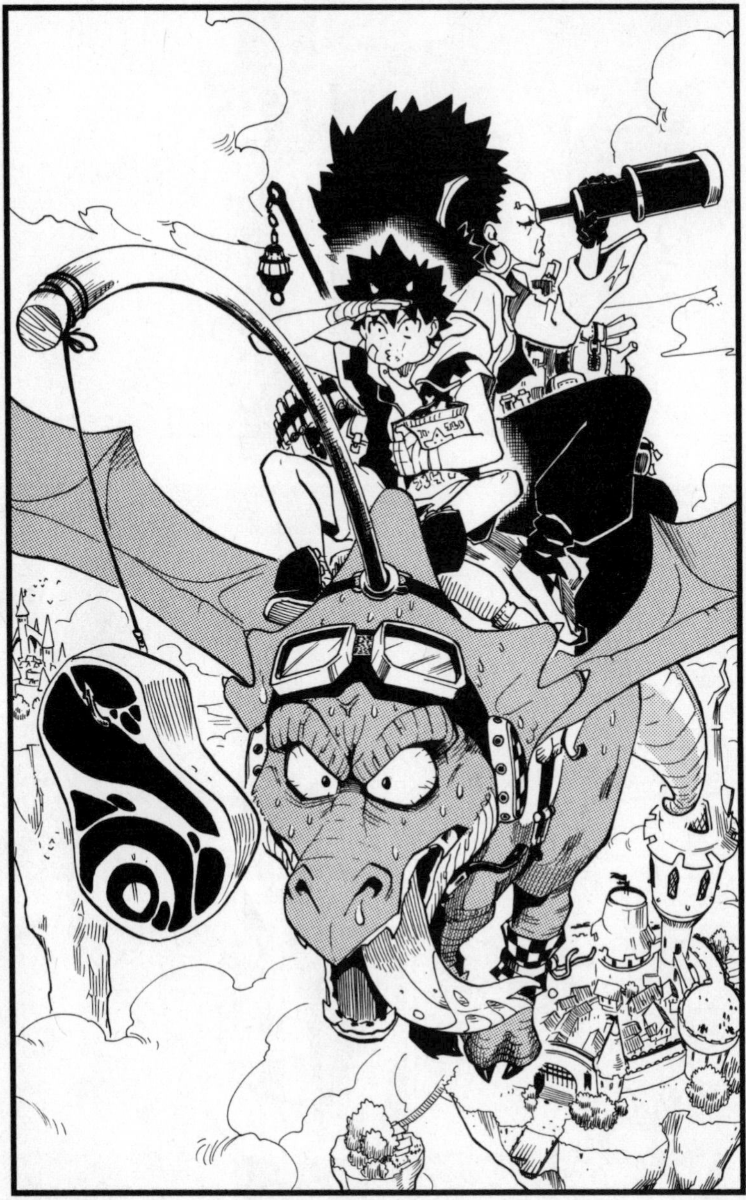

Chapter 2

Awakening

...

HNGH ...

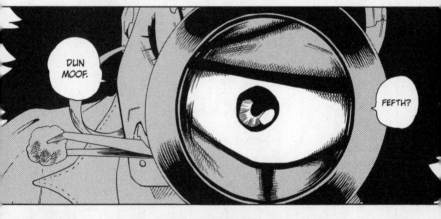

DUN MOOF.

FEFTH?

ZBAM

WHATTA HEKKF?!

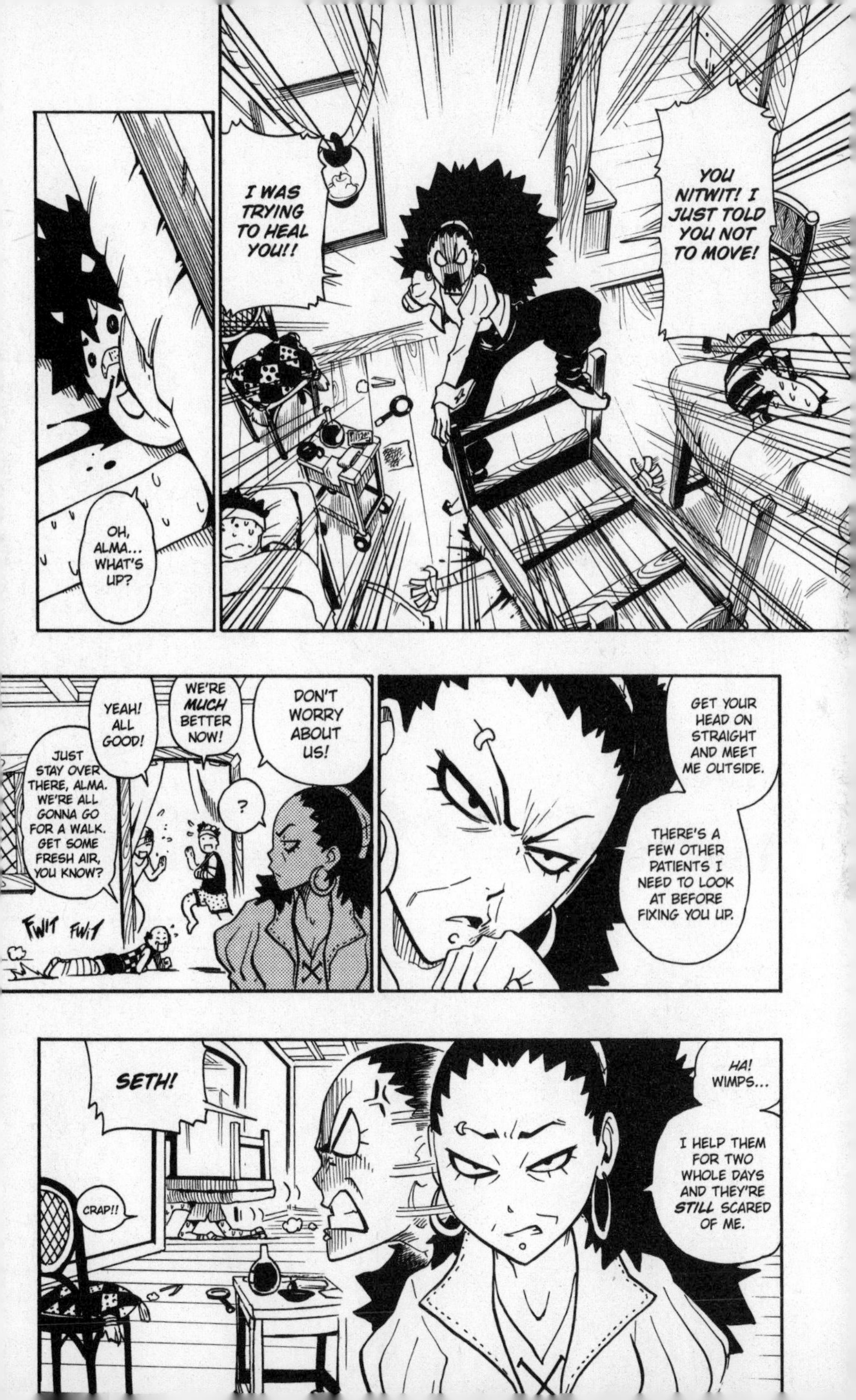
YOU NITWIT! I JUST TOLD YOU NOT TO MOVE!
I WAS TRYING TO HEAL YOU!!
OH, ALMA... WHAT'S UP?
GET YOUR HEAD ON STRAIGHT AND MEET ME OUTSIDE.
THERE'S A FEW OTHER PATIENTS I NEED TO LOOK AT BEFORE FIXING YOU UP.
DON'T WORRY ABOUT US!
WE'RE *MUCH* BETTER NOW!
YEAH! ALL GOOD!
?
JUST STAY OVER THERE, ALMA. WE'RE ALL GONNA GO FOR A WALK. GET SOME FRESH AIR, YOU KNOW?
FWIT FWIT
HA! WIMPS...
I HELP THEM FOR TWO WHOLE DAYS AND THEY'RE *STILL* SCARED OF ME.
SETH!
CRAP!!

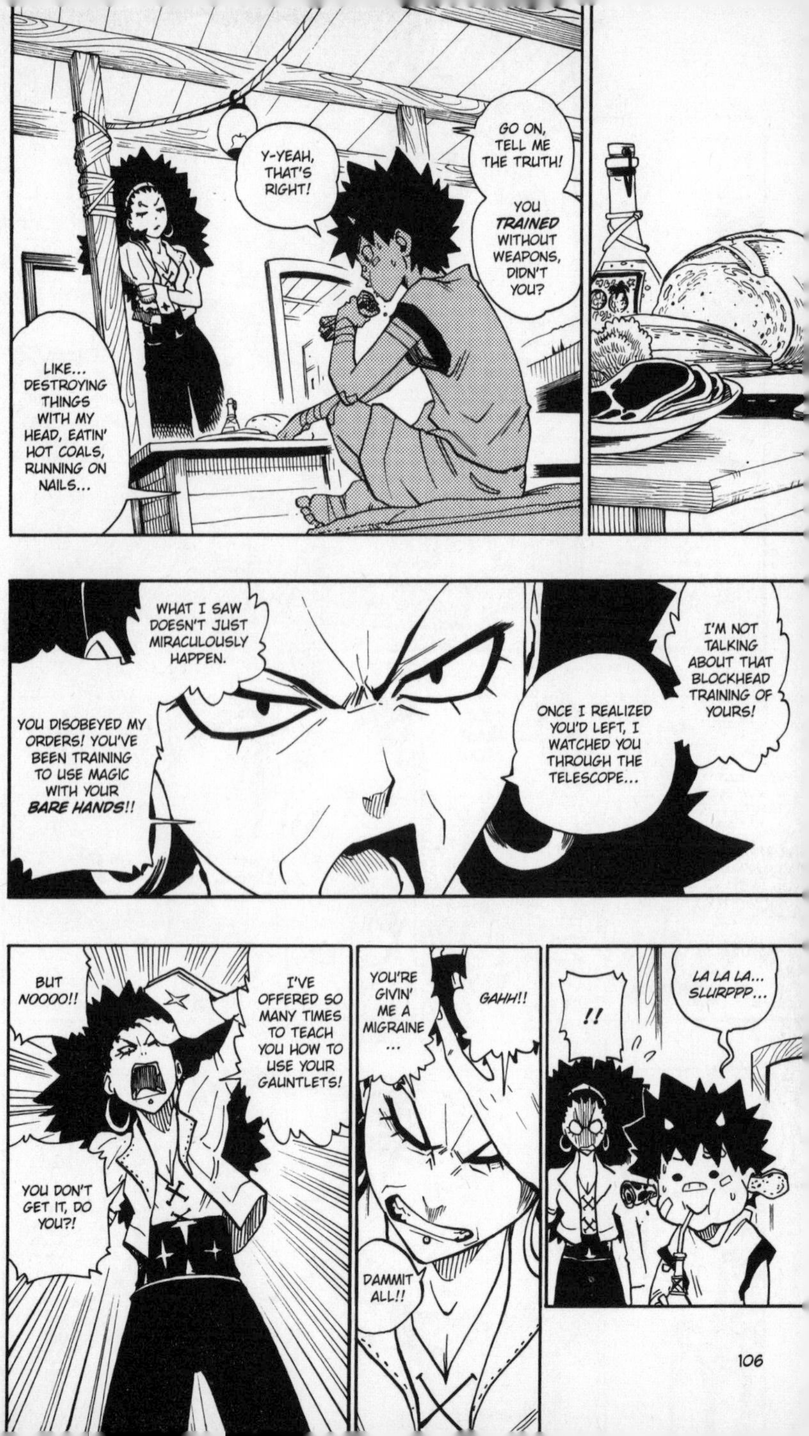
GO ON, TELL ME THE TRUTH!
YOU *TRAINED* WITHOUT WEAPONS, DIDN'T YOU?
Y-YEAH, THAT'S RIGHT!
LIKE... DESTROYING THINGS WITH MY HEAD, EATIN' HOT COALS, RUNNING ON NAILS...
I'M NOT TALKING ABOUT THAT BLOCKHEAD TRAINING OF YOURS!
ONCE I REALIZED YOU'D LEFT, I WATCHED YOU THROUGH THE TELESCOPE...
WHAT I SAW DOESN'T JUST MIRACULOUSLY HAPPEN.
YOU DISOBEYED MY ORDERS! YOU'VE BEEN TRAINING TO USE MAGIC WITH YOUR ***BARE HANDS***!!
LA LA LA... SLURPPP...
!!
GAHH!!
YOU'RE GIVIN' ME A MIGRAINE...
DAMMIT ALL!!
I'VE OFFERED SO MANY TIMES TO TEACH YOU HOW TO USE YOUR GAUNTLETS!
BUT *NOOOO*!!
YOU DON'T GET IT, DO YOU?!

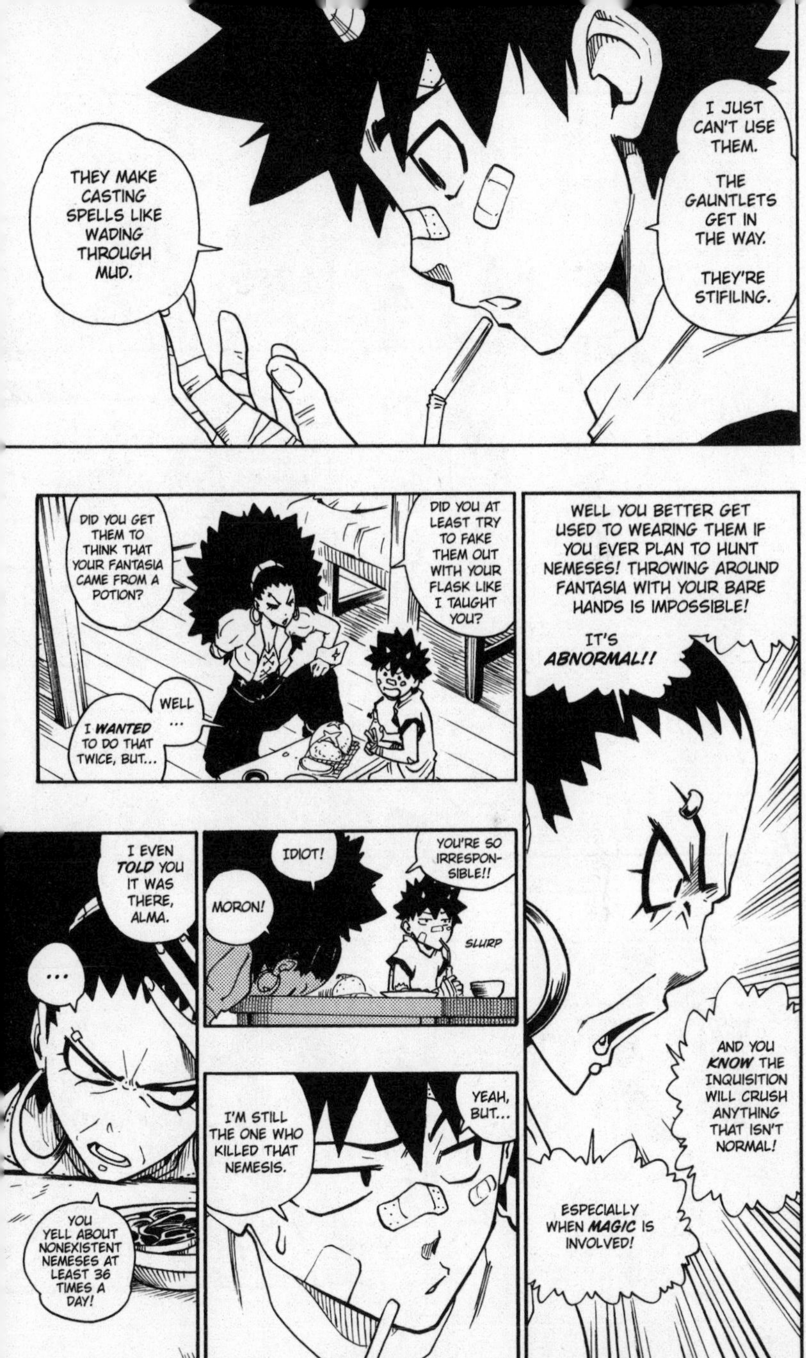
I JUST CAN'T USE THEM.
THE GAUNTLETS GET IN THE WAY.
THEY'RE STIFILING.
THEY MAKE CASTING SPELLS LIKE WADING THROUGH MUD.
WELL YOU BETTER GET USED TO WEARING THEM IF YOU EVER PLAN TO HUNT NEMESES! THROWING AROUND FANTASIA WITH YOUR BARE HANDS IS IMPOSSIBLE!
IT'S ABNORMAL!!
AND YOU KNOW THE INQUISITION WILL CRUSH ANYTHING THAT ISN'T NORMAL!
ESPECIALLY WHEN MAGIC IS INVOLVED!
DID YOU AT LEAST TRY TO FAKE THEM OUT WITH YOUR FLASK LIKE I TAUGHT YOU?
DID YOU GET THEM TO THINK THAT YOUR FANTASIA CAME FROM A POTION?
WELL...
I WANTED TO DO THAT TWICE, BUT...
YOU'RE SO IRRESPONSIBLE!!
IDIOT!
MORON!
SLURP
YEAH, BUT...
I'M STILL THE ONE WHO KILLED THAT NEMESIS.
I EVEN TOLD YOU IT WAS THERE, ALMA.
...
YOU YELL ABOUT NONEXISTENT NEMESES AT LEAST 36 TIMES A DAY!

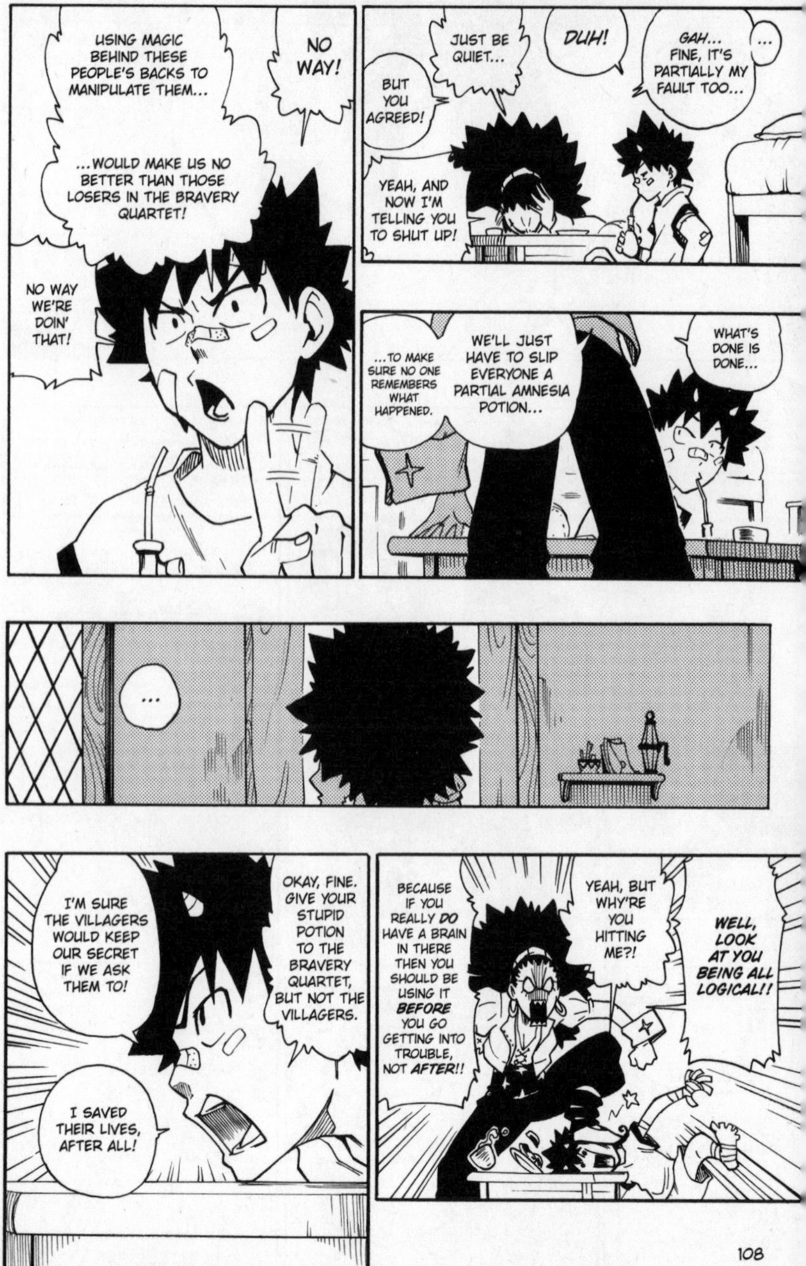
...
GAH... FINE, IT'S PARTIALLY MY FAULT TOO...
DUH!
JUST BE QUIET...
BUT YOU AGREED!
YEAH, AND NOW I'M TELLING YOU TO SHUT UP!
WHAT'S DONE IS DONE...
WE'LL JUST HAVE TO SLIP EVERYONE A PARTIAL AMNESIA POTION...
...TO MAKE SURE NO ONE REMEMBERS WHAT HAPPENED.
NO WAY!
USING MAGIC BEHIND THESE PEOPLE'S BACKS TO MANIPULATE THEM...
...WOULD MAKE US NO BETTER THAN THOSE LOSERS IN THE BRAVERY QUARTET!
NO WAY WE'RE DOIN' THAT!
...
WELL, LOOK AT YOU BEING ALL LOGICAL!!
YEAH, BUT WHY'RE YOU HITTING ME?!
BECAUSE IF YOU REALLY DO HAVE A BRAIN IN THERE THEN YOU SHOULD BE USING IT BEFORE YOU GO GETTING INTO TROUBLE, NOT AFTER!!
OKAY, FINE. GIVE YOUR STUPID POTION TO THE BRAVERY QUARTET, BUT NOT THE VILLAGERS.
I'M SURE THE VILLAGERS WOULD KEEP OUR SECRET IF WE ASK THEM TO!
I SAVED THEIR LIVES, AFTER ALL!

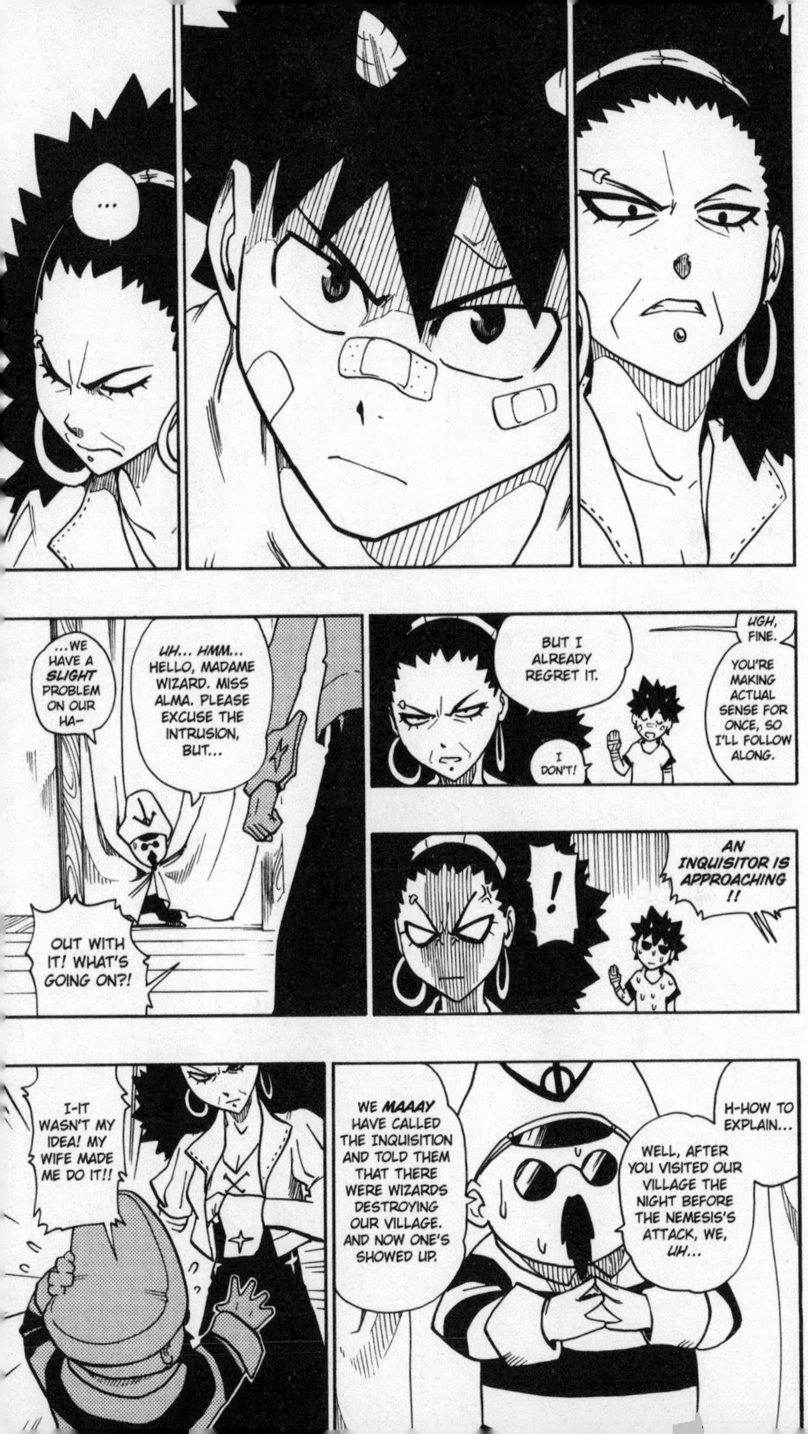
...
UGH, FINE.
YOU'RE MAKING ACTUAL SENSE FOR ONCE, SO I'LL FOLLOW ALONG.
BUT I ALREADY REGRET IT.
I DON'T!
AN INQUISITOR IS APPROACHING !!
!
UH... HMM... HELLO, MADAME WIZARD. MISS ALMA. PLEASE EXCUSE THE INTRUSION, BUT...
...WE HAVE A SLIGHT PROBLEM ON OUR HA-
OUT WITH IT! WHAT'S GOING ON?!
H-HOW TO EXPLAIN...
WELL, AFTER YOU VISITED OUR VILLAGE THE NIGHT BEFORE THE NEMESIS'S ATTACK, WE, UH...
WE MAAAY HAVE CALLED THE INQUISITION AND TOLD THEM THAT THERE WERE WIZARDS DESTROYING OUR VILLAGE. AND NOW ONE'S SHOWED UP.
I-IT WASN'T MY IDEA! MY WIFE MADE ME DO IT!!

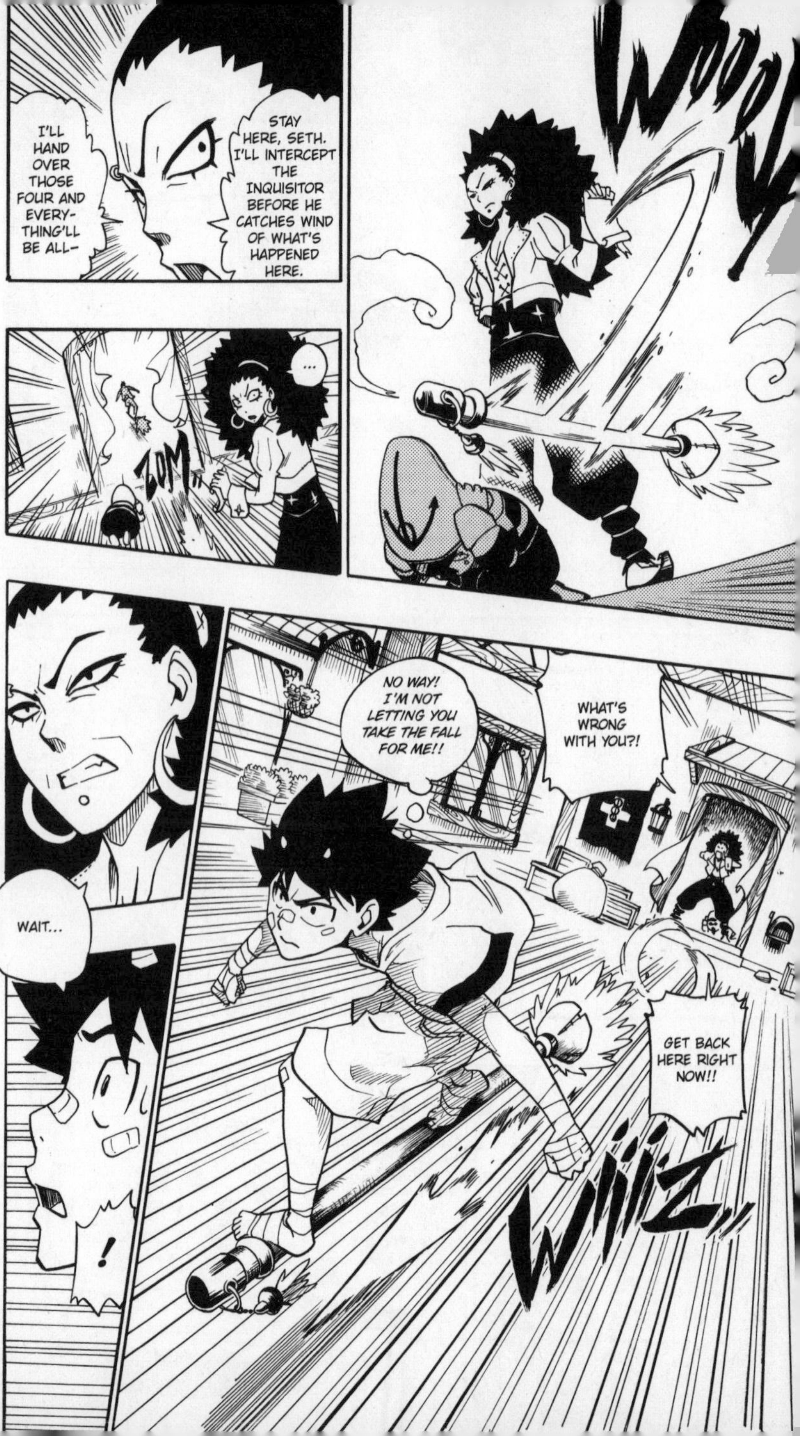
STAY HERE, SETH. I'LL INTERCEPT THE INQUISITOR BEFORE HE CATCHES WIND OF WHAT'S HAPPENED HERE.
I'LL HAND OVER THOSE FOUR AND EVERY-THING'LL BE ALL-
...
ZOM
WHAT'S WRONG WITH YOU?!
NO WAY! I'M NOT LETTING YOU TAKE THE FALL FOR ME!!
GET BACK HERE RIGHT NOW!!
WIIIZ..!!
WAIT...
!

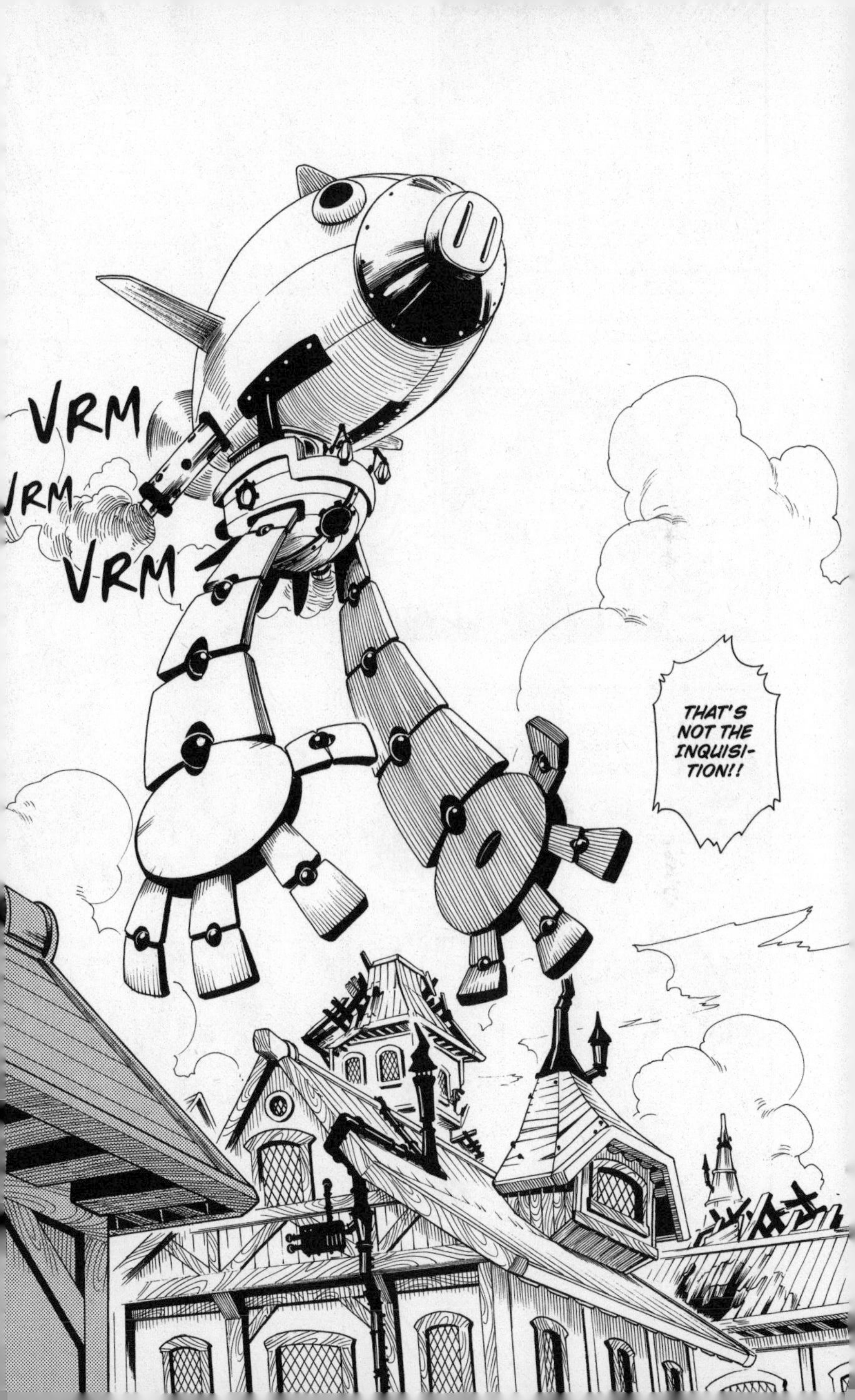
THAT'S NOT THE INQUISITION!!
VRM
VRM
VRM

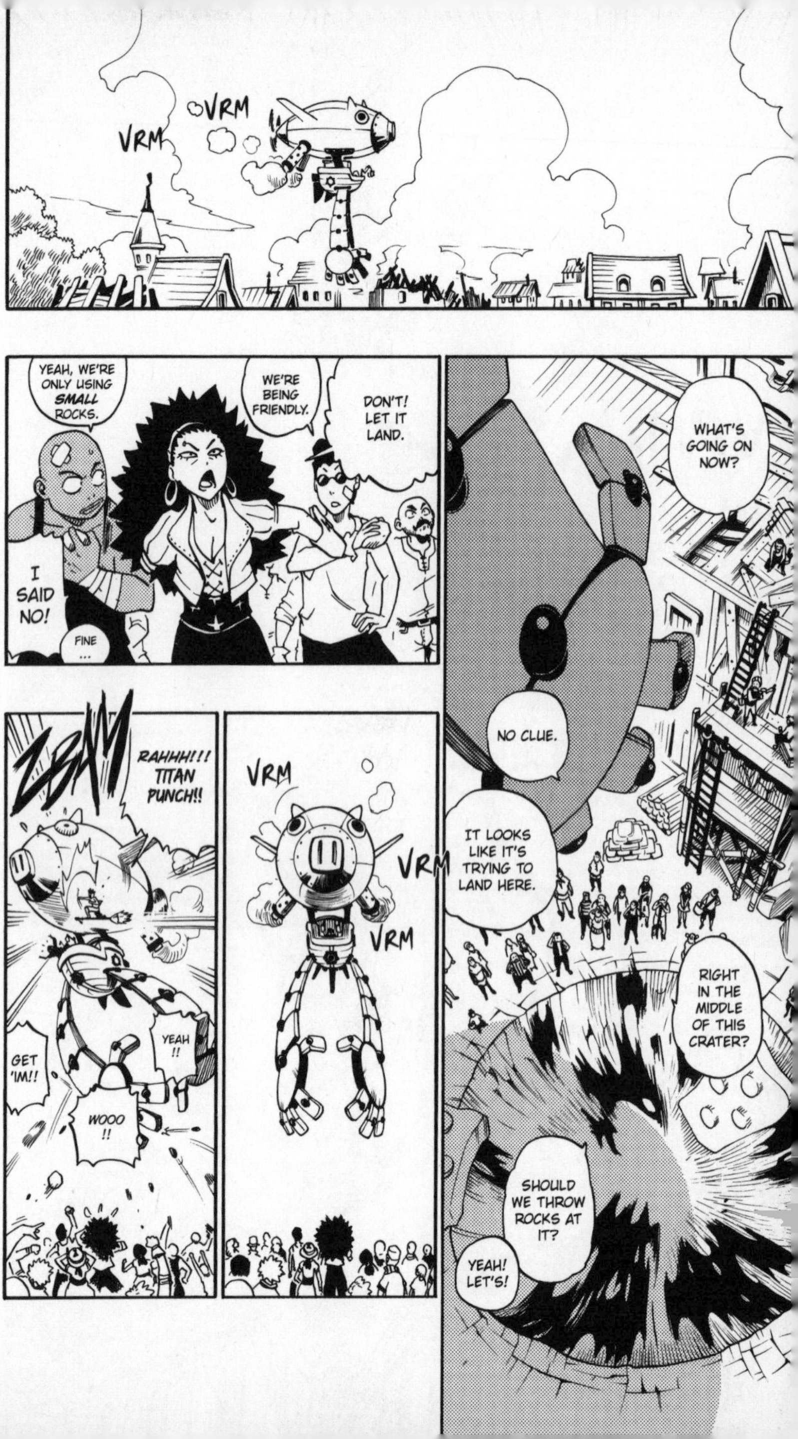
VRM
VRM
WHAT'S GOING ON NOW?
NO CLUE.
IT LOOKS LIKE IT'S TRYING TO LAND HERE.
RIGHT IN THE MIDDLE OF THIS CRATER?
SHOULD WE THROW ROCKS AT IT?
YEAH! LET'S!
DON'T! LET IT LAND.
WE'RE BEING FRIENDLY.
YEAH, WE'RE ONLY USING **SMALL** ROCKS.
I SAID NO!
FINE...
VRM
VRM
VRM
ZBAM
RAHHH!!! TITAN PUNCH!!
YEAH!!
GET 'IM!!
WOOO!!

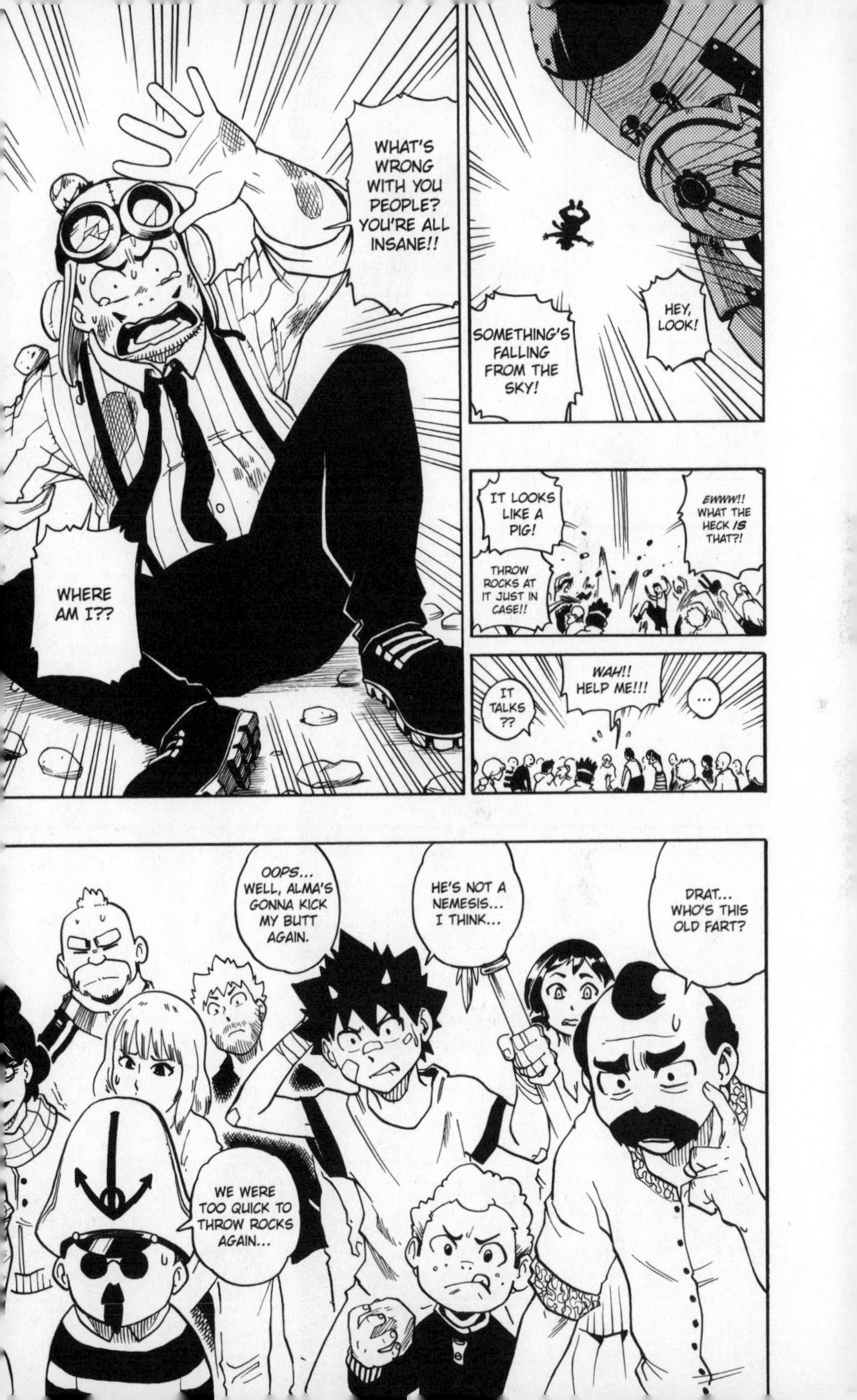
HEY, LOOK!
SOMETHING'S FALLING FROM THE SKY!
EWWW!! WHAT THE HECK IS THAT?!
IT LOOKS LIKE A PIG!
THROW ROCKS AT IT JUST IN CASE!!
...
WAH!! HELP ME!!!
IT TALKS??
WHAT'S WRONG WITH YOU PEOPLE? YOU'RE ALL INSANE!!
WHERE AM I??
DRAT... WHO'S THIS OLD FART?
HE'S NOT A NEMESIS... I THINK...
OOPS... WELL, ALMA'S GONNA KICK MY BUTT AGAIN.
WE WERE TOO QUICK TO THROW ROCKS AGAIN...

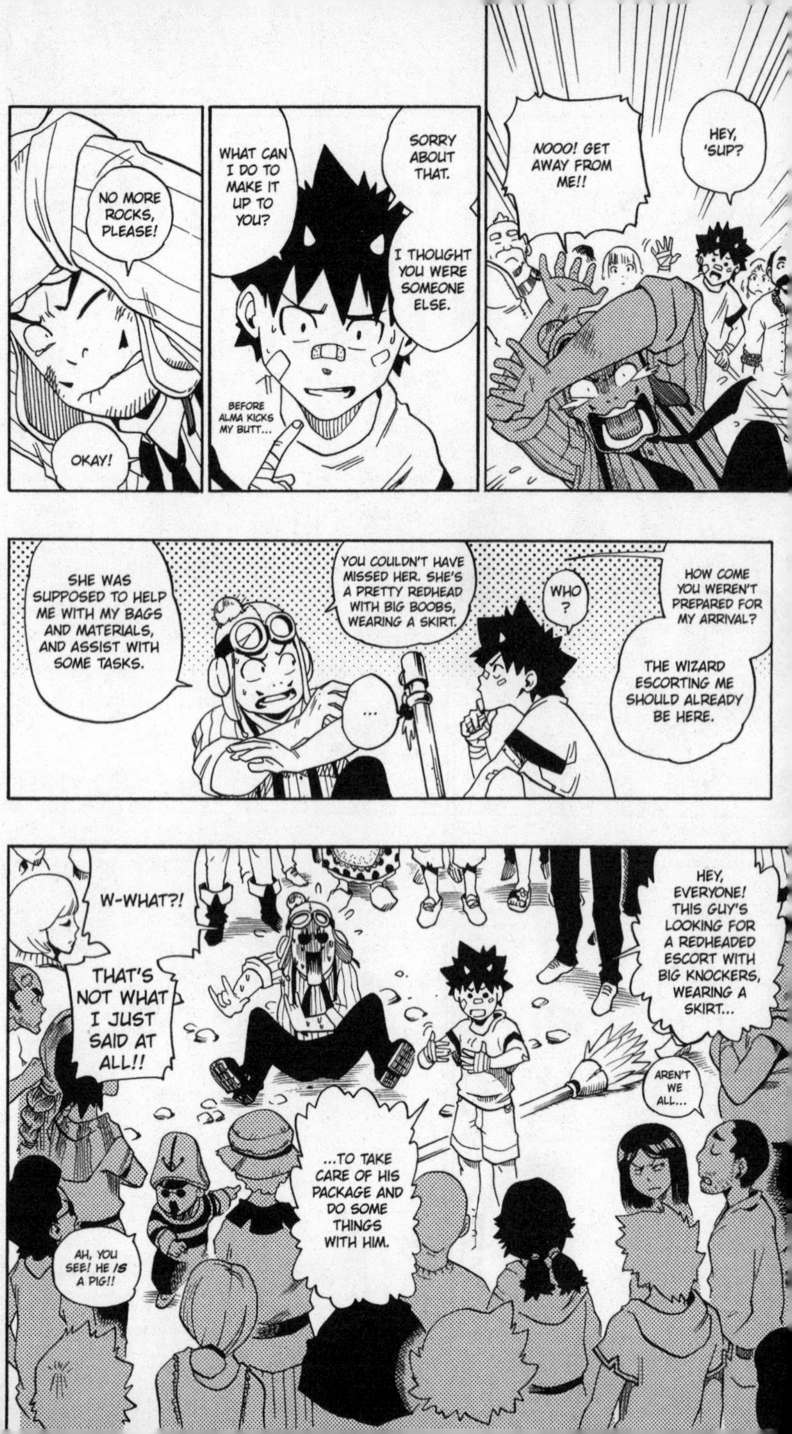
HEY, 'SUP?
NOOO! GET AWAY FROM ME!!
SORRY ABOUT THAT.
I THOUGHT YOU WERE SOMEONE ELSE.
WHAT CAN I DO TO MAKE IT UP TO YOU?
BEFORE ALMA KICKS MY BUTT...
NO MORE ROCKS, PLEASE!
OKAY!
HOW COME YOU WEREN'T PREPARED FOR MY ARRIVAL?
THE WIZARD ESCORTING ME SHOULD ALREADY BE HERE.
WHO?
YOU COULDN'T HAVE MISSED HER. SHE'S A PRETTY REDHEAD WITH BIG BOOBS, WEARING A SKIRT.
...
SHE WAS SUPPOSED TO HELP ME WITH MY BAGS AND MATERIALS, AND ASSIST WITH SOME TASKS.
HEY, EVERYONE! THIS GUY'S LOOKING FOR A REDHEADED ESCORT WITH BIG KNOCKERS, WEARING A SKIRT...
AREN'T WE ALL...
...TO TAKE CARE OF HIS PACKAGE AND DO SOME THINGS WITH HIM.
W-WHAT?!
THAT'S NOT WHAT I JUST SAID AT ALL!!
AH, YOU SEE! HE *IS* A PIG!!

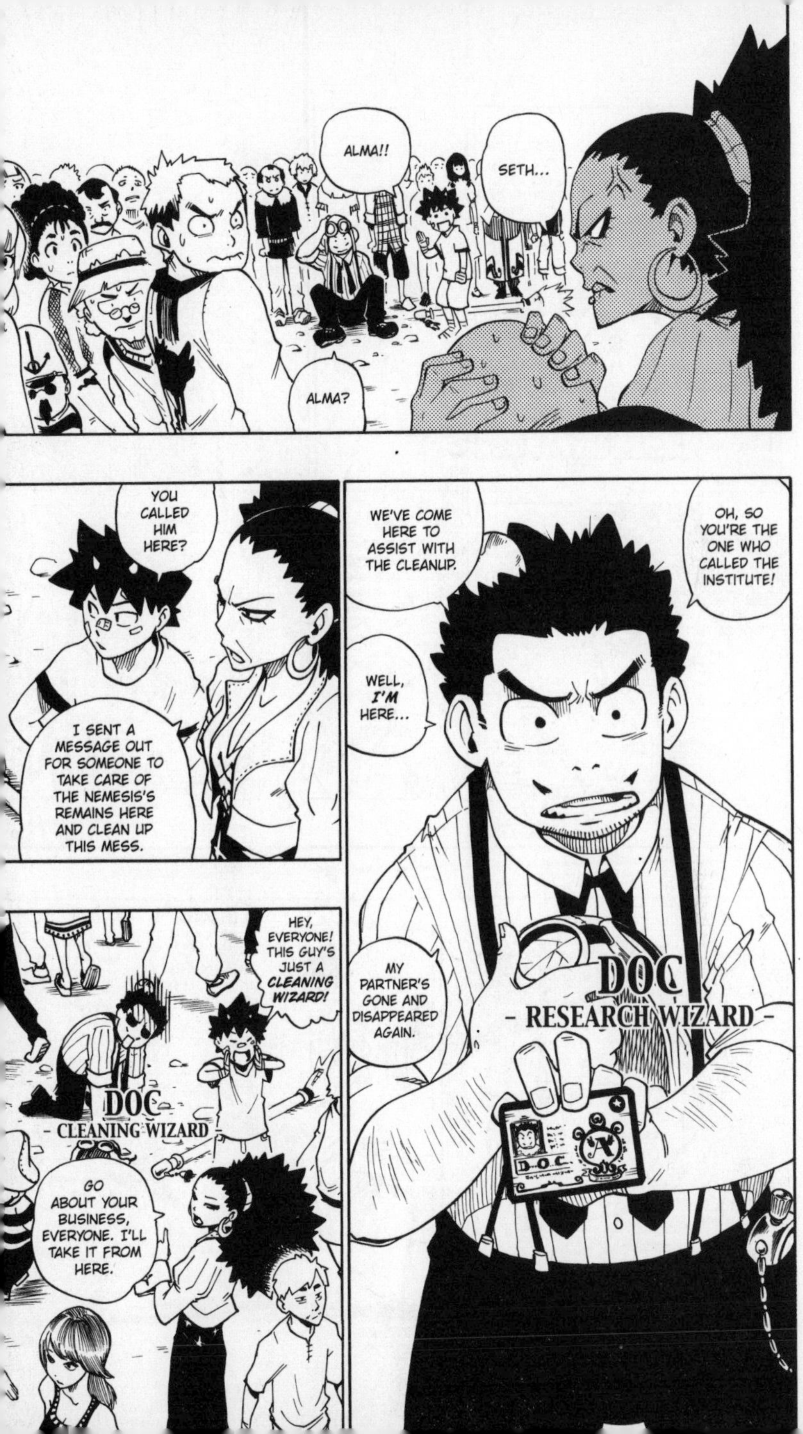
SETH...
ALMA!!
ALMA?
OH, SO YOU'RE THE ONE WHO CALLED THE INSTITUTE!
WE'VE COME HERE TO ASSIST WITH THE CLEANUP.
WELL, *I'M* HERE...
MY PARTNER'S GONE AND DISAPPEARED AGAIN.
DOC
- RESEARCH WIZARD -
D.O.C.
YOU CALLED HIM HERE?
I SENT A MESSAGE OUT FOR SOMEONE TO TAKE CARE OF THE NEMESIS'S REMAINS HERE AND CLEAN UP THIS MESS.
HEY, EVERYONE! THIS GUY'S JUST A *CLEANING WIZARD!*
DOC
- CLEANING WIZARD -
GO ABOUT YOUR BUSINESS, EVERYONE. I'LL TAKE IT FROM HERE.

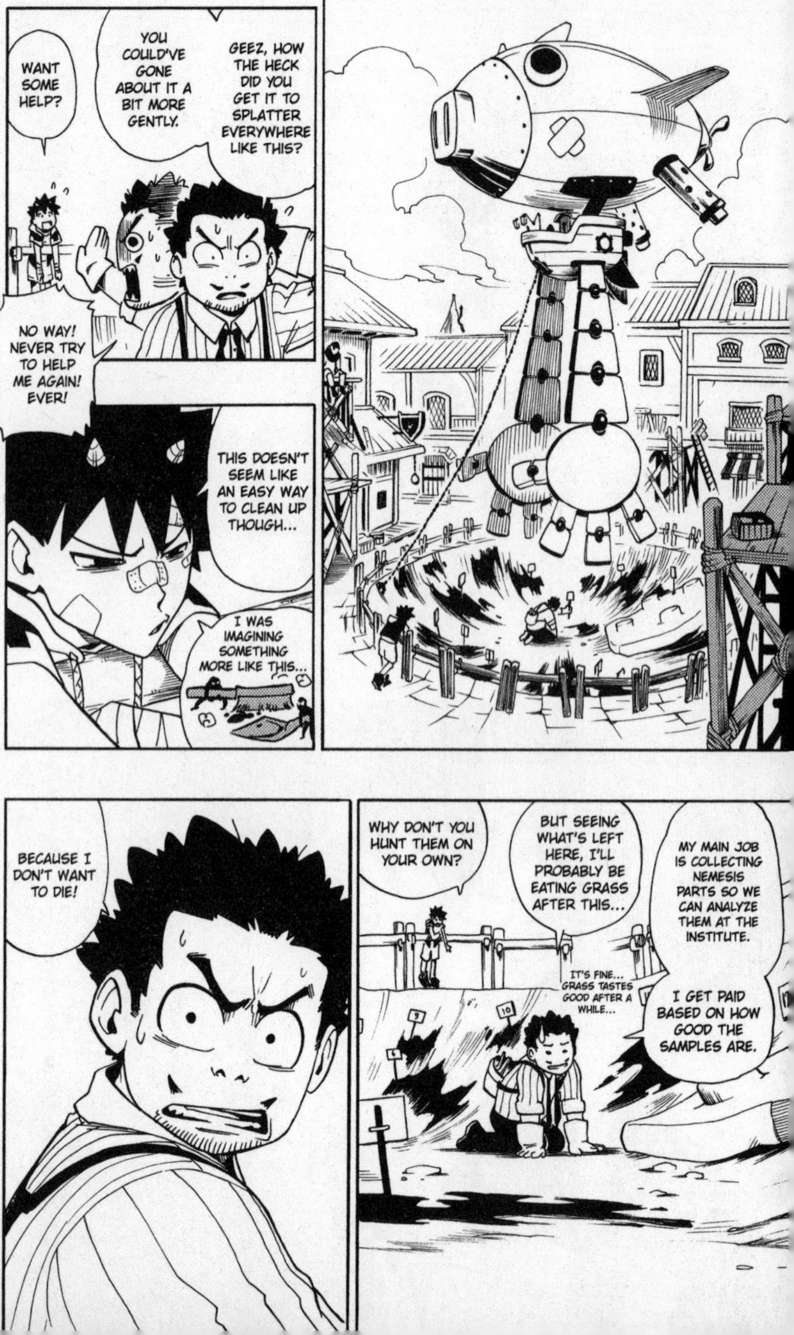
GEEZ, HOW THE HECK DID YOU GET IT TO SPLATTER EVERYWHERE LIKE THIS?
YOU COULD'VE GONE ABOUT IT A BIT MORE GENTLY.
WANT SOME HELP?
NO WAY! NEVER TRY TO HELP ME AGAIN! EVER!
THIS DOESN'T SEEM LIKE AN EASY WAY TO CLEAN UP THOUGH...
I WAS IMAGINING SOMETHING MORE LIKE THIS...
MY MAIN JOB IS COLLECTING NEMESIS PARTS SO WE CAN ANALYZE THEM AT THE INSTITUTE.
I GET PAID BASED ON HOW GOOD THE SAMPLES ARE.
BUT SEEING WHAT'S LEFT HERE, I'LL PROBABLY BE EATING GRASS AFTER THIS...
IT'S FINE... GRASS TASTES GOOD AFTER A WHILE...
WHY DON'T YOU HUNT THEM ON YOUR OWN?
BECAUSE I DON'T WANT TO DIE!

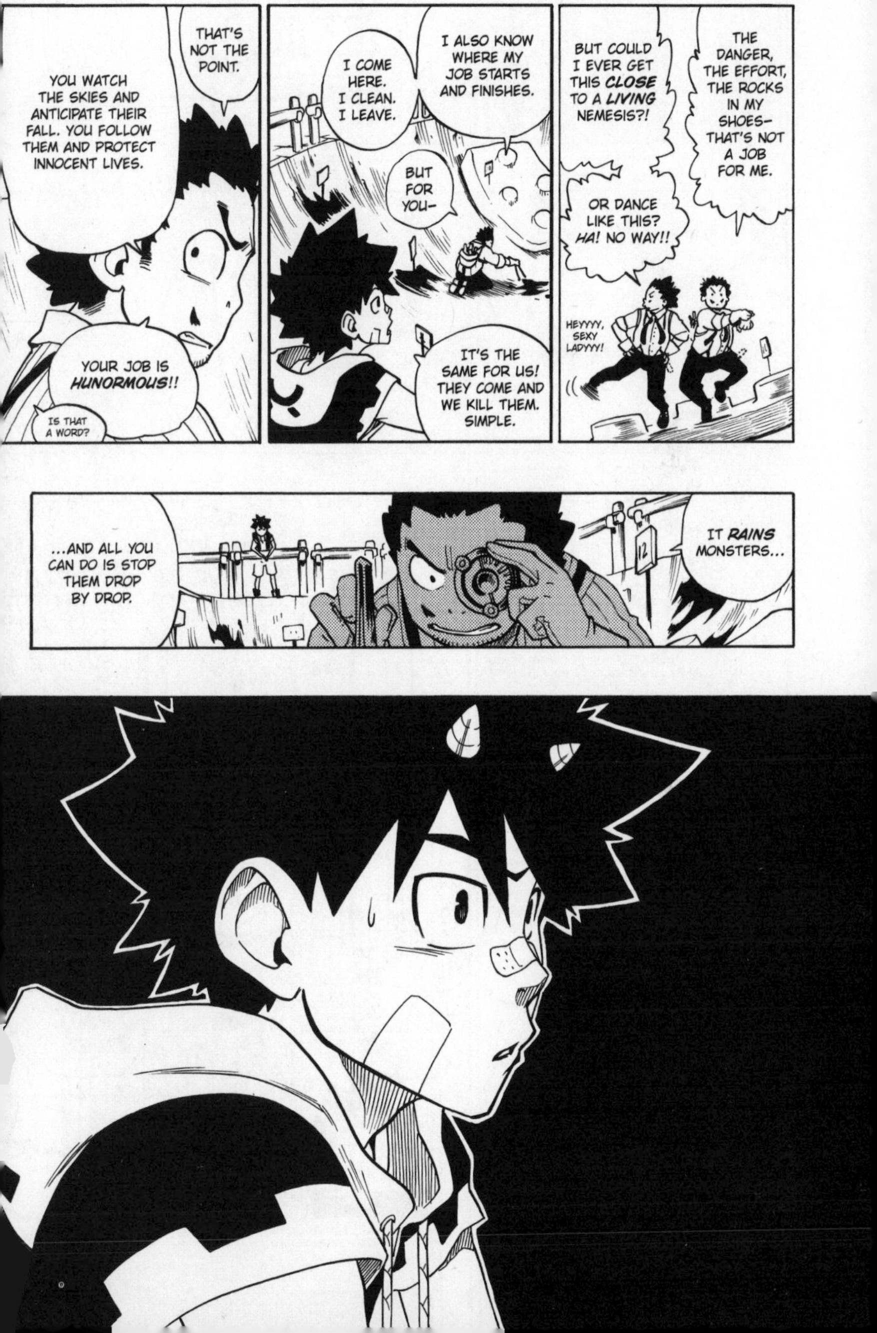
THE DANGER, THE EFFORT, THE ROCKS IN MY SHOES— THAT'S NOT A JOB FOR ME.
BUT COULD I EVER GET THIS CLOSE TO A LIVING NEMESIS?!
OR DANCE LIKE THIS? HA! NO WAY!!
HEYYYY, SEXY LADYYY!
I ALSO KNOW WHERE MY JOB STARTS AND FINISHES.
I COME HERE. I CLEAN. I LEAVE.
BUT FOR YOU–
IT'S THE SAME FOR US! THEY COME AND WE KILL THEM. SIMPLE.
THAT'S NOT THE POINT.
YOU WATCH THE SKIES AND ANTICIPATE THEIR FALL. YOU FOLLOW THEM AND PROTECT INNOCENT LIVES.
YOUR JOB IS HUNORMOUS!!
IS THAT A WORD?
IT RAINS MONSTERS...
...AND ALL YOU CAN DO IS STOP THEM DROP BY DROP.

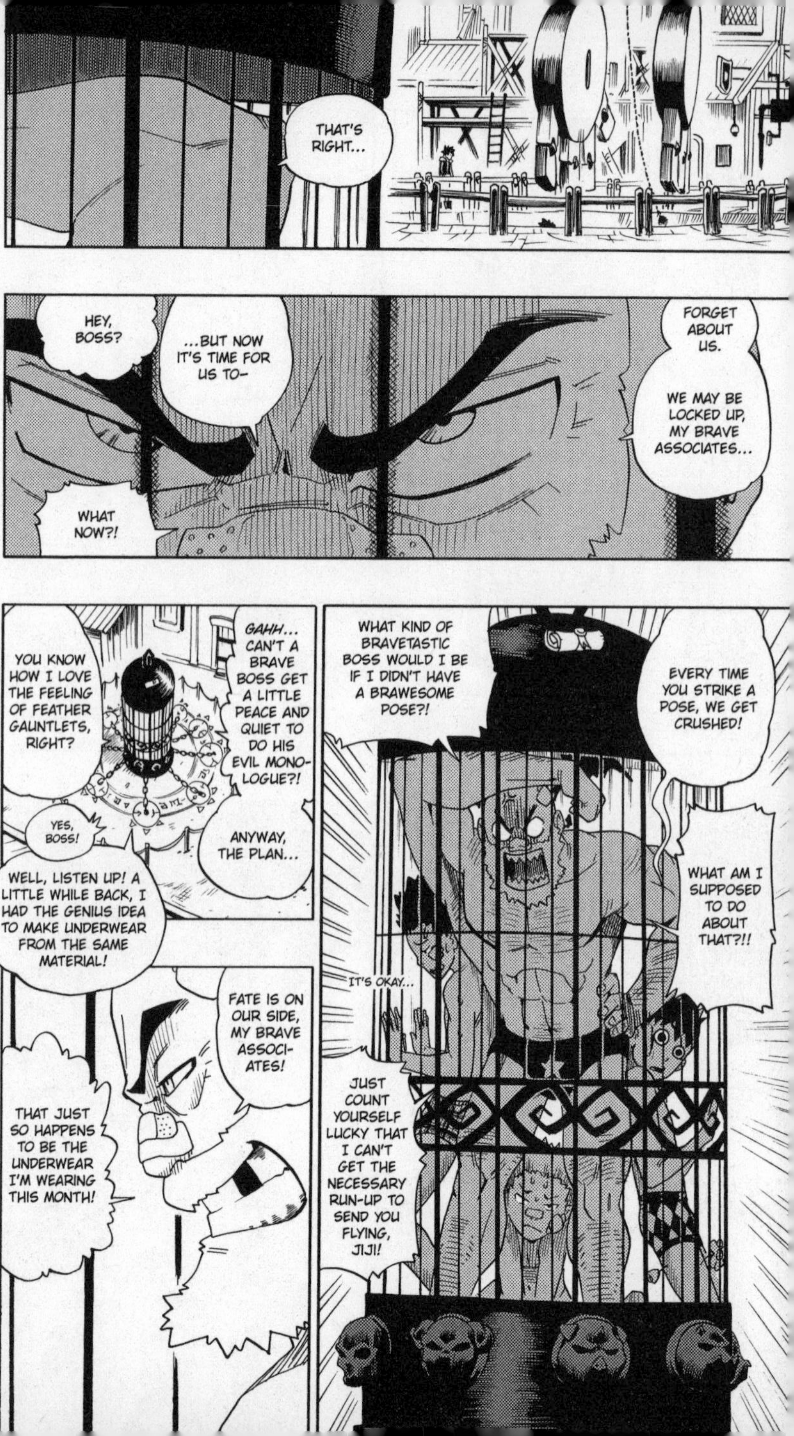

THAT'S RIGHT...
FORGET ABOUT US.
WE MAY BE LOCKED UP, MY BRAVE ASSOCIATES...
...BUT NOW IT'S TIME FOR US TO–
HEY, BOSS?
WHAT NOW?!
EVERY TIME YOU STRIKE A POSE, WE GET CRUSHED!
WHAT KIND OF BRAVETASTIC BOSS WOULD I BE IF I DIDN'T HAVE A BRAWESOME POSE?!
WHAT AM I SUPPOSED TO DO ABOUT THAT?!!
IT'S OKAY...
JUST COUNT YOURSELF LUCKY THAT I CAN'T GET THE NECESSARY RUN-UP TO SEND YOU FLYING, JIJI!
GAHH... CAN'T A BRAVE BOSS GET A LITTLE PEACE AND QUIET TO DO HIS EVIL MONO-LOGUE?!
ANYWAY, THE PLAN...
YOU KNOW HOW I LOVE THE FEELING OF FEATHER GAUNTLETS, RIGHT?
YES, BOSS!
WELL, LISTEN UP! A LITTLE WHILE BACK, I HAD THE GENIUS IDEA TO MAKE UNDERWEAR FROM THE SAME MATERIAL!
FATE IS ON OUR SIDE, MY BRAVE ASSOCI-ATES!
THAT JUST SO HAPPENS TO BE THE UNDERWEAR I'M WEARING THIS MONTH!

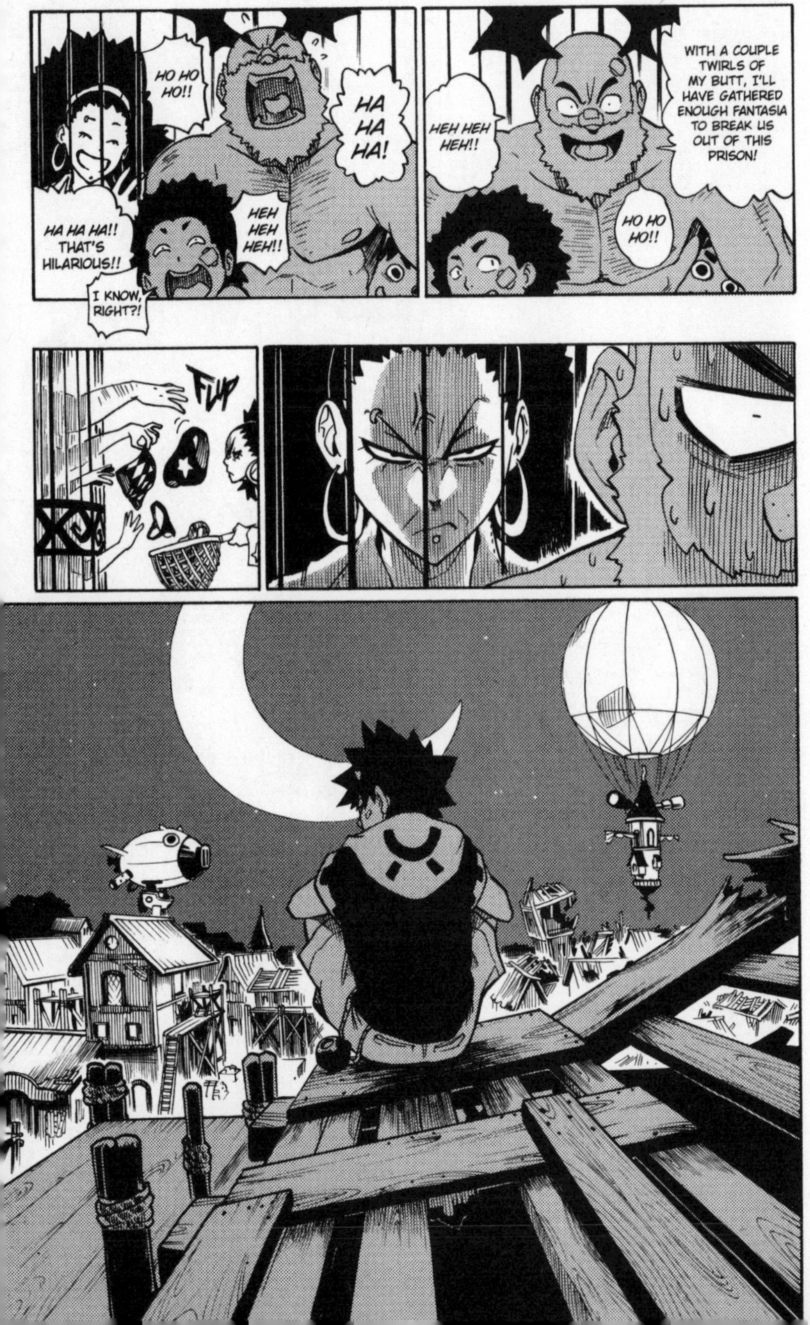
WITH A COUPLE TWIRLS OF MY BUTT, I'LL HAVE GATHERED ENOUGH FANTASIA TO BREAK US OUT OF THIS PRISON!
HEH HEH HEH!!
HO HO HO!!
HA HA HA!
HO HO HO!!
HEH HEH HEH!!
HA HA HA!! THAT'S HILARIOUS!!
I KNOW, RIGHT?!
FLIP

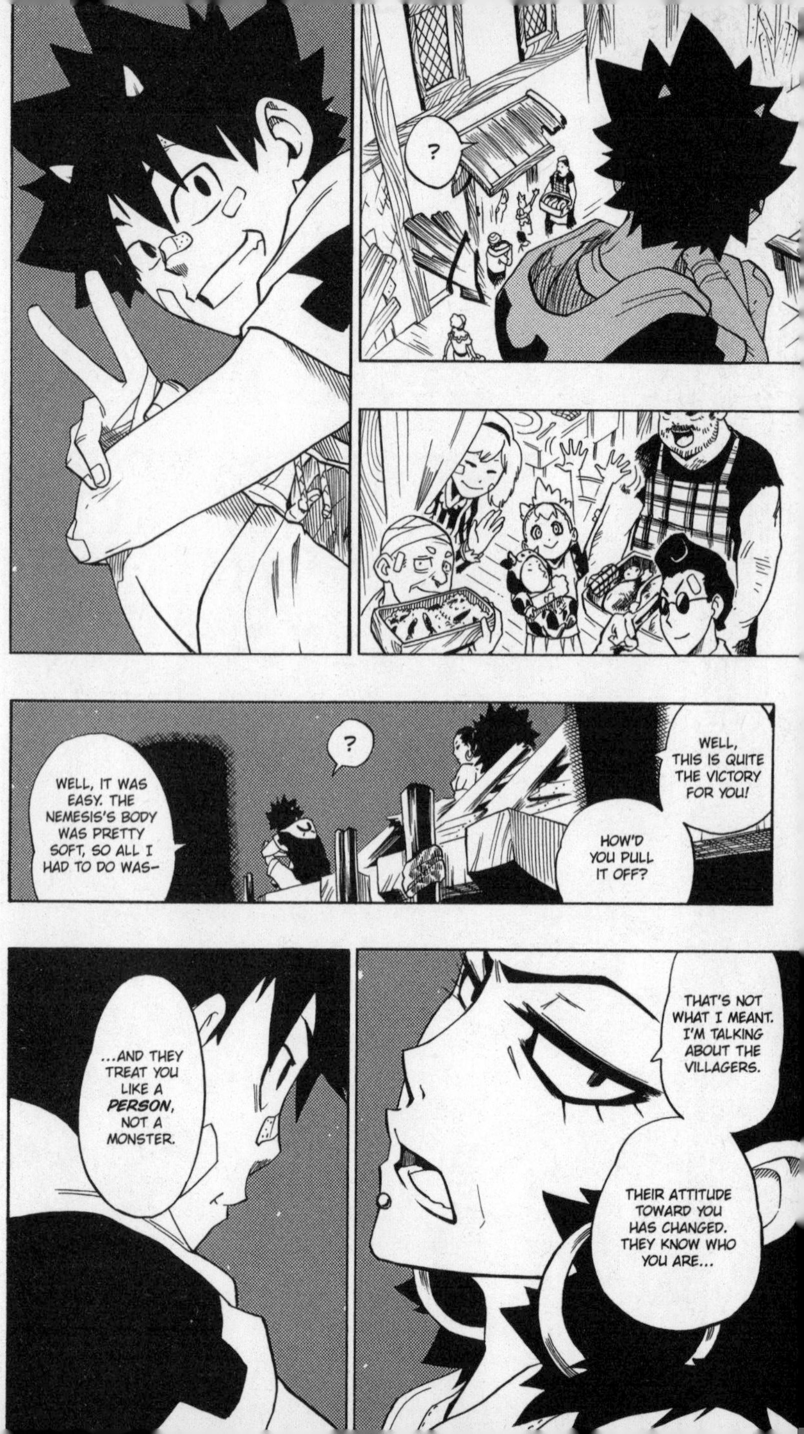
?
WELL, THIS IS QUITE THE VICTORY FOR YOU!
HOW'D YOU PULL IT OFF?
?
WELL, IT WAS EASY. THE NEMESIS'S BODY WAS PRETTY SOFT, SO ALL I HAD TO DO WAS-
THAT'S NOT WHAT I MEANT. I'M TALKING ABOUT THE VILLAGERS.
THEIR ATTITUDE TOWARD YOU HAS CHANGED. THEY KNOW WHO YOU ARE...
...AND THEY TREAT YOU LIKE A *PERSON*, NOT A MONSTER.

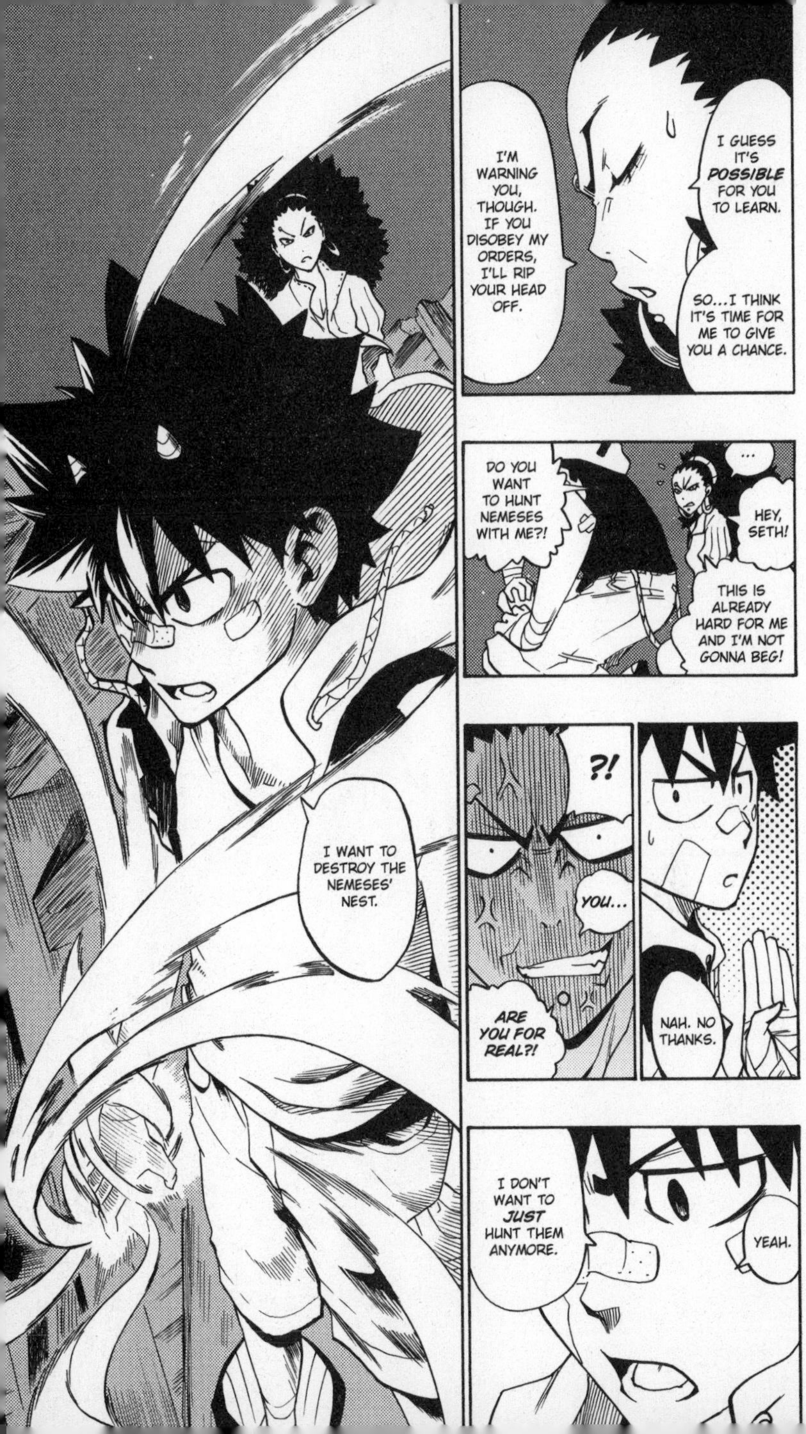
I GUESS IT'S POSSIBLE FOR YOU TO LEARN.
SO...I THINK IT'S TIME FOR ME TO GIVE YOU A CHANCE.
I'M WARNING YOU, THOUGH. IF YOU DISOBEY MY ORDERS, I'LL RIP YOUR HEAD OFF.
...
HEY, SETH!
THIS IS ALREADY HARD FOR ME AND I'M NOT GONNA BEG!
DO YOU WANT TO HUNT NEMESES WITH ME?!
NAH. NO THANKS.
?!
YOU...
ARE YOU FOR REAL?!
YEAH.
I DON'T WANT TO JUST HUNT THEM ANYMORE.
I WANT TO DESTROY THE NEMESES' NEST.

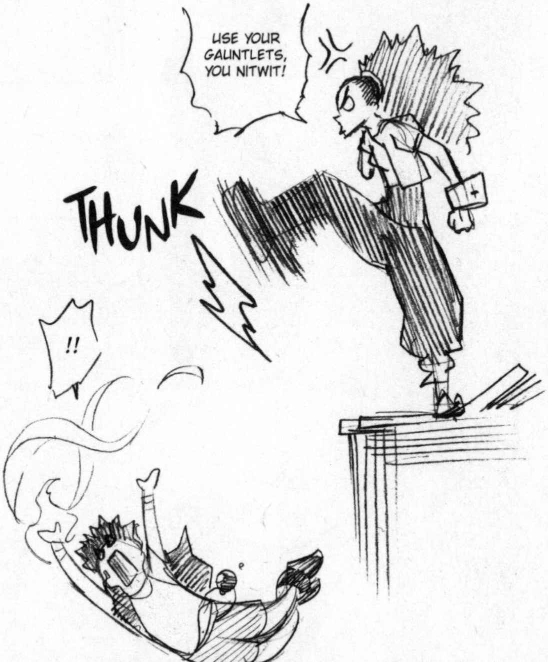
USE YOUR GAUNTLETS, YOU NITWIT!
THUNK
!!

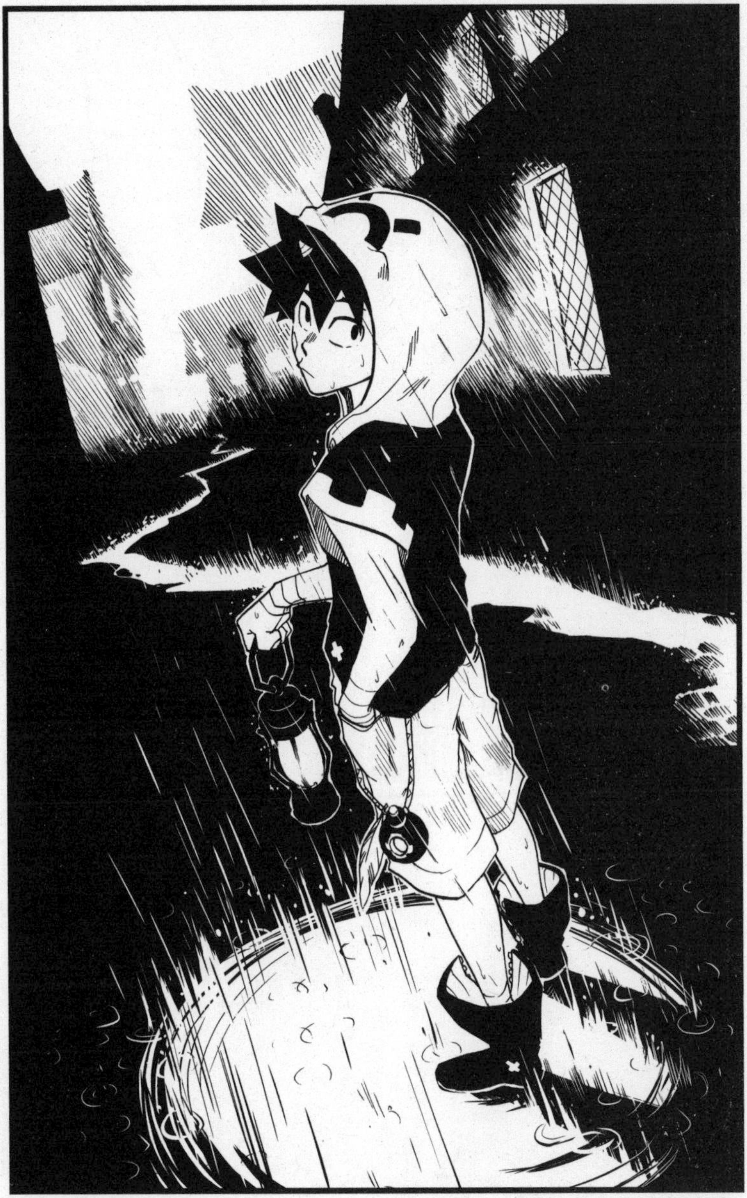

CHAPTER 3

SOMEONE HAIRY, SOMEONE HORNY

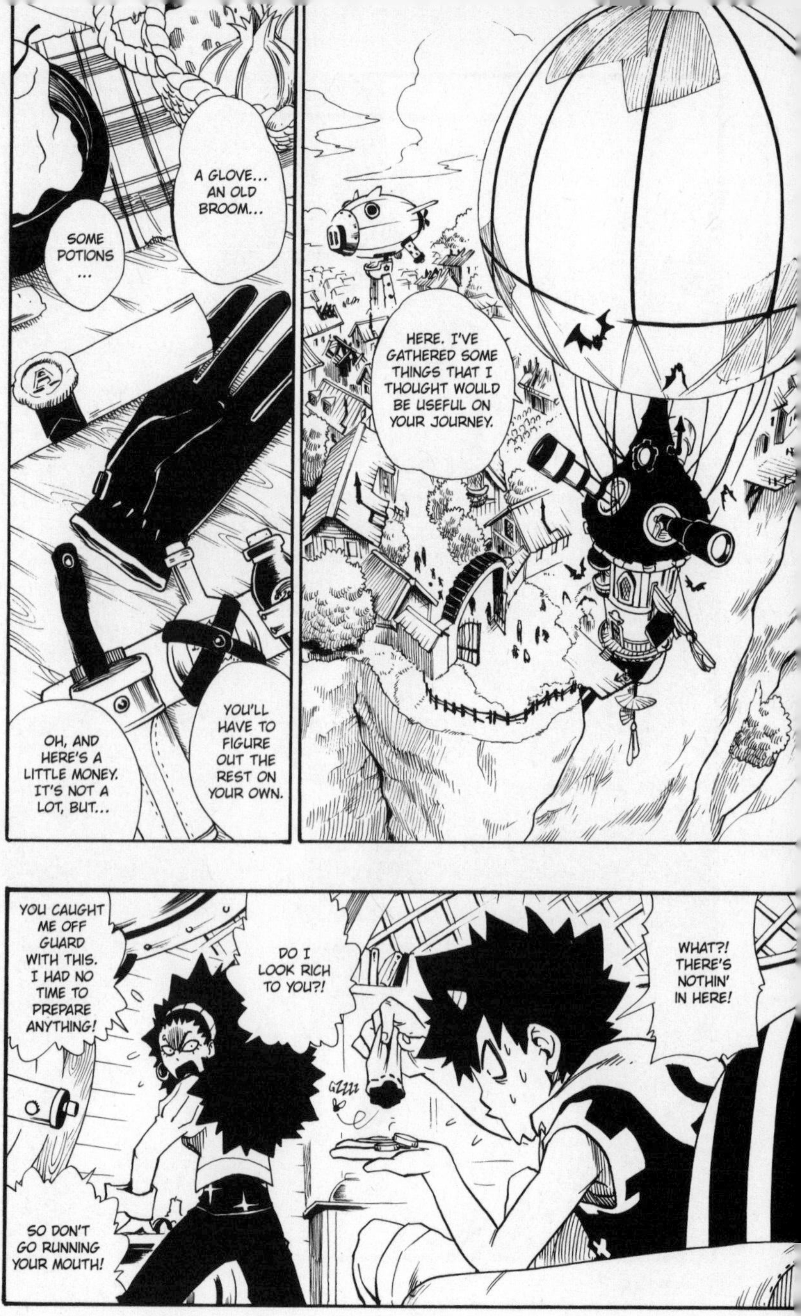
HERE. I'VE GATHERED SOME THINGS THAT I THOUGHT WOULD BE USEFUL ON YOUR JOURNEY.
A GLOVE... AN OLD BROOM...
SOME POTIONS ...
YOU'LL HAVE TO FIGURE OUT THE REST ON YOUR OWN.
OH, AND HERE'S A LITTLE MONEY. IT'S NOT A LOT, BUT...
WHAT?! THERE'S NOTHIN' IN HERE!
GZZZ
DO I LOOK RICH TO YOU?!
YOU CAUGHT ME OFF GUARD WITH THIS. I HAD NO TIME TO PREPARE ANYTHING!
SO DON'T GO RUNNING YOUR MOUTH!

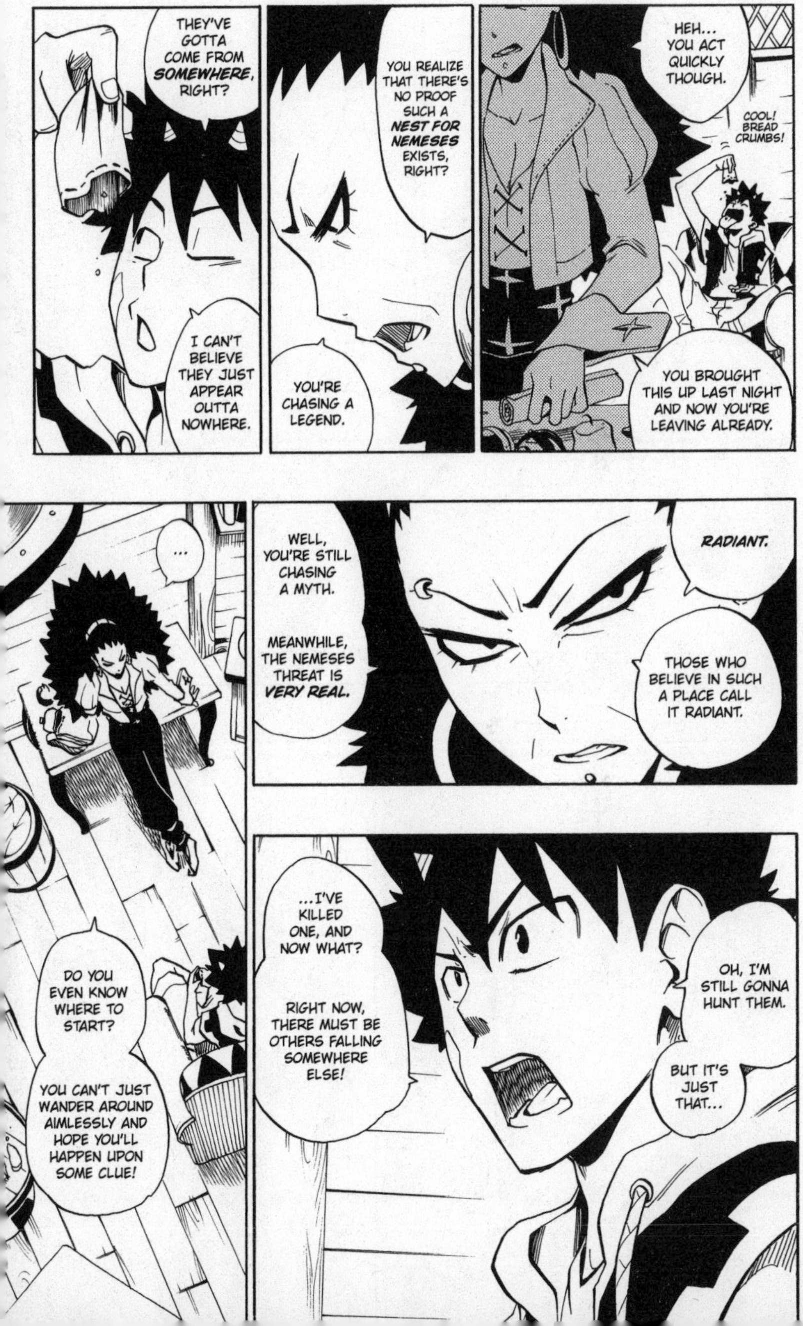
HEH... YOU ACT QUICKLY THOUGH.
COOL! BREAD CRUMBS!
YOU BROUGHT THIS UP LAST NIGHT AND NOW YOU'RE LEAVING ALREADY.
YOU REALIZE THAT THERE'S NO PROOF SUCH A ***NEST FOR NEMESES*** EXISTS, RIGHT?
YOU'RE CHASING A LEGEND.
THEY'VE GOTTA COME FROM ***SOMEWHERE***, RIGHT?
I CAN'T BELIEVE THEY JUST APPEAR OUTTA NOWHERE.
RADIANT.
THOSE WHO BELIEVE IN SUCH A PLACE CALL IT RADIANT.
WELL, YOU'RE STILL CHASING A MYTH.
MEANWHILE, THE NEMESES THREAT IS ***VERY REAL.***
OH, I'M STILL GONNA HUNT THEM.
BUT IT'S JUST THAT...
...I'VE KILLED ONE, AND NOW WHAT?
RIGHT NOW, THERE MUST BE OTHERS FALLING SOMEWHERE ELSE!
...
DO YOU EVEN KNOW WHERE TO START?
YOU CAN'T JUST WANDER AROUND AIMLESSLY AND HOPE YOU'LL HAPPEN UPON SOME CLUE!

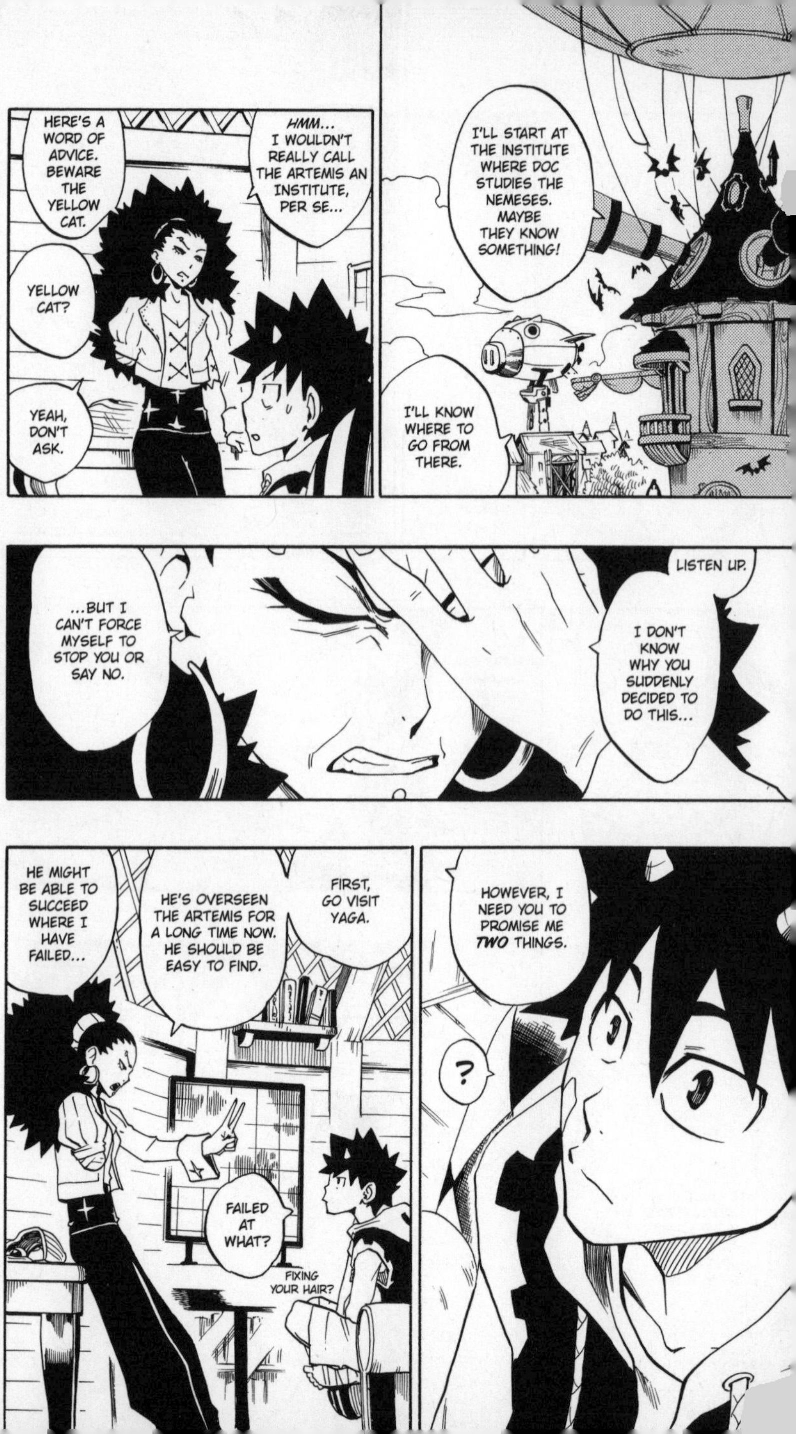
I'LL START AT THE INSTITUTE WHERE DOC STUDIES THE NEMESES. MAYBE THEY KNOW SOMETHING!
I'LL KNOW WHERE TO GO FROM THERE.
HMM... I WOULDN'T REALLY CALL THE ARTEMIS AN INSTITUTE, PER SE...
HERE'S A WORD OF ADVICE. BEWARE THE YELLOW CAT.
YELLOW CAT?
YEAH, DON'T ASK.
LISTEN UP.
I DON'T KNOW WHY YOU SUDDENLY DECIDED TO DO THIS...
...BUT I CAN'T FORCE MYSELF TO STOP YOU OR SAY NO.
HOWEVER, I NEED YOU TO PROMISE ME ***TWO*** THINGS.
?
FIRST, GO VISIT YAGA.
HE'S OVERSEEN THE ARTEMIS FOR A LONG TIME NOW. HE SHOULD BE EASY TO FIND.
HE MIGHT BE ABLE TO SUCCEED WHERE I HAVE FAILED...
FAILED AT WHAT?
FIXING YOUR HAIR?

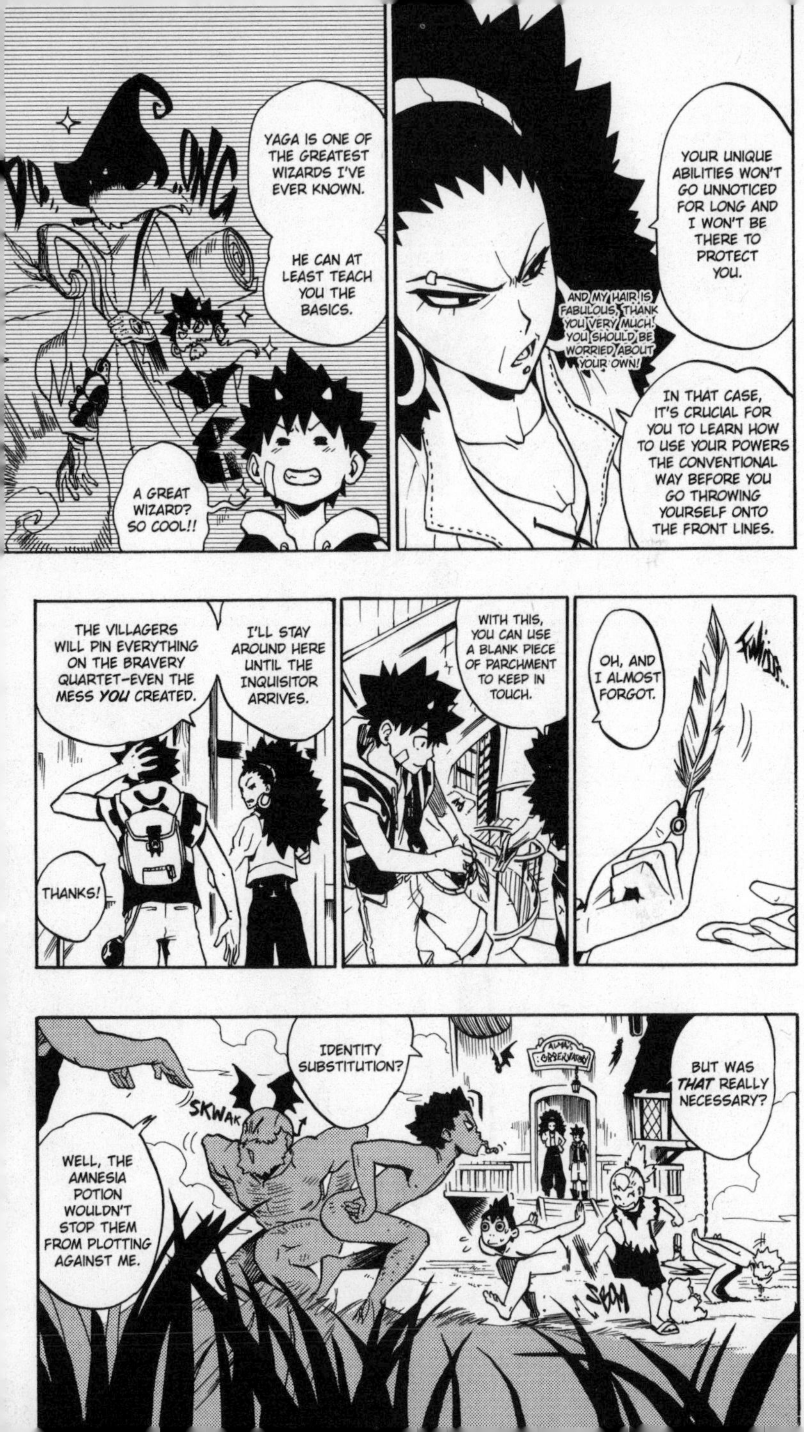
YOUR UNIQUE ABILITIES WON'T GO UNNOTICED FOR LONG AND I WON'T BE THERE TO PROTECT YOU.
AND MY HAIR IS FABULOUS, THANK YOU VERY MUCH! YOU SHOULD BE WORRIED ABOUT YOUR OWN!
IN THAT CASE, IT'S CRUCIAL FOR YOU TO LEARN HOW TO USE YOUR POWERS THE CONVENTIONAL WAY BEFORE YOU GO THROWING YOURSELF ONTO THE FRONT LINES.
YAGA IS ONE OF THE GREATEST WIZARDS I'VE EVER KNOWN.
HE CAN AT LEAST TEACH YOU THE BASICS.
A GREAT WIZARD? SO COOL!!
OH, AND I ALMOST FORGOT.
WITH THIS, YOU CAN USE A BLANK PIECE OF PARCHMENT TO KEEP IN TOUCH.
I'LL STAY AROUND HERE UNTIL THE INQUISITOR ARRIVES.
THE VILLAGERS WILL PIN EVERYTHING ON THE BRAVERY QUARTET—EVEN THE MESS *YOU* CREATED.
THANKS!
BUT WAS *THAT* REALLY NECESSARY?
IDENTITY SUBSTITUTION?
SKWAK
WELL, THE AMNESIA POTION WOULDN'T STOP THEM FROM PLOTTING AGAINST ME.

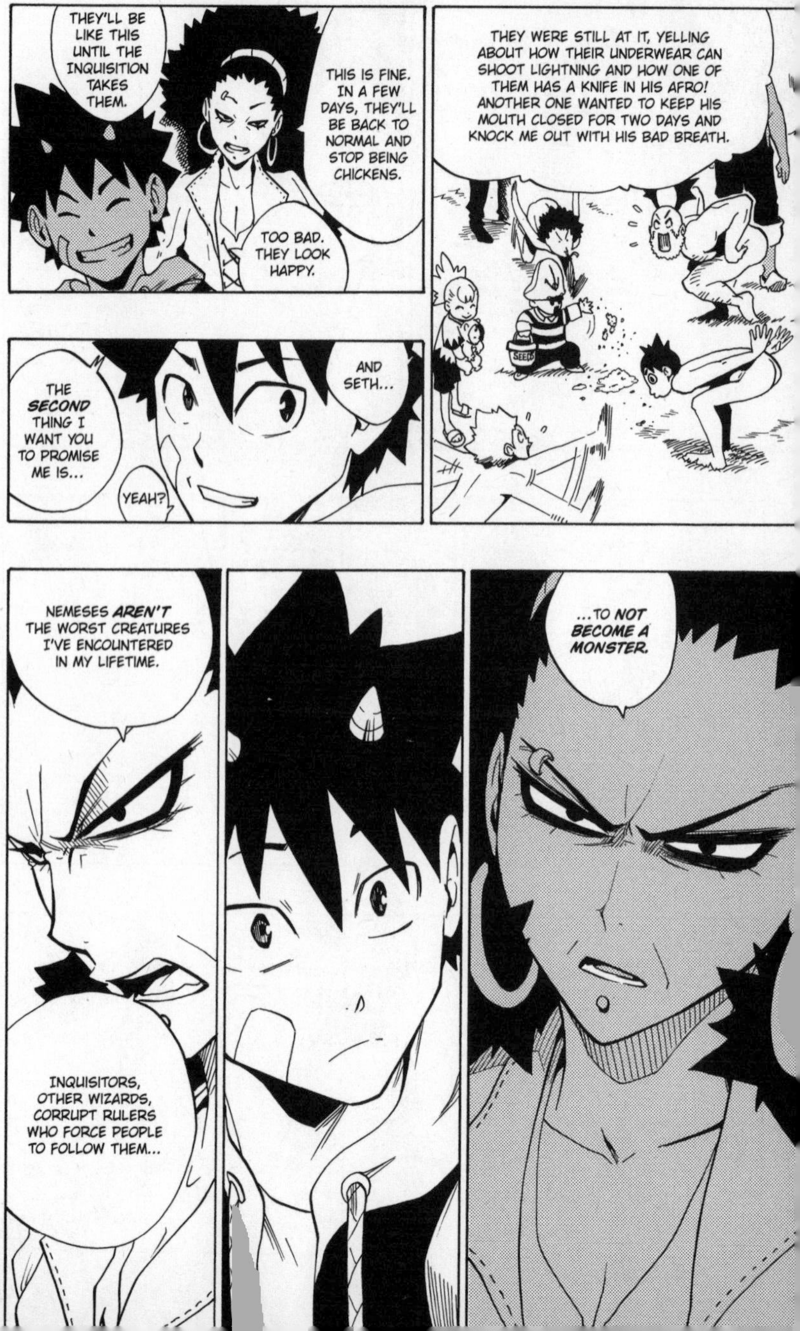
THEY WERE STILL AT IT, YELLING ABOUT HOW THEIR UNDERWEAR CAN SHOOT LIGHTNING AND HOW ONE OF THEM HAS A KNIFE IN HIS AFRO! ANOTHER ONE WANTED TO KEEP HIS MOUTH CLOSED FOR TWO DAYS AND KNOCK ME OUT WITH HIS BAD BREATH.
SEEDS
THIS IS FINE. IN A FEW DAYS, THEY'LL BE BACK TO NORMAL AND STOP BEING CHICKENS.
THEY'LL BE LIKE THIS UNTIL THE INQUISITION TAKES THEM.
TOO BAD. THEY LOOK HAPPY.
AND SETH...
THE *SECOND* THING I WANT YOU TO PROMISE ME IS...
YEAH?
...TO **NOT BECOME A MONSTER.**
NEMESES ***AREN'T*** THE WORST CREATURES I'VE ENCOUNTERED IN MY LIFETIME.
INQUISITORS, OTHER WIZARDS, CORRUPT RULERS WHO FORCE PEOPLE TO FOLLOW THEM...

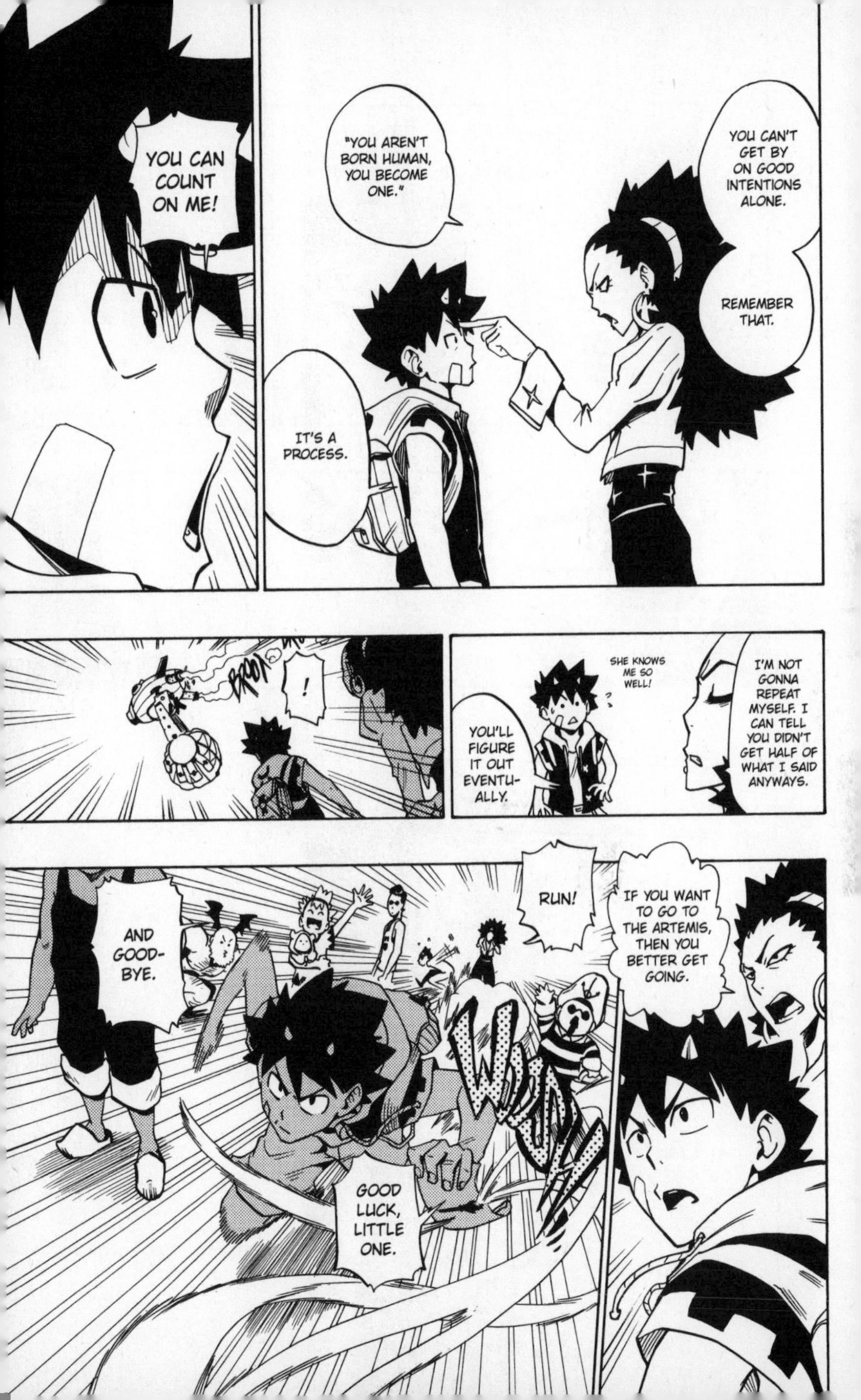
YOU CAN'T GET BY ON GOOD INTENTIONS ALONE.
REMEMBER THAT.
"YOU AREN'T BORN HUMAN, YOU BECOME ONE."
IT'S A PROCESS.
YOU CAN COUNT ON ME!
I'M NOT GONNA REPEAT MYSELF. I CAN TELL YOU DIDN'T GET HALF OF WHAT I SAID ANYWAYS.
SHE KNOWS ME SO WELL!
YOU'LL FIGURE IT OUT EVENTU-ALLY.
!
IF YOU WANT TO GO TO THE ARTEMIS, THEN YOU BETTER GET GOING.
RUN!
AND GOOD-BYE.
GOOD LUCK, LITTLE ONE.

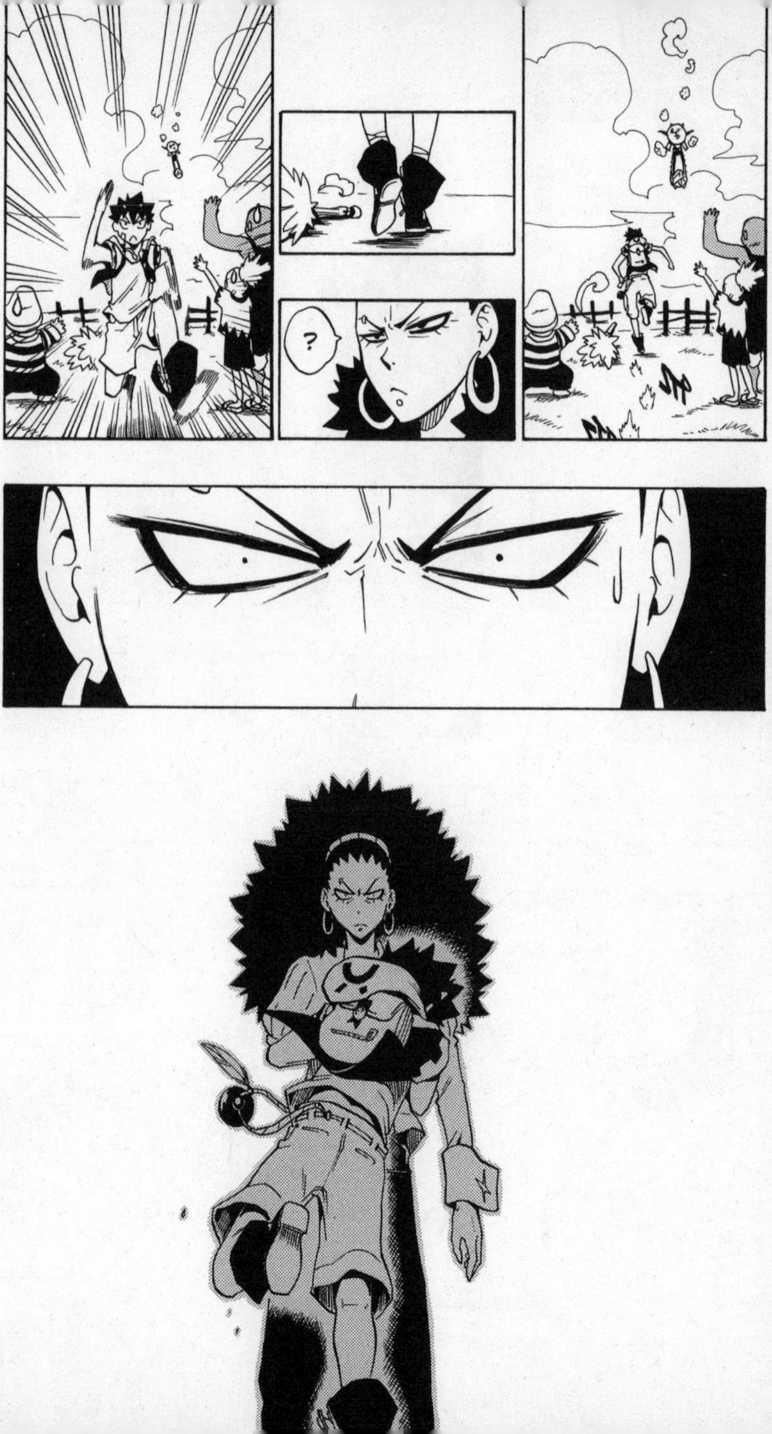
?

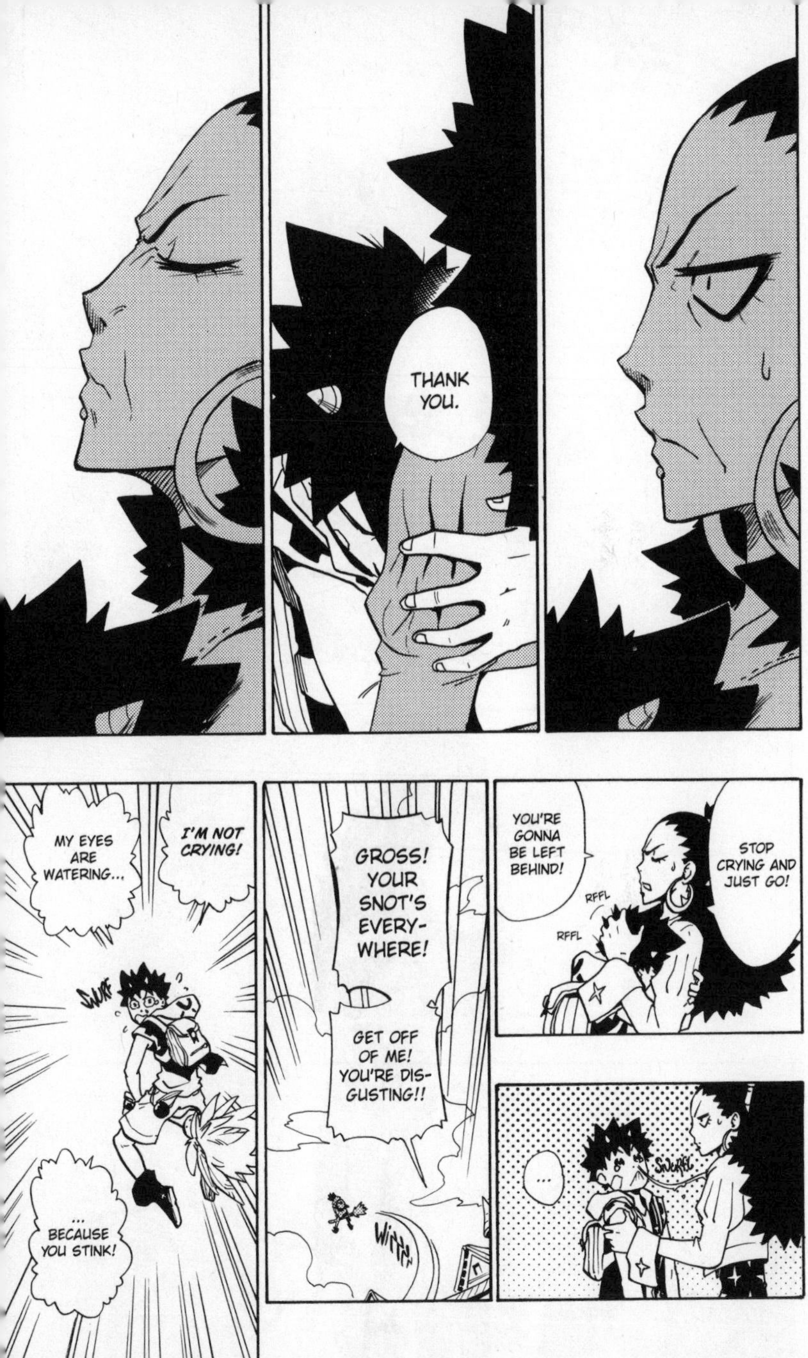
THANK YOU.
STOP CRYING AND JUST GO!
YOU'RE GONNA BE LEFT BEHIND!
RFFL
RFFL
...
GROSS! YOUR SNOT'S EVERY-WHERE!
GET OFF OF ME! YOU'RE DIS-GUSTING!!
I'M NOT CRYING!
MY EYES ARE WATERING...
... BECAUSE YOU STINK!

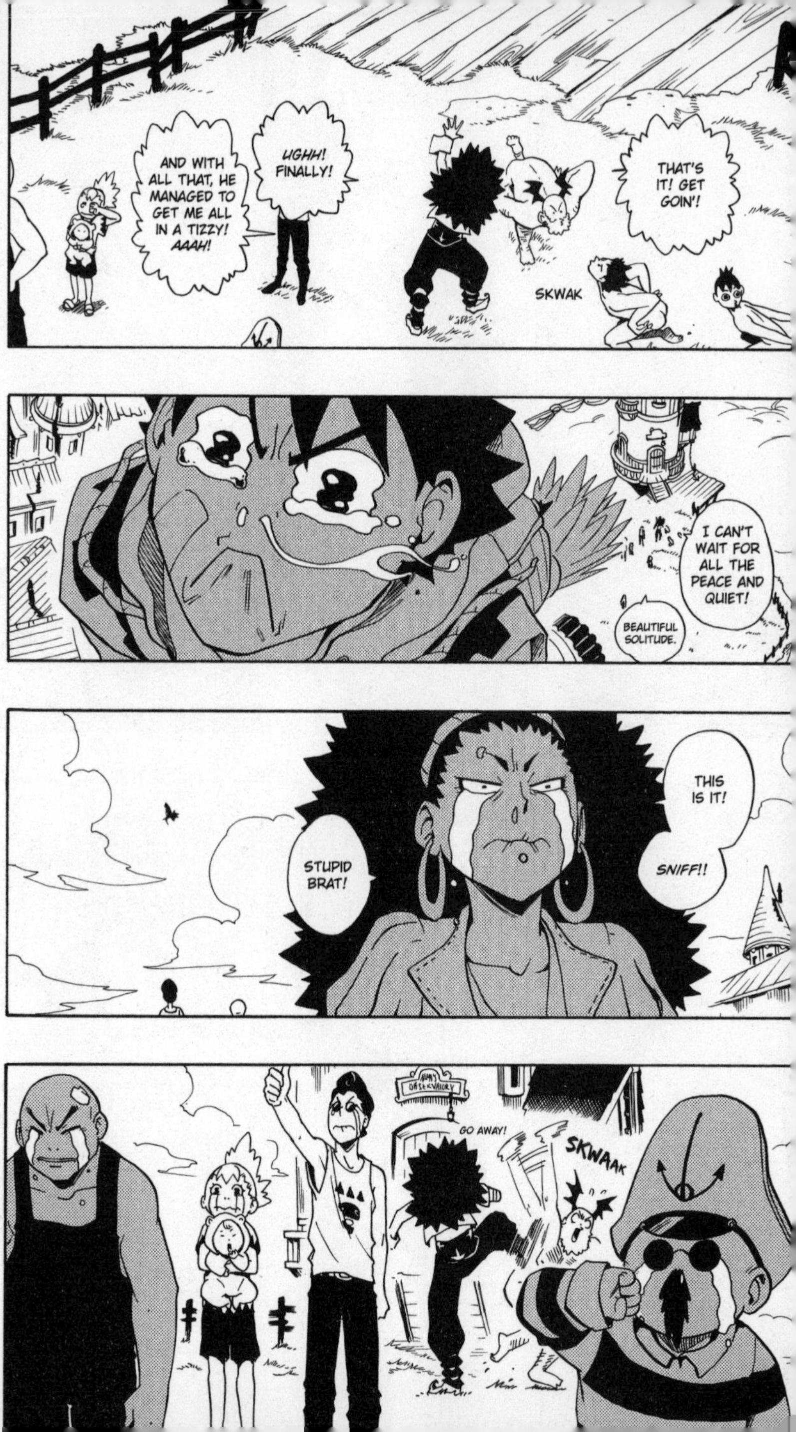
THAT'S IT! GET GOIN'!
SKWAK
UGHH! FINALLY!
AND WITH ALL THAT, HE MANAGED TO GET ME ALL IN A TIZZY! AAAH!
I CAN'T WAIT FOR ALL THE PEACE AND QUIET!
BEAUTIFUL SOLITUDE.
THIS IS IT!
SNIFF!!
STUPID BRAT!
SKWAAK
GO AWAY!

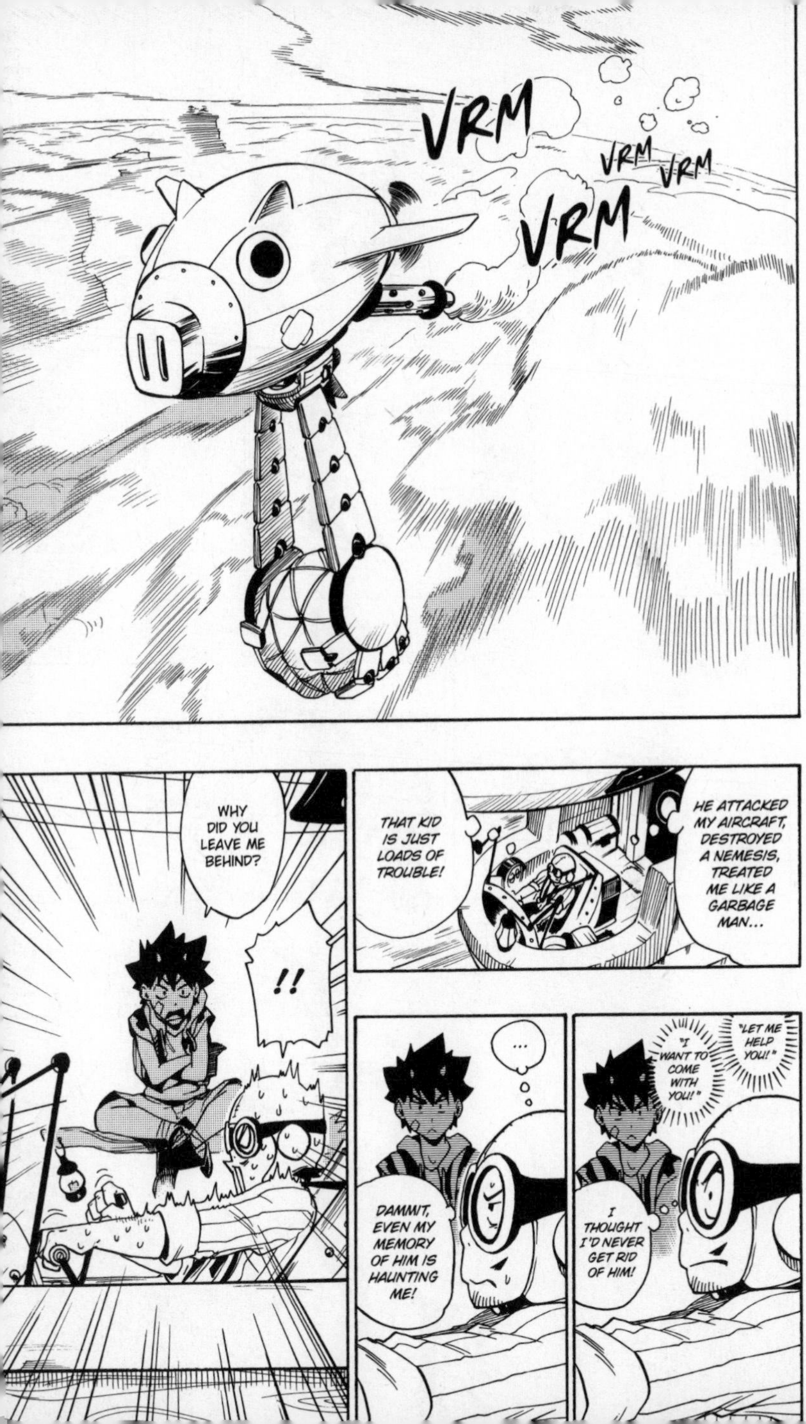
VRM
VRM VRM
VRM
HE ATTACKED MY AIRCRAFT, DESTROYED A NEMESIS, TREATED ME LIKE A GARBAGE MAN...
THAT KID IS JUST LOADS OF TROUBLE!
"LET ME HELP YOU!"
"I WANT TO COME WITH YOU!"
I THOUGHT I'D NEVER GET RID OF HIM!
...
DAMMIT, EVEN MY MEMORY OF HIM IS HAUNTING ME!
WHY DID YOU LEAVE ME BEHIND?
!!

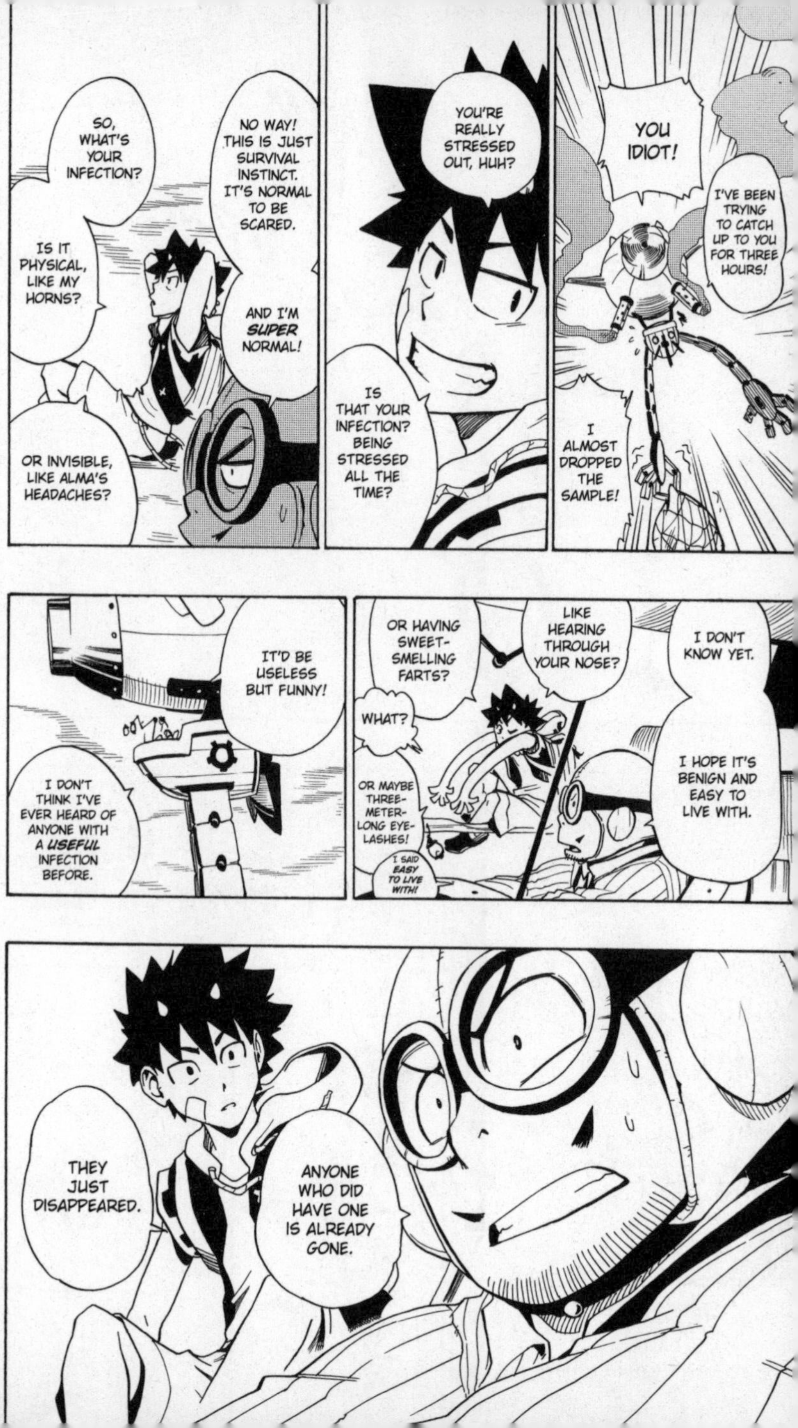
YOU IDIOT!
I'VE BEEN TRYING TO CATCH UP TO YOU FOR THREE HOURS!
I ALMOST DROPPED THE SAMPLE!
YOU'RE REALLY STRESSED OUT, HUH?
IS THAT YOUR INFECTION? BEING STRESSED ALL THE TIME?
NO WAY! THIS IS JUST SURVIVAL INSTINCT. IT'S NORMAL TO BE SCARED.
AND I'M *SUPER* NORMAL!
SO, WHAT'S YOUR INFECTION?
IS IT PHYSICAL, LIKE MY HORNS?
OR INVISIBLE, LIKE ALMA'S HEADACHES?
I DON'T KNOW YET.
I HOPE IT'S BENIGN AND EASY TO LIVE WITH.
LIKE HEARING THROUGH YOUR NOSE?
OR HAVING SWEET-SMELLING FARTS?
WHAT?
OR MAYBE THREE-METER-LONG EYE-LASHES!
I SAID *EASY TO LIVE WITH!*
IT'D BE USELESS BUT FUNNY!
I DON'T THINK I'VE EVER HEARD OF ANYONE WITH A *USEFUL* INFECTION BEFORE.
ANYONE WHO DID HAVE ONE IS ALREADY GONE.
THEY JUST DISAPPEARED.

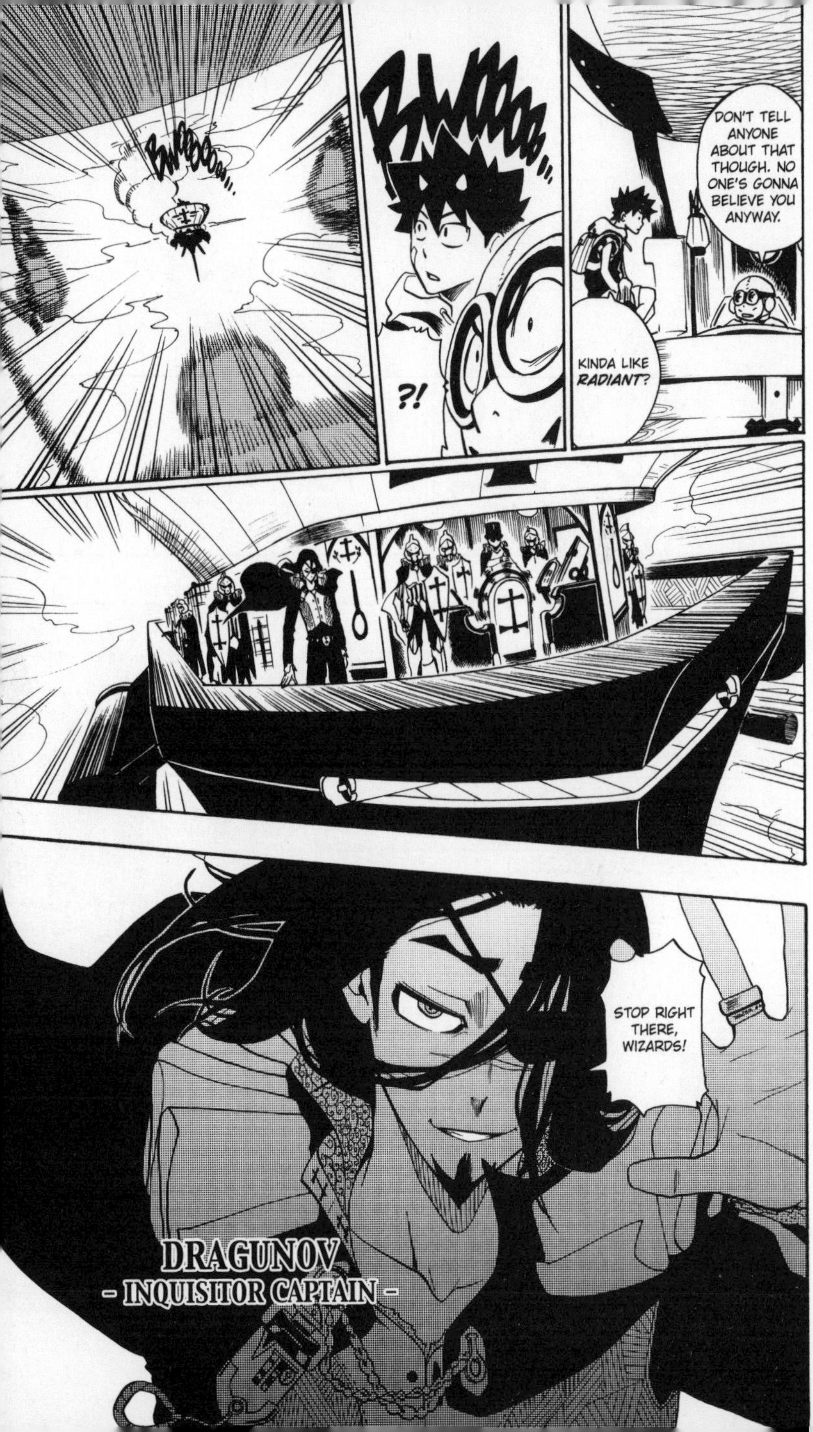
DON'T TELL ANYONE ABOUT THAT THOUGH. NO ONE'S GONNA BELIEVE YOU ANYWAY.
KINDA LIKE *RADIANT*?
BWOOOO...
?!
BWOOOO...
STOP RIGHT THERE, WIZARDS!
DRAGUNOV
- INQUISITOR CAPTAIN -

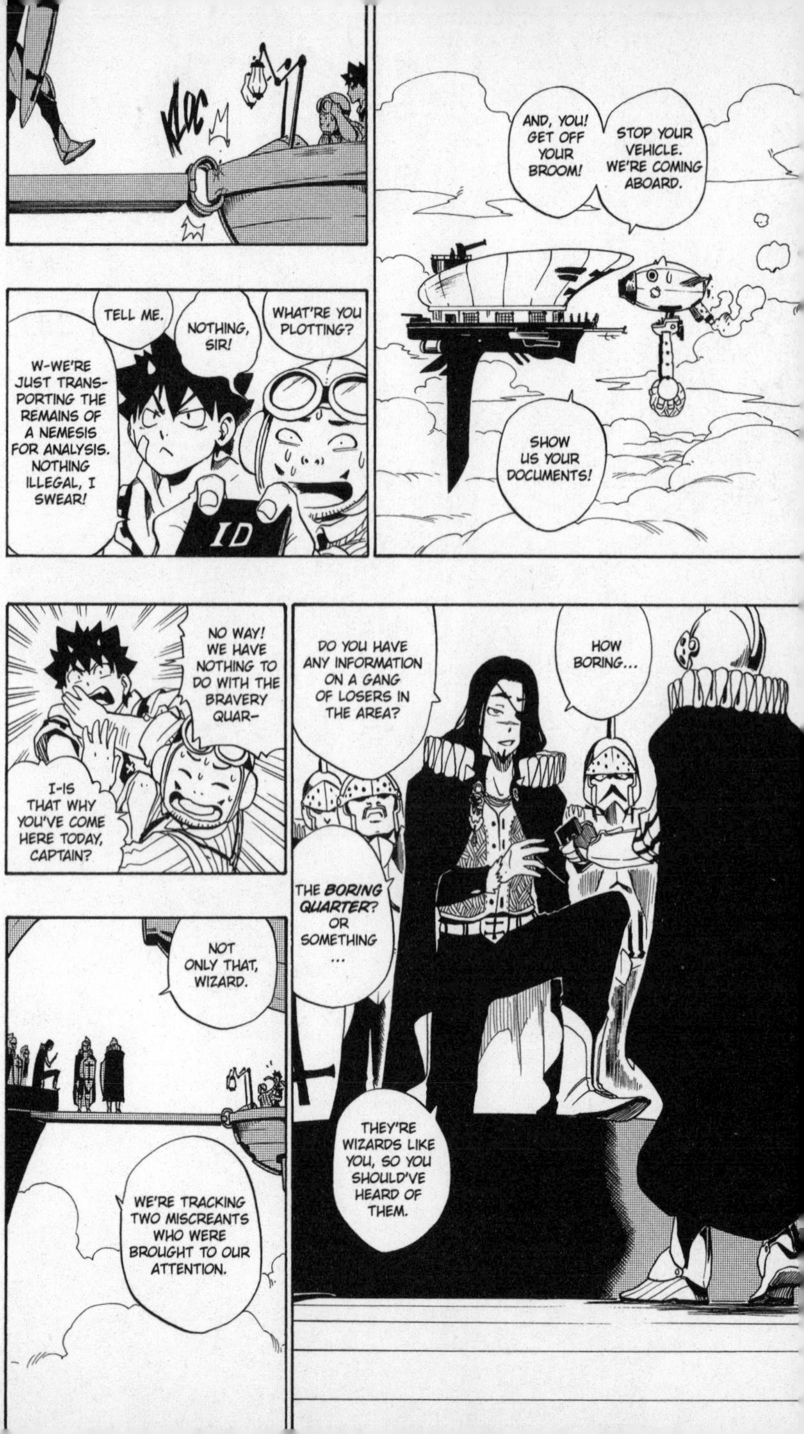
STOP YOUR VEHICLE. WE'RE COMING ABOARD.
AND, YOU! GET OFF YOUR BROOM!
SHOW US YOUR DOCUMENTS!
KLOC
WHAT'RE YOU PLOTTING?
NOTHING, SIR!
TELL ME.
W-WE'RE JUST TRANSPORTING THE REMAINS OF A NEMESIS FOR ANALYSIS. NOTHING ILLEGAL, I SWEAR!
ID
HOW BORING...
DO YOU HAVE ANY INFORMATION ON A GANG OF LOSERS IN THE AREA?
THE *BORING QUARTER*? OR SOMETHING ...
THEY'RE WIZARDS LIKE YOU, SO YOU SHOULD'VE HEARD OF THEM.
NO WAY! WE HAVE NOTHING TO DO WITH THE BRAVERY QUAR-
I-IS THAT WHY YOU'VE COME HERE TODAY, CAPTAIN?
NOT ONLY THAT, WIZARD.
WE'RE TRACKING TWO MISCREANTS WHO WERE BROUGHT TO OUR ATTENTION.

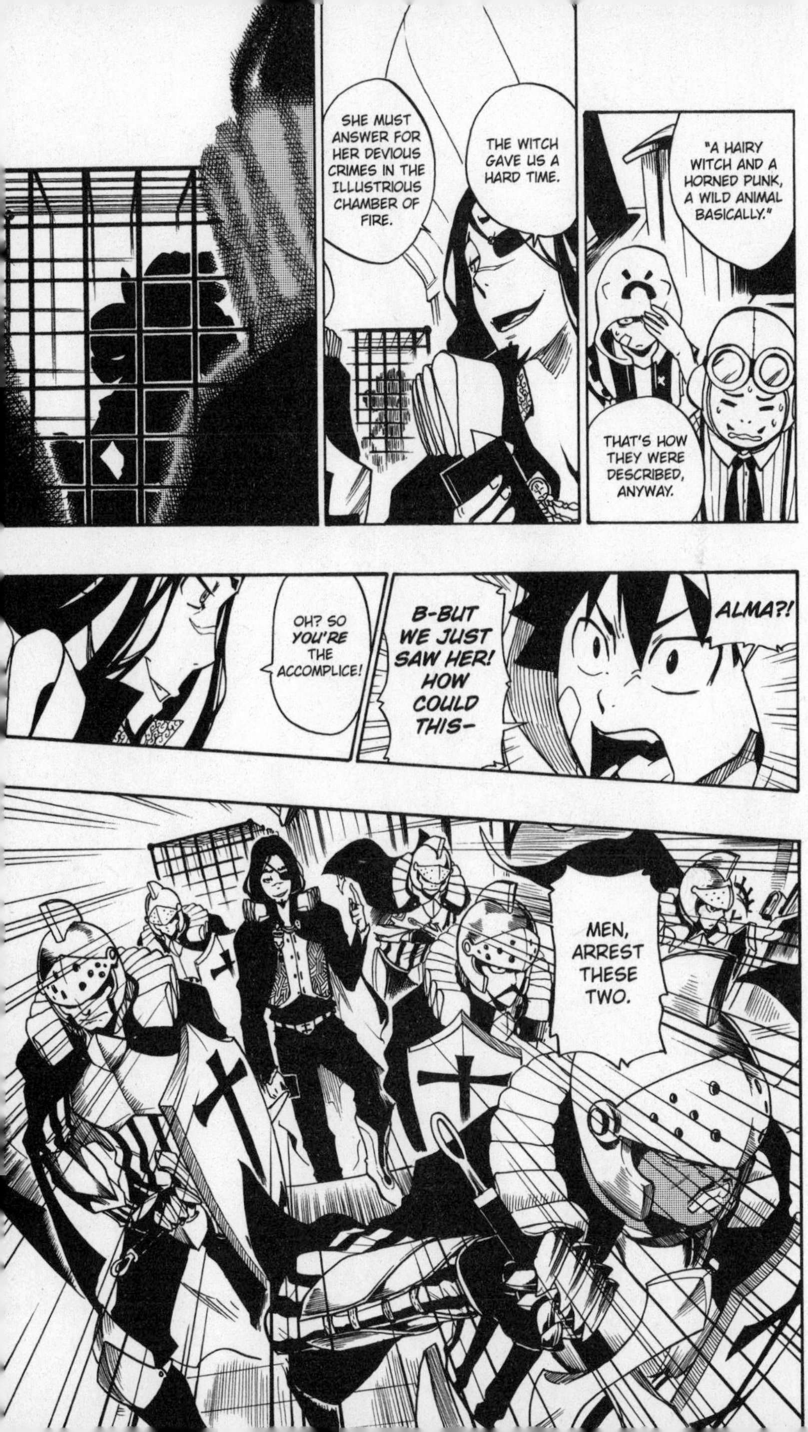
"A HAIRY WITCH AND A HORNED PUNK, A WILD ANIMAL BASICALLY."
THAT'S HOW THEY WERE DESCRIBED, ANYWAY.
THE WITCH GAVE US A HARD TIME.
SHE MUST ANSWER FOR HER DEVIOUS CRIMES IN THE ILLUSTRIOUS CHAMBER OF FIRE.
ALMA?!
B-BUT WE JUST SAW HER! HOW COULD THIS-
OH? SO YOU'RE THE ACCOMPLICE!
MEN, ARREST THESE TWO.

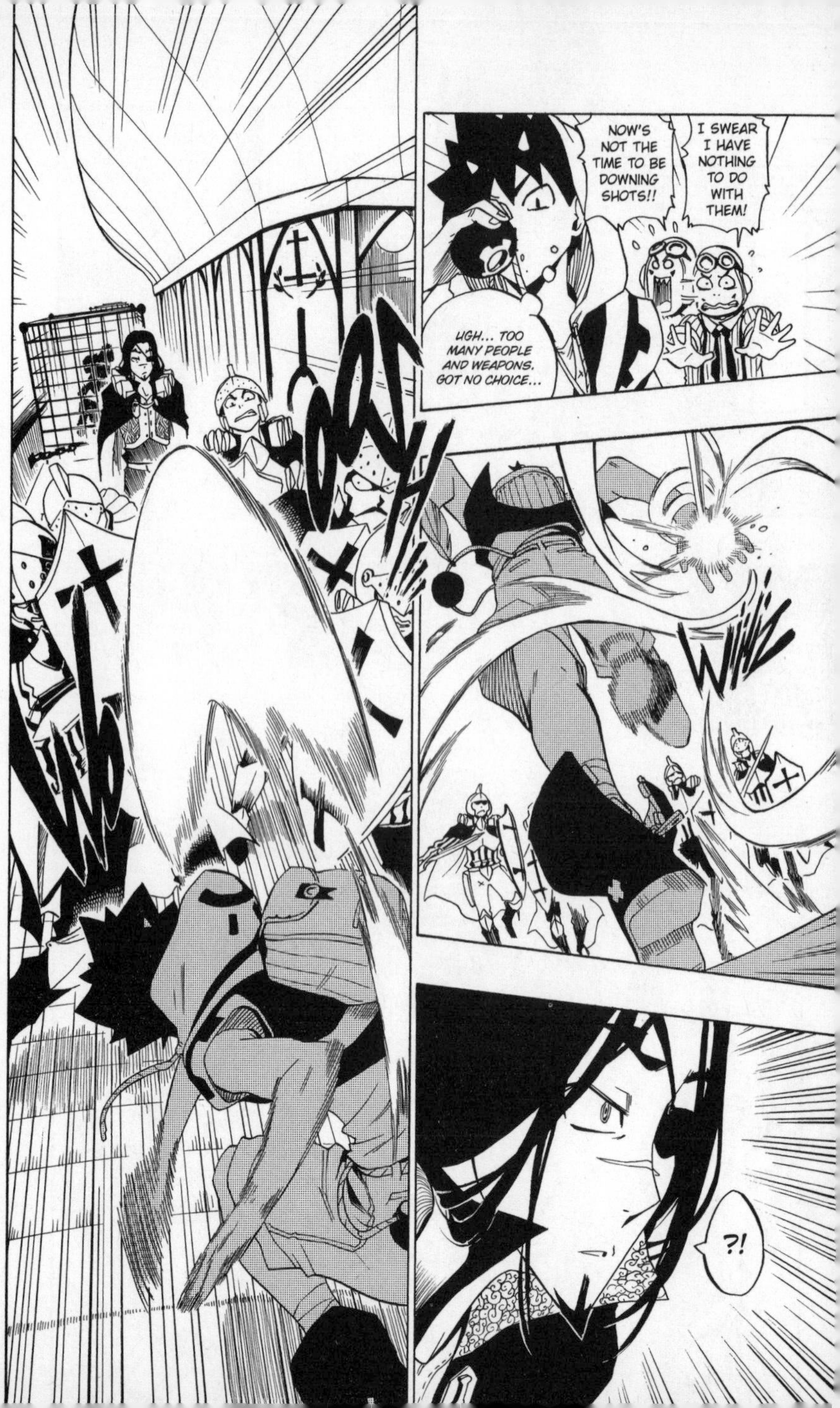
I SWEAR I HAVE NOTHING TO DO WITH THEM!
NOW'S NOT THE TIME TO BE DOWNING SHOTS!!
UGH... TOO MANY PEOPLE AND WEAPONS. GOT NO CHOICE...
?!

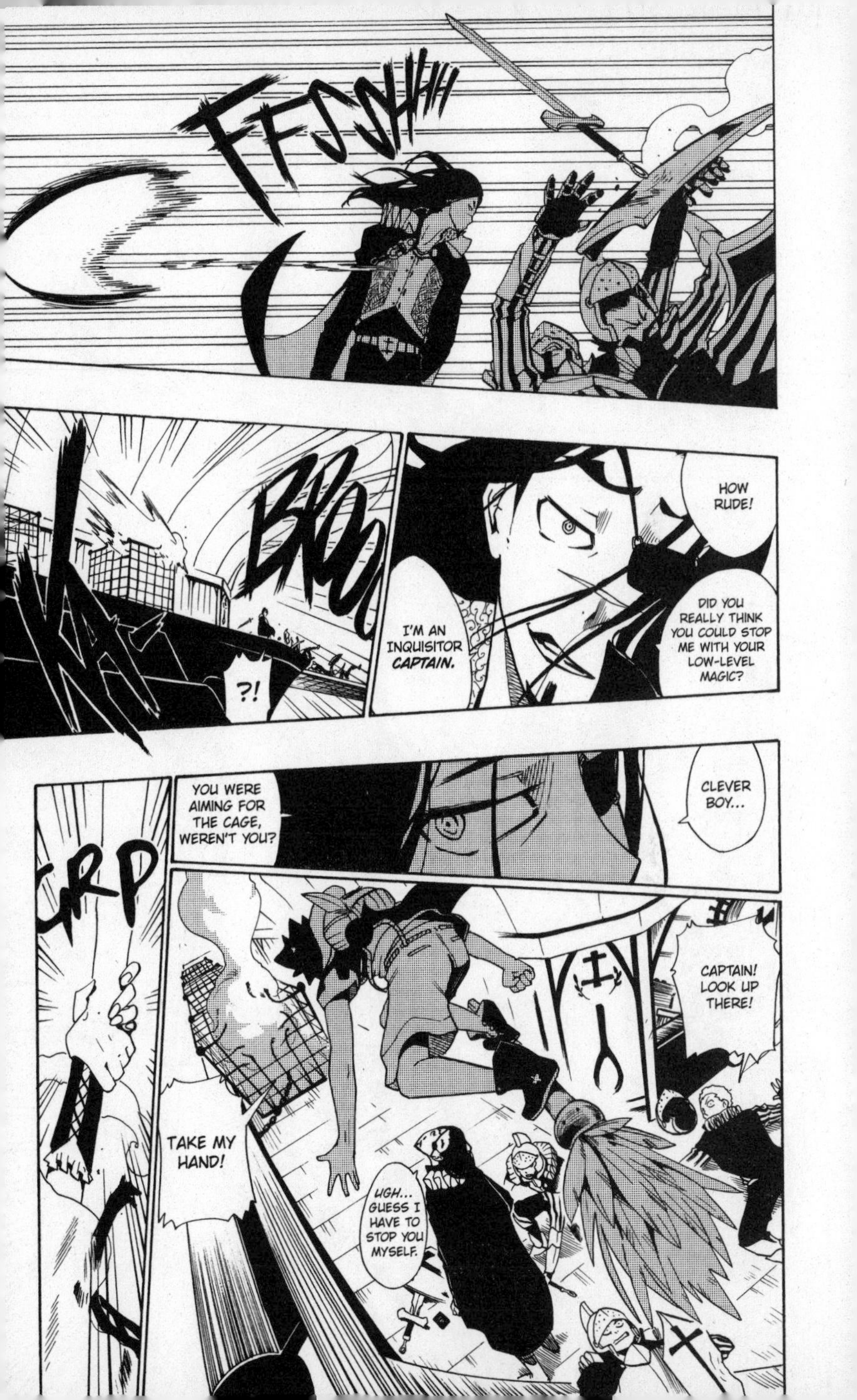
HOW RUDE!
DID YOU REALLY THINK YOU COULD STOP ME WITH YOUR LOW-LEVEL MAGIC?
I'M AN INQUISITOR CAPTAIN.
?!
CLEVER BOY...
YOU WERE AIMING FOR THE CAGE, WEREN'T YOU?
CAPTAIN! LOOK UP THERE!
UGH... GUESS I HAVE TO STOP YOU MYSELF.
TAKE MY HAND!

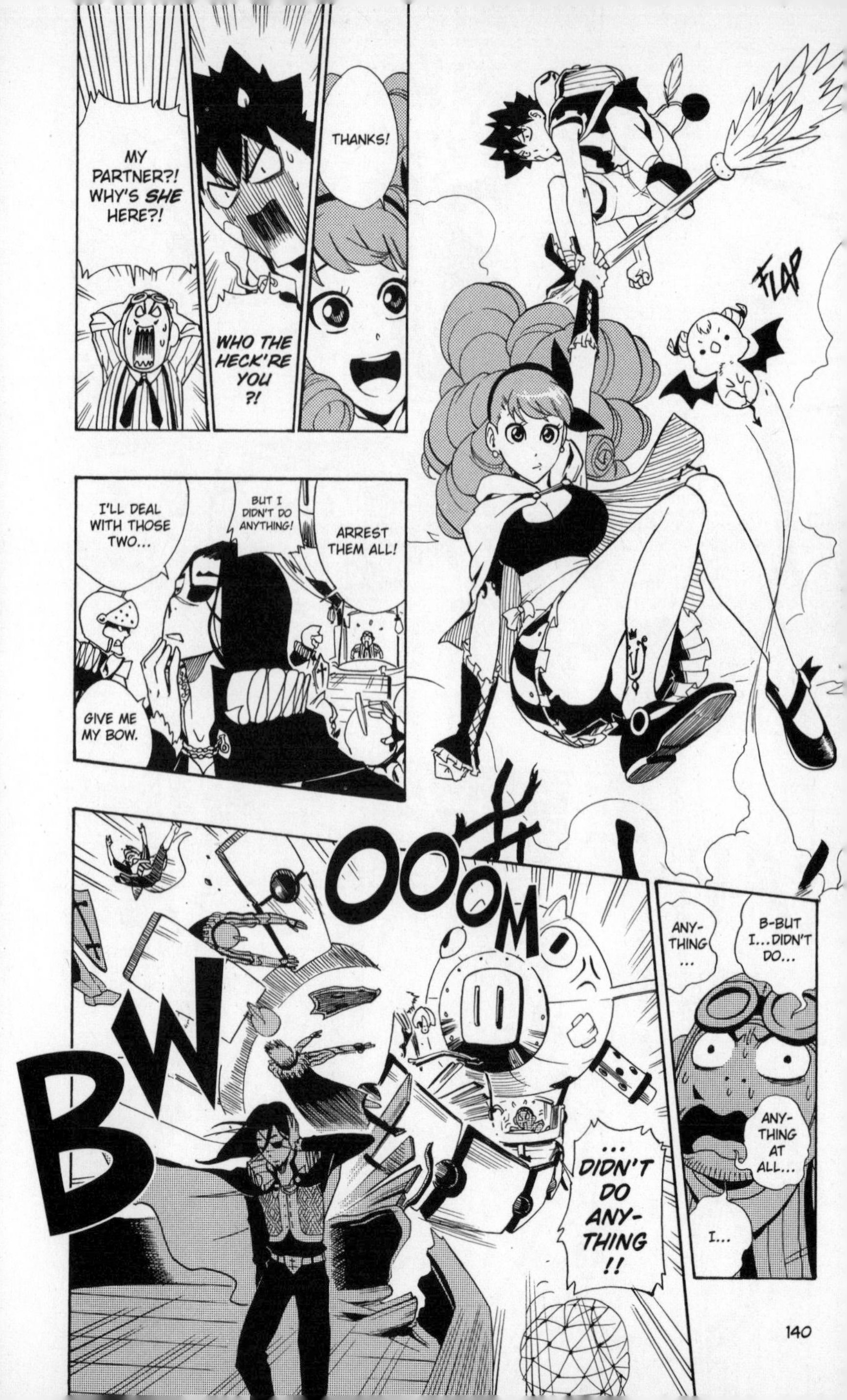
FLAP
THANKS!
WHO THE HECK'RE YOU ?!
MY PARTNER?! WHY'S SHE HERE?!
ARREST THEM ALL!
BUT I DIDN'T DO ANYTHING!
I'LL DEAL WITH THOSE TWO...
GIVE ME MY BOW.
B-BUT I...DIDN'T DO...
ANY-THING ...
ANY-THING AT ALL...
I...
BWOOOM
... DIDN'T DO ANY-THING !!

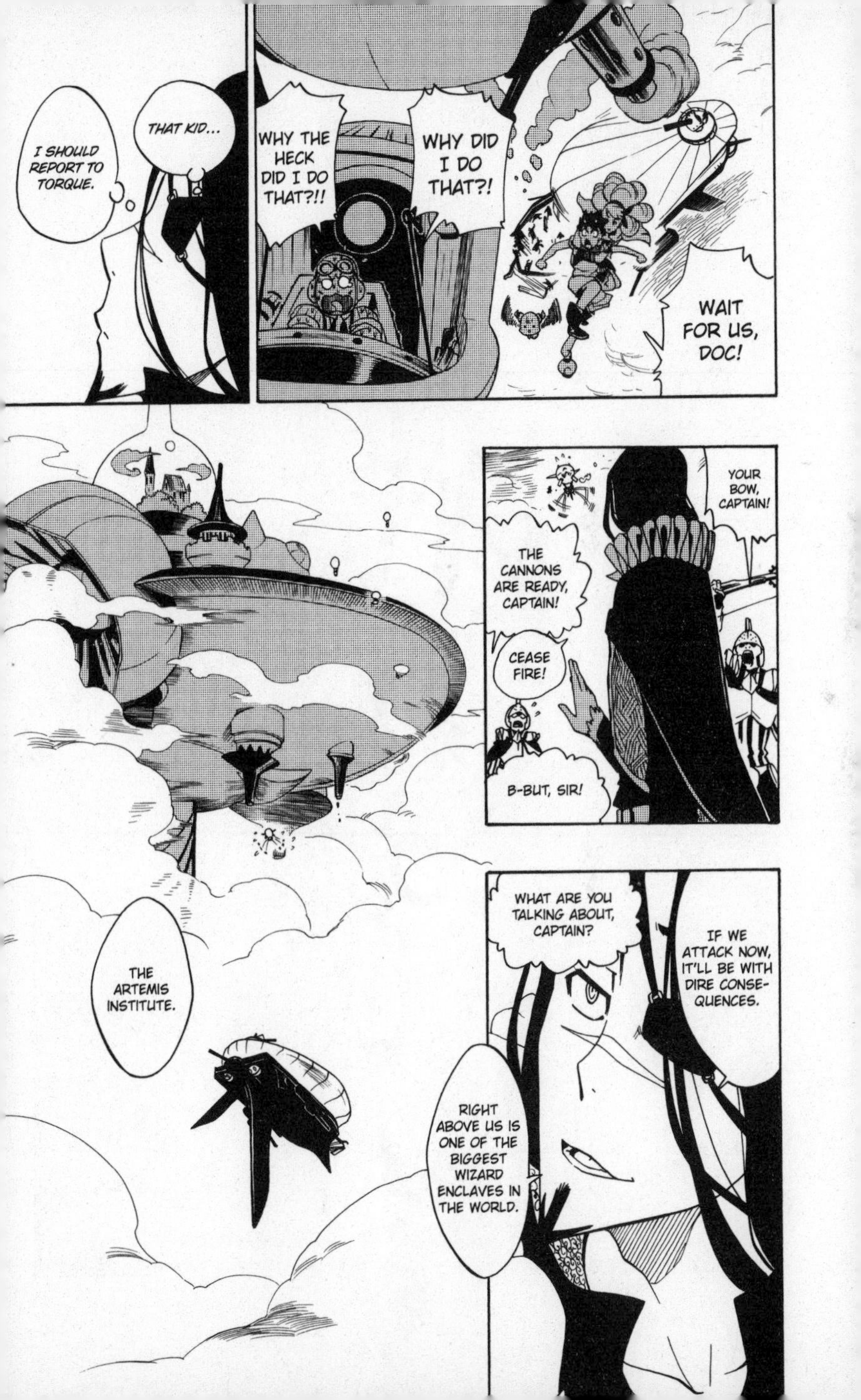
WAIT FOR US, DOC!
WHY DID I DO THAT?!
WHY THE HECK DID I DO THAT?!!
THAT KID...
I SHOULD REPORT TO TORQUE.
YOUR BOW, CAPTAIN!
THE CANNONS ARE READY, CAPTAIN!
CEASE FIRE!
B-BUT, SIR!
WHAT ARE YOU TALKING ABOUT, CAPTAIN?
IF WE ATTACK NOW, IT'LL BE WITH DIRE CONSE-QUENCES.
RIGHT ABOVE US IS ONE OF THE BIGGEST WIZARD ENCLAVES IN THE WORLD.
THE ARTEMIS INSTITUTE.

BLAM

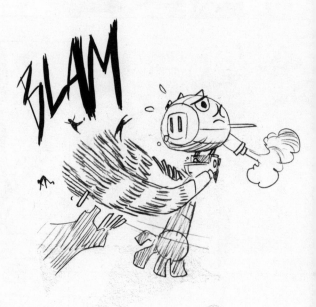

MEANWHILE...

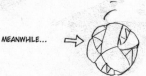

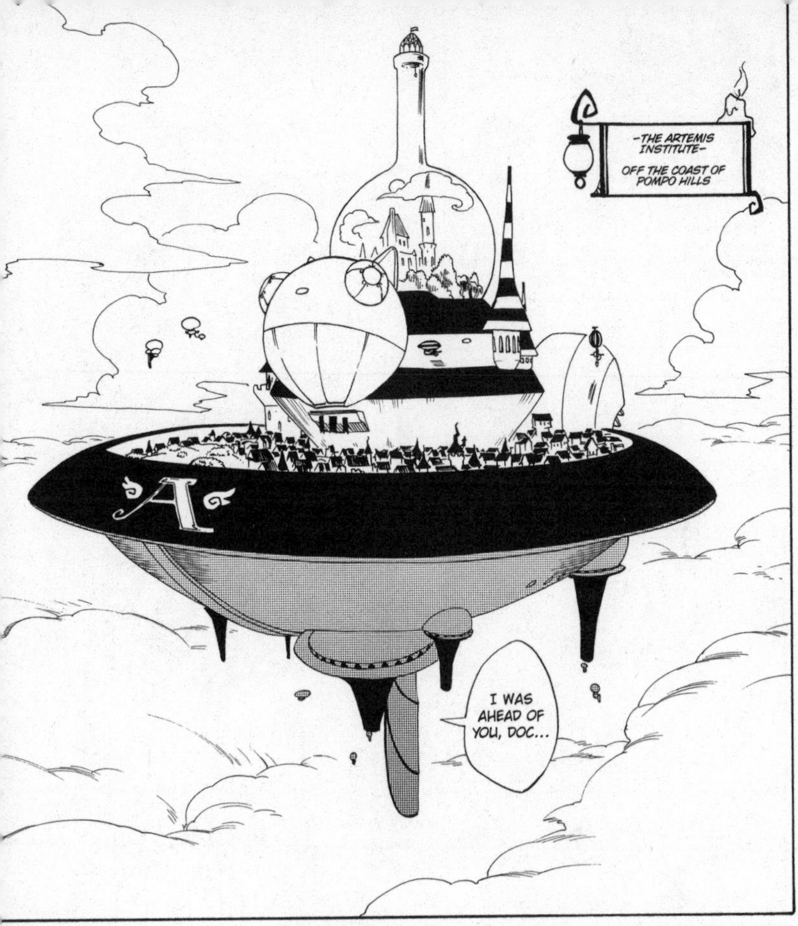
-THE ARTEMIS INSTITUTE-
OFF THE COAST OF POMPO HILLS
I WAS AHEAD OF YOU, DOC...

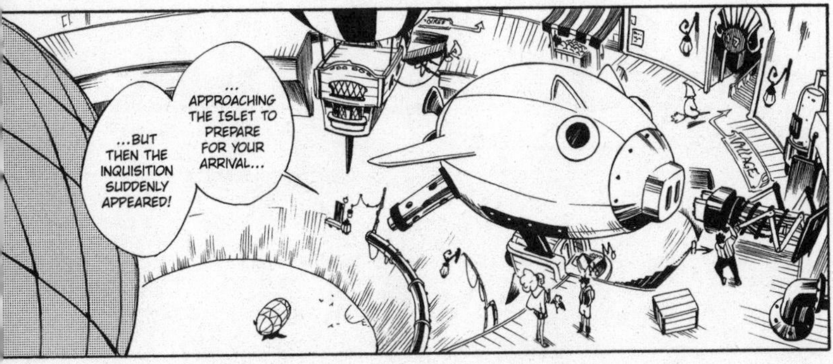
...APPROACHING THE ISLET TO PREPARE FOR YOUR ARRIVAL...
...BUT THEN THE INQUISITION SUDDENLY APPEARED!

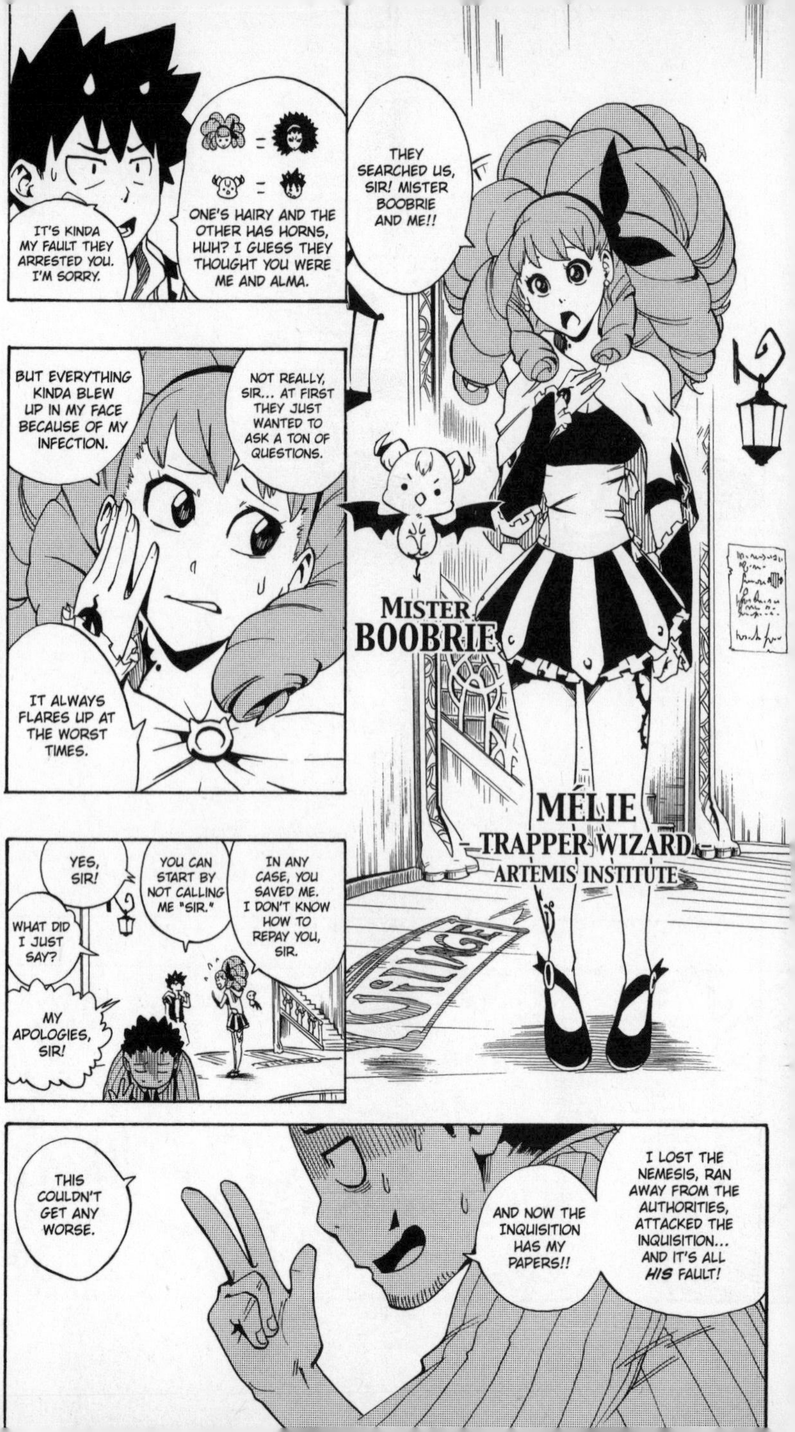
THEY SEARCHED US, SIR! MISTER BOOBRIE AND ME!!
MISTER BOOBRIE
MÉLIE
TRAPPER WIZARD
ARTEMIS INSTITUTE
ONE'S HAIRY AND THE OTHER HAS HORNS, HUH? I GUESS THEY THOUGHT YOU WERE ME AND ALMA.
IT'S KINDA MY FAULT THEY ARRESTED YOU. I'M SORRY.
NOT REALLY, SIR... AT FIRST THEY JUST WANTED TO ASK A TON OF QUESTIONS.
BUT EVERYTHING KINDA BLEW UP IN MY FACE BECAUSE OF MY INFECTION.
IT ALWAYS FLARES UP AT THE WORST TIMES.
IN ANY CASE, YOU SAVED ME. I DON'T KNOW HOW TO REPAY YOU, SIR.
YOU CAN START BY NOT CALLING ME "SIR."
YES, SIR!
WHAT DID I JUST SAY?
MY APOLOGIES, SIR!
I LOST THE NEMESIS, RAN AWAY FROM THE AUTHORITIES, ATTACKED THE INQUISITION... AND IT'S ALL *HIS* FAULT!
AND NOW THE INQUISITION HAS MY PAPERS!!
THIS COULDN'T GET ANY WORSE.

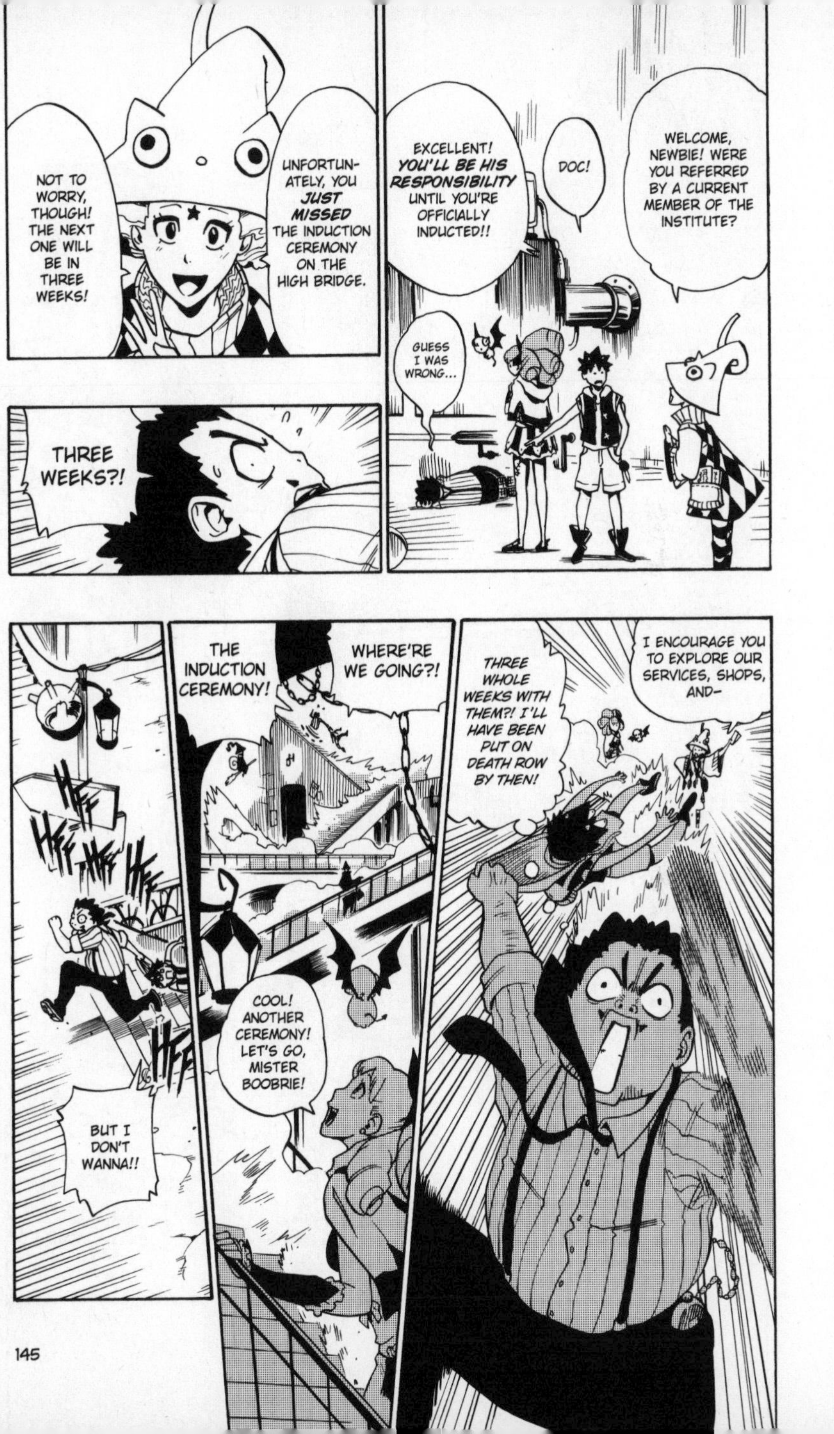
WELCOME, NEWBIE! WERE YOU REFERRED BY A CURRENT MEMBER OF THE INSTITUTE?
DOC!
EXCELLENT! ***YOU'LL BE HIS RESPONSIBILITY*** UNTIL YOU'RE OFFICIALLY INDUCTED!!
GUESS I WAS WRONG...
UNFORTUNATELY, YOU ***JUST MISSED*** THE INDUCTION CEREMONY ON THE HIGH BRIDGE.
NOT TO WORRY, THOUGH! THE NEXT ONE WILL BE IN THREE WEEKS!
THREE WEEKS?!
I ENCOURAGE YOU TO EXPLORE OUR SERVICES, SHOPS, AND–
THREE WHOLE WEEKS WITH THEM?! I'LL HAVE BEEN PUT ON DEATH ROW BY THEN!
WHERE'RE WE GOING?!
THE INDUCTION CEREMONY!
COOL! ANOTHER CEREMONY! LET'S GO, MISTER BOOBRIE!
HFF HFF HFF HFF HFF
HFF
BUT I DON'T WANNA!!

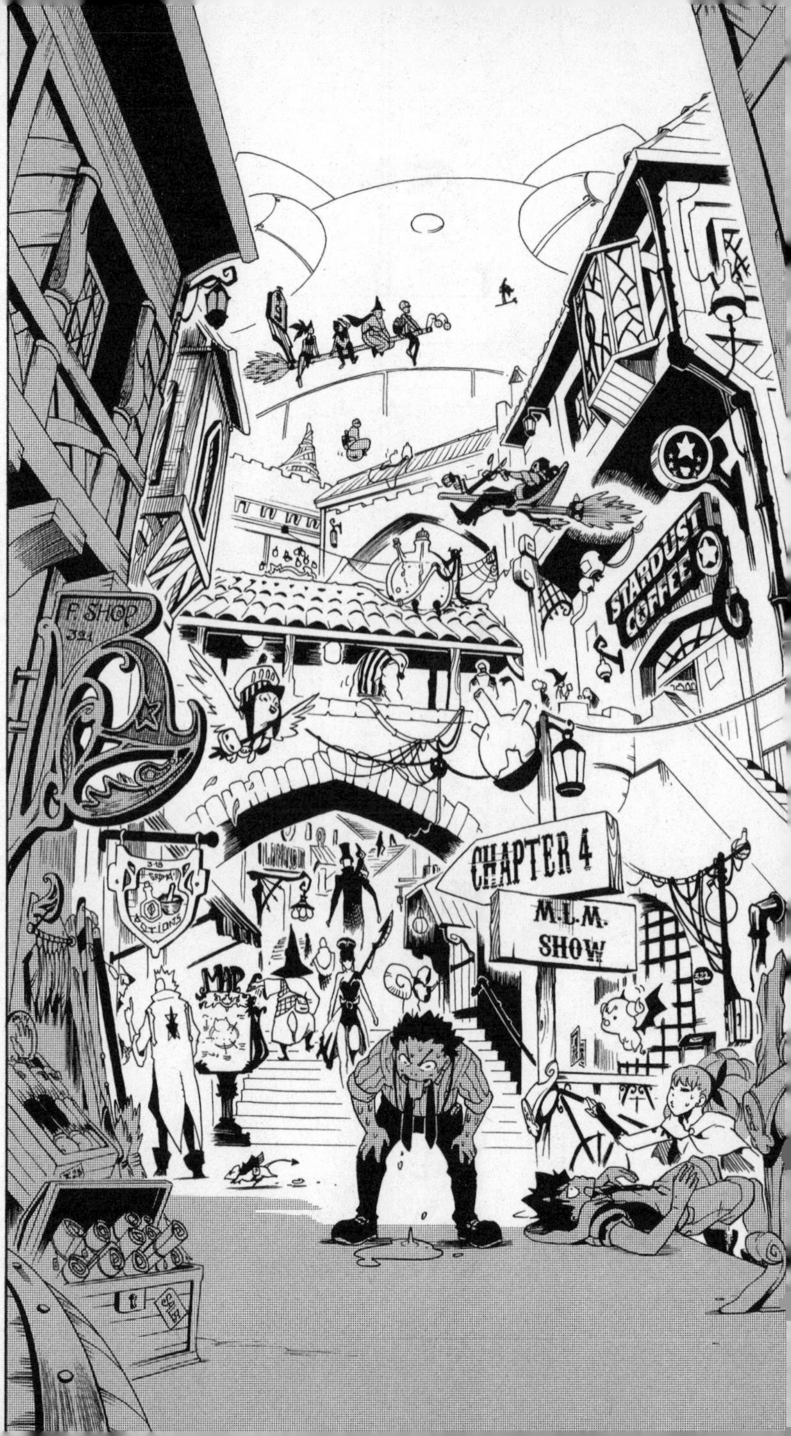
F. SHOP
321
POTIONS
MAP
STARDUST COFFEE
CHAPTER 4
M.L.M. SHOW
322

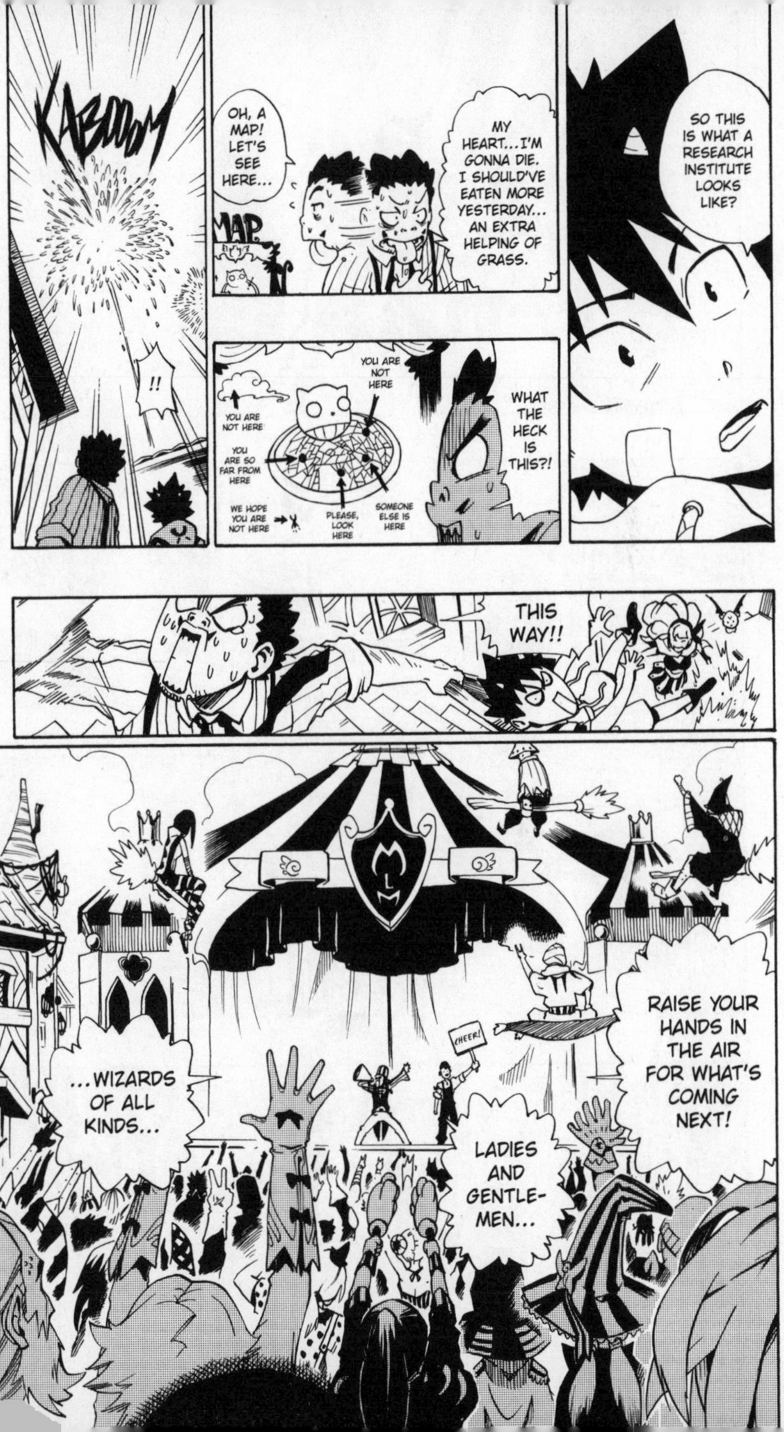
SO THIS IS WHAT A RESEARCH INSTITUTE LOOKS LIKE?
MY HEART...I'M GONNA DIE. I SHOULD'VE EATEN MORE YESTERDAY... AN EXTRA HELPING OF GRASS.
OH, A MAP! LET'S SEE HERE...
MAP
WHAT THE HECK IS THIS?!
YOU ARE NOT HERE
YOU ARE NOT HERE
YOU ARE SO FAR FROM HERE
SOMEONE ELSE IS HERE
PLEASE, LOOK HERE
WE HOPE YOU ARE NOT HERE
KABOOOM
!!
THIS WAY!!
RAISE YOUR HANDS IN THE AIR FOR WHAT'S COMING NEXT!
CHEER!
LADIES AND GENTLE-MEN...
...WIZARDS OF ALL KINDS...

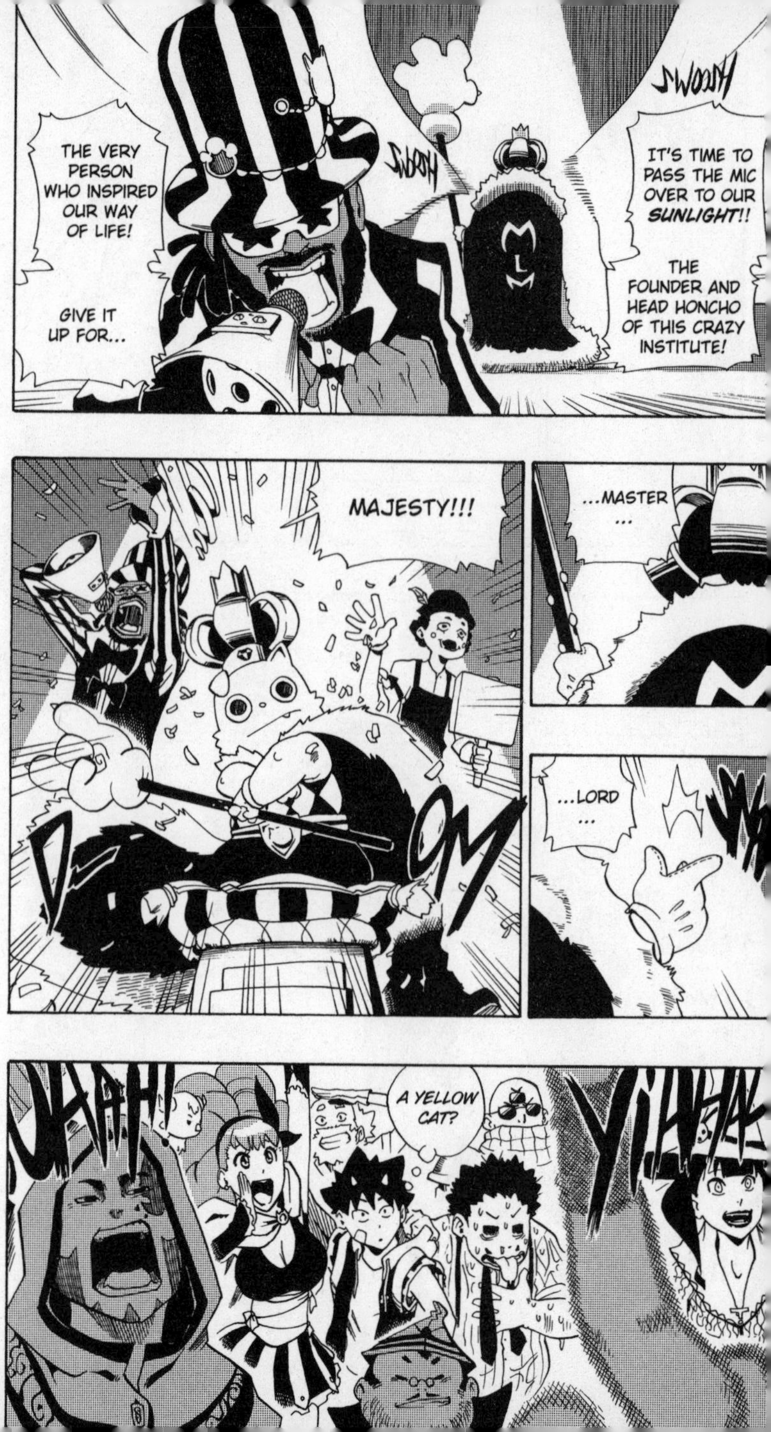

SWOOSH
IT'S TIME TO PASS THE MIC OVER TO OUR *SUNLIGHT!!*
THE FOUNDER AND HEAD HONCHO OF THIS CRAZY INSTITUTE!
SWOOSH
THE VERY PERSON WHO INSPIRED OUR WAY OF LIFE!
GIVE IT UP FOR...
...MASTER ...
...LORD ...
MAJESTY!!!
A YELLOW CAT?

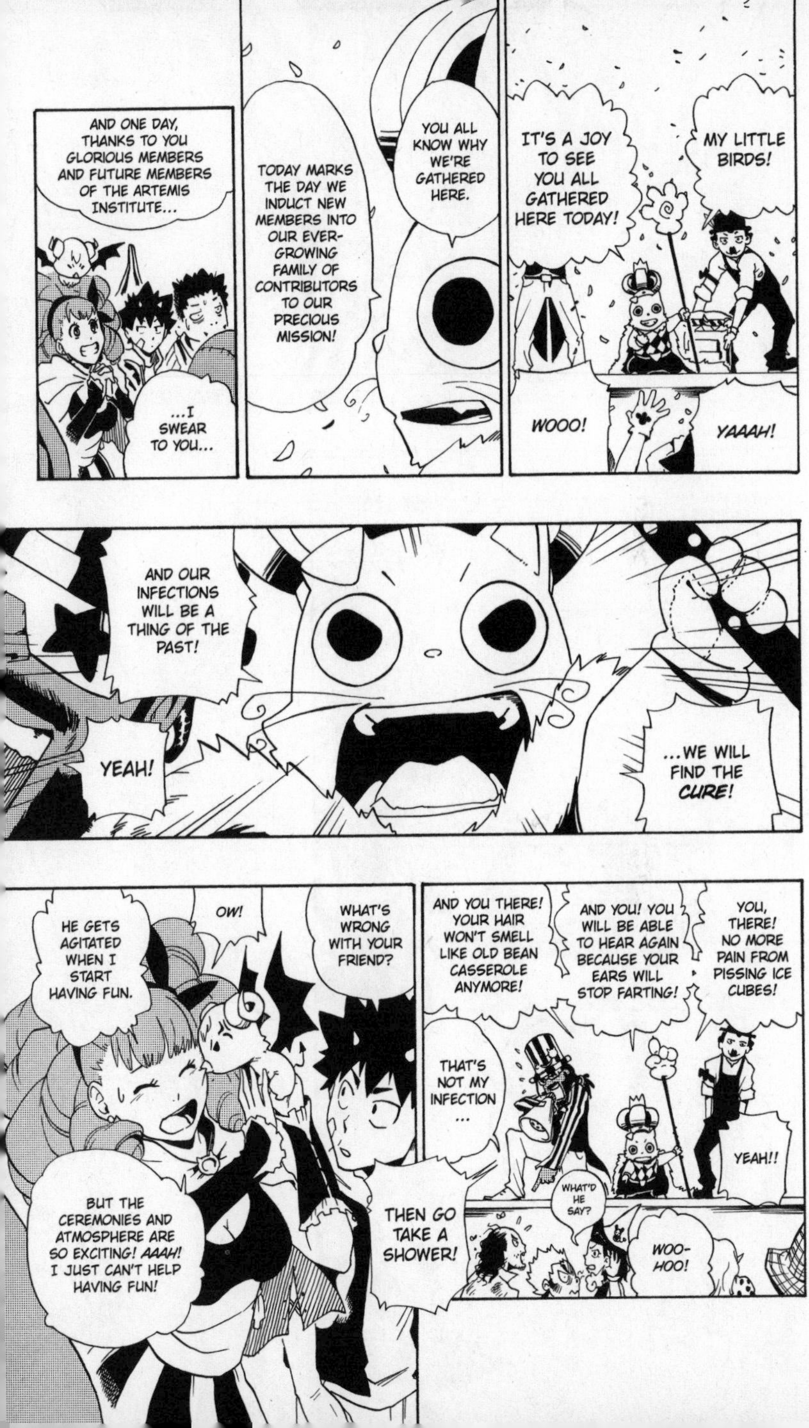
MY LITTLE BIRDS!
IT'S A JOY TO SEE YOU ALL GATHERED HERE TODAY!
YAAAH!
WOOO!
YOU ALL KNOW WHY WE'RE GATHERED HERE.
TODAY MARKS THE DAY WE INDUCT NEW MEMBERS INTO OUR EVER-GROWING FAMILY OF CONTRIBUTORS TO OUR PRECIOUS MISSION!
AND ONE DAY, THANKS TO YOU GLORIOUS MEMBERS AND FUTURE MEMBERS OF THE ARTEMIS INSTITUTE...
...I SWEAR TO YOU...
...WE WILL FIND THE *CURE*!
AND OUR INFECTIONS WILL BE A THING OF THE PAST!
YEAH!
YOU, THERE! NO MORE PAIN FROM PISSING ICE CUBES!
AND YOU! YOU WILL BE ABLE TO HEAR AGAIN BECAUSE YOUR EARS WILL STOP FARTING!
AND YOU THERE! YOUR HAIR WON'T SMELL LIKE OLD BEAN CASSEROLE ANYMORE!
THAT'S NOT MY INFECTION ...
YEAH!!
WHAT'D HE SAY?
WOO-HOO!
THEN GO TAKE A SHOWER!
WHAT'S WRONG WITH YOUR FRIEND?
OW!
HE GETS AGITATED WHEN I START HAVING FUN.
BUT THE CEREMONIES AND ATMOSPHERE ARE SO EXCITING! *AAAH!* I JUST CAN'T HELP HAVING FUN!

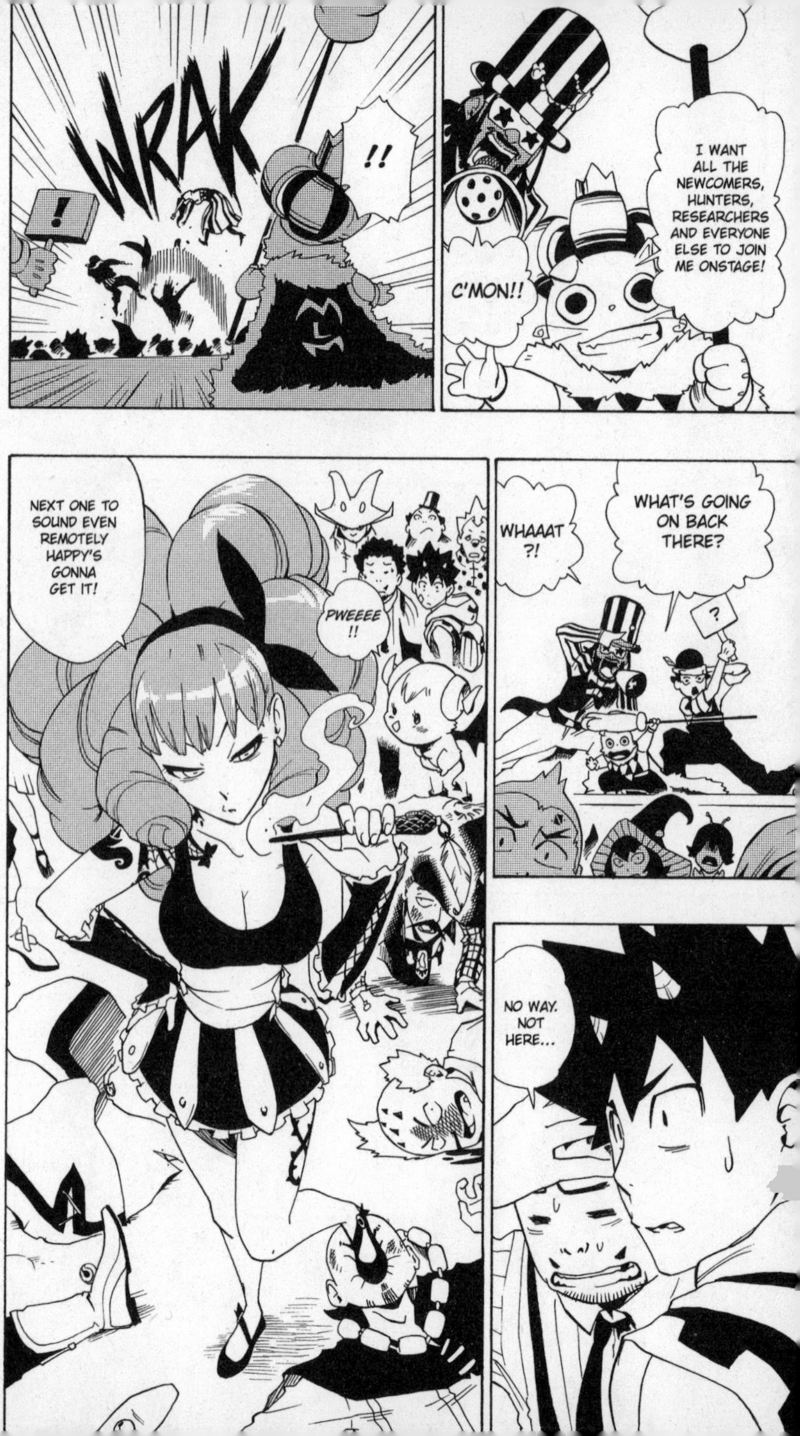
I WANT ALL THE NEWCOMERS, HUNTERS, RESEARCHERS AND EVERYONE ELSE TO JOIN ME ONSTAGE!
C'MON!!
!!
WRAK
!
WHAT'S GOING ON BACK THERE?
WHAAAT ?!
?
NO WAY. NOT HERE...
NEXT ONE TO SOUND EVEN REMOTELY HAPPY'S GONNA GET IT!
PWEEEE !!

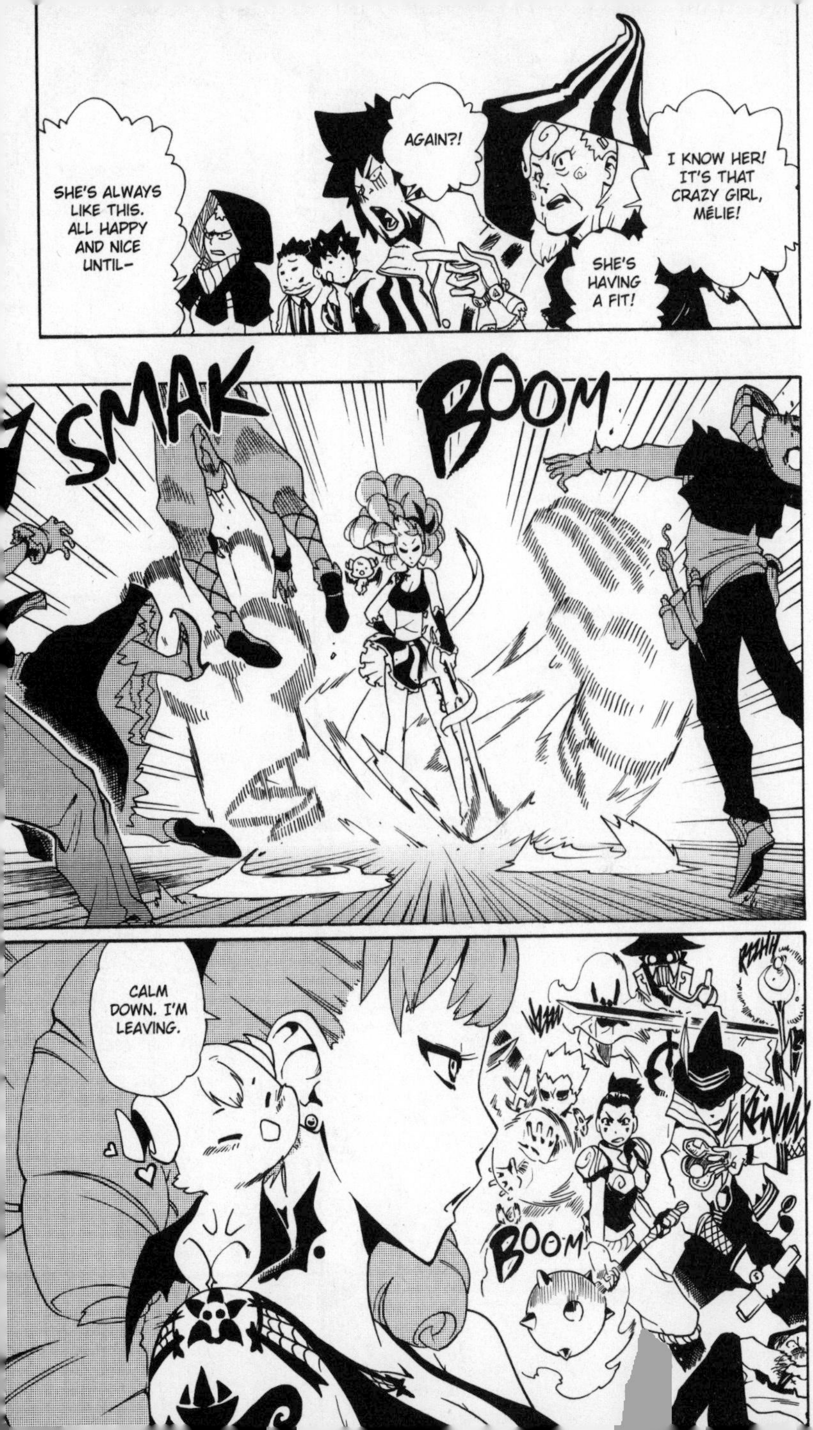
I KNOW HER! IT'S THAT CRAZY GIRL, MÉLIE!
SHE'S HAVING A FIT!
AGAIN?!
SHE'S ALWAYS LIKE THIS. ALL HAPPY AND NICE UNTIL-
BOOM
SMAK
BOOM
CALM DOWN. I'M LEAVING.

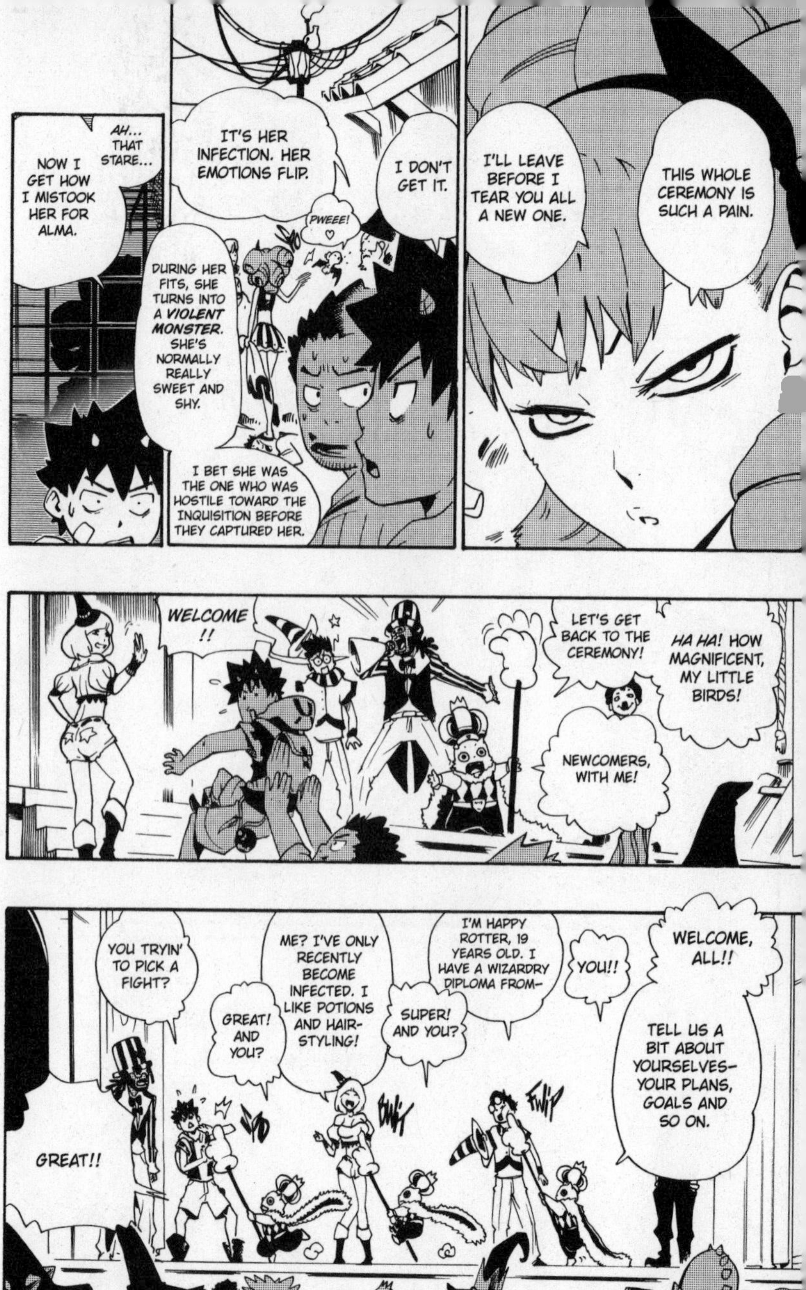
THIS WHOLE CEREMONY IS SUCH A PAIN.
I'LL LEAVE BEFORE I TEAR YOU ALL A NEW ONE.
I DON'T GET IT.
IT'S HER INFECTION. HER EMOTIONS FLIP.
PWEEE!
DURING HER FITS, SHE TURNS INTO A *VIOLENT MONSTER*. SHE'S NORMALLY REALLY SWEET AND SHY.
I BET SHE WAS THE ONE WHO WAS HOSTILE TOWARD THE INQUISITION BEFORE THEY CAPTURED HER.
AH... THAT STARE...
NOW I GET HOW I MISTOOK HER FOR ALMA.
HA HA! HOW MAGNIFICENT, MY LITTLE BIRDS!
LET'S GET BACK TO THE CEREMONY!
NEWCOMERS, WITH ME!
WELCOME!!
WELCOME, ALL!!
TELL US A BIT ABOUT YOURSELVES- YOUR PLANS, GOALS AND SO ON.
YOU!!
I'M HAPPY ROTTER, 19 YEARS OLD. I HAVE A WIZARDRY DIPLOMA FROM-
FWIP
SUPER! AND YOU?
ME? I'VE ONLY RECENTLY BECOME INFECTED. I LIKE POTIONS AND HAIR-STYLING!
GREAT! AND YOU?
YOU TRYIN' TO PICK A FIGHT?
GREAT!!

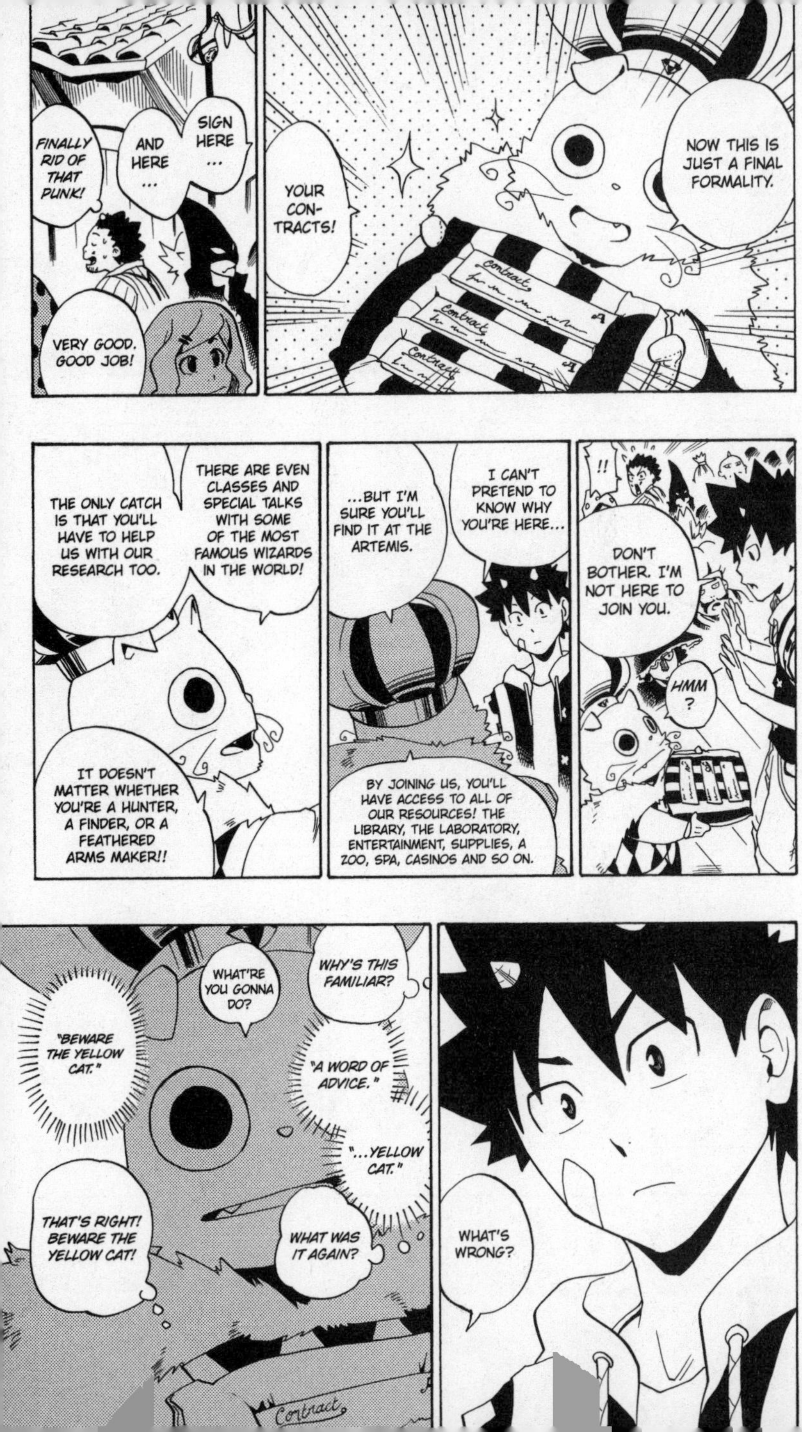
NOW THIS IS JUST A FINAL FORMALITY.
YOUR CONTRACTS!
SIGN HERE...
AND HERE...
FINALLY RID OF THAT PUNK!
VERY GOOD. GOOD JOB!
!!
DON'T BOTHER. I'M NOT HERE TO JOIN YOU.
HMM?
I CAN'T PRETEND TO KNOW WHY YOU'RE HERE...
...BUT I'M SURE YOU'LL FIND IT AT THE ARTEMIS.
BY JOINING US, YOU'LL HAVE ACCESS TO ALL OF OUR RESOURCES! THE LIBRARY, THE LABORATORY, ENTERTAINMENT, SUPPLIES, A ZOO, SPA, CASINOS AND SO ON.
THERE ARE EVEN CLASSES AND SPECIAL TALKS WITH SOME OF THE MOST FAMOUS WIZARDS IN THE WORLD!
THE ONLY CATCH IS THAT YOU'LL HAVE TO HELP US WITH OUR RESEARCH TOO.
IT DOESN'T MATTER WHETHER YOU'RE A HUNTER, A FINDER, OR A FEATHERED ARMS MAKER!!
WHAT'S WRONG?
WHY'S THIS FAMILIAR?
WHAT'RE YOU GONNA DO?
"A WORD OF ADVICE."
"BEWARE THE YELLOW CAT."
"...YELLOW CAT."
WHAT WAS IT AGAIN?
THAT'S RIGHT! BEWARE THE YELLOW CAT!

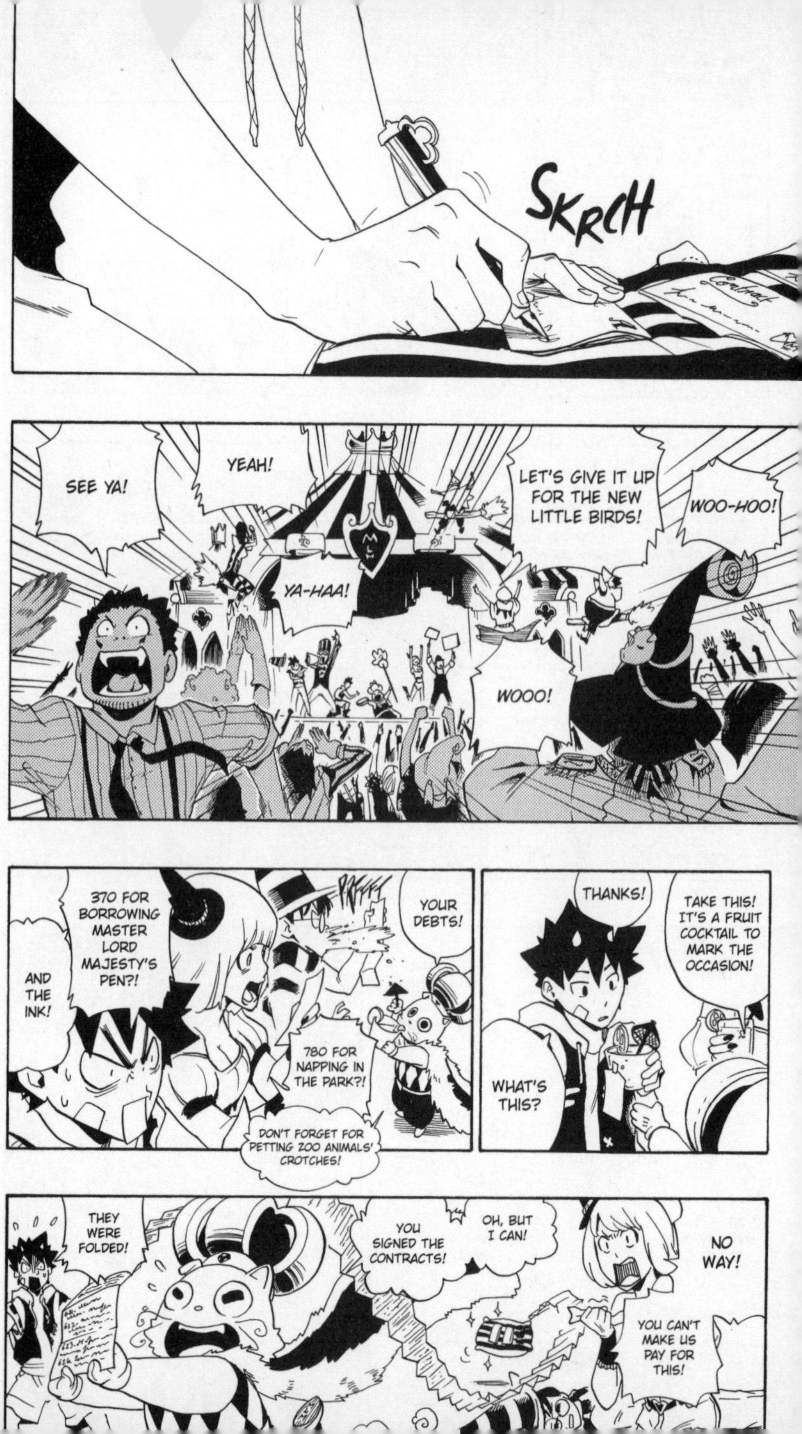
SKRCH
WOO-HOO!
LET'S GIVE IT UP FOR THE NEW LITTLE BIRDS!
YEAH!
SEE YA!
YA-HAA!
WOOO!
TAKE THIS! IT'S A FRUIT COCKTAIL TO MARK THE OCCASION!
THANKS!
WHAT'S THIS?
YOUR DEBTS!
370 FOR BORROWING MASTER LORD MAJESTY'S PEN?!
AND THE INK!
780 FOR NAPPING IN THE PARK?!
DON'T FORGET FOR PETTING ZOO ANIMALS' CROTCHES!
NO WAY!
YOU CAN'T MAKE US PAY FOR THIS!
OH, BUT I CAN!
YOU SIGNED THE CONTRACTS!
THEY WERE FOLDED!

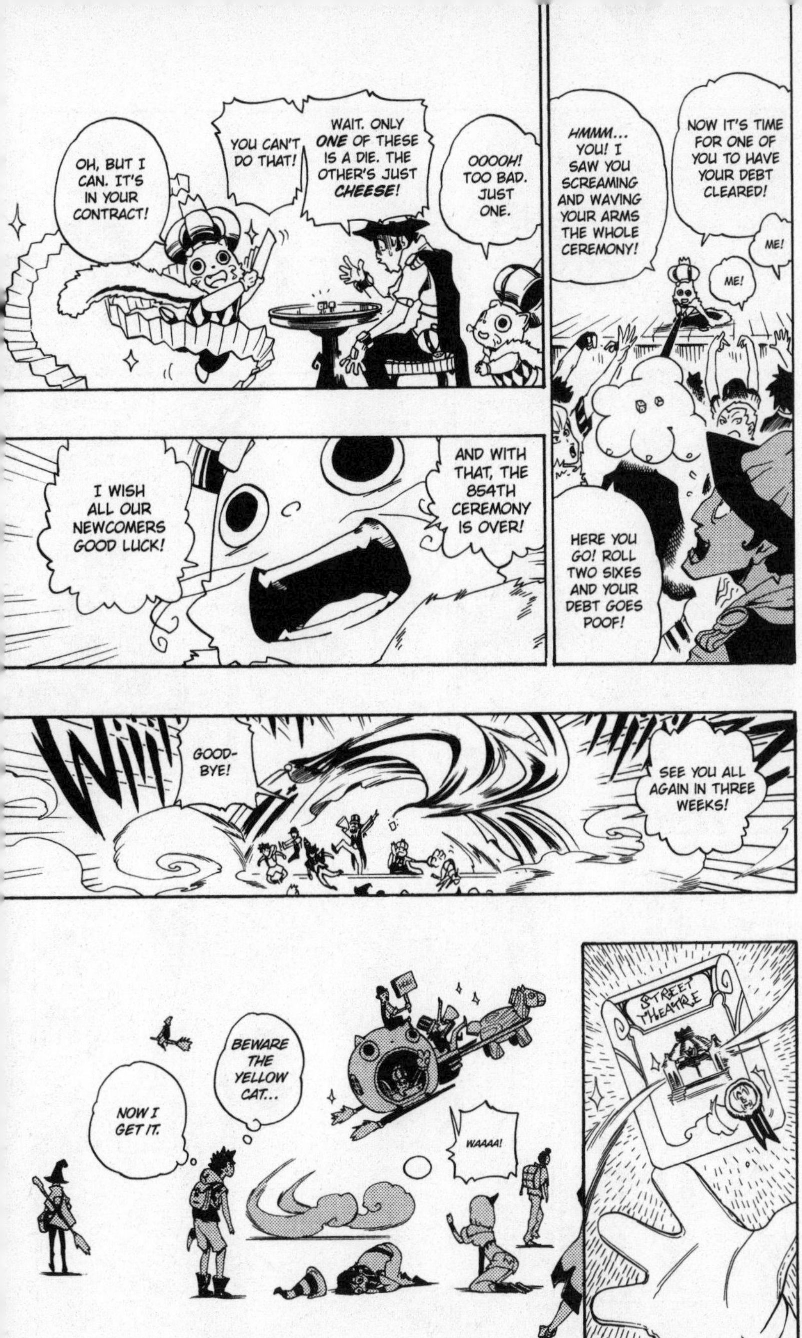
NOW IT'S TIME FOR ONE OF YOU TO HAVE YOUR DEBT CLEARED!
HMMM... YOU! I SAW YOU SCREAMING AND WAVING YOUR ARMS THE WHOLE CEREMONY!
ME!
ME!
HERE YOU GO! ROLL TWO SIXES AND YOUR DEBT GOES POOF!
OOOOH! TOO BAD. JUST ONE.
WAIT. ONLY *ONE* OF THESE IS A DIE. THE OTHER'S JUST *CHEESE*!
YOU CAN'T DO THAT!
OH, BUT I CAN. IT'S IN YOUR CONTRACT!
AND WITH THAT, THE 854TH CEREMONY IS OVER!
I WISH ALL OUR NEWCOMERS GOOD LUCK!
SEE YOU ALL AGAIN IN THREE WEEKS!
GOOD-BYE!
STREET THEATRE
WAAAA!
BEWARE THE YELLOW CAT...
NOW I GET IT.

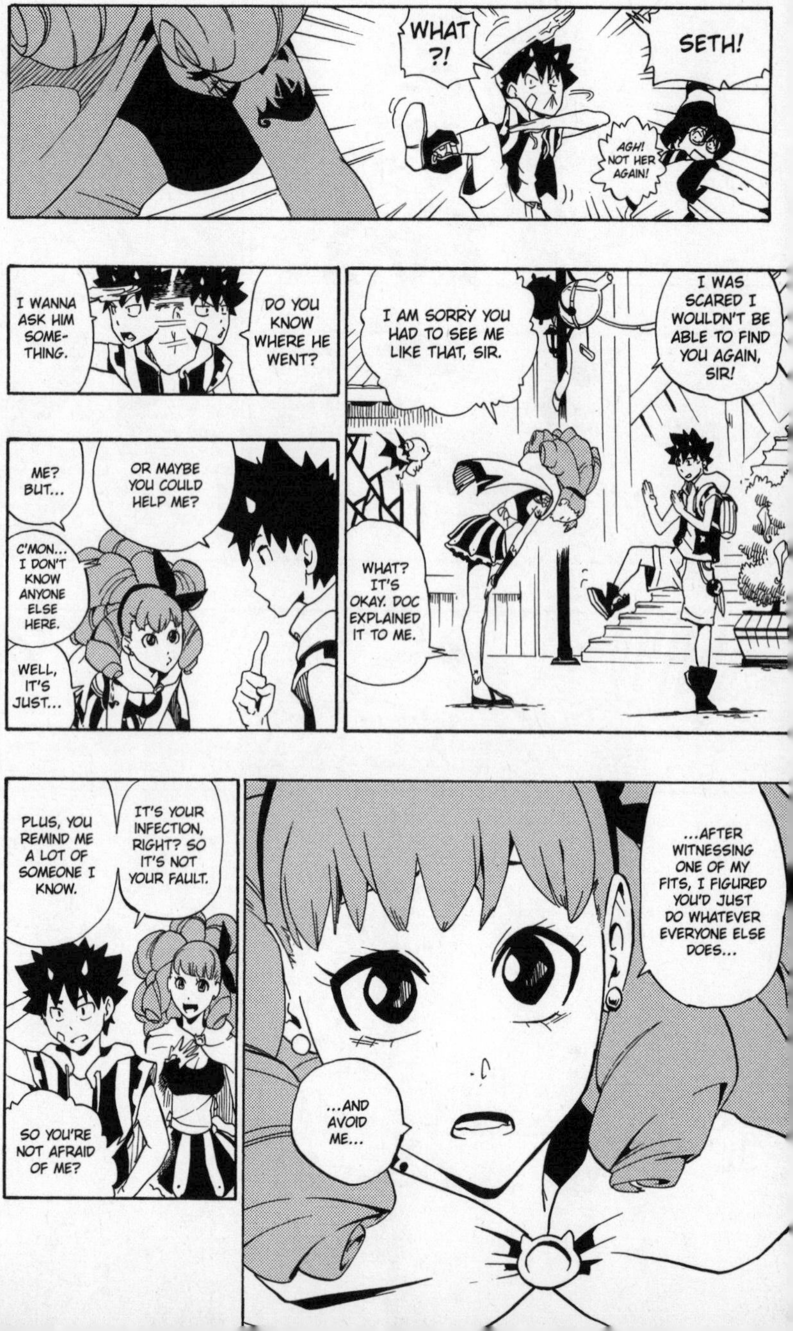
SETH!
AGH! NOT HER AGAIN!
WHAT ?!
I WAS SCARED I WOULDN'T BE ABLE TO FIND YOU AGAIN, SIR!
I AM SORRY YOU HAD TO SEE ME LIKE THAT, SIR.
WHAT? IT'S OKAY. DOC EXPLAINED IT TO ME.
DO YOU KNOW WHERE HE WENT?
I WANNA ASK HIM SOME-THING.
OR MAYBE YOU COULD HELP ME?
ME? BUT...
C'MON... I DON'T KNOW ANYONE ELSE HERE.
WELL, IT'S JUST...
...AFTER WITNESSING ONE OF MY FITS, I FIGURED YOU'D JUST DO WHATEVER EVERYONE ELSE DOES...
...AND AVOID ME...
IT'S YOUR INFECTION, RIGHT? SO IT'S NOT YOUR FAULT.
PLUS, YOU REMIND ME A LOT OF SOMEONE I KNOW.
SO YOU'RE NOT AFRAID OF ME?

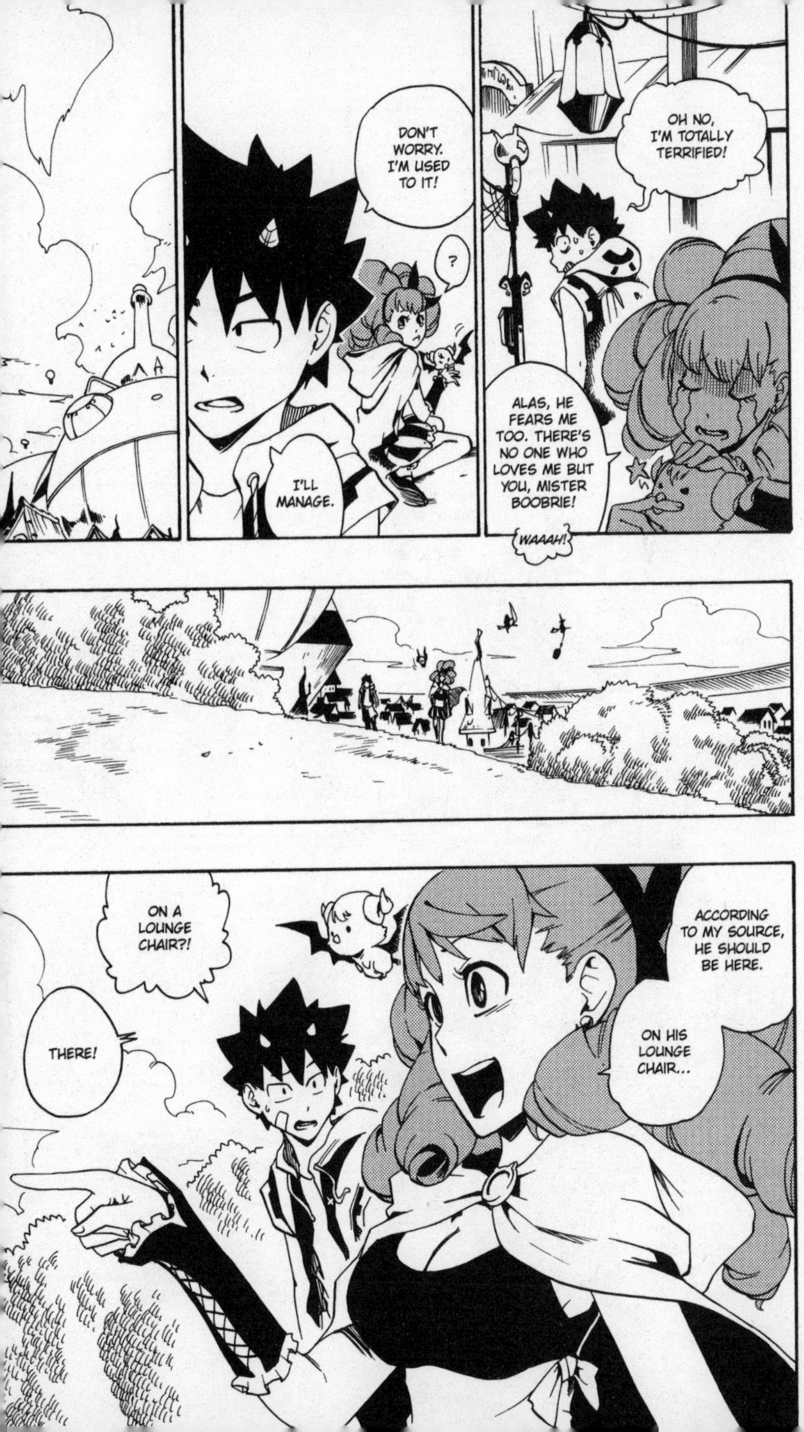
OH NO, I'M TOTALLY TERRIFIED!
ALAS, HE FEARS ME TOO. THERE'S NO ONE WHO LOVES ME BUT YOU, MISTER BOOBRIE!
WAAAH!
DON'T WORRY. I'M USED TO IT!
?
I'LL MANAGE.
ACCORDING TO MY SOURCE, HE SHOULD BE HERE.
ON HIS LOUNGE CHAIR...
ON A LOUNGE CHAIR?!
THERE!

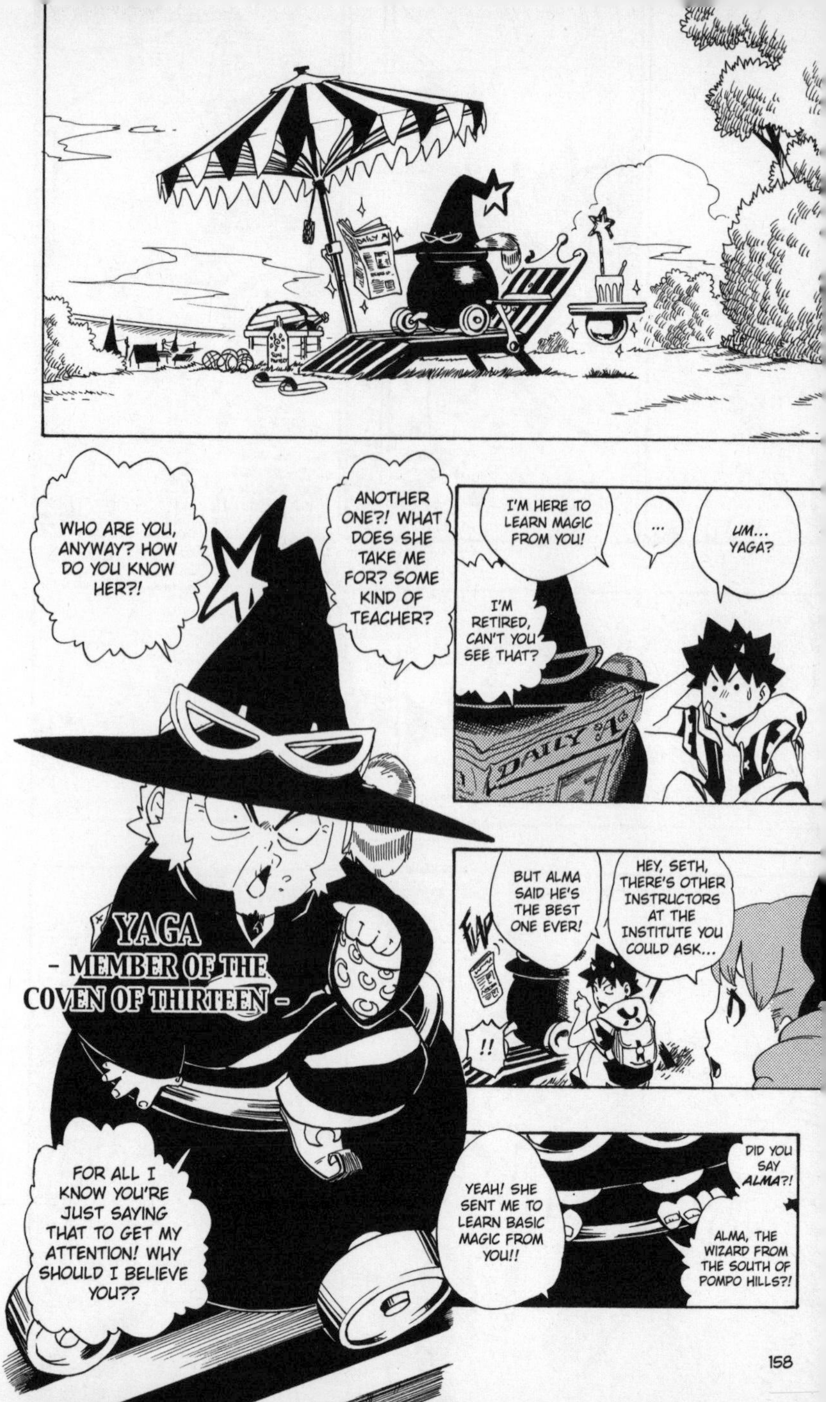
UM... YAGA?
...
I'M HERE TO LEARN MAGIC FROM YOU!
I'M RETIRED, CAN'T YOU SEE THAT?
HEY, SETH, THERE'S OTHER INSTRUCTORS AT THE INSTITUTE YOU COULD ASK...
BUT ALMA SAID HE'S THE BEST ONE EVER!
FLAP
!!
DID YOU SAY *ALMA*?!
ALMA, THE WIZARD FROM THE SOUTH OF POMPO HILLS?!
YEAH! SHE SENT ME TO LEARN BASIC MAGIC FROM YOU!!
ANOTHER ONE?! WHAT DOES SHE TAKE ME FOR? SOME KIND OF TEACHER?
WHO ARE YOU, ANYWAY? HOW DO YOU KNOW HER?!
YAGA
- MEMBER OF THE COVEN OF THIRTEEN -
FOR ALL I KNOW YOU'RE JUST SAYING THAT TO GET MY ATTENTION! WHY SHOULD I BELIEVE YOU??

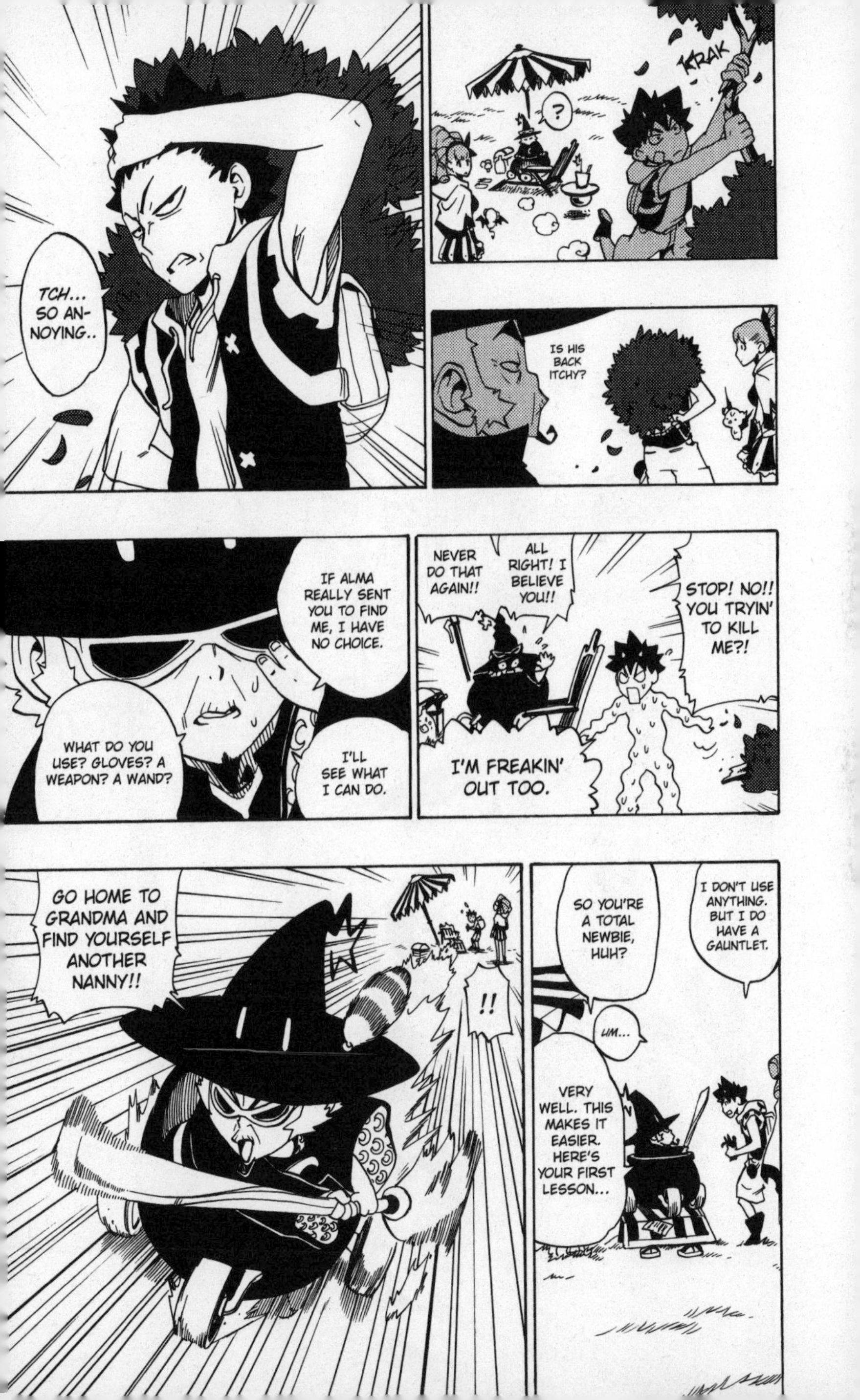
KRAK
?
IS HIS BACK ITCHY?
TCH... SO AN-NOYING..
STOP! NO!! YOU TRYIN' TO KILL ME?!
ALL RIGHT! I BELIEVE YOU!!
NEVER DO THAT AGAIN!!
I'M FREAKIN' OUT TOO.
IF ALMA REALLY SENT YOU TO FIND ME, I HAVE NO CHOICE.
I'LL SEE WHAT I CAN DO.
WHAT DO YOU USE? GLOVES? A WEAPON? A WAND?
I DON'T USE ANYTHING. BUT I DO HAVE A GAUNTLET.
SO YOU'RE A TOTAL NEWBIE, HUH?
UM...
VERY WELL. THIS MAKES IT EASIER. HERE'S YOUR FIRST LESSON...
!!
GO HOME TO GRANDMA AND FIND YOURSELF ANOTHER NANNY!!

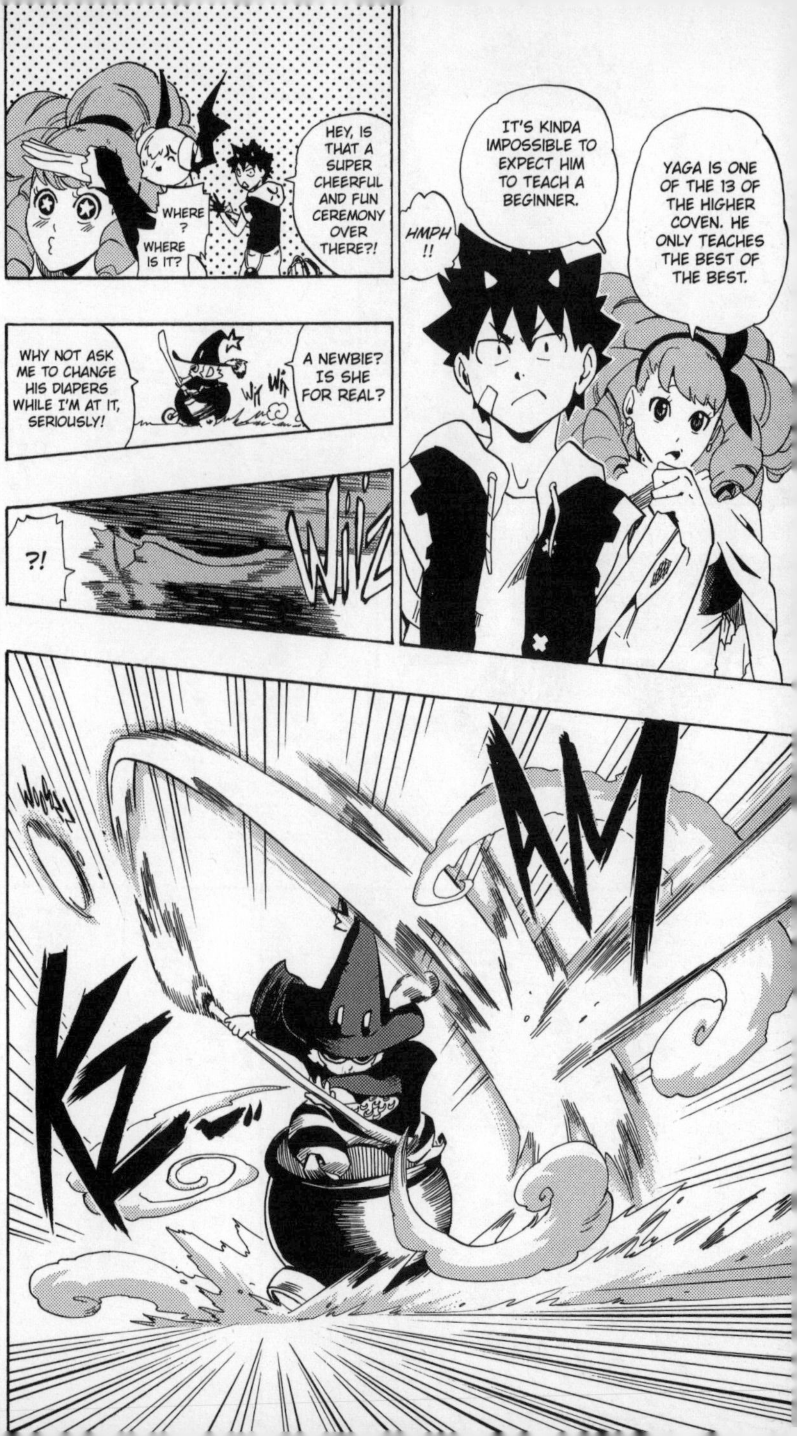
YAGA IS ONE OF THE 13 OF THE HIGHER COVEN. HE ONLY TEACHES THE BEST OF THE BEST.
IT'S KINDA IMPOSSIBLE TO EXPECT HIM TO TEACH A BEGINNER.
HMPH !!
HEY, IS THAT A SUPER CHEERFUL AND FUN CEREMONY OVER THERE?!
WHERE ? WHERE IS IT?
A NEWBIE? IS SHE FOR REAL?
WIT WIT
WHY NOT ASK ME TO CHANGE HIS DIAPERS WHILE I'M AT IT, SERIOUSLY!
WIIZ
?!
AM
KA

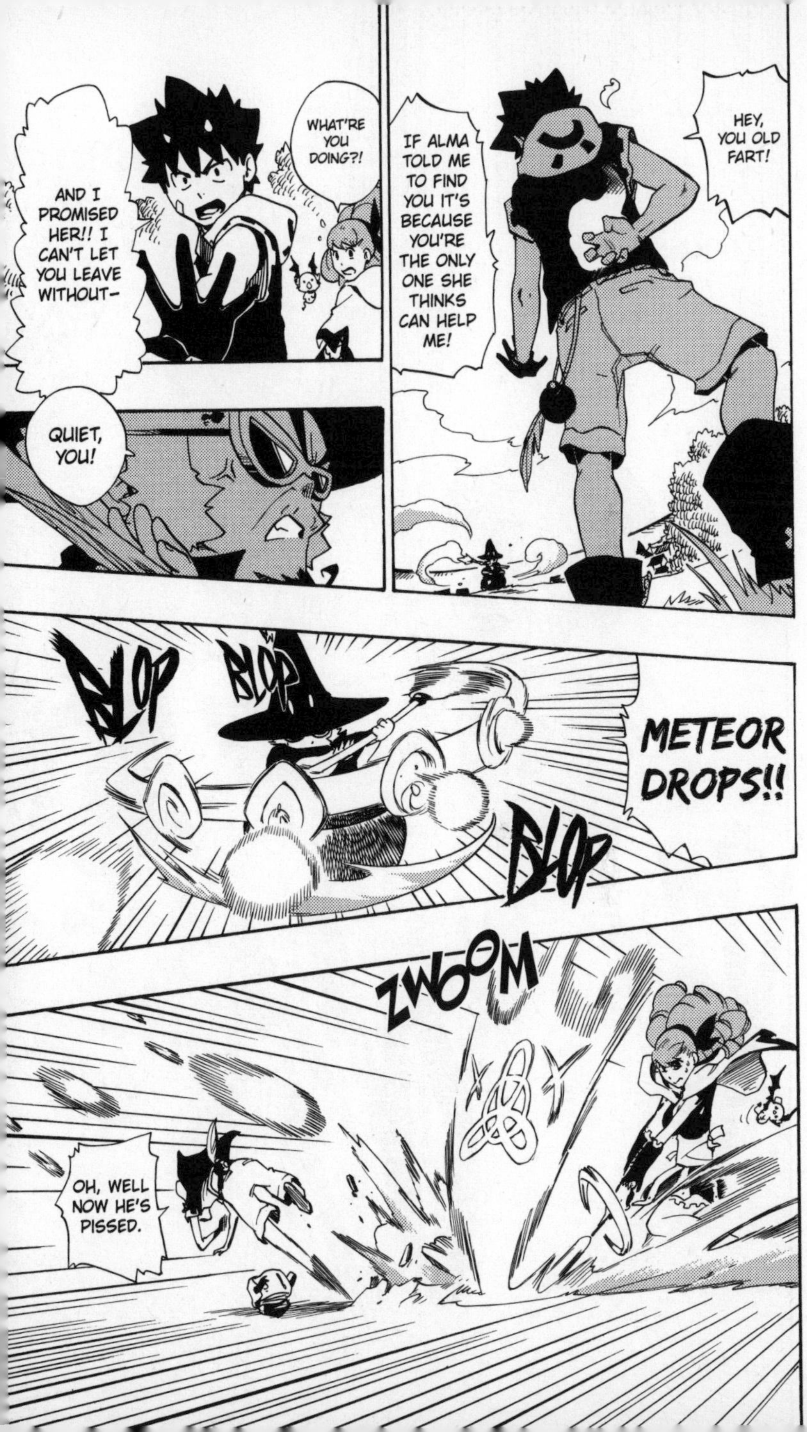
HEY, YOU OLD FART!
IF ALMA TOLD ME TO FIND YOU IT'S BECAUSE YOU'RE THE ONLY ONE SHE THINKS CAN HELP ME!
WHAT'RE YOU DOING?!
AND I PROMISED HER!! I CAN'T LET YOU LEAVE WITHOUT-
QUIET, YOU!
METEOR DROPS!!
BLOP
BLOP
BLOP
ZWOOM
OH, WELL NOW HE'S PISSED.

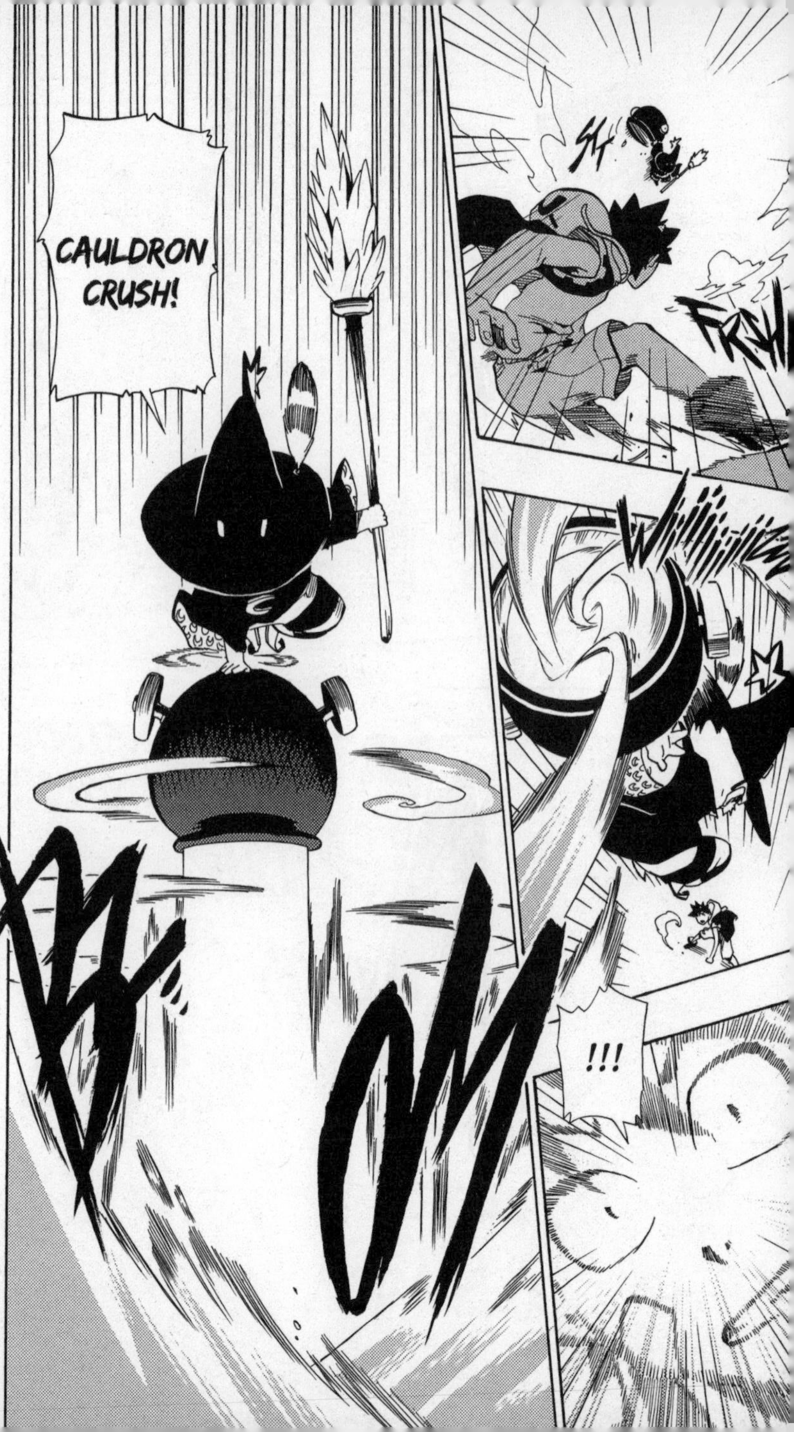
!!!
CAULDRON CRUSH!

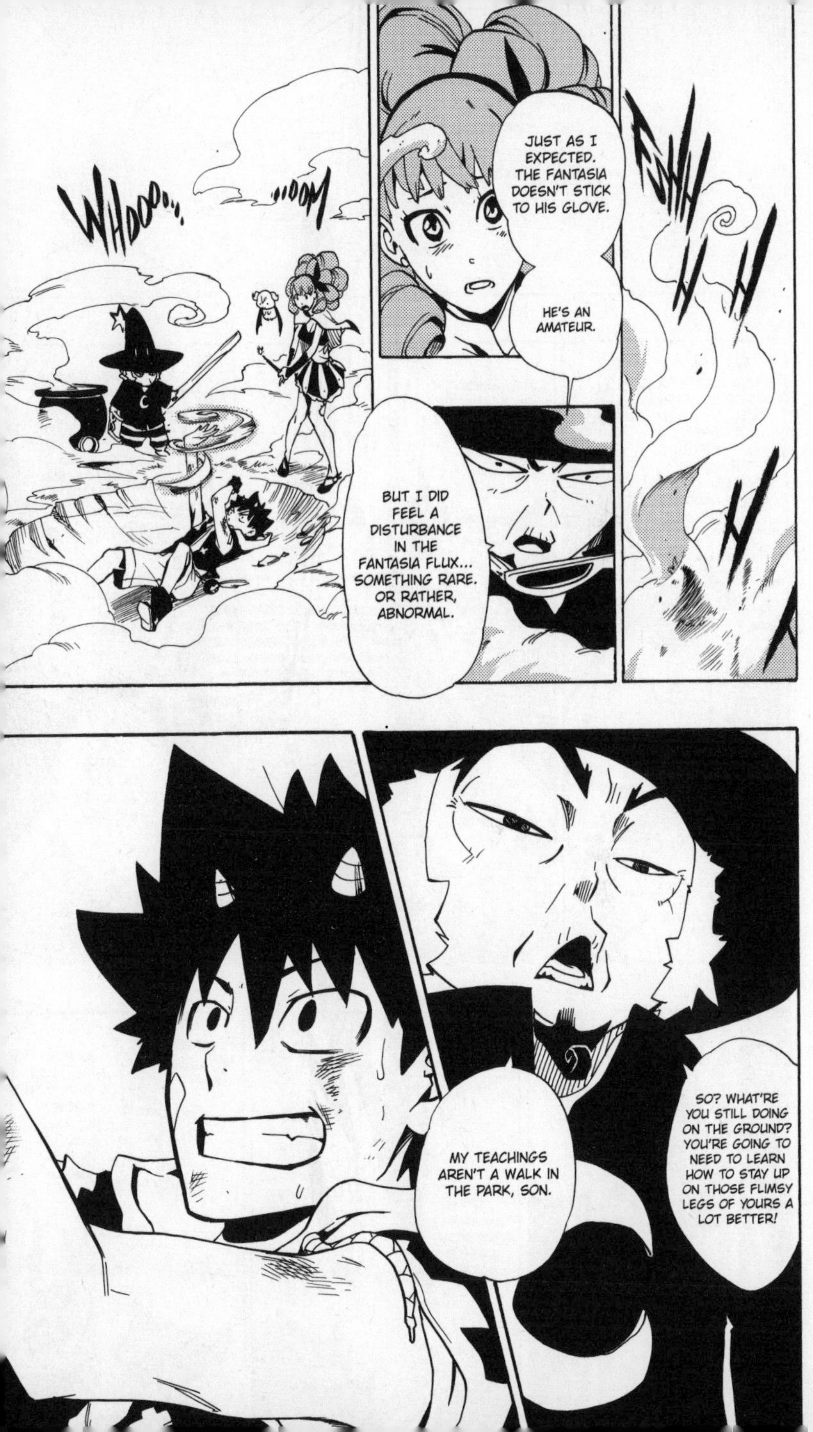
FSHHH
JUST AS I EXPECTED. THE FANTASIA DOESN'T STICK TO HIS GLOVE.
HE'S AN AMATEUR.
BUT I DID FEEL A DISTURBANCE IN THE FANTASIA FLUX... SOMETHING RARE. OR RATHER, ABNORMAL.
WHOOO...
...OOM
SO? WHAT'RE YOU STILL DOING ON THE GROUND? YOU'RE GOING TO NEED TO LEARN HOW TO STAY UP ON THOSE FLIMSY LEGS OF YOURS A LOT BETTER!
MY TEACHINGS AREN'T A WALK IN THE PARK, SON.

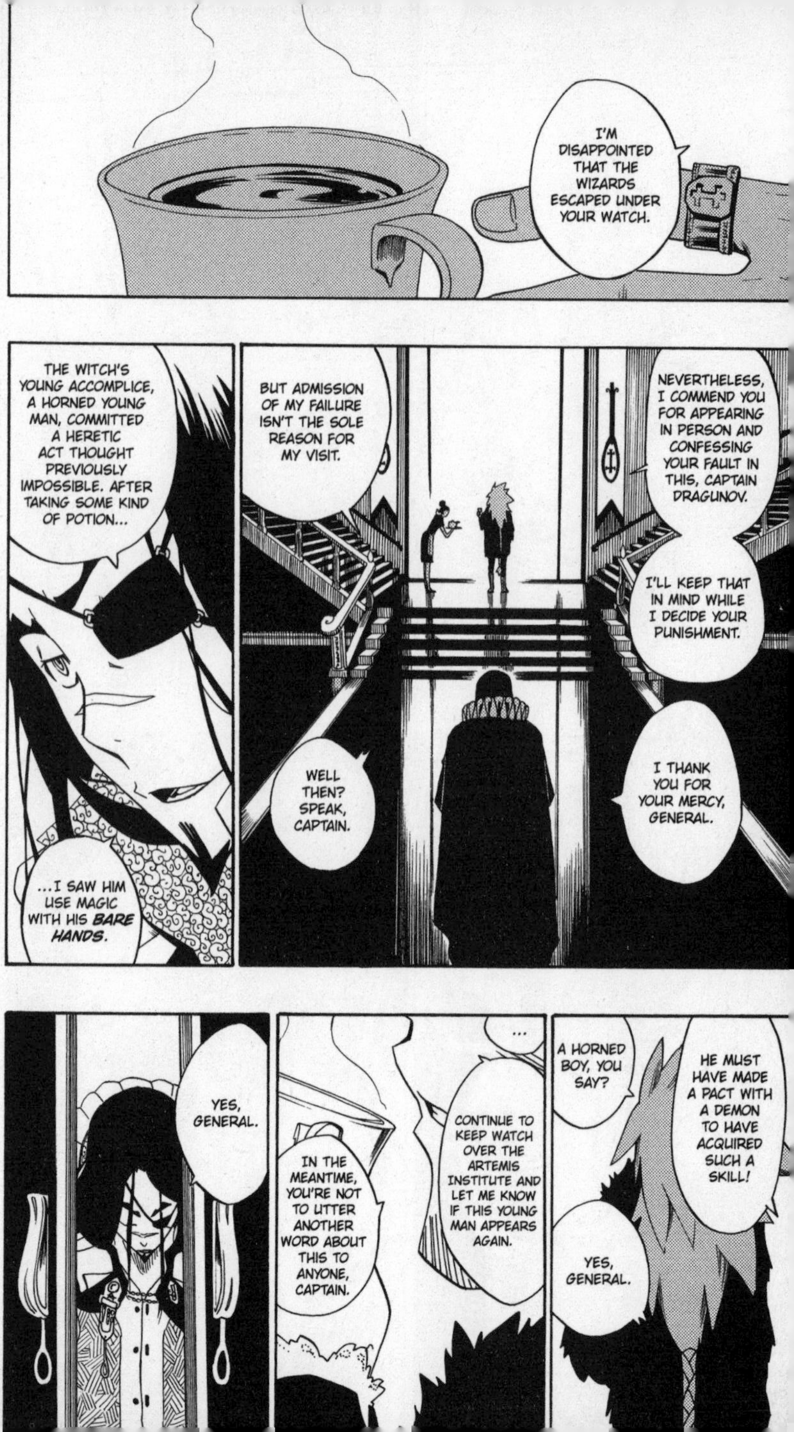
I'M DISAPPOINTED THAT THE WIZARDS ESCAPED UNDER YOUR WATCH.
NEVERTHELESS, I COMMEND YOU FOR APPEARING IN PERSON AND CONFESSING YOUR FAULT IN THIS, CAPTAIN DRAGUNOV.
I'LL KEEP THAT IN MIND WHILE I DECIDE YOUR PUNISHMENT.
I THANK YOU FOR YOUR MERCY, GENERAL.
BUT ADMISSION OF MY FAILURE ISN'T THE SOLE REASON FOR MY VISIT.
WELL THEN? SPEAK, CAPTAIN.
THE WITCH'S YOUNG ACCOMPLICE, A HORNED YOUNG MAN, COMMITTED A HERETIC ACT THOUGHT PREVIOUSLY IMPOSSIBLE. AFTER TAKING SOME KIND OF POTION...
...I SAW HIM USE MAGIC WITH HIS *BARE HANDS*.
A HORNED BOY, YOU SAY?
HE MUST HAVE MADE A PACT WITH A DEMON TO HAVE ACQUIRED SUCH A SKILL!
YES, GENERAL.
...
CONTINUE TO KEEP WATCH OVER THE ARTEMIS INSTITUTE AND LET ME KNOW IF THIS YOUNG MAN APPEARS AGAIN.
IN THE MEANTIME, YOU'RE NOT TO UTTER ANOTHER WORD ABOUT THIS TO ANYONE, CAPTAIN.
YES, GENERAL.

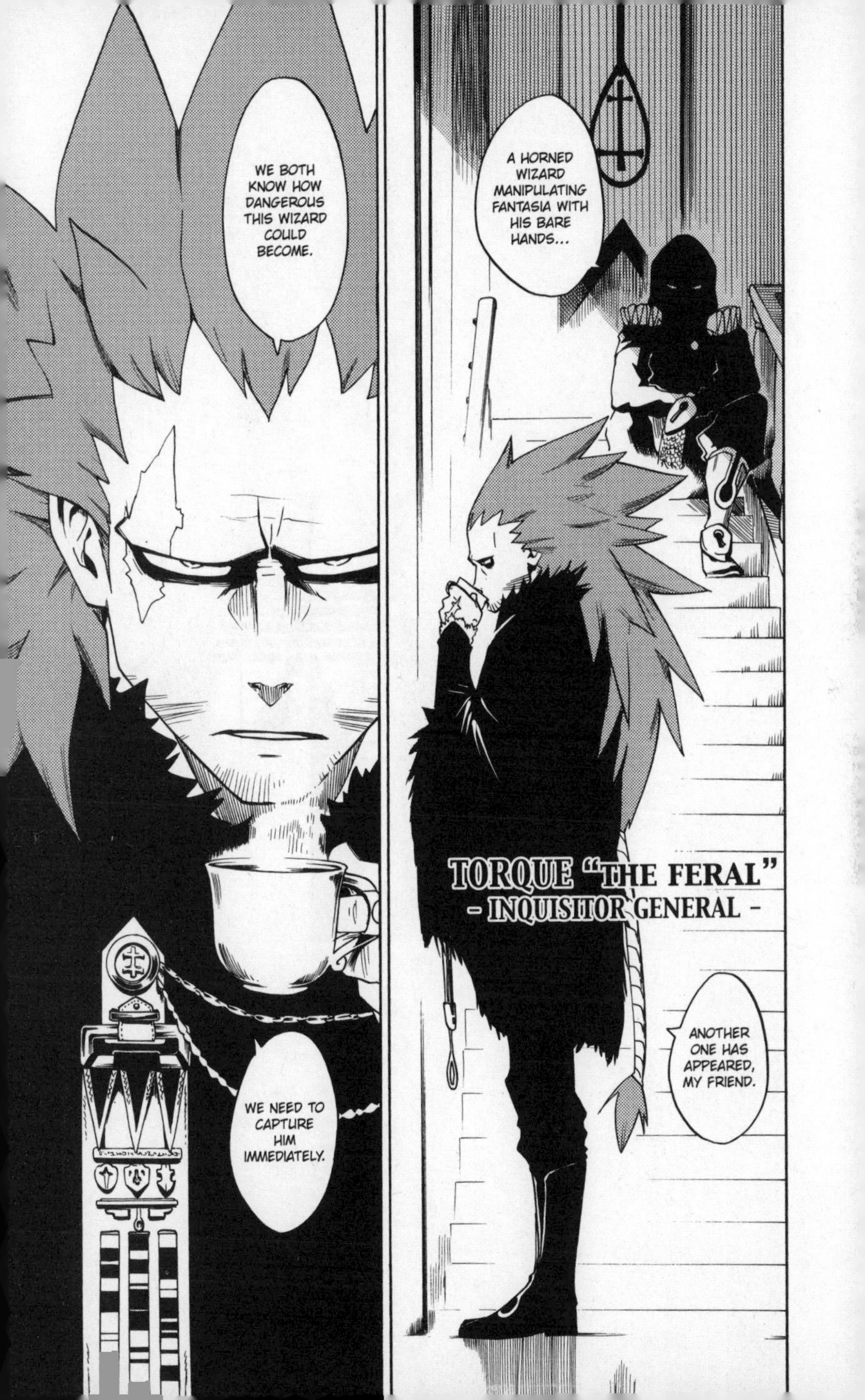
A HORNED WIZARD MANIPULATING FANTASIA WITH HIS BARE HANDS...
TORQUE "THE FERAL"
- INQUISITOR GENERAL -
ANOTHER ONE HAS APPEARED, MY FRIEND.
WE BOTH KNOW HOW DANGEROUS THIS WIZARD COULD BECOME.
WE NEED TO CAPTURE HIM IMMEDIATELY.

TO BE CONTINUED...

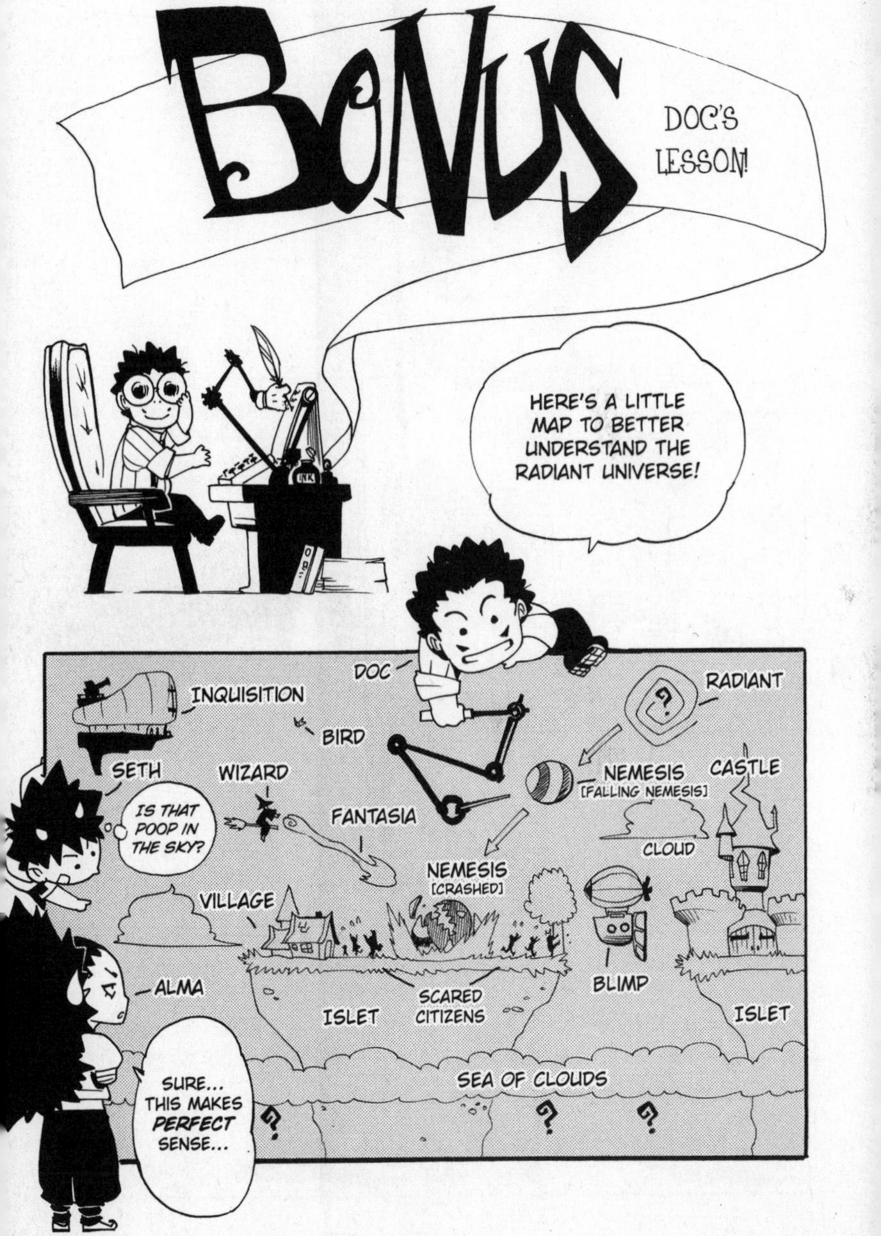
BONUS
DOC'S LESSON!
HERE'S A LITTLE MAP TO BETTER UNDERSTAND THE RADIANT UNIVERSE!
INK
DOC
RADIANT
INQUISITION
BIRD
SETH
WIZARD
NEMESIS
[FALLING NEMESIS]
CASTLE
IS THAT POOP IN THE SKY?
FANTASIA
CLOUD
NEMESIS
[CRASHED]
VILLAGE
ALMA
SCARED CITIZENS
BLIMP
ISLET
ISLET
SURE... THIS MAKES *PERFECT* SENSE...
SEA OF CLOUDS

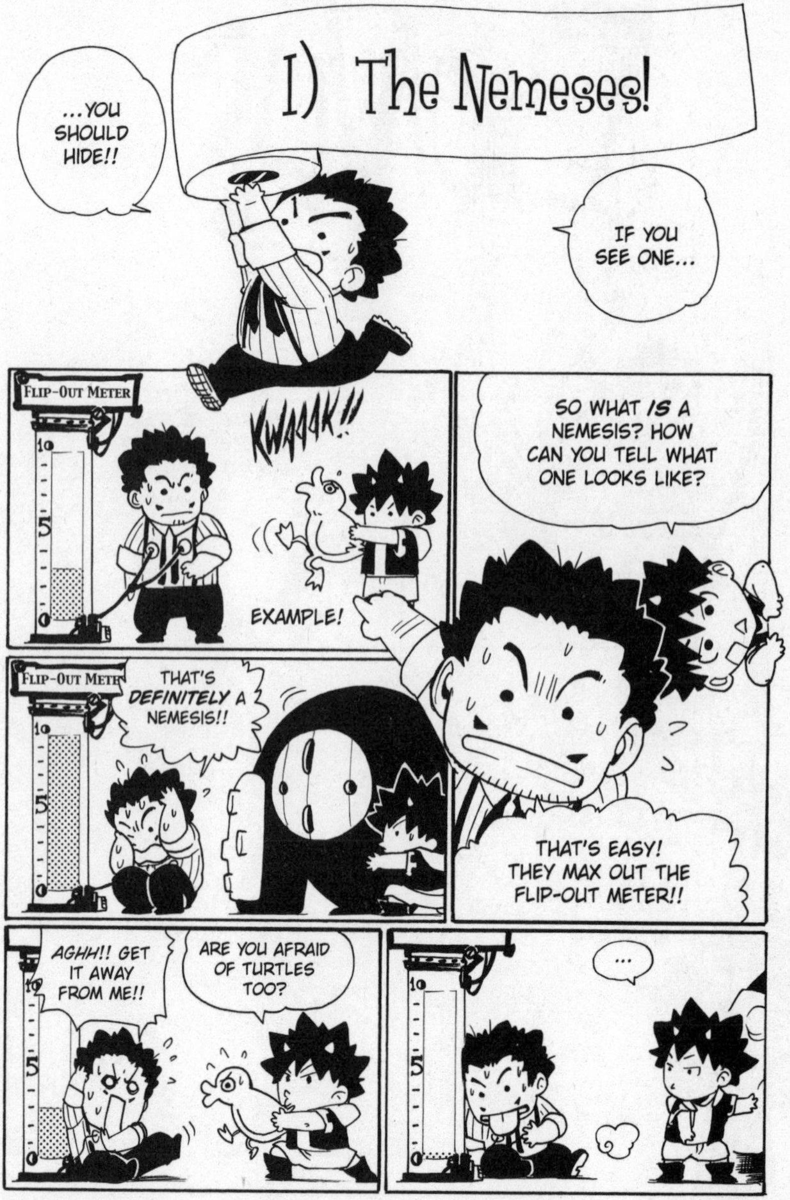
1) The Nemeses!
IF YOU SEE ONE...
...YOU SHOULD HIDE!!
SO WHAT IS A NEMESIS? HOW CAN YOU TELL WHAT ONE LOOKS LIKE?
THAT'S EASY! THEY MAX OUT THE FLIP-OUT METER!!
FLIP-OUT METER
10
5
0
KWAAAK!!
EXAMPLE!
FLIP-OUT METER
10
5
0
THAT'S DEFINITELY A NEMESIS!!
...
10
5
0
ARE YOU AFRAID OF TURTLES TOO?
AGHH!! GET IT AWAY FROM ME!!
10
5
0

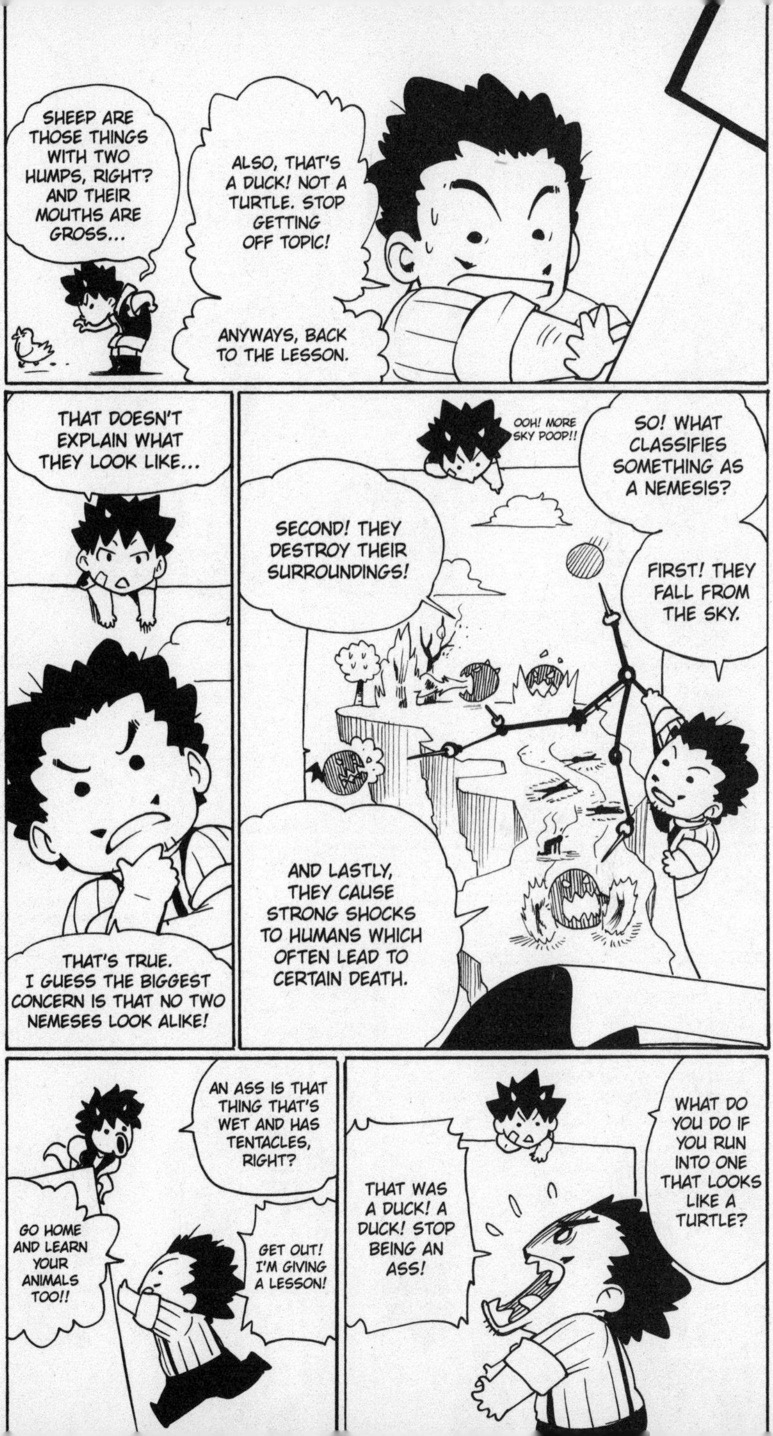
ALSO, THAT'S A DUCK! NOT A TURTLE. STOP GETTING OFF TOPIC!
ANYWAYS, BACK TO THE LESSON.
SHEEP ARE THOSE THINGS WITH TWO HUMPS, RIGHT? AND THEIR MOUTHS ARE GROSS...
SO! WHAT CLASSIFIES SOMETHING AS A NEMESIS?
OOH! MORE SKY POOP!!
FIRST! THEY FALL FROM THE SKY.
SECOND! THEY DESTROY THEIR SURROUNDINGS!
AND LASTLY, THEY CAUSE STRONG SHOCKS TO HUMANS WHICH OFTEN LEAD TO CERTAIN DEATH.
THAT DOESN'T EXPLAIN WHAT THEY LOOK LIKE...
THAT'S TRUE. I GUESS THE BIGGEST CONCERN IS THAT NO TWO NEMESES LOOK ALIKE!
WHAT DO YOU DO IF YOU RUN INTO ONE THAT LOOKS LIKE A TURTLE?
THAT WAS A DUCK! A DUCK! STOP BEING AN ASS!
AN ASS IS THAT THING THAT'S WET AND HAS TENTACLES, RIGHT?
GET OUT! I'M GIVING A LESSON!
GO HOME AND LEARN YOUR ANIMALS TOO!!

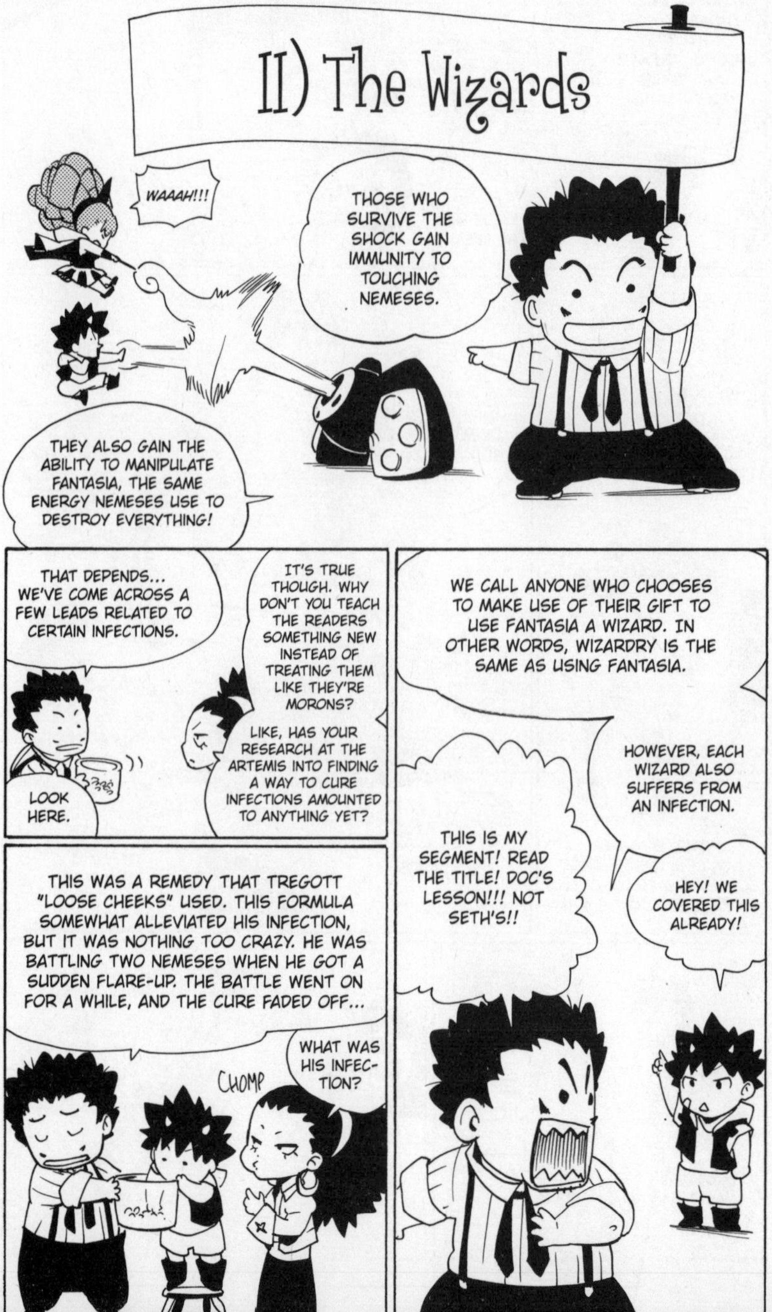
II) The Wizards
THOSE WHO SURVIVE THE SHOCK GAIN IMMUNITY TO TOUCHING NEMESES.
WAAAH!!!
THEY ALSO GAIN THE ABILITY TO MANIPULATE FANTASIA, THE SAME ENERGY NEMESES USE TO DESTROY EVERYTHING!
WE CALL ANYONE WHO CHOOSES TO MAKE USE OF THEIR GIFT TO USE FANTASIA A WIZARD. IN OTHER WORDS, WIZARDRY IS THE SAME AS USING FANTASIA.
HOWEVER, EACH WIZARD ALSO SUFFERS FROM AN INFECTION.
HEY! WE COVERED THIS ALREADY!
THIS IS MY SEGMENT! READ THE TITLE! DOC'S LESSON!!! NOT SETH'S!!
IT'S TRUE THOUGH. WHY DON'T YOU TEACH THE READERS SOMETHING NEW INSTEAD OF TREATING THEM LIKE THEY'RE MORONS?
LIKE, HAS YOUR RESEARCH AT THE ARTEMIS INTO FINDING A WAY TO CURE INFECTIONS AMOUNTED TO ANYTHING YET?
THAT DEPENDS... WE'VE COME ACROSS A FEW LEADS RELATED TO CERTAIN INFECTIONS.
LOOK HERE.
THIS WAS A REMEDY THAT TREGOTT "LOOSE CHEEKS" USED. THIS FORMULA SOMEWHAT ALLEVIATED HIS INFECTION, BUT IT WAS NOTHING TOO CRAZY. HE WAS BATTLING TWO NEMESES WHEN HE GOT A SUDDEN FLARE-UP. THE BATTLE WENT ON FOR A WHILE, AND THE CURE FADED OFF...
WHAT WAS HIS INFECTION?
CHOMP

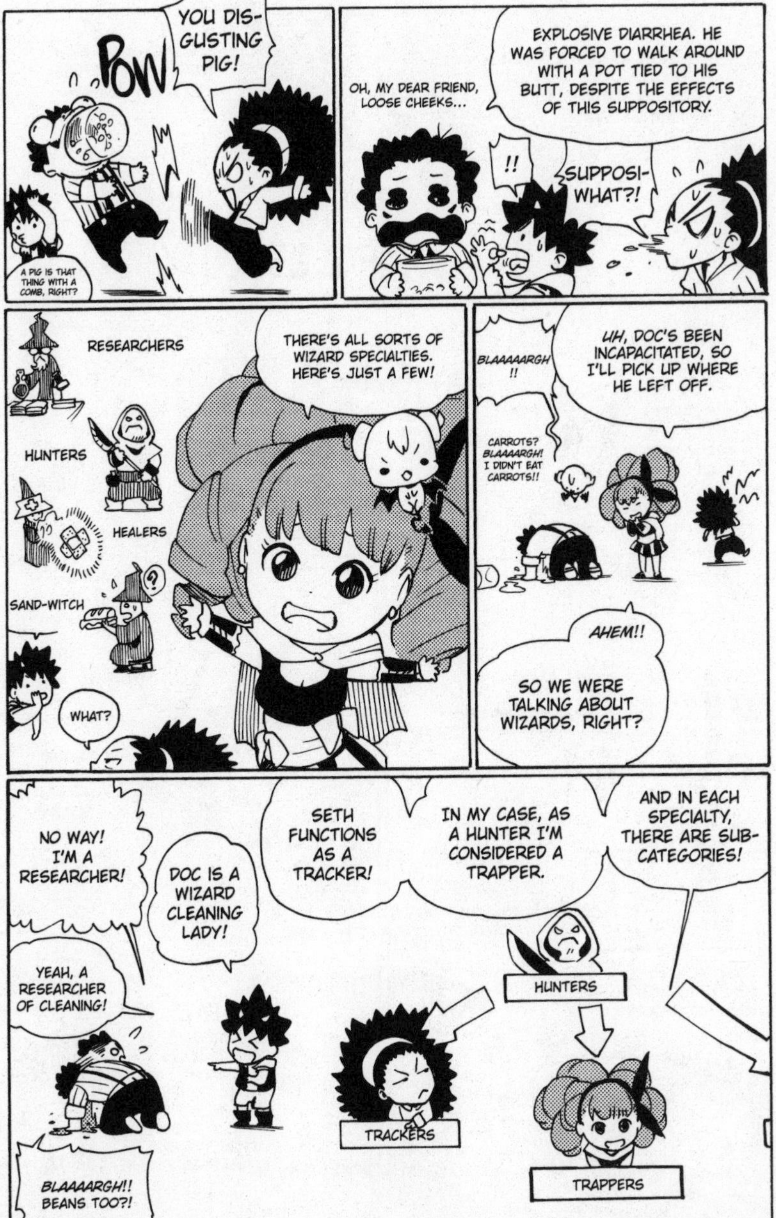
EXPLOSIVE DIARRHEA. HE WAS FORCED TO WALK AROUND WITH A POT TIED TO HIS BUTT, DESPITE THE EFFECTS OF THIS SUPPOSITORY.
OH, MY DEAR FRIEND, LOOSE CHEEKS...
SUPPOSI-WHAT?!
!!
YOU DIS-GUSTING PIG!
POW
A PIG IS THAT THING WITH A COMB, RIGHT?
UH, DOC'S BEEN INCAPACITATED, SO I'LL PICK UP WHERE HE LEFT OFF.
BLAAAAARGH!!
CARROTS? BLAAAARGH! I DIDN'T EAT CARROTS!!
AHEM!!
SO WE WERE TALKING ABOUT WIZARDS, RIGHT?
THERE'S ALL SORTS OF WIZARD SPECIALTIES. HERE'S JUST A FEW!
RESEARCHERS
HUNTERS
HEALERS
SAND-WITCH
WHAT?
AND IN EACH SPECIALTY, THERE ARE SUB-CATEGORIES!
IN MY CASE, AS A HUNTER I'M CONSIDERED A TRAPPER.
SETH FUNCTIONS AS A TRACKER!
DOC IS A WIZARD CLEANING LADY!
NO WAY! I'M A RESEARCHER!
HUNTERS
TRAPPERS
TRACKERS
YEAH, A RESEARCHER OF CLEANING!
BLAAAARGH!! BEANS TOO?!

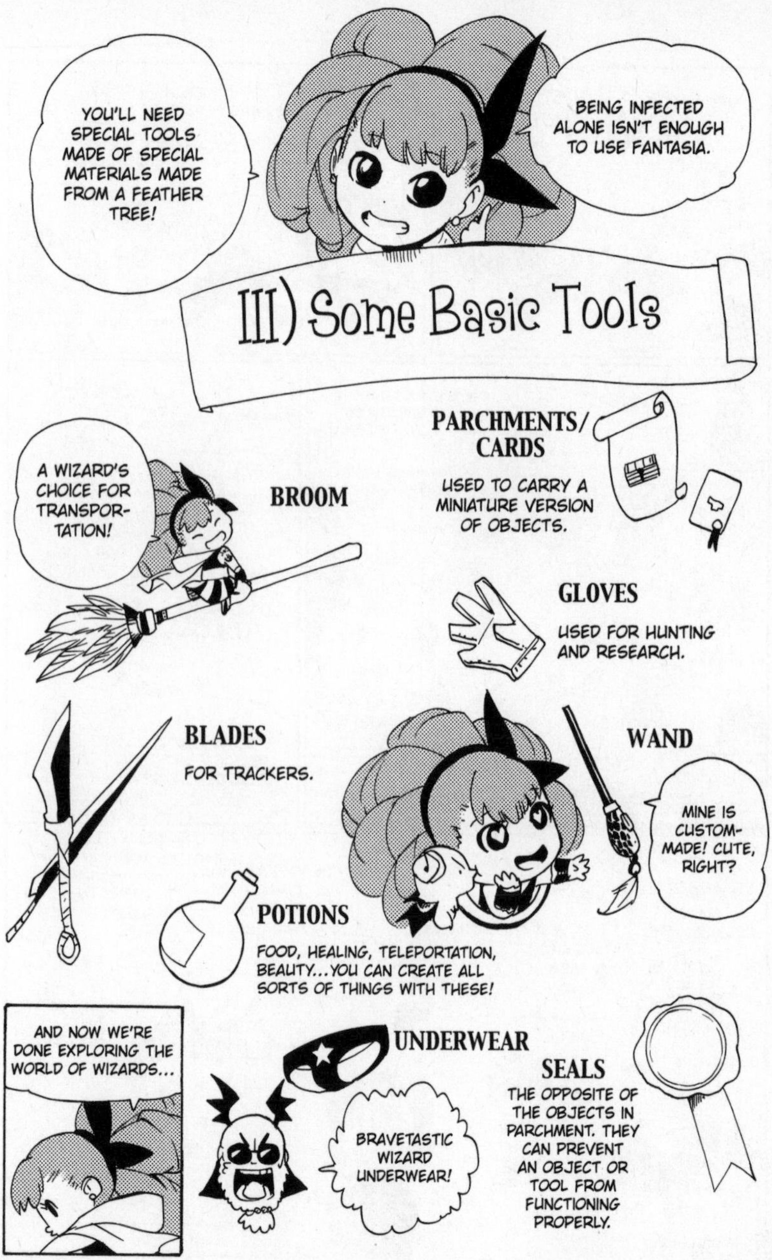
BEING INFECTED ALONE ISN'T ENOUGH TO USE FANTASIA.
YOU'LL NEED SPECIAL TOOLS MADE OF SPECIAL MATERIALS MADE FROM A FEATHER TREE!
III) Some Basic Tools
PARCHMENTS/ CARDS
USED TO CARRY A MINIATURE VERSION OF OBJECTS.
BROOM
A WIZARD'S CHOICE FOR TRANSPORTATION!
GLOVES
USED FOR HUNTING AND RESEARCH.
WAND
MINE IS CUSTOM-MADE! CUTE, RIGHT?
BLADES
FOR TRACKERS.
POTIONS
FOOD, HEALING, TELEPORTATION, BEAUTY...YOU CAN CREATE ALL SORTS OF THINGS WITH THESE!
SEALS
THE OPPOSITE OF THE OBJECTS IN PARCHMENT. THEY CAN PREVENT AN OBJECT OR TOOL FROM FUNCTIONING PROPERLY.
UNDERWEAR
BRAVETASTIC WIZARD UNDERWEAR!
AND NOW WE'RE DONE EXPLORING THE WORLD OF WIZARDS...

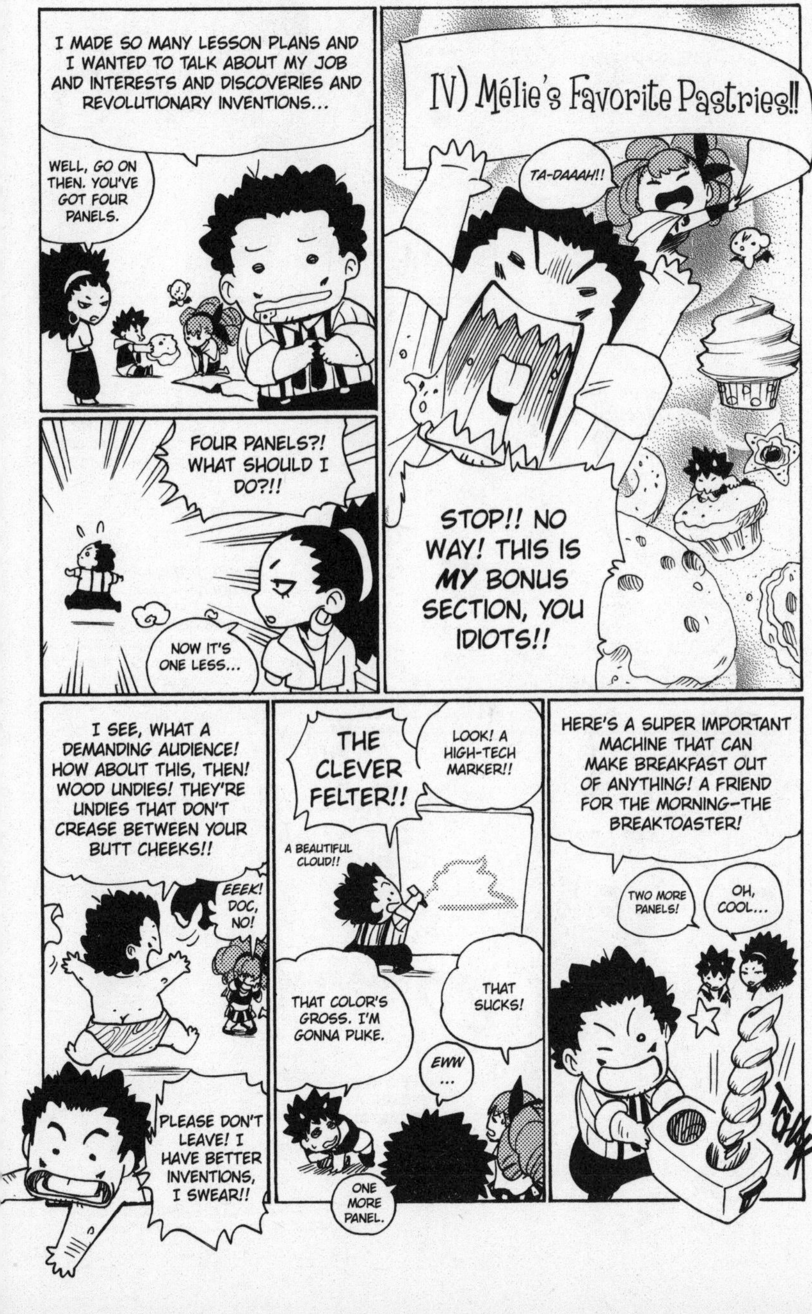
IV) Mélie's Favorite Pastries!!
TA-DAAAH!!
STOP!! NO WAY! THIS IS *MY* BONUS SECTION, YOU IDIOTS!!
I MADE SO MANY LESSON PLANS AND I WANTED TO TALK ABOUT MY JOB AND INTERESTS AND DISCOVERIES AND REVOLUTIONARY INVENTIONS...
WELL, GO ON THEN. YOU'VE GOT FOUR PANELS.
FOUR PANELS?! WHAT SHOULD I DO?!!
NOW IT'S ONE LESS...
HERE'S A SUPER IMPORTANT MACHINE THAT CAN MAKE BREAKFAST OUT OF ANYTHING! A FRIEND FOR THE MORNING—THE BREAKTOASTER!
OH, COOL...
TWO MORE PANELS!
TCHAK
LOOK! A HIGH-TECH MARKER!!
THE CLEVER FELTER!!
A BEAUTIFUL CLOUD!!
THAT SUCKS!
THAT COLOR'S GROSS. I'M GONNA PUKE.
EWW...
ONE MORE PANEL.
I SEE, WHAT A DEMANDING AUDIENCE! HOW ABOUT THIS, THEN! WOOD UNDIES! THEY'RE UNDIES THAT DON'T CREASE BETWEEN YOUR BUTT CHEEKS!!
EEEK! DOC, NO!
PLEASE DON'T LEAVE! I HAVE BETTER INVENTIONS, I SWEAR!!

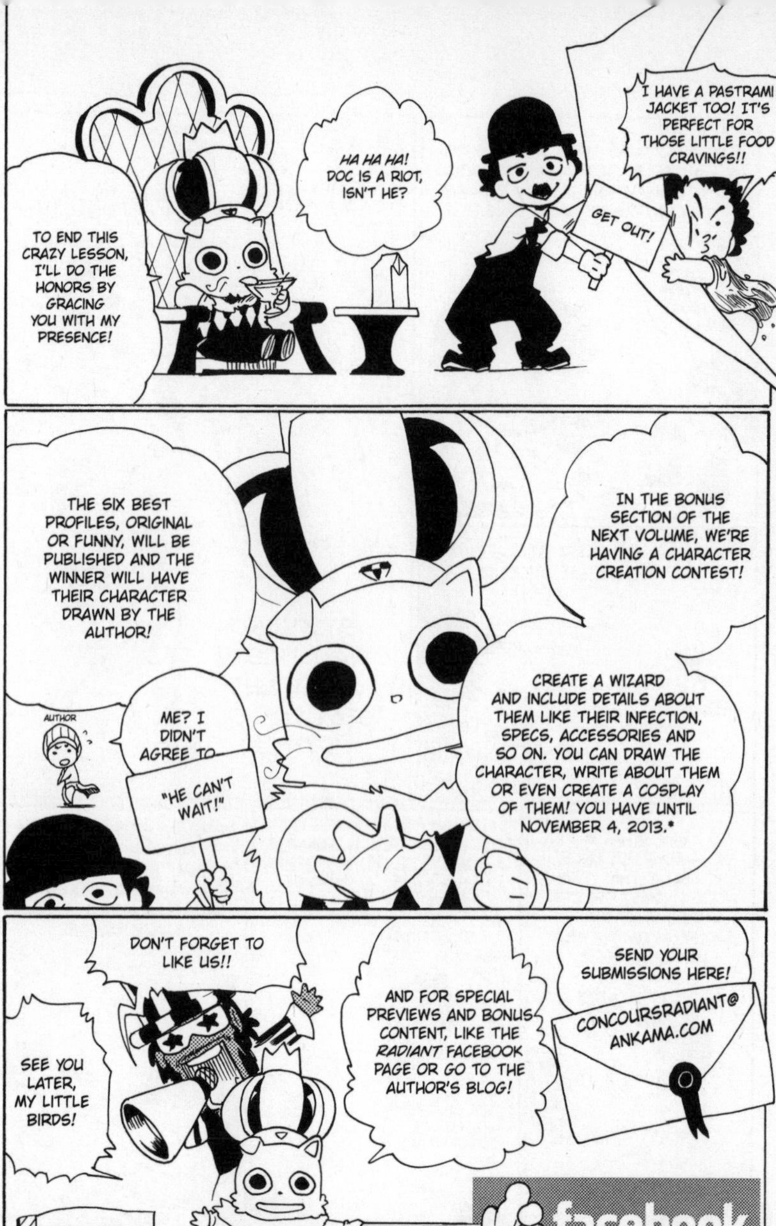
I HAVE A PASTRAMI JACKET TOO! IT'S PERFECT FOR THOSE LITTLE FOOD CRAVINGS!!
GET OUT!
HA HA HA! DOC IS A RIOT, ISN'T HE?
TO END THIS CRAZY LESSON, I'LL DO THE HONORS BY GRACING YOU WITH MY PRESENCE!
IN THE BONUS SECTION OF THE NEXT VOLUME, WE'RE HAVING A CHARACTER CREATION CONTEST!
THE SIX BEST PROFILES, ORIGINAL OR FUNNY, WILL BE PUBLISHED AND THE WINNER WILL HAVE THEIR CHARACTER DRAWN BY THE AUTHOR!
CREATE A WIZARD AND INCLUDE DETAILS ABOUT THEM LIKE THEIR INFECTION, SPECS, ACCESSORIES AND SO ON. YOU CAN DRAW THE CHARACTER, WRITE ABOUT THEM OR EVEN CREATE A COSPLAY OF THEM! YOU HAVE UNTIL NOVEMBER 4, 2013.*
"HE CAN'T WAIT!"
ME? I DIDN'T AGREE TO-
AUTHOR
SEND YOUR SUBMISSIONS HERE!
CONCOURSRADIANT@ ANKAMA.COM
AND FOR SPECIAL PREVIEWS AND BONUS CONTENT, LIKE THE *RADIANT* FACEBOOK PAGE OR GO TO THE AUTHOR'S BLOG!
DON'T FORGET TO LIKE US!!
SEE YOU LATER, MY LITTLE BIRDS!
facebook
THE END!

HTTP://VALENTE.CANALBLOG.COM

*THIS CONTEST RAN IN 2013. SUBMISSIONS ARE CLOSED.

RADIANT

RADIANT VOL. 1
VIZ MEDIA Manga Edition

STORY AND ART BY **TONY VALENTE**

Translation/**Anne Ishii**
Additional Translation/**(´・∀・`)ｻｧ?**
Touch-Up Art & Lettering/**Erika Terriquez**
Design/**Julian [JR] Robinson**
Editor/**Marlene First**

Published by arrangement with MEDIATOON LICENSING/Ankama.
RADIANT T01

Printed in the U.S.A.

Published by VIZ Media, LLC
P.O. Box 77010
San Francisco, CA 94107

10 9 8 7 6 5 4 3 2 1
First printing, September 2018

VIZ MEDIA
viz.com

ratings.viz.com
RATED T TEEN

PARENTAL ADVISORY
RADIANT is rated T for Teen and is recommended for ages 13 and up. This volume contains fantasy violence.

MY CAPE IS ALWAYS BLOWING IN THE WIND!

" I want to make mangaaaaa!" I spent years screaming this from every rooftop. And now, here I am! You're holding the first book in your hands! It's satisfaction! It's satisfactastic! It's satisfactionistic! There aren't enough words to describe my joy. Well, now that I've realized one of my greatest dreams, there's nothing left but to move on to the next one: "I want to sleeeeeep!!"

—Tony Valente

Tony Valente began working as a comic artist with the series *The Four Princes of Ganahan*, written by Raphael Drommelschlager. He then launched a new three-volume project, *Hana Attori*, after which he produced *S.P.E.E.D. Angels*, a series written by Didier Tarquin and colored by Pop.

In preparation for *Radiant*, he relocated to Canada. Through confronting caribou and grizzlies, he gained the wherewithal to train in obscure manga techniques. Since then, his eating habits have changed, his lifestyle became completely different and even his singing voice has changed a bit!

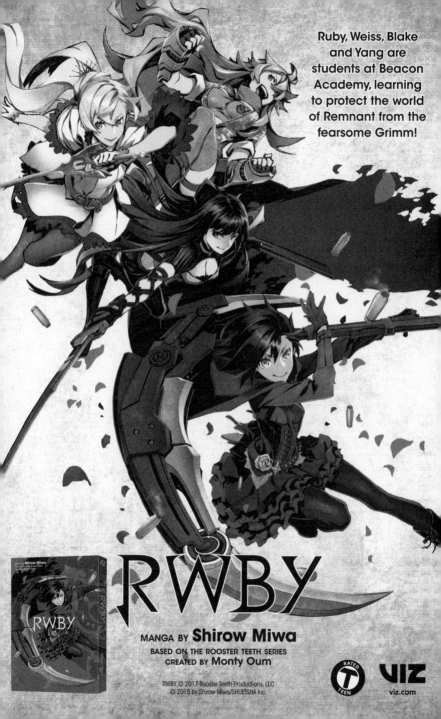

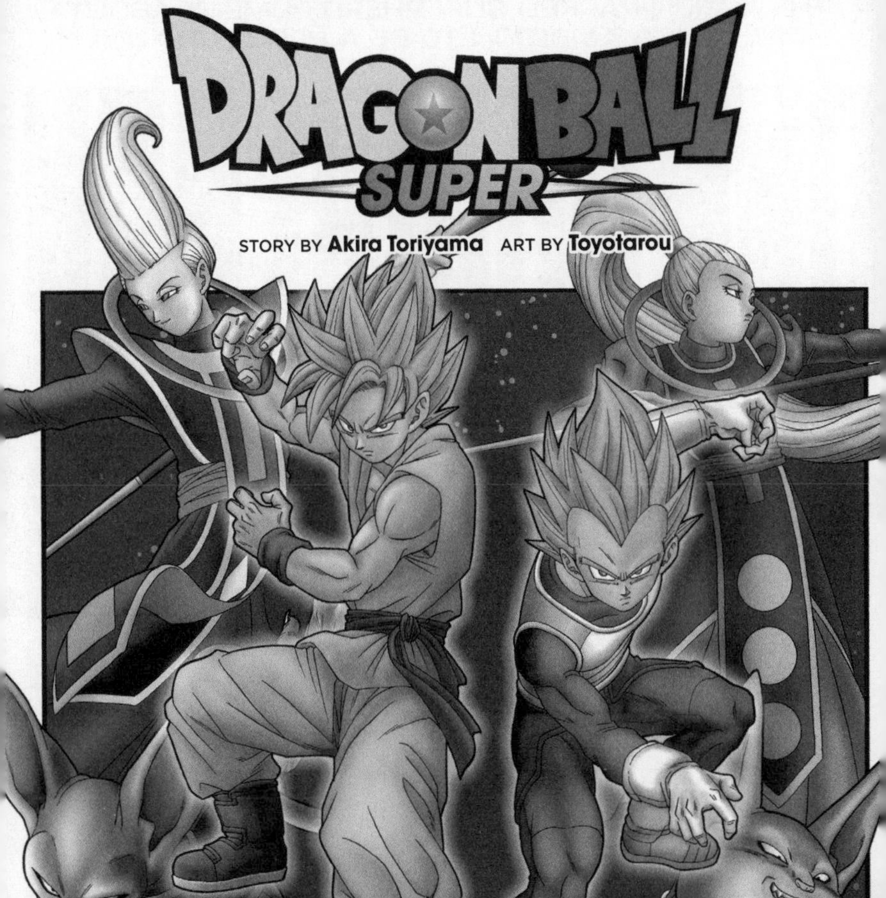
DRAGON BALL SUPER
STORY BY Akira Toriyama ART BY Toyotarou

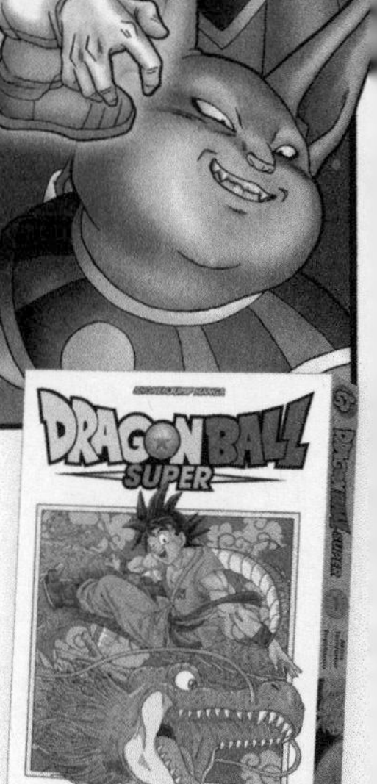
DRAGON BALL SUPER
STORY BY Akira Toriyama
ART BY Toyotarou
1

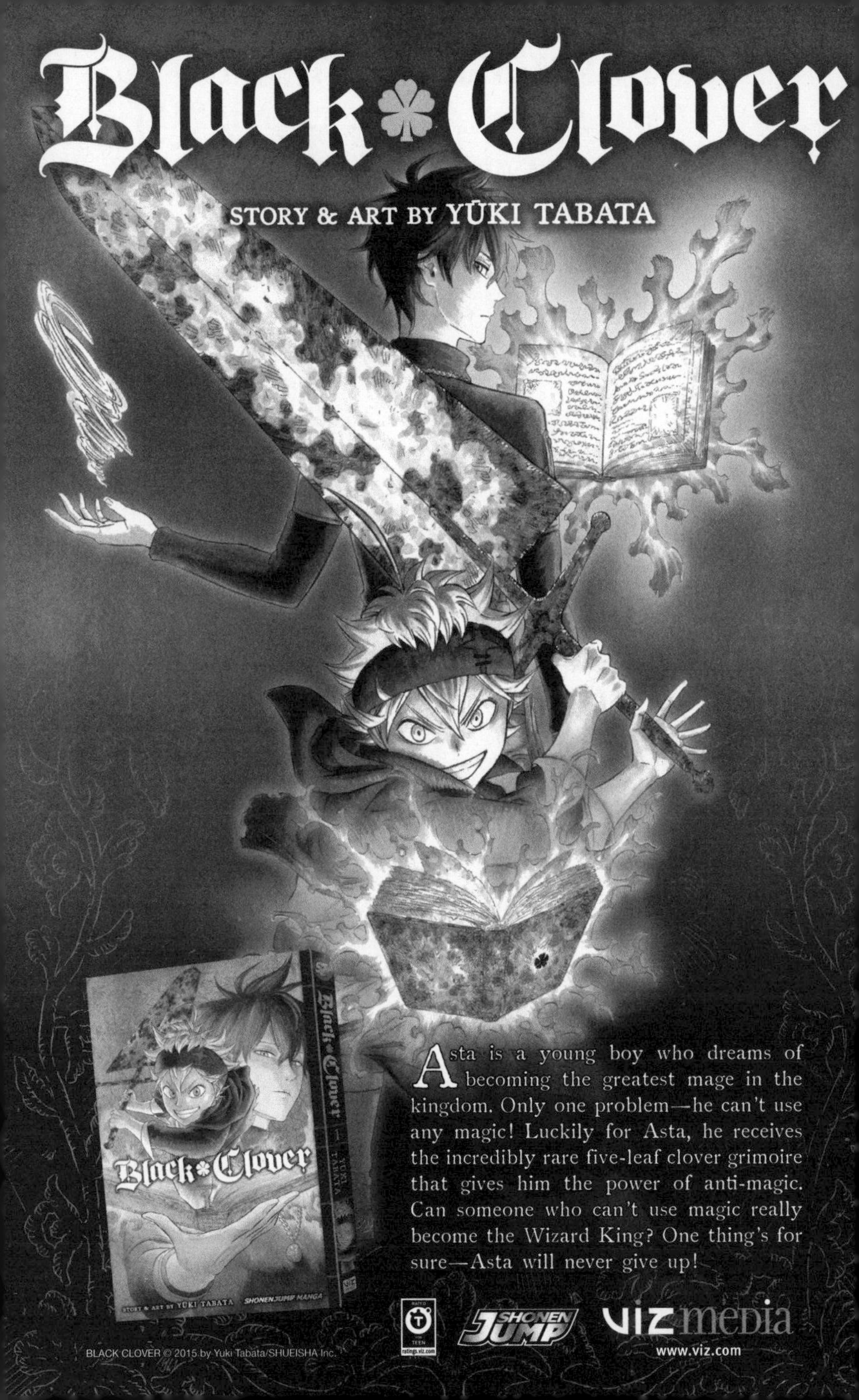
Black Clover
STORY & ART BY YŪKI TABATA
Asta is a young boy who dreams of becoming the greatest mage in the kingdom. Only one problem—he can't use any magic! Luckily for Asta, he receives the incredibly rare five-leaf clover grimoire that gives him the power of anti-magic. Can someone who can't use magic really become the Wizard King? One thing's for sure—Asta will never give up!
Black Clover
STORY & ART BY YŪKI TABATA
SHONEN JUMP MANGA
SHONEN JUMP
VIZ media
www.viz.com
BLACK CLOVER © 2015 by Yuki Tabata/SHUEISHA Inc.

A PREMIUM BOX SET OF THE FIRST TWO STORY ARCS OF ONE PIECE!

A PIRATE'S TREASURE FOR ANY MANGA FAN!

STORY AND ART BY EIICHIRO ODA

Comes with
EXCLUSIVE POSTER
and the **ROMANCE DAWN**
mini-comic!

As a child, Monkey D. Luffy dreamed of becoming King of the Pirates.
But his life changed when he accidentally gained the power to stretch like
rubber...at the cost of never being able to swim again! Years later, Luffy sets off
in search of the "One Piece," said to be the greatest treasure in the world...

**This box set includes VOLUMES 1-23, which comprise
the EAST BLUE and BAROQUE WORKS story arcs.**

EXCLUSIVE PREMIUMS and GREAT SAVINGS
over buying the individual volumes!

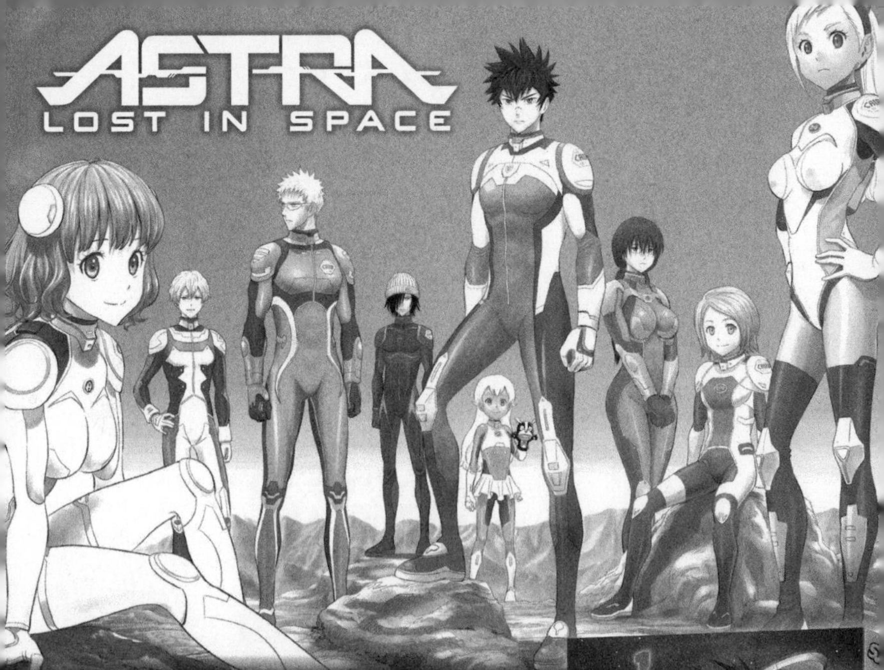
ASTRA
LOST IN SPACE

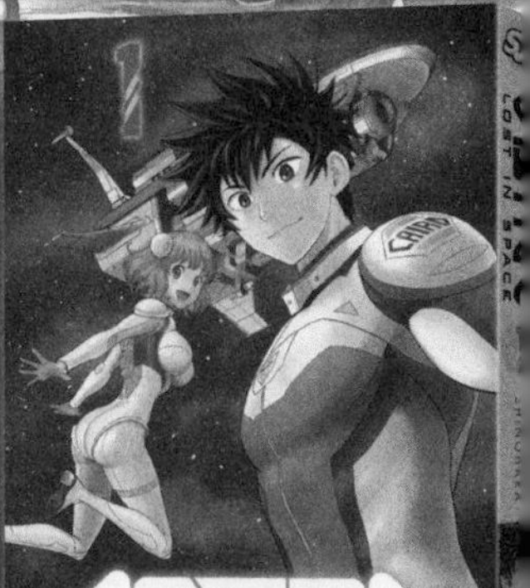
ASTRA
LOST IN SPACE
Story and Art by KENTA SHINOHARA

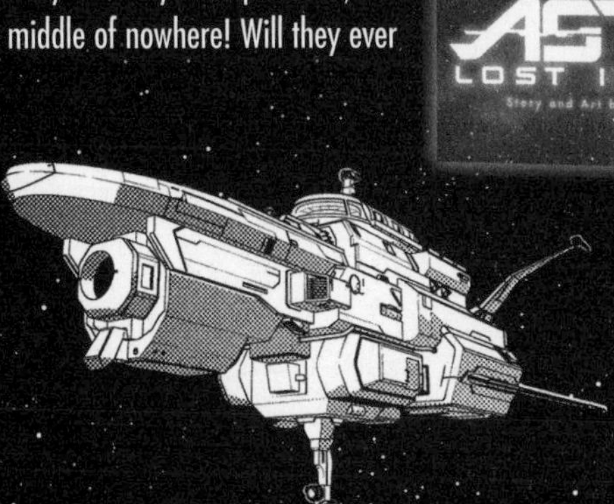

YOU'RE READING THE WRONG WAY

RADIANT reads from right to left, starting in the upper-right corner, meaning that action, sound effects, and word-balloon order are completely reversed from English order.

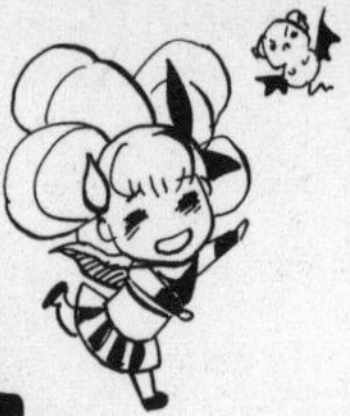

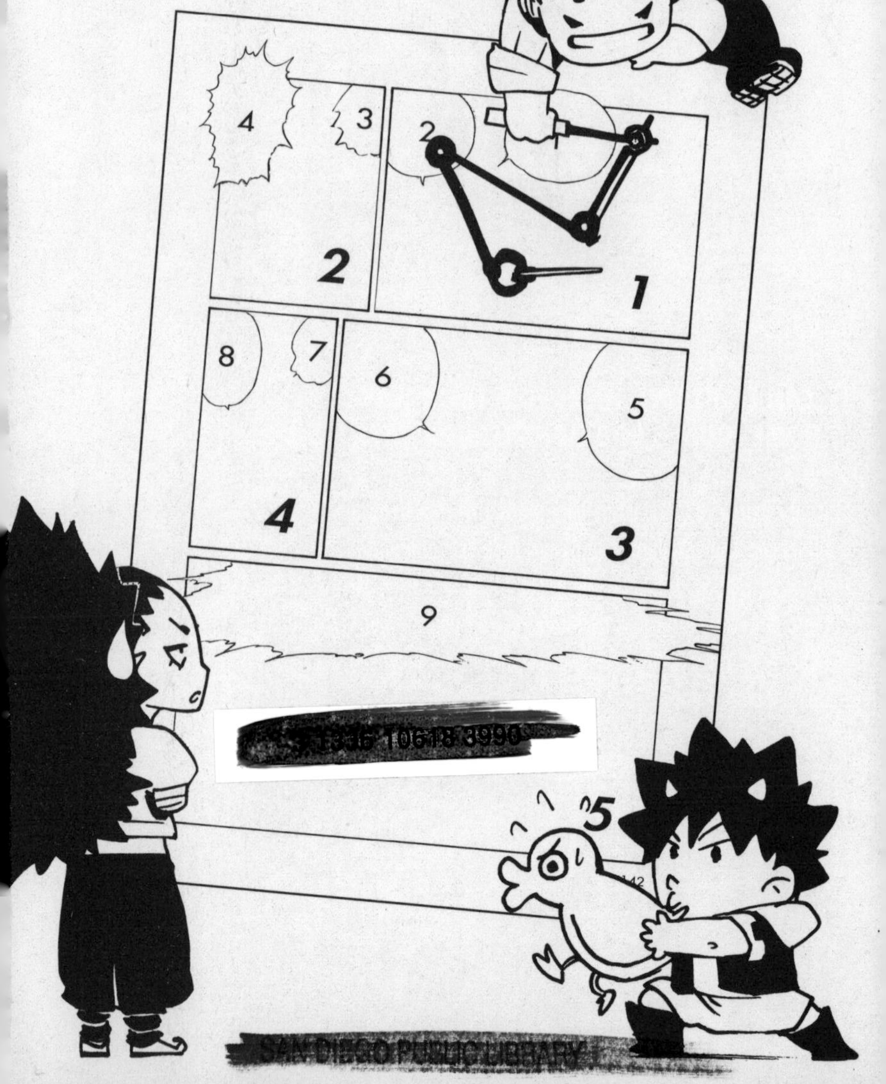
2
1
3
4
2
5
3
6
7
8
4
9
5